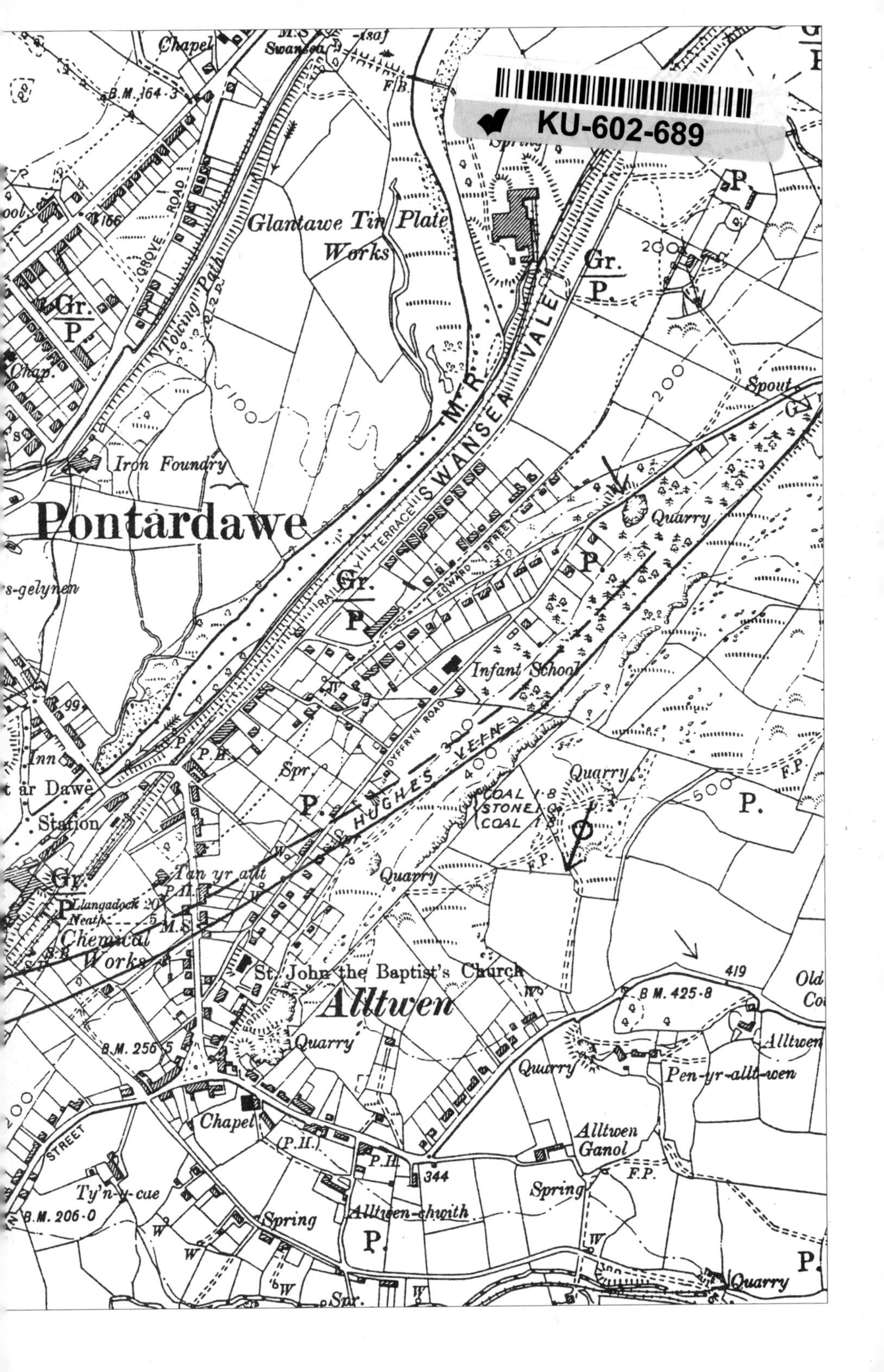
KU-602-689
Chapel
Swansea
F.B.
B.M. 164·3
GROVE ROAD
Towing Path
Glantawe Tin Plate Works
Spring
Gr. P.
M.R.
SWANSEA VALE
Spout
Iron Foundry
Pontardawe
-gelynen
RAILWAY TERRACE
EDWARD STREET
Quarry
Infant School
DYFFRYN ROAD
HUGHES VEIN
Spr.
Inn
P.H.
ar Dawe
Station
COAL 1·8
STONE
COAL 1·8
Quarry
F.P.
Tan yr allt
Llangadock
Neath
M.S.
Chemical Works
St. John the Baptist's Church
Alltwen
B.M. 425·8
419
Old
B.M. 256·5
Quarry
Pen-yr-allt-wen
Chapel
(P.H.)
STREET
Alltwen Ganol
344
Ty'n-y-cae
Spring
B.M. 206·0
Spring
Alltwen-chwith
W
Spr.
Quarry

Publications of the South Wales Record Society

No. 16

THE LETTER-BOOKS OF W. GILBERTSON & CO. LTD., PONTARDAWE

Pontardawe Steelworks, c.1925 *(Edwin Hartland)*

The Letter-Books of W. Gilbertson & Co. Ltd., Pontardawe 1890-1929

Edited by

P. W. Jackson

Cardiff:
South Wales Record Society
Swansea:
West Glamorgan Archive Service
2001

Published by West Glamorgan Archive Service
County Hall, Oystermouth Road, Swansea SA1 3SN
and the South Wales Record Society
12 The Green, Radyr, Cardiff CF15 8BR

First published 2001

ISBN 0 9521783 8 9 (West Glamorgan Archive Service)
ISBN 0 9525961 6 4 (South Wales Record Society)

Printed in Wales by
Dinefwr Press Ltd, Llandybie, Carmarthenshire

Dedicated to the memory
of my Parents

CONTENTS

LIST OF ILLUSTRATIONS

PREFACE

The ten Letter-Books of W. Gilbertson and Company Limited which form the major part of this book span the period from 13 August 1890 to 7 October 1929, and comprise 6,751 pages and approximately 5,000 copies of outgoing letters. The method adopted for retaining copies of company letters was to impress them onto the dampened leaves of a Letter-Book. Copies were thus 'filed' chronologically, with no attempt to categorise them into discrete functional or thematic areas.

From the flimsy pages of the Letter-Books emerges a record of the day-to-day issues and problems which confronted a family of tinplate and steel producers through four decades of technical development, home and foreign trade and competition, a world war and its aftermath and an increasingly organised labour force. Most of the letters were hand-written by Arthur Gilbertson and his sons and capture their perceptions of these events and give a uniquely personal insight into their opinions, values, feelings and prejudices. It has been suggested that ". . . the real, central theme of History is not what happened, but what people thought about it when it was happening".[1] Judged by this assessment the letters reveal their writers' thoughts and their reactions to the manifold production, financial, human and commercial problems of managing a competitive enterprise and also include a commentary on the life of the community of Pontardawe which was largely dependent upon the Gilbertson family's personal stewardship of the business for its continued employment and financial security. The letters also illustrate the nature and influence of a particular managerial ideology which was essentially paternalist, both in its supply and control modes, and firmly rooted in traditional values and hierarchical relationships at a time of considerable social change.

THE SELECTION

The selection of a balanced and representative sample of letters from the vast miscellany available posed several problems, not the least of which was the need to produce a narrative which was comprehensive, which reflected the dynamic features of the company's activities and the roles of its major participants at work and in the community, and to present these in a coherent structure. A preliminary review and indexing of the letters suggested three discrete yet interactive environments, namely the Gilbertson family, the company and the community. The family letters were

1. G. M. Young, *Victorian England: Portrait of an Age*, (OUP, 1960), vi.

modestly limited in number and mainly reflected Arthur Gilbertson's concern to perpetuate the family's control of the company. These form the substance of Chapter 1. Letters which dealt with company issues comprised a large and heterogeneous mass and covered many, often overlapping, details of the company's work. The choice of which letters to include was invariably difficult, and their final resolution into work-related developmental and functional areas constitute Chapters 2 to 7. Some of the letters in these chapters refer to Pontardawe's inhabitants and imply the community's dependence upon the works. This relationship is more closely focussed in the final three chapters where the selected letters illustrate the Gilbertson family's involvement in several aspects of community life.

TRANSCRIPTION

Each transcribed letter is prefaced by the names of the writer and the addressee, and referenced in square brackets by the index number of the appropriate Letter-Book (see Appendix 1) and its page number(s). The date line has been standardised, and the opening salutation and concluding valediction have been omitted as these would have taken up valuable space. The original spelling, punctuation and underlining have been retained. Where letters have not been fully transcribed the omissions are shown by ellipsis points (. . .). The transcribed letters have been arranged chronologically in their respective chapters and editorial comment on certain letters has been italicised.

ACKNOWLEDGEMENTS

Whilst the processes of selecting and transcribing the letters have necessarily been solitary pursuits, my commitment has been reinforced by the ready assistance of many people to whom I owe a great debt of gratitude. Foremost among these are Professor George Thomason, who guided my earlier research into the Gilbertson letter-books and has remained a much valued friend and adviser. I also wish to record my thanks to the staff of the West Glamorgan Archive Service, headed by Susan Beckley, for their professionalism and gracious response to all requests for information, and similarly to the library staff of Swansea Institute of Higher Education, Swansea Reference Library and the University of Wales Swansea. Several descendants of Arthur Gilbertson willingly verified relationships and dates, and I am especially grateful to Mrs. Nanette Pearce, daughter of the late Commander G. N. Gilbertson, for her kindness in permitting the reproduction of family photographs. I am also grateful to former colleagues Eric Roberts, who provided invaluable advice on financial procedures, and Ryan Griffiths for creating the Index. Tinplate historian Paul Jenkins willingly helped to resolve technical questions on the ferrous industry and local historians Jeff Childs, Keri Thomas, Clive Reed and Bill Harding were always generously prepared to discuss aspects of community development. I am indebted too to Beth James for her patience and skill in deciphering my longhand and producing a legible typescript, and to my editor, Brian James, who has shepherded the book with meticulous care through all its production stages. Finally, may I thank my family of Audrey, Caroline, Catherine and David, historians all, for their constant encouragement, and my especial gratitude goes to my wife who has tolerated the domestic accumulation of papers, books and disintegrating letter-books with good humour, and has consistently supported my enthusiasm for the project. For all errors and misinterpretations I am solely responsible.

P. W. JACKSON
April 2001

The South Wales Record Society is grateful to the Church Trust and the Ethel and Gwynne Morgan Trust for their generous grants, which have been partly put towards the publication of this volume.

THE FAMILIES OF WILLIAM, ARTHUR AND FRANK GILBERTSON

William Gilbertson
1810-82
m. Eliza Bramah 1835
1816-68

- Matthias 1836-?
- Francis Bramah 1838-1921
- Emily 1839-41
- Arthur 1841-1912
  m. 1872 Ellen Lloyd 1850-94
- Owen 1842-43
- Fanny 1844-1937
- Catherine Anne 1845-1933
  m. William Fisk Richardson
- Alice Mary 1849-59
- John Henry June-December 1852
- Ellen Louisa 1853-?
- William Onslow 1855-1904
- Madelina 1856-1936
- Edward Collings 1859-87
- Emily Maude 1862-1940

Arthur Gilbertson
1841-1912
m. Ellen Lloyd 1872
1850-94

- Francis William 1873-1929
  m. 1896 Isabel Frances de Winton Thomas 1869-1955
- Arthur Howel 1874-1923
  m. 1897 Harriet May Lloyd 1871-1949
- Cecil Frederick 1876-1948
  1. m. 1903 Gwladys Ellen Gwyn Moore-Gwyn 1881-1916
  2. m.1918 Gertrude Adshead 1887-1960
- Colin Richard 1877-1906
- Harriet Florence 1878-1918
  m. 1904 Rice Mansel Dillwyn
- Lettice Mary 1880-1885
- Olive 1881-1946
  m. 1907 Joseph Gwyn Moore-Gwyn 1879-1937
- Winifred 1883-1964
  m. 1918 Howel Gwyn Moore-Gwyn 1886-1956
- Charles Geoffrey 1884-1963
  m. 1908 Ellen Christabel Moore-Gwyn 1883-1963
- Marguerite Ellen 1885-1960
  m. 1911 William Giffard Wynne 1882-1972
- George Noel 1886-1955
  m. 1925 Helen Morris
- Sylvia Maude 1888-1950
  m. 1919 Frank Choat
- Phyllis 1890-1973
  m. Douglas (Robert) Dunlop
- John 1891 (died at birth)

Francis William Gilbertson
1873-1929
m. Isabel Frances de Winton
Thomas 1896
1869-1955

- Mary Dulcibel Frances 1898-1975
  m. 1917 Hugh Vivian 1884-1956

INTRODUCTION

For the greater part of its history W. Gilbertson and Company was a family firm where executive control was exclusively retained by family members. In this respect the Company typified an entrepreneurial pattern which was common in nineteenth-century western capitalist society where the majority of companies were family enterprises which initially drew capital from family holdings and expanded largely by self-financing. William Gilbertson laid the foundations of what became in the late nineteenth and early twentieth centuries a medium-size limited company which remained essentially a family firm.

This pattern of development is observable in British and American iron and steel, textiles, brewing, chemicals, newspapers, with the big "names" such as Guinness, Forte, Lever, Fraser, Cadbury, Kemsley, Du Pont, Swift, Armour, Anheuser-Busch and so on beginning as family businesses. Capitalism, as Marx observed, was not only an economic system with class formation on economic lines, but a social system in which power was transferred by patrilineal inheritance through the family. Transmitted family property has, since Roman times, bequeathed social and economic power, and the linked institutions of property and family have invariably been seen as the necessary preconditions for established society. Family and firm were likewise a symbolic and real biunity, and family firms became the architects not only of British industrialisation but also of the communities which coalesced about them and came to depend upon them for their economic survival.

Pontardawe became a company village dominated by the tinplate, steel and galvanizing works of W. Gilbertson and Company, and its chief executive and his family headed the social hierarchy in the village.[1] There were other local leaders, such as landowners, church and chapel ministers and several professional men, but all knew that the viability of the community depended upon the company. Whilst not always agreeing with the family, all appreciated the need for the firm to be prosperous and to pay regularly. For their part, the Gilbertson family members perceived themselves to be the natural leaders of the community, believed they knew what was good for the community and were influential in supervising and contributing to its development. Every social issue came under their critical scrutiny and was subjected to their sometimes censorious opinions. William, Arthur and Frank Gilbertson, in their respective ways, were benevolently supportive and coercively regulative, fulfilling a paternalistic role and its diffuse obligations according to their own normative standards.

WILLIAM GILBERTSON: FOUNDER OF AN INDUSTRIAL DYNASTY

William Gilbertson was born on 10th June 1810 and baptised at All Saints' Church, Hertford, on 9 December 1810, the sixth child of Matthias and Fanny Gilbertson.[2] The family's origins are obscure, but it has been suggested that Matthias was the son of James Gilbertson, a factor to the Marquis of Tweeddale,[3] and Fanny was the daughter of Robert Collings, a King's Messenger and London merchant.[4] From 1803 to 1824 Matthias appears in the land tax assessments as occupier and owner of several properties in Hertford, whilst in the Register of Baptisms at All Saints' Church he is described in 1812 as a draper by occupation. Matthias was also paying land tax in Egham, Surrey, from 1810 and was registered to vote in respect of his house, named in the register as Elm Cottage, in 1835. He did not relinquish his properties in Hertford, however, and subsequent land tax assessments show that he continued to extend his holdings there.[5] Pigot's Directory for 1826-27 lists his first son, James Matthias, as a grocer and tallow chandler in Fore Street, Hertford, and Gilbertson and Palmer are shown as linen drapers in the same street. Matthias Gilbertson of Fore Street also appears as agent for the Norwich Union insurance company. Subsequent assessments confirm his increasing ownership of properties in Hertford, and by 1863-4 he is shown as being "of Staines" near Egham.[6]

These records suggest that William Gilbertson grew up in a comfortably affluent and secure middle-class environment where commercial values would have predominated. At the age of fifteen he entered Shrewsbury School which, under the headship of Dr. Samuel Butler, the eminent scholar and later Bishop of Lichfield and Coventry, was one of the finest public schools in Britain with a high scholastic reputation.[7] The school records show that William remained there from August 1825 to Christmas 1828, but unfortunately there is no indication of his scholastic achievements as the school lists do not start until 1831. Dr. Butler's register merely states that William came from 'Egham Hill' and that he was placed in the Fifth. He does not appear to have progressed further and Dr. Butler's prize examination mark register does not record him in 1827 or 1828, omissions which prompted a former School Librarian to speculate that William "was not a roaring success as a classical scholar, when this was the raison d'etre of Shrewsbury".[8] After leaving Shrewsbury School, William appears to have served articles for the legal profession, for he was admitted to the Roll of Attorneys on 9 May 1834. He is recorded in the Law Lists for 1835 to 1840 as a partner in the firm of Weeks and Gilbertson at 12, Cook's Court, Lincoln's Inn.[9] In 1835 the young solicitor married Eliza Bramah, the daughter of Francis and the granddaughter of the celebrated inventor Joseph Bramah, and in the following year she gave birth to Matthias, the first of their fourteen children. At some stage during those critical first years of independence, when the problems of developing a law practice and of coping with new marital responsibilities and parenthood must have dominated his life, he decided to abandon his profession and embark upon a radically different and challenging career in industrial management. In 1839 he removed his family from Hanover Square and its genteel Mayfair society

William Gilbertson *(Mrs Nanette Pearce)*

Eliza Gilbertson *(Mrs Nanette Pearce)*

to the harsh and alien environment of Cwmavon in a remote and rapidly industrialising South Wales valley. There he took over the unaccustomed position of manager of the recently constituted and extensive copper works of Vigurs, Batten, James and Company,[10] and the associated role of main employer in a community of 2,000 people.[11] He was never again to practise law as a solicitor for there is no further reference to him in the Law Society's records after 1840. His partnership with Weeks ceased from the same date, although Weeks continued to practise on his own account at Cook's Court.

Some explanation for his radical change of career may be found in the suggestion that he went to Cwmavon not as a salaried manager but as a partner in the company.[12] There are no extant company records to corroborate the claim, nor any indication of his capacity to buy a partnership in a speculative venture. However, entry into the metal trades was not excessively costly and in the tinplate trade the capital cost of building a works was small, production was small scale and the operational costs could be largely funded on a credit basis.[13] Gilbertson's financial status at this time is not known but his family background suggests a sufficient degree of affluence to have made his entry into the metallurgical trades reasonably easy. By 1841, when the business and the works of Vigurs, Batten, James & Company were made over to the Governor and Company of Copper Miners in England, the Company's prospectus showed a capital issue of £1m in 10,000 shares of £100 each, and included among the chief shareholders were John Vigurs and his son Lewis, B. P. Batten, Trevenen James and William Gilbertson.[14] Unfortunately their individual holdings were not specified, but William was designated in the prospectus as one of the twelve Assistant Governors of the Company and in that capacity he undertook "sole and undivided management" of the enterprise at Cwmavon until April 1844.[15] Under his management the coal, iron, tinplate and copper operations of the company were extended, the rolling of copper plates and sheets was introduced and he probably played a part in the completion of Port Talbot Docks, as the Copper Company owned 80% of the Port Talbot Harbour Company. By 1842 Gilbertson was well established as a major metal and tinplate producer and was also shipping approximately 1,000 tons of coal weekly to European and Baltic ports. His Cwmbuchan (Cwmavon) works employed 880 workers and the village was almost entirely dependent for employment on the works and its collieries. Gilbertson resigned in April 1844 and the partnership was dissolved in January 1846.[16] A financial crisis in the following year forced the Company to mortgage its property to the Bank of England which carried on production until 1851 when statutory authority was obtained by the Company to repurchase the works from the Bank.

On 13 May 1852 the Company's directors returned to be met by scenes of jubilation, and a cavalcade of carriages, preceded by banners and the local band, escorted them along the long road from Aberavon railway station to Cwmavon. One of the recipients of the cheers was William Gilbertson, and a spokesman for the Glanafan Lodge referred to ". . . the name of our old and respected master, William Gilbertson, Esq., for the care he has shown towards the inhabitants of this valley and we sincerely hope the zeal and efforts and his unswerving self-denial which he showed in his honourable efforts to bring about the circumstances for which we have met today will be long remembered in the hearts of a thankful people". At a celebratory dinner many speeches referred to William Gilbertson's abilities and to his "suitability to deal with all kinds of business matters". When Gilbertson rose to respond the entire concourse of six hundred diners "rose with a hip, hip, hooray, again and again, to show their respect for the new manager . . . ".[17] There followed several halcyon years of prosperity for the Afan Valley. From 1852 to 1860 the net profits realised by the works totalled £215,527.2s.2d., a preference dividend of 7½% was regularly paid and "a considerable sum" was distributed as dividend to ordinary shareholders.[18] William's personal contribution as chief executive to these years of financial success can only be inferred, but his status as a popular employer and public benefactor are explicitly revealed in a poem dedicated to him at a local eisteddfod in 1857 and published as a pamphlet entitled *A Tribute of Gratitude, or Workingman's Estimate of a Kind Master*. It extols his "good deeds" in restoring the Cwmavon Works to the "old company", in providing drinking water throughout the village, in erecting baths for use by the workmen, in establishing schools for the workmen's children "without infringing upon their religious liberty", and in giving financial support to the Bible Society "to spread this blessed volume" to his workmen. Gilbertson was a devout Anglican and was the driving force behind the building of a new church at Cwmavon. At its opening and consecration in June 1856 the Governor and Company of Copper Miners were praised for having transformed Cwmavon from a small village of a few hundred people to a populous community of "6,000 souls", and for providing "for the spiritual wants of their workmen". The Company had apparently refused all financial aid "from any of the Societies" and had funded the building of the church "solely by the voluntary contributions of the individual Proprietors of the Works". For the opening services, all the shops were closed and the main part of the works shut for the day. Gilbertson had expressly stated, however, that no man should be compelled to leave his work or to lose his pay "if his conscience or other scruples prevented his attending the services of the Established Church, or if his circumstances were such he could not, in justice to his wife and family, afford to lose a day's earnings".[19]

William Gilbertson's paternalism undoubtedly owed much to his deeply held religious principles. At the Company's anniversary dinner on 13 May 1857 one speaker commended Gilbertson's "anxiety for both the temporal and spiritual welfare of his workpeople". Another referred to his "moral·principles and religious conduct [which] were exemplary and conspicuous, and whilst they served to guide the judgement, they, at the same time, sustained him during those laborious exertions which are so necessary to the successful carrying on of works of such magnitude". In proposing the health of the agents and clerks of the Company, Gilbertson referred to a previous speaker's remark about "the necessity of harmony and love amongst them" and asked them to give him "credit for entertaining the same feeling". It was his earnest desire that all who co-operated with him "should flourish and prosper".

He then spoke at length about the need to observe the Sabbath, particularly when there were so many temptations to work on that day, and asked the agents and clerks to co-operate with him "in putting down to the lowest possible ebb all labour on that day". He was sure that all who desired Cwmavon's prosperity and the Company's success would do so. They were all aware that "there were certain departments which could not be carried on without a certain amount of Sabbath labour", but he "wished that amount to be brought down to the very smallest point", and he "should feel deeply and personally indebted to them if they would lay their heads together" and present him with "any plan by which the labour of even a single man would be done away with on the Sabbath-day". He then referred his listeners to the Bible where "they would see that no work whatever should be done upon the Sabbath without the sternest necessity". He therefore implored them "each to say 'I will help Mr. Gilbertson in putting down labour on the Sabbath-day'". He concluded by saying that he thought "every working man had a right to enjoy the Sabbath as he wishes, provided it was in accordance with the word of God".[20]

Gilbertson was not only managing a successful company but was also deeply involved in the everyday life of Cwmavon, contributing largely to its religious, educational and social development and attempting to improve the quality of life generally for his employees and their families. A population of approximately 8,000 was now dependent upon his works, and the company was paying about one-sixth of the entire rate assessment of the borough of Aberavon within which Cwmavon was situated. As resident manager and major employer the mantle of community leadership and its consequent responsibilities fell naturally upon his shoulders. One major factor which made the assumption of this obligation imperative was the absence of any significant alternative. The agencies of government which today provide the environmental facilities which sustain healthy communities were non-existent or only rudimentarily developed. Central government's interest was minimal and all-purpose local authorities providing an array of supportive services had yet to be developed. The parish vestry, the ancient boroughs and the chaos of ad hoc authorities were inadequate to cope with the demands of an industrialising urban society. Moreover, the calibre of local representatives did not always inspire confidence in the propertied ratepayers. Gilbertson too had no confidence in the abilities of the burgesses. In 1859 he signed a petition to the Privy Council for the grant of a new charter of incorporation to Aberavon because the existing corporation was "utterly inadequate to the wants of the population". At a public meeting in July 1859 he stated that he felt Aberavon was not as prosperous as other towns because the existing corporation "required an infusion of new blood (hear, hear). The position of the present Corporation as regards the education of its members was a great drawback to the prosperity of the town". He thought that they were not sufficiently educated "to be entrusted with the management of property" and that the granting of the charter would be of immense importance to the prosperity of the town: "Aberavon had great facilities for the erection of works, but with such a Corporation as at present, what inducement was there for men of capital?".[21] Later, at a public inquiry in January

1860, he submitted that "the town was managed exceedingly badly", and added, "The members of the present Corporation, particularly those who resided in the neighbourhood, are exceedingly illiterate men, and in my judgement totally unfitted to have charge of the borough." He acknowledged that one or two public improvements had taken place within the last five or six years, "but altogether irrespective of the Corporation", and believed the town would greatly improve under a better system of management. Holding such a low opinion of the quality of Aberavon's governing body, Gilbertson felt that there was no alternative but to accept the role of leader within his isolated enclave at Cwmavon. Thus, when questioned at the same municipal inquiry about Cwmavon being brought within the terms of the Municipal Corporations Act of 1835 and having a properly elected council, he replied enigmatically that he would "still desire as far as his connection with the Company was concerned to be 'Alexander Selkirk'". Asked if he meant his remark to mean 'Lord of the beast and the brute', Gilbertson replied "No, there is another line, 'Monarch of all he surveyed'".[22]

This response nicely encapsulated his perception of the community role which his managerial position had created for him. His company was dependent on the labour of that community, and he willingly accepted the reciprocal obligations to be its developer, its spiritual and moral protector and its ultimate arbiter in all aspects of its social and economic life.[23] Seeking to illustrate the community's dependence on Gilbertson, the Rev. William Llewellyn of Cowbridge applied Wren's epitaph to him and said that if people were to seek a monument to Gilbertson they need to do no more than to look around Cwmavon: "If they looked at the schools, the children of the place were well taught; and as to the masters, they need not desire better. If they turned again to the church, the services were well conducted, in season and out of season. Indeed, to have such a man amongst them, was a great acquisition, both to the directors and to the valley at large".[24] Gilbertson bequeathed to his successor not only a profitable industrial complex but one which, according to a correspondent to *The Cambrian*, had no equal in Wales in its concern for the rights of its workmen. Every worker was paid in cash, "without being shackled by the infamous truck system which grinds the workmen down to the condition of the Carolinian slave"; there were excellent schools where the children were educated "without having their faith pinned to the sleeve of any bigot"; there were two churches and numerous nonconformist chapels which had been built on land given freely "through the liberality of the Company"; and a "liberal fund . . . for the assistance of the poor and afflicted" and other individual charities were "daily bestowed by the manager and his agents to worthy and deserving families".[25]

For his part, Gilbertson's motives for leaving Cwmavon at this particularly favourable time and buying his own tinplate works in Pontardawe are not recorded. He would have evaluated the potential risks and rewards of investing his capital in what he must have perceived to be a stable and expanding market for tinplate. He may also have had the foresight to realise that the good trading conditions for the Cwmavon Works were not to last, but not even the most percipient of entrepreneurs could have predicted the massive losses that 'the old company' was to experience. In six of the next nine years his successor, W. P. Struvé, was to endure net losses owing to lower demand for iron, coal and copper, exacerbated by increased competition from the iron industry in the north of England and by a continual depreciation in copper prices from 1866 to 1869. One further factor emerges from the Company Report for 1870 which may have been influential in stimulating Gilbertson to leave. It refers to the organisational difficulties which beset large and heterogeneous, vertically integrated enterprises where the "extent and multifarious character of the works" created major problems of co-ordination and supervision. It has been suggested that one common factor contributing to a founder's intention to achieve entrepreneurial independence was a basic anti-bureaucratic antagonism towards large, complex organisations. The main features of this antagonism were a desire to start a small enterprise where short means-ends chains allowed the decision-maker to see the consequences of his decisions, where personal affective relationships predominated in place of the large organisation's impersonal instrumental rationality, and where a restrictive bureaucratic role might be expanded to encompass several social roles and so satisfy "a yearning for a new moral order in business relationships".[26] One may only conjecture that William Gilbertson, given his business experience and his sense of social duty, may have harboured similar thoughts. He was now aged fifty and may well have felt the need for autonomous control of a small manageable concern where he would be responsible to himself only and where the benefits of his labours would accrue to himself and his family.

THE GILBERTSON FAMILY AND PONTARDAWE, 1861-1890

In 1861 William Gilbertson left Cwmavon for the Swansea Valley which was being extensively industrialised, with many iron forges and tinplate works, collieries and several populous villages. On 8 May he leased the Pontardawe tinplate works comprising nine mills from William Parsons. The works ledger of W. Gilbertson and Company starts with a contra-entry dated May 1861, transferring £10,000 from his private account at the Neath branch of the Glamorganshire Banking Company "in a/c of partnership" with John Harris of Durham and George Lawrence of Hereford.[27] The locational factors were attractive, for the works were situated between the Swansea valley canal, for the conveyance of raw materials directly to the works via a branch canal and for shipping its output to the port of Swansea eight miles away, and the River Tawe which provided water power. The main valley road lay alongside the canal, and on the other side of the works the single line of the Swansea Valley Railway had been opened in February 1860 to the acclaim of local workmen and the expectation that it would prove advantageous to "enterprising proprietors" and to "the inhabitants of a fertile mineral district that has yet scarcely been explored".[28] Moreover, the village of Pontardawe, which was partly situated in the three parishes of Llanguicke, Cilybebyll and Rhyndwyclydach, contained an experienced workforce and an increasing population.

Gilbertson transferred his family and servants to Ynysderw House which had been built by William Parsons on a slope overlooking the works.[29] At that time the village of Pontardawe had a population of 1,500 inhabitants and, according to a much later newspaper report, was "a ramshackle old place somewhat of the wigwam style of architecture". The same source suggested that the works were "as old-fashioned and as remarkable as they well could be, dilapidated, and everything of the most ancient order."[30] The new owner embarked on a process of modernisation and within four years Pontardawe was being described as "a rising and populous village" with the Gilbertson tinplate works "giving employment to a great number of men".[31] Contemporary newspaper reports show that the Gilbertson family entered fully into the social life of the compact community. In 1865 the 300 or so children of the National School, the night school and the Sunday schools in Pontardawe were "regaled with tea and cake", and among the "several ladies and gentlemen" who "readily assisted in distributing the good things provided", were Mr. and Mrs. William Gilbertson, third son Arthur and his sisters.[32] A week later, before a full audience including the Gilbertson family in the Oddfellows Hall, "Mr. Arthur Gilbertson rendered, with his usual feeling, 'The Reefer' and 'Harp of Wales', "and also sang with his sisters 'The Sea Flower' and 'Sleep, gentle lady'", while the eldest son Matthias Gilbertson "presided at the pianoforte". The proceeds of this concert, which was "a most decided success", went to the Church Choir and Choral Society and to the Church organ fund. Arthur Gilbertson also sang at a grand concert in Briton Ferry in the same week.[33]

William's early achievements were commemorated at the Alltwen Eisteddfod in April 1867 where a *Song of Praise to W. Gilbertson, Esquire* recorded in twelve stanzas his contributions to Pontardawe and offered a paean of praise to his character. He was referred to as a "Gentleman worthy of every respect" and "His workmen and neighbours revere his person". He was a staunch Christian who was possessed of "unwavering justice", while his "inflexible principles" led him to close the tinworks on Sundays so that his employees, unlike the "thousands of workmen in servile submission to worldly employers", should attend church. He re-established the "grossly neglected" Reading Room and encouraged "All movements which tend to diffuse education, or cultivate morals". Although a Churchman "he still is no bigot, But loves every Christian as brother and kin". As a county magistrate and presiding magistrate at the Pontardawe sessional division "his name is impeachless" and his administration was just, though "felons before him are stricken with awe". He was generous to philanthropic bodies and "radiant with charity". Such literary appraisals of industrialists were not uncommon at that time and it is difficult, if not impossible, to separate reality from what today would be regarded as obsequious hyperbole. The image which materialises from these stanzas, from the *Tribute of Gratitude* written at the Cwmavon Eisteddfod in 1857, and from his many community provisions in Cwmavon and Pontardawe, suggests a man of firm moral rectitude wholly committed to the industrial, social and religious improvement of the communities over which he exercised his authority. Moreover, the structural features which were most likely to enhance his authority existed in Cwmavon and Pontardawe. Both were relatively isolated and "retired spots", and both were being colonised by a largely immigrant, heterogeneous and proletarian work-force which was totally reliant upon the sole major employer for subsistence. Traditional power relationships were replicated in these communities and the workers, accustomed to respect authority, were generally acquiescent to employer regulation.

Like all other valley masters or owner-managers William Gilbertson lived near the works, his daily relationships were personalised, and his proximity served to maximise his social control and to cloak the contractual and functionally specific relationship which overtly typified the urban factory owner whose home was segregated from those of his workmen and their subcultures. The economic exchange which was basic to the relationship was seen to be complementary to the social exchange whose obligations were not only unspecified but appear to have been unlimited. In the prototypical manner of many paternalist employers, he assumed responsibilities beyond the contractual provision of wages and conditions of work and became the universal provider of religious, educational and social amenities, and in return he expected deference and the acceptance of his authority. The eisteddfod poems and the ebullient celebration in Cwmavon when "the old company" returned may be interpreted as the spontaneous and unforced expressions of a social exchange which tend to engender feelings of personal obligation, gratitude and trust.[34]

William's move to Pontardawe coincided, however, with the emergence of a rival source of leadership which was about to challenge the traditional authority of the masters. Trade unionism in the tinplate trade dates from 1862 with the formation of the Amalgamated Malleable Ironworkers Union in the North of England. By 1874 there were 113 branches in Wales. In South West Wales, however, a competitive and separatist union, the Independent Association of Tinplate Workers, was registered in Swansea in 1871 and was led by the charismatic William Lewis (Lewys Afan). During the union's brief existence (to 1887) its activities were confined to works within fifteen miles of Swansea, but there is no record of a branch being established in Pontardawe and contemporary journals and newspapers give no indication of union activity in Pontardawe. The union's emergence marks the beginning of formalised collective bargaining in the tinplate trade, but it was essentially a fund-raising organisation to support its members during strikes and lockouts, and as there were frequent localised disputes, "the union never had enough 'powder and shot' to engage in a real contest with the employers".[35] Each dispute weakened the union's financial strength and it was unable to enforce a settlement on individual employers. In 1874 the union demanded wage parity for its members with the rates paid in Staffordshire and Monmouthshire, but the employers refused. Agitation in Carmarthenshire over the creation of a standard uniform pay scale spread to works in West Glamorgan and the employers responded with notices to terminate contracts and on their expiration 20,000 iron and tinplate workers were locked out and over 30 works were idle.[36] By late August the masters were holding meetings to formulate a uniform wage scale for tinplate millmen,[37] and "particulars have been already agreed upon provisionally which will lead to an increase in the remuneration of certain workmen".[38]

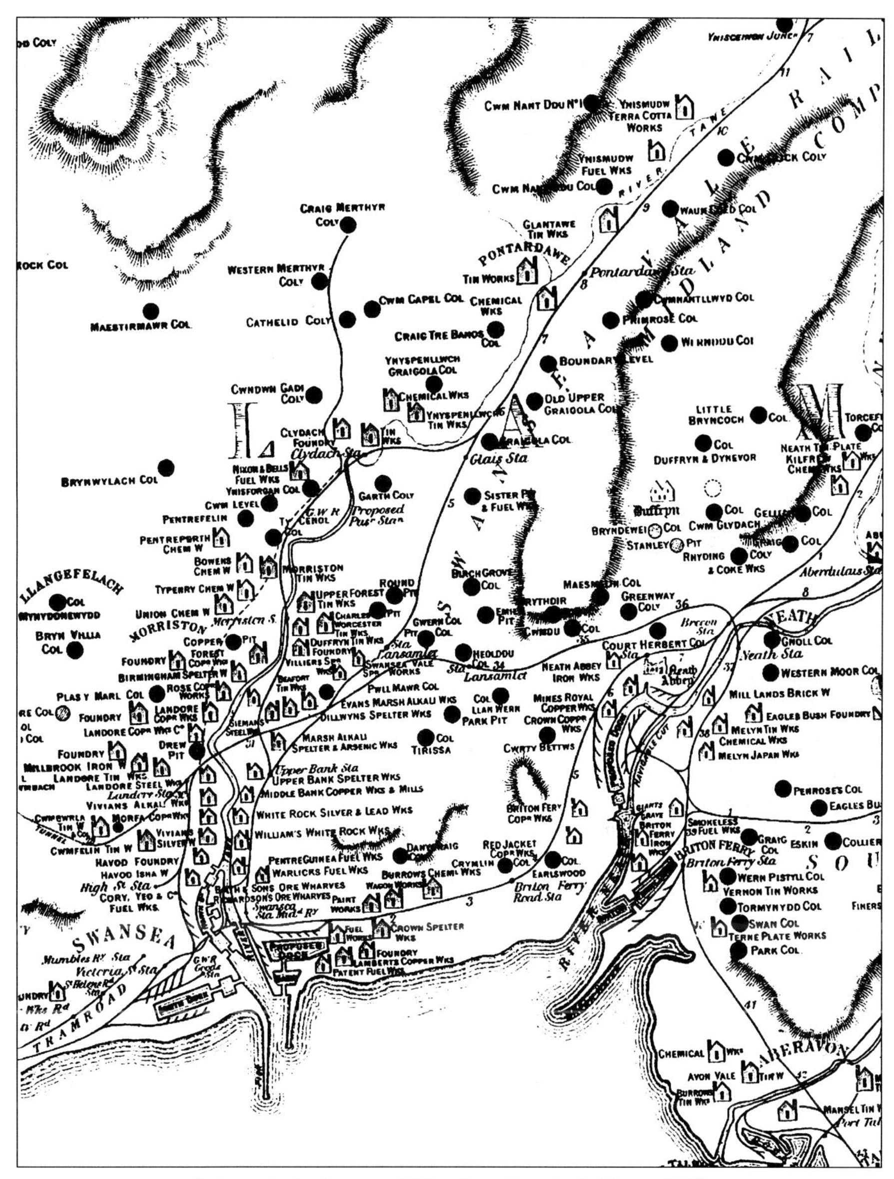

Industry in the Swansea Valley from Campion's Map, c.1875
(West Glamorgan Archive Service)

In these deliberations Arthur Gilbertson played a leading role and was one of the three signatories to the scale of rates which was finally agreed with the workers' representatives on 24 November 1874, and became known subsequently as 'The 1874 List' (Appendix 2).

William died on 4 February 1882. His obituary in *The Cambrian*, claimed that Pontardawe had benefited from being under his "kindly eye", and by "precept and example" he had "spread his silent but civilising influence around him – commencing at a time when such influence, and when some steady moral control was much needed in the locality". Although his "personal status in the county, his almost solitary position in his immediate neighbourhood, and his intellectual attainments might be expected to render him, apparently at least, a man much to himself so far as concerned people generally", he was seen to be a fair manager of men. His long experience as an employer "had amply taught him that some sternness as well as sympathy was essential to obtain punctuality and exactitude from employees". His tinplate works were "second to none in the pursuance of a steady, as well as successful, run of business, carried on principles of rigid integrity and honour – a business in which the limit of distinction of master and man has always been distinctly observed, but a distinction in which the limit formed no barrier to sympathy when required, not only as expressed by words, but by good deeds, though done in silence. It is certain that no appeal was made to Mr. Gilbertson, that he did not scrutinize, and then reward on its merits". The obituary suggested that his qualities would be difficult to replace because: "Such characters, taking them for all in all, are becoming rarer day by day. Gentlemen by birth, education, worldly means by position and at the same time honourable men of business, at the head of extensive works, are valuable members of the community, and deserve cherishing while living . . . We claim all this for the very honourable man whose loss we now deplore."[39]

William Gilbertson's personal estate was valued at £75,923. He bequeathed to his son Arthur all his shares, amounting to seven-fifteenths of the partnership, in W. Gilbertson and Company, and thus ensured the continuity of family control. For nearly a quarter of a century Arthur had shadowed his father in the management and development of the Pontardawe works which, by 1880, comprised twelve iron puddling furnaces and six rolling mills. Arthur's emergence to such prominence owed as much to his natural aptitude for the tinplate business as to his elder brothers' defection from it. The eldest son Matthias, although described in the 1861 census for Pontardawe as a 'Tinplate Manufacturer', left the area.[40] The second son Francis Bramah seems to have shunned managerial responsibility, travelled widely and was later given a position as the company's agent in Liverpool.[41] Arthur was the first of William's sons to be born in Wales, at Coed Park, Cwmavon, and was educated locally at Cowbridge Grammar School and for a year (1857-8) at Christ College, Brecon. From the age of 17 he had understudied his father and reportedly combined "the energy of his youth with the mature experience of his father".[42] In the following years he established a sufficiently prominent reputation to be chosen as a vigorous advocate of the masters' cause in the formulation of the 1874 List and to be elected

Arthur Gilbertson, J.P. *(Mrs Nanette Pearce)*

President of the South Wales Tinplate Association in 1877. In the eight years following his father's death, Arthur embarked upon a process of industrial expansion. In May 1883 he bought the adjacent Glantawe tinplate works with three mills, and registered it as the Glanrhyd Tin Plate Company with £21,000 capital. In November 1885 W. Gilbertson and Company was registered as a limited company with a nominal capital of £35,000 divided into 700 shares of £50 each. The share allotment of 1891 shows that 426 shares were held by Arthur Gilbertson, 210 by his father's business partner George Lawrence of Cheltenham, and the remaining shares were distributed among members of the two families and their associates.

From the 1880s Pontardawe, like many other villages on the coalfield, grew in population and prosperity as the coal and tinplate trades expanded to meet an apparently insatiable world demand. Aided by the tinplate boom in the 1880s, with prices rising rapidly and large profit margins, Arthur Gilbertson reaped the benefits of his enterprise and his workers were guaranteed regular employment and steady wages. In March 1890 he built the Glynbeudy tinplate works in Brynamman with four mills, and in October of the same year introduced the Siemens open-hearth process in his Pontardawe works by building two basic steel furnaces. The substitution of mild steel sheet for puddled wrought iron sheet as the base material for the manufacture of tinplates was of fundamental importance to the firm and to the local community. In addition to guaranteeing his supplies of steel for tinplating and later galvanizing, he could ensure higher quality standards, reduce his manufacturing costs and be more responsive to new developments and product opportunities.

Arthur Gilbertson was now a well-established leader in the industrial and social life of the district. He was a Justice of the Peace, sitting with his brother-in-law Herbert Lloyd on the bench of Pontardawe Petty Sessions, where he was able to maintain a judicial overview of the miscreant life of the community and of any of his workmen who were unfortunate enough to be brought before him. At the close of 1888 he became a candidate for election to Glamorgan County Council, stating that he was "not a Tory but a mild Conservative, and a staunch supporter of our present admirable Government"[43] – that of the Marquis of Salisbury. His success in the January 1889 election added another dimension to his authority, which was further enhanced by his appointment as High Sheriff in 1892.

Supporting his early ambitions was his wife Ellen whom he had married at Cilybebyll Parish Church on 25 July 1872. Ellen was the second daughter of Francis Edwardes Lloyd (1805-65) and sister of Herbert Lloyd (1838-1914), the main landowner in the Pontardawe area. In the following five years Ellen bore him four sons and in 1878 Arthur moved his young family from their Danygraig home to a newly erected mansion at Glanrhyd House where ten more children were born. The house became a centre of social activity for the most prominent families of the district. In 1888 *The Cambrian* reported "The grandest event hitherto of the season" when "The whole of the leading families in the neighbourhood were represented . . . including several fair *debutantes*, a gay phalanx of beauty, whose presence imparted additional lustre to an already fairy-like scene; the house being brilliantly illuminated with gas

Arthur Gilbertson as High Sheriff of Glamorganshire, 1892
(Mrs Nanette Pearce)

Ellen Gilbertson, c.1890 *(Mrs Nanette Pearce)*

and Chinese lanterns". Ellen "received her guests in the entrance-hall, and dancing, for the first time, took place in the oak room, a large building recently erected by Mr. Gilbertson, and in every way fitted for an assemblage of this kind. The gay terpsichoreans commenced to dance about 10 o'clock to the strains of Mr. F. W. Hulley's famous band, and all 'went as merry as a marriage bell,' until the 'wee' small hours of morning, when the party dispersed, thoroughly pleased with the great treat which Mr. and Mrs. Gilbertson had provided for them".[44] One can only speculate about the reactions of his employees to this lavish display of conspicuous consumption.

As the first lady of the village Ellen fulfilled her interlocking roles of wife, mother and hostess, and was noted for "her kindness to the poor of the district". She took a particular interest in the welfare of the works' girls and from 1882 was the moving spirit behind the Girls' Friendly Society in Pontardawe (Appendix 3). The Tinplate Union's newspaper expressed its gratitude to her for establishing instruction classes and for her many benevolent activities on the girls' behalf, stating that "this lady has proved to be a good angel to many of them".[45] Later it referred to her "high reputation for the good that she is doing to better the conditions of our female workers", and applauded another of "her many acts of generosity" when she invited all the works' girls to a Saturday tea "in the big room that was given for their use some years ago by their honoured mistress".[46] During their married life of twenty-two years Ellen bore Arthur seven sons and seven daughters, and so helped to ensure the dynastic succession of the family business. In her public sphere she symbolised for Pontardawe's inhabitants the softer supply side of paternalism by actively supporting good causes, providing moral leadership and displaying a devotion for the traditional integrating institutions of family and church. She died on 15 March 1894 at the age of 44, and her gravestone in All Saints cemetery is inscribed with the beatitude 'Blessed are the pure in heart'. Her death was a personal tragedy from which Arthur never fully recovered, and his remaining years were devoted to his large family and the development of his expanding business.

THE LETTER-BOOKS: INDUSTRIAL AND SOCIAL CONTEXT 1890-1929

The value system within which Arthur Gilbertson worked was changing from that experienced by his father. The emergence of new unionism and changing social expectations created a more critical environment than that which William had dominated. William had acquired a monopoly of power over his employees, and, as his successor, Arthur claimed the unique vicarious right to exercise a comparable power. Believing his authority to be legitimate, reliable and fair, he felt that he could apply and enforce his authoritative and unilateral decisions without challenge.[47] The Independent Association of Tinplate Workers was succeeded in 1887 by the South Wales, Monmouthshire and Gloucestershire Tinplate Workers' Union under the general secretaryship of Thomas Phillips. When the union's first weekly newspaper *The Welsh Industrial Times*, edited by J. H. John, began publishing in August 1888 there were no trade unionists in Arthur Gilbertson's Pontardawe or Glanrhyd works. The issue for 6 October 1888 said that both works were well managed and "every workman is having his rights, and in consequence no disputes arise between employers and employed". The writer lamented the fact that the men were not unionists but hoped they might "improve their childish ways and show they are men", by joining the union. The appeal was repeated intermittently in succeeding years but produced little response from the majority of the workmen.

By 1890 the imminent loss of the American domestic market and overproduction in the trade had produced a glut of tinplates, and there was considerable discussion of the employers' proposal to stop their works for a fortnight "to give a fillip to the trade".[48] With the active support of the Tinplate Workers' Union a stop week was agreed for mid-March 1890 and 32 of the 45 works were closed. Neither Pontardawe works stopped production, nor did Gilbertson delay the start of his new Glynbeudy works in Brynamman. In a letter to *The Western Mail* he argued that although two-thirds of the works had been stopped, losing 200,000 boxes, the trade remained "in a languishing condition" and "ruin would overtake some of the manufacturers" unless stocks were further reduced. As he was "personally indifferent to the success of the stoppage movement, and inclined to doubt its expediency on broad principles, I kept my works going, and am in a position to do so for some months again". He pointed out that tinplate stocks had increased to such an extent that the Midland Railway's vans in Swansea were full, as were the Harbour Trust's sheds, and predicted that buyers would exploit the situation and "works less fortunately placed than others will have to be added to the astonishing number of failures (77 works bankrupt in 12 years)". He had "orders to go on with" because "our exceptional connection with foreign parts enables us to work without adding to the American glut".[49]

A fortnight later *The Welsh Industrial Times* referred once more to the Pontardawe men's indifference to unionism and attributed it to Gilbertson's qualities "as an employer [who] is recognised by the men as one of the best in the trade".[50] This opinion was to change radically over subsequent months as Gilbertson continued to refuse stop weeks, and the general reluctance of his workmen to join the Tinplate Workers' Union was further reinforced in October 1890 with the start-up of his two new steel furnaces and the expectation of continued employment opportunities. In describing the event the Union's paper unwittingly underlined the community's dependence on Arthur Gilbertson who had "always endeavoured to further the interests of Pontardawe". Not only did he employ "constant men" but the conversion to steel was "looked upon with much satisfaction by the shopkeepers and others in Pontardawe". Commenting on the celebratory fireworks display held in the eight acre Recreation Ground provided by the company, the reporter suggested that as the new works was lit by electricity, Gilbertson "should now be approached with a view to having the streets of the rising little town lit by electricity".[51] He appeared to be oblivious of the possibility that public benefaction on such a scale might require a reciprocal display of deferential gratitude. By July 1891 he had recouped the outlay on the steelworks and confirmed that "All is going well here & Steel Works a grand success" [1 : 131]. He profited from the boom demand which preceded the enforcement of the protectionist McKinley Act from 1 July 1891, but the subsequent contraction of the American tinplate market overshadowed and exacerbated localised tensions throughout the trade. A duty of 2·2 cents per lb. on imported tinplates and terneplates (equivalent to a 70% increase in the selling price) and 1·65 cents per lb. on finished blackplates was imposed by the U.S. Congress, and immediately British exports of these goods fell from a peak of 325,143 tons in 1891 to 85,472 tons in 1897. The South Wales tinplate trade, having benefited as the world's leading manufacturer of tinplates and virtually monopolising the American trade, suffered substantial hardship. Many employers were forced to close down their mills or to reduce wages and wrest concessions and allowances from their employees. Gilbertson ignored the Union's further calls for stop weeks and the restoration of the '36 box rule', limiting output per eight hour shift. In his three tinplate works production remained buoyant, stimulated by the high prices paid by the United States, prior to the imposition of its tariff, and his alternative markets in South America and the colonies [1 : 77-8]. Nevertheless, the McKinley tariff did require some cost cutting and when contacted by J. H. John, the editor of *The Industrial World*, which had superseded *The Welsh Industrial Times* in January 1892, Arthur Gilbertson asserted that, "I don't think there is any agitation among my men. I pay very liberal wages, and afford absolutely regular work. I did not avail myself of the reduction in wages, when others did, but the terrible competition just now compels me to reduce my costs. I trust it won't last long".[52] He then reduced the price of dipping a box of tinplates, and the Pontardawe correspondent to *The Industrial World*, writing in Welsh under the pseudonym of 'Tawe', stated that unionists and non-unionists alike were "enthusiastic in their disgust", and he reported one of the workmen as saying that ". . . this is our reward for complying with the master's request not to join the Union".[53]

Gilbertson's action presaged a strike which lasted nearly two months at the Pontardawe works, but the majority of his workmen remained apathetic to the Union, whose appeal may have been limited by its own narrow perception of its role as a 'strike' or 'wage protecting' organisation. Moreover, the trade was improving and most of his workmen were reluctant to jeopardise their wages at such a volatile time. Earlier in February 1892 Gilbertson had confessed that "Everything is very depressed now" [1 : 74], but five months later the company paid a final dividend of 10% and he admitted that "We are doing exceedingly well, in spite of the state of trade generally" [1 : 185-7]. In the same month, he confided to a fellow employer that, "I don't despair of beating America in cost, in spite of her tariff" [1 : 200].

A strike of assorters in August 1892 and their replacement by non-unionist labour produced an editorial in *The Industrial World* which suggested that "It is his misfortune and not his fault that he lives in a democratic age, an age in which workmen dare to think and act as if they also had rights, and are not prepared to bow the knee in adoration even of the High Sheriff of Glamorgan".[54] It was incongruent with Gilbertson's frame of reference to visualise his company as a pluralism containing related but separate interests. He saw a corporate unity with himself as the single focus of authority and loyalty, and failed to accept the legitimacy of rival sources of leadership or of sectional groups with divergent objectives. However, democratic and egalitarian ideals were now challenging years of deferential respect, and his traditional expectations and strategies for enforcing authority were becoming more and more unrealistic before the crystallising power of organised labour. Arthur Gilbertson remained implacably opposed to the Tinplate Workers' Union and its leaders, seeing them to be irrelevant to his workers' financial security and a potential threat to his managerial prerogative. His attitude was obdurately rooted in his belief, sustained by convention if not law, that he was the *master* with proprietary control over his subordinate *servants*. Since 1875 these titles had been replaced in legislation by *employers* and *workmen* as equal partners in a civil contract, but even in 1892 Arthur still referred to himself as *master* and was allegedly incensed when addressed by the ten dismissed assorters "as our employer". He was said to have replied, "I am accustomed to be addressed as 'master' (not employer) in my Works".[55] This curt admonition conveyed his *de facto* interpretation of what was *de jure* an obsolete relationship.

The dispute dragged on until October 1893 when the Union admitted it had lost the battle. Seven of the ten tinplate mills and nine pots at Pontardawe were being worked by non-unionists, but the trade was generally unconcerned over the plight of one tinplate works where the millmen had previously been "indifferent Unionists". On 4 October Gilbertson wrote to the *Cambria Daily Leader* claiming that the strike "instigated by the spirit of 'New Unionism' has completely broken down . . . and all the men we require have tendered their regret for the steps they were induced to take by the Union Leaders". In its review of the year *The Industrial World* admitted that "for the first time in the history of the Union, a strike became a failure, and Blacklegging triumphed".[56] Labour relations for the remaining years of the century were comparatively quiescent and the infrequent references to Pontardawe in *The Industrial World* suggest the union's reluctant recognition that Arthur Gilbertson's authority was unassailable. However, his workmen at the Glynbeudy works expressed their independence by joining the Tinplate Workers' Union, and he later accounted for this apostasy by admitting that "I am too far off to get influence over the men" [2 : 18-9].

Shortly after his wife's death in March 1894, Arthur was joined in the Company by his eldest son Frank who was completing his undergraduate studies at Oxford. At Frank's deferred coming of age celebration on Easter Day 1894, a supper party attended by Arthur's employees and local notabilities heard him state how important the event was to them and the village "whose prosperity depends mostly upon these works". The occasion enabled him to give his son "a vested interest in the business carried on here . . . I am thankful to say he has entered upon the work, as you will know, with hearty interest and has already suggested some important improvements in the modes of manufacture: especially he is useful to me as possessing a scientific education, and a good practical knowledge of chemistry". That summer Frank was awarded a B.A.(Hons.) in Natural Science, specialising in Chemistry.[57] His scientific knowledge was unusual in a future owner-manager and rare in an industry which was generally bedevilled by the inability of owners to adapt to technological change.[58] Arthur appreciated the necessity of keeping abreast of technical developments to maintain his competitiveness, for as he told the assembly, "You know, in these days, old fashioned ideas as to manufacture can only lead to grief and failure".[59] To have an eldest son with the commitment and ability to guide the family business into an unparalleled third generation of tinplate and steel manufacturing must have been immensely gratifying for Arthur, and fulfilled his overriding desire, expressed in his letters in Chapter 1, of ensuring that the Company should remain in his family's control.

Despite the McKinley tariff and the suggested weekly loss of 225 tons of tinplate exports to the United States,[60] the company's annual returns to the Special Commissioner of Tax show a consistently healthy level of gross profits from 1892 to 1896, averaging £11,350 p.a. and peaking to £14,251 in 1896, while paying its shareholders final dividends of 10% for each of the three years from 1892 to 1894 and 22½% and 20% in 1895 and 1896 respectively. In March 1896 Arthur Gilbertson stated that "Our success is greatly owing to certain results from our Steel Works recently", and attributed much of his good fortune to his son Frank's "special scientific knowledge" [2 : 222-3]. Earlier that year he was planning to build a galvanizing department because the U.S. was now "rapidly making its own Tinplates & in a year's time, we shall want an outlet for our Steel, instead of part of our present Tinplates" [2 : 208-9]. He proposed to raise £17,000 to erect sheet mills and a galvanizing works because "The profits on 'Sheets' and 'Galvanizing' are more than Tinplates!! and all go to our <u>Colonies</u>, instead of America". The galvanizing trade was based in the Midlands, but Gilbertson was convinced that "We can beat the <u>Midlands</u> down here, hollow . . ." [2 : 208-9]. However, the fear of local competition and his wish to learn from the experience of others delayed his decision to build the galvanizing works, planned to produce 200 tons a week, and sheet mills until 1897. By February 1899 they were producing successfully and profitably [2 : 382-3].

The first stirrings of a recovery in the tinplate trade began in the last years of the century, with 1899-900 marking the start of a boom period. Improvements overseas in food canning techniques and the increase in motor car production stimulated demand for tinplate. Between 1891 and 1913 the home consumption of tinplate increased by 250% and exports rose by 10%. The USA continued to be the largest importer, but new and growing markets developed throughout the Far East, Asia, India and South America. From its dependency on one market in 1891 the British tinplate industry had by 1913 become the major supplier to a global market. During the same period exports of blackplates increased and the demand for terneplate, mainly for roofing, remained constant.[61] The tonnage of tin, terne and blackplates exported through Swansea docks rose from 209,400 tons in 1902 to 330,350 tons in 1912.[62] As the Welsh tinplate and steel industries prospered, so too did Arthur Gilbertson's works. In 1899 he responded to sheet developments in West

Francis William Gilbertson *(Michael Vivian)*

Wales by converting his tinplate mills to sheet mills, and by the eve of the new century he viewed the future with considerable optimism.

In 1900 Arthur Gilbertson sought to expand his steelmaking capacity by building a new steelworks on a twelve-acre site adjacent to the Port Talbot dock and the main Great Western Railway line. His choice of Port Talbot was influenced by its locational advantages, particularly for ore imports, and by major infrastructure improvements which had recently been completed by the Port Talbot Railway and Docks Company. Formed in 1890, the Company had based its strategy for regenerating the depressed economy of the borough and its coal-rich hinterland upon the enlargement and improvement of the dock to take ocean-going vessels and the laying of rail track into the neighbouring Ogwr and Garw valleys. A private bill to effect these changes was passed in 1894 and the new dock was opened in 1898.[63] The production and shipping advantages offered by these developments were persuasive, as was the personal intervention of Thomas Mansel Franklen, the Clerk to Glamorgan County Council, who fully appreciated the employment and other local multiplier advantages of a large modern steelworks for the locality and for the shareholders of the Docks Company. Moreover, his approaches to Gilbertson were encouraged by the site landowner, Miss Emily Charlotte Talbot, the wealthy heiress of the Margam Estate, and Franklen's first cousin.[64] She was already the largest shareholder in the new Port Talbot Railway and Docks Company and was prepared to invest substantially in the new steelworks.

The Port Talbot Iron and Steel Company was incorporated as a limited company in August 1900 with a nominal capital of £10,000 divided into 200 ordinary shares of £50 each. The share list shows that Arthur Gilbertson held 60 shares, with sons Frank holding 35 shares, Cecil 20 shares, Colin 20 shares and Howel 5 shares. The remainder were held by Miss Talbot's solicitor Charles Cheston with 58 shares, whilst Alfred Beesly, solicitor, and Christopher William Morgan, accountant, held one share each. The Register of Directors for 8 January 1901 shows Arthur Gilbertson as Managing Director, with three of his sons as co-directors, and T. M. Franklen as a nominee director for Miss Talbot. In January 1902 the capital was increased to £40,000 by the creation of 300 preference shares of £100 each, with a fixed cumulative dividend of 6% p.a. Franklen was allotted 130 of these shares, Cheston held 20 and Beesly 5, whilst the Gilbertson sons and daughters were allotted 130 shares.

The plant was designed to produce 650 to 700 tons of steel per week by the Pourcell method, a modified Bertrand-Thiel process, and comprised a battery of three cupolas with blowing plant for the supply of molten iron, and two 60 ton open-hearth furnaces. A three-stand rolling mill was built to produce steel sections, tinplate bars and billets, and was probably the first in Britain to be equipped with electrically driven auxiliaries.[65] The enterprise was to prove a costly failure, and Arthur Gilbertson's letters in Chapter 2 vividly illustrate the risks and uncertainties of entrepreneurial speculation and their attendant anxieties. An innovative process with unpredictable technical difficulties, labour problems, increasing cash liabilities and Miss Talbot's refusal to increase her investment, led inexorably to the company's liquidation in March 1904. John Hodge, General Secretary of the British Steel Smelters Association, later wrote that he had been invited by Arthur to inspect the new works and had "condemned with all my heart" the relatively untried process, which he dismissed as "a sort of bastard Bertrand Thiel process of steel making". With all the assurance of hindsight, he added that Gilbertson's "proposals were utterly bad and that his cost of working the cupola alone would double his melting costs". He suggested that it would have been "Far better to work the two furnaces as independent units; his output would be at least doubled and his costs a half less". Adding further insult to injury, he also condemned the mill, the proposed ingot size and the rolling method! After the venture had proved unsuccessful, Gilbertson was alleged to have said, "Hodge, you're a bit of a fraud; if you had described yourself as an expert adviser and charged me a fee of 3,000 guineas, I would have paid it, and saved £80,000".[66]

Despite Arthur Gilbertson's appeals to Franklen to intercede and persuade Miss Talbot to guarantee additional bank overdraft facilities, she appears to have been reluctant to commit herself further. The Margam Estate Papers show that in addition to an existing loan of £20,000 and the share purchases, the Estate had borrowed £70,000 from Lloyd's Bank, Birmingham, to invest in the steelworks and on 5 April 1902 had invested another £20,000. As these transactions appear in the Estate papers it might be appropriate to infer that Franklen, Cheston, Beesly and Morgan held their shares not in their own right but had acted as agents for the Estate and Miss Talbot.[67]

The Port Talbot venture had been a chastening experience for Arthur and his sons. They were forced to reappraise their corporate strategy and abandon their grand scheme of acquiring a coastal site. Thereafter, their energies were focussed on developing the Pontardawe works. In February 1903 two additional basic furnaces were planned and by May two more steel mills were being installed to augment the existing eleven mills.[68] Frank was now taking a more prominent role in works management and in public affairs. He was already a county councillor (since 1898) and was being groomed to succeed his father by gradually acquiring more responsibility for day-to-day general management and for the firm's technical supervision and direction. He was also emerging as a spokesman for the domestic ferrous industry which, at the turn of the century, was experiencing internal pressures for structural change and external threats from increasing foreign competition. The economic power of the United States and Germany in the last quarter of the nineteenth century and the rapidity of their industrial development, protected by high tariffs, increasingly challenged Britain's leadership in world markets. Moreover, their exports of steel to Britain, which had averaged 300,000 tons in the 1880s and early 1890s, rose sharply from 1896-97 to a million tons in 1900, and called into question Britain's continued maintenance of the free trade policy which had served its manufacturers so well throughout the halcyon years of Victorian trade supremacy.

From 1900 to 1904 there were growing concerns being voiced over the stagnation of the British iron and steel industry. In November 1900 Arthur Gilbertson suggested boycotting American steel imports and British tinplate makers who used American bars [3 : 140-1], and in October 1903 repeated his arguments in a letter to *The Western Mail* [4 : 128-30]. Earlier in 1903 Frank Gilbertson had joined the prevailing debate and attacked free trade for crippling the competitiveness of the independent steelmaker. He recalled the ruinous impact of the McKinley tariff on tinplate production in South Wales and its continuing baleful influence which had "checked the progress of our prosperous tinplate industry, stopped from that day to this the erection of new works, and enabled the United States to manufacture, by 1902, 400,000 tons a year, which would otherwise have gone to swell – nay, double – our Welsh production . . .". Additionally, he condemned "the effect of foreign tariffs" which had been "disastrous to this industry" by providing British tinplate and galvanized sheet manufacturers with the opportunity "to buy his supply of raw steel from a highly protected country . . . at a price less than the cost in his own country or the one that produces it". German steel was available at ten shillings a ton below home produced steel and its purchase by home manufacturers had led to "the stoppage today, in South Wales, of no less than nine steel works all built within the last twenty years for the production of steel for the tinplate industry, of which seven were in operation when the foreign influx commenced".[69]

When the iron and steel industry was investigated in 1904 by Joseph Chamberlain's unofficial advisory "Tariff Commission", Frank Gilbertson gave evidence and emphasised the need for government protection against unfair and unrestrained foreign competition.[70] Later, in 1906, he reiterated his protectionist arguments at the Swansea Royal Metal Exchange, but the local political establishment regarded his stance as unacceptable and unnecessarily controversial. The landslide victory of a Liberal government in 1906, pledged to preserve free trade, led the South Wales steelmakers to group together for self-preservation by forming the South Wales Siemens Steel Association to control output and prices and prevent price cutting.[71] The new steel combine was immediately criticised by the recently enobled Lord Glantawe (Sir John Jones Jenkins, a former Swansea tinplate manufacturer) as a self-serving device which "in the long run would prosper neither the Welsh Siemens tin bar manufacturer nor the Welsh tinplate maker".[72]

Apart from the buoyancy in tinplate, the early years of the twentieth century were demoralizing for the British iron and steel industry. Cheap imports, static exports in a growing world market, low prices and an apparently uncaring government, exacerbated the growing insecurity of steelmakers and drained all confidence in future improvement. Set against this background of deteriorating trade and the failure of his Port Talbot venture, Arthur Gilbertson attempted to maintain and expand his markets. In December 1902 he wrote to one of his major shareholders, Walter Lawrence, who was the viceroy's private secretary at the India Office, to ask if his electrical steel sheet, which he was exporting to Canada and extensively to Japan, would "be useful in India" [3 : 767-8]. In the following summer he attempted to negotiate a contract with an Australian merchant house to supply galvanized sheets from "the most modern Mills" which were due to come into production [3 : 873-4, 882-3]. In 1904 the company began to produce high carbon steel billets and in the following year Frank Gilbertson was again using the Lawrence connection "to put in a word at the India Office" to verify the quality of the company's steel for conversion to springs for the Indian railway system [5 : 150-1]. Membership of the Galvanized Sheet Association, which regulated competition by allocating production quotas and controlled prices, was proving profitable with prices rising steadily to 1907, a year which, according to the *Iron & Coal Trades' Review* (11 October 1907) was "outdistancing all previous years as one of vast international commerce". Gilbertson's shareholders profited from those years with final dividends of 100% in 1906 and an unprecedented 150% in 1907.

Nationally, however, there were signs of a recession in the steel industry from 1907 when UK exports of iron and steel products were 5,152,000 tons, falling to 4,097,000 tons in 1908. The Cyfarthfa and Blaenavon works closed in 1908, there was a partial suspension of operations at Landore, output was cut at Dowlais and Cardiff, and there was a large drop in the export of galvanized sheets. The situation was worsened by imports, chiefly through Newport docks, of 350,000 tons of foreign iron and steel, mainly semi-finished bars, which were welcomed by the independent tinplate makers.[73] Gilbertson's tinplate production had for several years been confined to the Glynbeudy works, but in July 1908 the continual and increasing demand for tinplates and the depressed condition of the steel trade, prompted Frank Gilbertson to add six tinplate mills "& a new tinplate department complete" in Pontardawe. This initiative was seen by the directors as a "very considerable addition to the Works", and was moreover to be undertaken without increasing the capital or debt of the company. The cost of the six mill works, met from profits, amounted to £40,000 [7 : 202], but production did not start until February 1910. Possibly to offset the start-up costs of his new investment and to concentrate all the company's interests in Pontardawe the Glynbeudy tinplate works was sold in April 1910 to Theodore Gibbins and others.

Britain's trading position relative to other iron and steel producing countries continued to deteriorate. Whilst UK exports of iron and steel products increased incrementally from 1908 to 4,934,000 tons in 1913, imports doubled from 1,119,000 tons to 2,231,000 tons over the same period. The issue of dumping remained a contentious problem and during the two general elections of 1910 the Unionists made tariff reform a major agenda requirement. The successive return of Liberal administrations dampened any hope the steelmakers might have had of a retaliatory tariff or licensing system. In 1911 the *Iron & Coal Trades' Review* (16 June) devoted its editorial to "The Dumping Evil", and during that year imports totalled 1,760,000 tons. Most affected were the South Wales steelmakers, with Ebbw Vale closing in the second half of the year and Blaenavon and part of its blast furnace plant being shut down. In West Wales there was a lesser impact on steelmakers such as Gilbertson who used their own steel in their finishing works.[74] Among concerns expressed in the letters at this time were the company's absence from the Colonial Office's list of approved suppliers, which solicited another request for the help of Sir Walter

Lawrence; the possible effect of a Japanese tariff on galvanized sheets as the company was "by far the largest exporter to Japan", exacerbated by the apparently preferential treatment given to American imports to Japan; and the "unremunerative" and "unpleasant" features of the galvanizing trade resulting from the "dishonesty" of members of the Galvanized Sheet Association who circumvented the rules.

On 2 March 1912 Arthur Gilbertson died. He had been an invalid from about 1907 when a stroke restricted him to a passive role in the company's management. The burden of executive control had immediately been assumed by Frank, helped by his brothers, but not until his father's death did Frank become managing director. Arthur's death marked a watershed in the style of management which had typified the leadership of the firm and the supervision of the community. Arthur was one of the last of the Victorian autocrats. His will prevailed and his centralised authority and abrasive individualism were sustained by an exclusive corporate nepotism.[75] Frank Gilbertson was the antithesis of his father in personality and contemporary reports refer to his modesty and integrity.[76] He created a more collaborative internal control system, sharing collective responsibility for strategic decisions with his brothers, and extended his influence externally in a variety of collegiate roles in the wider and increasingly more complex industrial environment. Like his parents and his grandfather, he had a strongly developed awareness of his social responsibilities, fulfilling a paternalist-supply function in Pontardawe. Like his father and grandfather, he was a county councillor (1898-1912) and a J.P., and was an active churchman. He was secretary of the Congress of the Anglican Church in Swansea in 1909, and its success, for which he was personally thanked by the Archbishop of Canterbury, was largely attributed to "his foresight, zeal and mastery of detail". He had taken an early interest in the work of the Young Men's Christian Association, of which he was vice-president, and was also the local secretary of the Society for the Prevention of Cruelty to Children where "he has in more than one instance been instrumental in preventing the abuse and ill-treatment of children". He encouraged thrift by establishing a savings bank in the works for girl employees, which paid 5% interest, and a similar bank was organised for the local Sunday Schools.[77] His only remaining tangible monument in Pontardawe is the Public Hall and Institute, which originally housed a branch of the Swansea Savings Bank, and as chairman of its building committee he had guided and financially sponsored its erection to its festive opening in May 1909.[78]

One major respect in which Frank Gilbertson differed from his father was in his attitude to his employees and their unions. Following a dispute in 1901 it was Frank who proposed the establishment of a Consultative Committee to help in pre-empting future problems. Its apparent success might be inferred from the minutes of a meeting in October 1903 when an employee representative "expressed his satisfaction at the way the Committee had carried on, and thanked Mr. Gilbertson for allowing them to speak their minds freely without ill-feeling". He hoped that the Committee "would be a means of continuing good relations between Masters and Men". Frank responded by thanking the men's representatives "for their co-operation in making the meetings

Cecil, Frank and Charles Gilbertson *(Mrs Nanette Pearce)*

a success and expressed the pleasure it had been to him".[79] When the company joined the South Wales Siemens Steel Association in 1906, the Committee was suspended by Frank Gilbertson because "we thought the need for such a committee had ended".[80] It is not recorded if there had been consultation to suspend consultation and to substitute unilaterally what would appear to have been a form of district collective bargaining with John Hodge's Steel Smelters' Union, the only union the Association recognised.[81]

Unlike his father, Frank was more circumspect and respected Hodge's strategic command and the potential power of his union. Over subsequent years a co-operative relationship was to develop between the two men, as was apparent from Frank's evidence to the Industrial Council's Enquiry into Industrial Agreements in 1913. Frank was then vice-chairman of the Association and met officers of the union annually to discuss trade matters and on an ad hoc basis to attempt to resolve disputes over changes of rates or conditions. He felt that "the Steel Smelters' Union is a very efficient, well-organised body, and on the whole maintains very good discipline, and we have every confidence in making arrangements with them".[82] An important factor in the Gilbertson family's continued paternalism emerged in another answer when, commenting on the union's "anxiety to maintain discipline" during unofficial stoppages, he stated that "in our works, as a rule, there is a very good feeling existing between us and our men. We live among them, and we are very friendly with them". This close proximity helped to maintain the family's paternalistic style of management and, unlike his father, he saw the union as an aid to the promotion of a disciplined work force. Far from seeking to reduce the union's power, he wanted its enhancement when unofficial action was being taken by its members. He also accepted that unions had matured to become the equals of management in the contractual relationship, stating that "the unions and the workmen are able to treat with us on terms of absolute equality. They are intellectually on the up grade, and I think that the penalties for breach ought to be equal on either side".[83] His father's response to such an admission would have been enlightening, but he had died just five months before Frank gave his evidence to the Council.

The main developments in the company's history under Frank Gilbertson's direction from 1912 are presented in Chapter 3. In that year the demand for iron and steel from home shipbuilding and the Admiralty boosted steel production, and steel prices advanced to their highest levels since 1900. Additionally, there was an increased demand for galvanized sheet, while rail demand was high at home and overseas, particularly in the colonies. Despite hostilities in the Balkan States, Frank Gilbertson referred in November 1912 to the "very large business" conducted in that "most difficult market", and by March 1913 had resolved to visit Romania to assess the feasibility of building a galvanizing plant at Galatz on the Danube. Trading conditions for British steelmakers remained favourable, and 1913 brought greater prosperity with new production records and increased steel exports. In tinplate too exports increased, but the trade's bedevilling problems of overproduction and falling prices brought reduced profits.[84] By the end of 1913 iron and steel prices began to fall and there were complaints of foreign imports, especially from Germany, in most districts and particularly in South Wales. Prospects for 1914 were not promising, and with continued competition in the home market from Germany and Belgium and exports falling, British steelmakers viewed the future with pessimism. Nevertheless, despite deteriorating commercial and political conditions, Frank Gilbertson was resolved on expansion, and in February 1914 joined London merchants, Bessler, Waechter & Company, to form the Roumanian Sheet & Galvanizing Company Limited which was registered with £75,000 capital.[85] Frank and Cecil Gilbertson became directors and together with Charles as a shareholder the brothers embarked on a potentially long-term investment abroad, in the heart of a politically fragile but profitable Eastern European market. However, 1914 marked the first year of a cyclical decline which would probably have become a protracted depression had it not been for the outbreak of war in August,[86] when steel became a crucial determinant of victory in what Winston Churchill was later to call "A Steel War".

Shortages of labour and raw materials, particularly gas coal, were early problems, but the government's reduction of tinplate production and the removal of tinplate workers from the reserved list in 1916, allowed some transfers into the steelworks. The company was already a recognised supplier of steel products to the War Office and the Admiralty, and worked to full capacity throughout the war producing shell steel, boiler tubes, gas bottles, steam pipes, gun parts, ingots and high carbon billets, tinplate bars, sheet bars, tinplates, blackplates and galvanized sheets. The income tax returns, detailed in Chapter 4, provide an indication of the bonuses earned during the war years and suggest the high tonnages produced. The estimated net profit for the year ending 26 May 1917 was £99,803, and averaged £78,373 for the three years on which the 1918-19 assessment was to be based [10 : 519]. In February 1918 Frank Gilbertson confided that the steelworks had "largely increased its production during the War, probably by 80%". He added that "we have just been instructed to commence an Extension of our works, which will prove a new industry for the District of rather an important nature", requiring the expenditure of £85,000 on plant alone [10 : 525]. By July, after a reorganisation of the company's capital, he was able to inform the shareholders of the erection of an "important new Works adding an entirely new branch of trade to its activities". This new works was to become known locally as "The Alloy", where a mill for rolling alloy steel round bars for artillery shells was erected, but the war ended before the works came into operation.[87] He visualised that "the resumption of normal conditions in the Tinplate and Galvanizing Trades after the War is likely to be attended with serious difficulty and delay, and a large absorption of Capital in refinancing the working stocks in the Departments now idle". He concluded optimistically, stating that "the Company's operations will be on a much larger scale than before" and contemplated having to make financial provision "for increased housing accommodation for the workpeople" [10 : 556-60].

Frank Gilbertson emerged from the war with a considerably enhanced reputation, having attained national prominence as a spokesman for the South Wales sheet steel and tinplate industries. He was already President of the Swansea Royal Metal Exchange and in 1915 was elected Acting Chairman of the Welsh Plate & Sheet Manufacturers' Association, and from 1916 to 1918 was Chairman of the South Wales Steel Allocation Committee which was responsible for co-ordinating the distribution of all steel orders throughout South Wales. During this time he established and directed the Swansea National Shell Factory, managed the Cyfarthfa Iron & Steel Works for the Ministry of Munitions, was an executive council member of the Federation of British Industries and in 1917 the first Chairman of its Employers' Advisory Council. He was undoubtedly a man of immense energy, considerable technical ability and organisational skill. A month before the armistice was signed a press report referred to his "statesmanlike speech" at the Swansea Royal Metal Exchange, and to his "happy, almost boyish temperament which made him a most delightful companion". The report concluded ". . . few would imagine him to be the principal of one of the largest steel and tinplate firms in the Principality. But he has great ability, is far-sighted and broad-minded, all of which carry authoritative weight with his opinions. Most of all, he has preserved a happy urbanity of temperament which makes him popular among all circles, not least among his own extensive body of workpeople".[88]

Despite his reported happy temperament, the strain of the war years had seriously affected his health and left him with a weakened heart.[89] In recognition of his contribution to the war effort he was recommended for an award, rumoured in the family to be a knighthood, but he declined the honour. However, he accepted an award from the French Government for his work in the control of steel production for France during the war. He was asked in 1918 to stand as a Conservative candidate for

Parliament but was stated to be "more interested in the welfare of the community generally than he is in party politics".[90]

The principal theme in his presidential address to the Royal Metal Exchange in October 1918 was 'Reconstruction' and he predicted that the approaching transition to peace would produce "a situation of extraordinary difficulty in coping with the changes involved".[91] He could not have visualised the scale of the problems which were to follow the inflated post-war boom and which were to destroy all his hopes for the continued prosperity of his company. The Board of Trade index of iron and steel prices peaked in June 1920 but from October they dropped continuously to a catastrophic low point by December 1922.[92] In his Presidential address that month he referred to "the immensely complex situation that faces civilisation today". Despite the vast increase in productive capacity there was "a world shrinkage of purchasing power", and an essential need to establish "confidence in a reasonably stable economic order". Among the many problems confronting Welsh industry was that of increasing foreign competition from within old markets. They had lost "a valuable and expanding market" in Japan which had "learnt to galvanize", and in India which "has learnt to make steel and has made 83,000 tons of rails in a year, with nearly an equal tonnage of other steel products". India was also expanding its plant building programme, aiming for "an annual production of steel of 1,000,000 tons a year", increasing its tinplate output and "protecting its industries with tariffs". He warned the Labour Party, whose seemingly "amateurish" attitude to industrial problems he deplored, of these developments, as "low wages and protection are the basis on which these developments are growing, and if we lose our markets faster than we can replace them ever lower wages will be earned in Great Britain and no one can prevent it". In contrast to the continued expansion of steel capacity in the USA, Canada, Australia, embryonic beginnings in China and South Africa and the erection of new plant in Europe, "Great Britain has not a great deal of really modern plant except what has been put down under the ill-advised war scheme of 1916, and that has cost more than its real value". He concluded by emphasising that future prospects of improvement in the iron and steel trades lay with "the intelligent co-operation of our work-people to produce steel by some means cheaper than other countries, and reduce costs of coal and transit".[93]

These latter factors had been identified by the Scoby-Smith Committee in 1918 as anticipated problems which would impede the post-war reconstruction of the iron and steel trades. During the eight years after 1920-21 the industry struggled to regain its pre-war stability as prices dropped to unsustainable levels and wages followed suit. There was a considerable increase in home and foreign competition, and British steel production fell from 10·2% of the world total in 1913 to 8% in 1928. Over the same period total world output increased nearly 42% while British output increased by 11·1%. Moreover, in relation to its pre-war export trade, on which the industry largely depended, its share fell from 30·3% of the world's iron and steel exports in 1913 to 20·6% in 1928, and was exceeded by that of every exporting country except the U.S. France and Belgium in particular had increased their share, mainly at the expense of Germany and Britain, and had become Britain's chief competitors in the home market by 1929. Britain's failure to recover her share of world trade was partly due to the deflationary policy pursued by Britain from 1920, whilst its continental competitors benefited from their inflated currency which enabled them to clear much of their internal debts, to lay down new plant at low capital cost and to maintain low prices in their external markets.[94]

The post-war years were ones of unprecedented difficulty, but evidence of the fate of W. Gilbertson & Company is unfortunately sparse as entries in the tenth and last Letter-Book are infrequent after 15 July 1918. In September 1922 a final dividend of 3% was recommended as trading results over the previous year had shown a small profit. Frank Gilbertson expressed his worries that losses were being incurred "on a substantial scale, and the prospects of the Steel Trade are very bad . . . at present our new plant and our interests in colliery companies are idle or unproductive". Attempts to secure new outlets were "difficult and discouraging" when "demands for steel are not more than half the productive capacity of Great Britain" [10 : 580]. A year later, on 22 August 1924 he was anticipating the imminent readiness of new sheet mills and a steel furnace [10 : 594], but within a few days reported salary reductions [10 : 596-7]. By January 1925 Frank admitted to being "uneasy sometimes at our failure to earn an adequate return on the very large sums we have spent on our Steel Works while we can hold our own very well in Tinplates" [10 : 598-9]. On 16 March 1925 he wrote to his steel works manager admitting that "I have been very little at business for a long time, but I have been aware of the difficulties that face us". Trade was so seriously reduced that it appeared "doubtful if we can go on making steel", adding that "the time has come for very drastic measures". Production costs were unsustainably high and he required his manager to prepare a detailed analysis "<u>sparing no one</u>" in an effort to mitigate their effects. By October 1925 the company secretary stressed the gravity of conditions in steel and tinplate " and the future prospects present no hope of any immediate recovery" [10 : 610]. In June 1927 Cecil Gilbertson confirmed that orders were "very scarce" and the "prices for Tinplates and Galvanized Sheets reduced considerably" [10 : 621]. As the industry slipped into a major recession, the Company struggled to maintain a precarious viability but was finally forced into debt, owing the bank £250,000 "with little more security than Frank Gilbertson's personal word".[95]

During these aptly-named 'locust years'[96] Frank Gilbertson maintained his status as one of South Wales's industrial and educational leaders. He was president of the South Wales Siemens Steel Association from 1918 to 1929, became a director of the Great Western Railway Company in 1922, was president of the South Wales Steel Trade Conciliation Board at a particularly difficult period from 1924 to 1925, and vice-chairman of the Welsh Plate and Sheet Manufacturers' Association. He was also chairman of the Tinplate Stabilisation Committee to its suspension in 1925, when he felt "convinced that a great deal of underselling is going on, and we have evidence that such lamentable tricks have been resorted to as the handling of money through certain well-known brokers (whose names we know) for merchants' orders".[97]

Throughout this period he was also influential in promoting intermediate, technical, commercial and university education, advocating the extension of educational opportunity and the co-ordination of educational provisions into a unified system of public education. He had been co-opted as an employer governor of Swansea Technical College in 1916 and, following the Haldane Commission's report, campaigned for the College to become a constituent of the University of Wales's federal structure. He was also the founder and chairman of the Education Board of South Wales Manufacturers, and in January 1920 presented a comprehensive analysis of the vocational needs of industry which stressed the "paramount importance" of "all educational effort upon industrial efficiency". Classifying the different technical and commercial skills required of his own workforce, he proposed that "In the case of working men generally . . . whole-time general education to 16 years of age, with every subsequent opportunity for attending voluntary continuation and particularly voluntary technical classes, is the best suited for our industrial population". He wanted the provision of as broad a subject base in industrialised village communities as in more densely populated areas "if every one is to have the opportunity of making the best of his life". The costs of providing classes were to be met from public funds and supplemented if necessary by employer contributions.[98]

As Chairman of the Promotion Committee and later the first President of the University College Court of Governors, Frank Gilbertson worked tirelessly to attract industrial funding for the Singleton Abbey site of the new Swansea University College, which initially was to have had a technological bias. At a meeting in the Royal Metal Exchange in 1920 he urged the assembled industrialists to realise that "it was time, in spite of the Excess Profits Duty and heavy burdens of taxation" to "contribute handsomely . . . in a work that would be one of the most important agencies for improving the social conditions of the district". He suggested that the Steel Association should contribute £2,500 p.a. over five years and committed his firm to giving £5,000 a year, with additional "capital sums from time to time".[99] His dedication and drive led ultimately to £70,000 being raised, and on 19 July 1920 he presided over George V's visit to lay the foundation stone of the University College where he was to remain President until 1929.[100]

In August 1928 Frank Gilbertson's last two letters referred to colliery losses, to "a serious development in steel rolling in Belgium" where wage rates were undercutting those in Britain and leaving "little or no profit to English makers" [10 : 625-6], and to his company's interest in repurchasing the Glanrhyd Tinplate Works [10 : 627]. Earlier that year he had been chosen to lead a delegation to the USA to investigate the results of revolutionary new production methods which had culminated in the successful introduction in 1923-24 of a continuous hot-strip mill capable of rolling sheets 36 inches wide and up to 30 feet long from steel slabs. This innovation was to have a profound significance for all steel producing countries, as was the further U.S. development of the continuous cold reduction process, perfected by 1929, which produced steel strip to a gauge suitable for tinning. The significantly improved output, cost and quality implications of these capital-intensive methods were immediately apparent, but their applicability in Britain appeared doomed by entrenched attitudes, traditional work methods and obsolescent plant. However, the amalgamations of the 1920s, which had reduced the number of small independent producers in Wales, had created a concentration of ownership and had prepared the way for the possibility of a co-operative scheme to introduce continuous wide strip rolling. A committee was established under the chairmanship of Frank Gilbertson to consider such a scheme, but his death in 1929 and the onset of the depression deferred further progress.[101] It has been suggested that some steelmasters were of the view that "Gilbertson rather than the more ebullient Sir William Firth could have been the man to achieve the co-operation among steelmasters in accepting technical change without the controversy it eventually caused".[102]

Frank Gilbertson had suffered from ill-health for much of the previous decade as a result, suggested *The Cambrian*, of "over-strain during the war period",[103] when he travelled to London as often as three times a week by night train on war-related business.[104] There was a gradual deterioration from the early 1920s but against medical advice he maintained an active working life, and continued to enjoy his leisure pursuits. One of these latter interests entailed long motoring holidays in Europe, and on his last such journey to Romania he contracted diphtheria. He returned to Paradise Meadow, his home in Bishopston, Swansea, where he died on 8 October 1929, leaving his family "to mourn the loss of one who in his day and generation played a great role in the industrial and educational life of Wales".[105]

Cecil Gilbertson became chairman of the company on his brother's death. By 1933 it was appreciated that the future of the tinplate and sheet trade depended upon the establishment of a modern sheet mill which would require greater capital investment than a family concern could mobilize.[106] On 27 December 1933 Cecil Gilbertson wrote to each employee to confirm that the company had "concluded an amalgamation" with Richard Thomas & Co. Ltd., and that Sir William Firth would take over as chairman to direct its policy while he and brother Charles would continue as local directors (Appendix 4). The entire share capital was acquired by Richard Thomas & Co., and the family firm, which had dominated Pontardawe's economy since 1861, ceased to exist as an independent producer. The Gilbertson title was retained until 1946 when the works were absorbed by Richard Thomas & Baldwins Ltd. In May 1947 the tinplate works were acquired by the Steel Company of Wales and closed ten years later, whilst the steelworks continued until September 1962.

NOTES

1. D. C. Miller & W. H. Form, *Industrial Sociology: The Sociology of Work Organisations* (New York, Harper, 1964), 93-7.
2. The Hertford Parish Registers for the period are badly damaged but provide some information which is shown on the genealogical table.
3. The Yester (Tweeddale) Papers, deposited in the National Library of Scotland, show that a William Gilbertson was employed as Factor to Lord Tweeddale between 1814 and 1823. The connection with James has not been established. J. Muir, *Gifford 1750-1850* (Wm. Sinclair, 1913), refers to William as Factor and Baron Baillie, but not to James. William was possibly James's son.
4. The London directories from 1775 to 1820 showed only one person named Robert Collings and he was a horse hair manufacturer of 14, Whitecross Street in the parish of St. Giles Cripplegate. A list of liverymen of London published in 1792 as a supplement to the *Universal British Directory* showed that a Robert Collins (sic) of the same address was a liveryman of the Drapers' Company. In *Roll of the Drapers' Company of London*, compiled by Percival Boyd (1934), he is shown as having been apprenticed in the Company in 1770 and as still living in 1824.
5. Hertfordshire Record Office.
6. Hertfordshire Record Office, Land Tax assessments.
7. Dr. Samuel Butler (1774-1839) was Headmaster from 1798 to 1836. *D.N.B.*
8. Correspondence with J.B. Lawson, former School Librarian.
9. Henry Weeks was admitted to the roll in 1833.
10. John Vigurs (1779-1848) of Penzance had been associated with the tin and copper mining industries in Cornwall before going to South Wales where he and Leonard Smith owned the Ynysygerwn Tinplate Works in the Vale of Neath. They purchased S. F. Lettsom's blast furnace in Cwmavon in 1820 and built a small forge, containing an iron mill and a tin mill. In 1825 they transferred their Ynysygerwn tinplate plant to Cwmavon and began manufacturing tinplates there. Batten is alleged to have owned a banking business in Penzance and may have provided some of the capital for the Cwmavon copper works which they started building in October 1835. The production of copper started on 19 March 1838. M. Phillips, *The Copper Industry in the Port Talbot District* (Neath Guardian Press, 1935), 39-46, and C. Wilkins, *The History of the Iron, Steel and Tinplate Trades of Wales* (Merthyr Tydfil, Joseph Williams, 1903), 336-7.
11. In 1841 there were 347 dwellings in the hamlet of Lower Michaelston (containing Cwmavon) housing 2,132 persons. By 1851 there were 871 houses and a population of 5,421.
12. "Yr oedd Mr. Gilbertson yn un o ran feddianwyr y gweithiae" [Mr. Gilbertson was one of the part owners of the works]. Rev. John Rowlands in *Aeron Afan, Eisteddfod Iforaidd, Aberafan, 1853* (Caerfyrddin, William Thomas, 1855), 99.
13. W. E. Minchinton (ed.), *Industrial South Wales 1750-1914* (Cass, 1969), 109-110.
14. G. C. Boase, *Collectanea Cornubiensis* (1890), 824, 949, and M. Phillips, *ibid*, 48. The Company records are not deposited in the Guildhall Library and it does not appear in the *Stock Exchange Yearbook*. Entries in the London trade directories show that the company was first listed between 1842 and 1848 at 57½ Old Broad Street and Castle Baynard Wharf, 12 Upper Thomas Street. There is no entry in directories between 1849 and 1852, but in 1853 the company reappears at 10 New Broad Street Mews.
15. C. Wilkins, *ibid*, 337.
16. M. Phillips, *ibid*, 49-51.
17. *Cambrian*, 13 May 1852.
18. West Glamorgan Archives, D/D GV/10:48, *Company Report 1870*. The profits were: 1852-3 – £18,418; 1853-4 – £37,620; 1854-5 – £25,544; 1855-6 – £27,227; 1856-7 – £31,809; 1857-8 – £24,513; 1858-9 – £23,916; 1859-60 – £26,478.

19. *Cambrian*, 13 June 1856.
20. *Cambrian*, 15 May 1857.
21. *Cambrian*, 8 July 1859.
22. *Cambrian*, 13 January 1860.
23. *Welsh Industrial Times*, 27 April 1889, acknowledged the same relationship in respect of James Shaw, one of Gilbertson's successors in Cwmavon, and repeated the full stanza: "I'm monarch of all I survey, / My right there is none to dispute; / From the centre right down to the sea, / I am Lord o'er the fowl and the brute".
24. *Cambrian*, 15 May 1857.
25 *Cambrian*, 9 November 1860.
26. M. Scott, 'Independence and the flight from large scale: some sociological factors in the founding process', in A. Gibb and T. Webb (eds.), *Policy Issues in Small Business Research* (Saxon House, 1980).
27. The indenture comprises 60 pages of parchment. On 31 December 1868 John Harris sold all his shares to William Gilbertson and George Lawrence.
28. *Cambrian*, 24 February 1860.
29. The 1861 Census returns for the parish of Llangyfelach show the occupants of Ynysderw House as William Gilbertson (50), wife Eliza (45) and children Matthias (25), Ellen Louisa (7), Madeline (4) and Edward Colling (1). William is listed as Magistrate for the County of Glamorgan, while his eldest son Matthias is designated 'Tinplate Manufacturer'. There is no reference to Arthur (20) who was to succeed his father.
30. *Cambria Daily Leader*, 24 April 1896. On his walk through Wales in 1854 George Borrow passed through "the village of Tawy Bridge" and referred briefly to the valley's beauty and to "Pearson's" iron works. It was "an enormous edifice . . . [which] had huge chimneys, which were casting forth smoke, and from within I heard the noise of a steam-engine and the roar of furnaces".
31. Webster, *Directory*, 1865, 620.
32. *Cambrian*, 18 January 1865.
33. *Cambrian*, 21 January 1865.
34. P.M. Blau, *Exchange and Power in Social Life* (New York, Wiley, 1964), 93.
35. A. Pugh, *Men of Steel* (Iron & Steel Trades Confederation, 1951), 13.
36. P. S. Thomas, *Industrial Relations in Swansea* (Cardiff, University of Wales Press Board, 1940), 46.
37. *Engineer*, 28 August 1874.
38. *Cambrian*, 28 August 1874.
39. *Cambrian*, 10 February 1882.
40. He was born in Hanover Square, London in 1836 and lived in Pontardawe from 1861 to 1865. His life thereafter is obscure. William's will of 1881 provided an annuity of £200 p.a. for him. He died intestate.
41. Francis Bramah Gilbertson was born in London in 1838. In 1860 he left Cwmavon for Pernambucco, Brazil (*The Cambrian*, 27 January 1860) and there is no further local reference to him until 13 January 1865 when *The Cambrian* shows that he was in residence in Ynysderw House (see Biographical Notes).
42. *Cambria Daily Leader*, 24 April 1896.
43. *Cambrian*, 7 December 1888.
44. *Cambrian*, 31 August 1888.
45. *Welsh Industrial Times*, 22 September 1888.
46. *Welsh Industrial Times*, 14 December 1889.
47. R. Nozick, *Anarchy, State and Utopia* (Oxford, Blackwell, 1974), 109.
48. *Welsh Industrial Times*, 8 February 1890.
49. *Western Mail*, 22 March 1890.
50. *Welsh Industrial Times*, 5 April 1890.

51. *Welsh Industrial Times*, 1 November 1890
52. *Industrial World*, 29 February 1892.
53. *Industrial World*, 4 March 1892.
54. *Industrial World*, 26 August 1892.
55. *Industrial World*, 17 March 1893.
56. *Industrial World*, 29 December 1893. The Tinplate Workers' Union was dissolved in 1899 and many of its members joined John Hodge's British Steel Smelters' Association, whilst others joined Ben Tillett's Dockers' Union and a small number joined the Gas Workers' & General Labourers' Union. Two branches of the Steel Smelters' Union were formed in Pontardawe, but *The South Wales Daily News* expressed a generally accepted opinion when it stated that "At Pontardawe Labour leaders are not looked upon with favour" (19 April 1899).
57. Educated at Charterhouse 1886-8 and entered Magdalen College, Oxford, 1891.
58. W.E. Minchinton, 'The Tinplate Maker and Technical Change', in W. E. Minchinton (ed.) *Industrial South Wales 1750-1914* (Cass, 1969), 107-120
59. *Cambria Daily Leader*, 4 April 1894.
60. K. Warren, *The British Iron & Steel Sheet Industry since 1840* (Bell & Sons, 1970), 75.
61. W. E. Minchinton, *The British Tinplate Industry* (Oxford, Clarendon Press, 1957), 78-9.
62. K. O. Morgan, *Wales 1880-1980: Rebirth of a Nation* (Oxford, Oxford University Press, 1982), 64.
63. A. L. Evans, *The Story of Taibach & District* (Port Talbot, the author, 1963), 76-7.
64. J. V. Hughes, *The Wealthiest Commoner: CRM Talbot 1803-1890* (Talbot Printing, 1977), 34. *The Iron & Coal Trades' Review*, Vol. 64, 1902, 1148, refers to 'Port Talbot Redivivus' under "the tutelary guidance of Miss Talbot". The blast furnace plant being built "under the direction of Mr. Frank Gilbertson" was expected to produce an output of 650 to 700 tons a week and would be "in operation in the course of the present year".
65. D. Brinn, *Development of Iron & Steel in the Port Talbot Area* (B.S.C., 1972), 4-5.
66. J. Hodge, *Workman's Cottage to Windsor Castle* (Sampson Low, 1931), 114.
67. West Glamorgan Archives, Margam Estate Papers, D/D Ma 171. Details of share allotments are included in Company papers deposited in the P.R.O.
68. *Iron & Coal Trades' Review*, 27 February and 8 May 1903.
69. F. W. Gilbertson, 'Foreign Tariffs and Welsh Industries', *The Nineteenth Century & After*, LIV, July–December 1903, 854-66.
70. *Report of the Tariff Commission*, 1904, i, questions 851-902.
71. W. E. Minchinton, *ibid*, 86.
72. *The Times*, 19 September 1906. Sir John Jones Jenkins and his brother-in-law Rice Daniel took control of the Cwmfelin Tinplate & Colliery Co. in 1883.
73. J. C. Carr *et al.*, *A History of the British Steel Industry* (Oxford, Blackwell, 1962), 232-4.
74. *Ibid*, 234-5.
75. J. Vaizey, *The History of British Steel* (Weidenfeld & Nicolson, 1974), 22, refers to the 1920s as "the last decade in which major firms were customarily managed by one man without an effective managerial structure . . . steel leaders tended to be 'dictators'." D.L. Burn, *Economic History of Steelmaking 1867-1939* (1940), 298-301, comments on "The domination of old men and of men who became important by inheritance".
76. G. M. Holmes in *Dictionary of Business Biography* (Butterworths, 1984).
77. *Western Mail*, 26 February 1904.
78. *South Wales Daily Post*, 7 May 1909.
79. J. H. Davies, *ibid*, 560-1.
80. Industrial Council, *Report on Industrial Agreements*, 1913, Cd. 6953, Questions 6003 & 6004.
81. J. C. Carr, *ibid*, 275, 286.

82. Industrial Council, *ibid*, Question 5702.
83. *Ibid*, Question 5752.
84. Discussions to establish a scheme for regulating production proved abortive until early 1914 when a pooling system was agreed, and an allocation scheme named the Tinplate Conference was established.
85. In March 1887 W. Gilbertson & Co., had entered into an agreement with Bessler, Waechter & Co., giving them the sole right to sell their tinplates in Russia. *Cambrian*, 17 August 1888.
86. W. W. Rostow, *British Economy of the Nineteenth-Century* (Oxford, Clarendon Press, 1966), 33-6.
87. In 1921 six sheet mills were built on the site. J. Childs et al., *Around Pontardawe* (Stroud, Chalford Publishing Co., 1996), 40. Holmes has suggested that the original expansion was "not a little responsible for the firm's final difficulties in the 20's" when early expectations of continued growth were radically reversed by adverse trading conditions.
88. *Western Mail*, 4 October 1918.
89. *DBB*, 560.
90. *Western Mail*, 4 October 1918.
91. *Cambria Daily Leader*, 7 October 1918.
92. J. C. Carr, *ibid*, 346.
93. *South Wales Daily Post*, 12 December 1922.
94. ISTC Evidence, *Inquiry into the Iron & Steel Industry*, 1929, 3-7.
95. G. M. Holmes, 'The Achievement of Frank Gilbertson', unpublished Anniversary Lecture at the University College of Swansea on 9 October 1969.
96. K. O. Morgan, *ibid*, 210-219.
97. *Iron & Coal Trades' Review*, 8 May 1925, 784; Minchinton, *op.cit.* 140-4.
98. F. W. Gilbertson, *The Effects of Educational Effort upon Industrial Efficiency* (Harrison, 1920), also published in *Engineering*, 23 January 1920.
99. *Cambria Daily Leader*, 23 June 1920.
100. *DBB*, 560-1; D.W. Dykes, *op.cit.*, 349-354.
101. J. C. Carr, *op.cit.*, 407, 543; P. Jenkins, *Twenty by Fourteen* (Llandysul, Gomer, 1995) 50-1; also note Warren, *op.cit.* 190-1, who refers to reorganisation plans discussed at a tinplate committee convened by Frank Gilbertson in 1928.
102. G. M. Holmes, *DBB*, 560.
103. *Cambrian*, 11 October 1929.
104. G. M. Holmes, draft for *DBB* entry, 1980. In May 1919 Frank Gilbertson was elected as the first President of the Rotary Club of Swansea but was forced to resign in January 1921 owing to his continued ill-health. W. T. M. Hughes, *The Growth of a Notion* (Morriston, Crown Printing, 1955), 11-17.
105. *Cambrian*, 11 October 1929.
106. *South Wales Evening Post*, 23 June 1950.

Chapter 1

A FAMILY BUSINESS

Among the most crucial decisions which face family businesses are those which determine management succession and the allocation of executive responsibilities. In a patrilineal society structural authority is vested in the eldest son, and family control is perpetuated by dynastic succession. The managerial ability of the eldest son and his willingness to accept the pressures of command are thus of paramount importance, for whilst primogeniture bestows its privileges it also demands the acceptance of duties and of obligations towards the immediate family, the extended family of employees and the dependent community. Family, business and community form an interlocking system within which the chief executive is expected to provide "the dynamic, life-giving element."[1] Family expectations and confidence, and the distribution of voting equity among its members help to determine his degree of autonomy, whilst such variables as his managerial competence, technical ability, capacity to develop markets and to anticipate problems will be of major concern to his family and community whose security and future are reliant upon his operational effectiveness.

The preparation of one's successors is thus a major management responsibility, and Arthur Gilbertson was concerned to ensure that the business he inherited from his father should be passed on to sons who were competent to run it. In this respect, Arthur was especially favoured in his sons, particularly his talented eldest son, Francis William (Frank), who had been educated at Charterhouse and Magdalen College, Oxford.[2] The second son, Howel, was to emigrate to farm in Australia,[3] whilst the third and fourth sons, Cecil and Colin, entered the works to learn the trade. Colin's death at the age of 29 in 1906 led to Charles Geoffrey, the fifth son, being appointed a director while completing a BA Pass degree at Queen's College, Oxford.[4] In the following year, Arthur suffered a stroke and control passed to the three brothers. Two decades later they were joined by the sixth son, George, on his retirement from the Royal Navy. The company's simple management structure and the majority of its shares remained in family hands until Frank's death in 1929. Following the company's amalgamation with Richard Thomas and Company Limited in 1933 Cecil and Charles maintained a family influence and community presence as local directors.

Most of the selected letters in this chapter reflect Arthur Gilbertson's concerns for his children's future and are mainly addressed to his London solicitor, S. B. Barlow.

Arthur Gilbertson and his children in 1895. *From the left (standing)*: Colin, Frank, Arthur, Cecil, Howel; *(seated)*: Marguerite, Harriet, Olive; *(front)*: George, Phyllis, Sylvia, Charles, Winifred *(Mrs Nanette Pearce)*

They include details of his will and the need to ensure a continuation of family control (momentarily jeopardised, it seemed, by Frank's impending marriage and his future mother-in-law's "inspiration for control"!), and his views on his sons' executive designations and remuneration.

Arthur Gilbertson to William Williams, Pump Hotel, Llandrindod Wells — **28 July 1892 [1 : 200]**

I have your letter of yesterday and think you are wise to do as you say. I am simply "Sole Director" for life and provision made for appointing Directors after my death. Our articles were drawn up by my Solicitors, Messrs. Barlow & James, 49 Lime Street, London & settled by Counsel. If you like to apply to them to act for you, they are well posted. I purposely avoided local Solicitors.

You probably know more about American moves than I do, for I fancy your Son-in-Law is erecting Works there.

I dont despair of beating America in cost in spite of her tariff.

Arthur Gilbertson to S. B. Barlow — **8 May 1894 [2 : 3-4]**

I return my Will executed, for you to make sure it is right, and I have burnt my old Will and Codicil.

One question you did not answer – clause 17. Does this always leave my Daughters under Trustees, even if married? My Father did not do this, and I doubt it. I think it would be better to defer their coming of age to 25 years & then to let them have entire control, or upon marriage with consent of Guardians.

One other point, clause 10, does not restrict my Trustees as to £1000? I think clause 22 allows further money if needful, for school fees & maintenance?

Clause 31, is I conclude usual, but I think does not bind the Exors. to employ any certain Solicitor – I remember in my Father's case, it would have been convenient to have employed one, not a Trustee or Exor?

Arthur Gilbertson to M. Lough, Chicago, U.S.A. — **n.d. (c. Nov. 1894) [2 : 34]**

Seeing your advertisement, I think we might make some arrangement as to buying & selling Tinplates.

I have two Sons conversant with the manufacture & sale of Tinplates, as well as myself, and ultimately one of my Sons might proceed to America.

Will you write me your views and in what way capital would be employed, and how much.

Arthur Gilbertson to M. Lough. — **17 Dec. 1894 [2 : 41]**

I have your letter of 6th inst. and am giving the matter serious consideration.

Meanwhile you could give me an idea of the smallest amount of capital I should have to provide for a Son, & idea of profits.

If things took shape, I would send my Son out, in the Spring, to see you.

I am a Justice of the Peace for Glamorgan & was High Sheriff for the County 1892/1893, but I am a man of business, and my Sons, are being taught the Steel & Tinplate Trades, under me. They are intelligent, energetic and well principled – my eldest Son will succeed me here, but my second & third Sons (one or other) must go further afield.

Arthur Gilbertson to E. P. Martin, Dowlais. 31 Dec. 1894 [1 : 319-20]

I hear that Mr. Forester is retiring from the Dowlais Agency – I do not know if it is the case. If it is, could we not do our business with you direct? We consume a good quantity of your Pigs. My eldest son, whom you once were good enough to show over Dowlais, is now with me, and would be very glad to call on you at any time. He has taken his degree at Oxford, and Honours in final Science School, and has several times asked me if you would let him see Cardiff Works.

I fear the Tinplate Trade, in which you and I first made acquaintance, is in a serious state.

Best wishes of the Season to you.

Arthur Gilbertson to National Provincial Bank. 31 Aug. 1895 [1 : 389]

You will see by enclosed notice, that my Sons join me in the Directorate here.

No change in any way will ensue, but after this date all checks will be signed by two Directors & the Secretary (Mr. John Philip Davies) and checks will be endorsed by one Director.

Arthur Gilbertson to S. B. Barlow. 31 Oct. 1895 [2 : 147-8]

Your letter of yesterday.

Queensland purchase. I wired you to return Policy & letters and I will sell some Railway Bonds & carry out matter myself, with the Banks – it will be more simple.

Howel has decided to become a Farmer, under his Uncle's inspiration, who has been in Queensland some 25 years. I will tell you all about it when I call. I hope to call on you, about 12th November with Frank. Howel's plan upsets all mine, but Cecil can take the place in the Works: he is shaping well & especially gets on with the Workmen.

My Will must now have a codicil (as Howel will now get from £3000 to £3500 in cash & Farm) reducing his shares in W. Gilbertson & Co. Ltd.

Say Howel 30 shares (not 70)

Cecil, increased to 57 shares (not 47)

Colin, increased to 50 shares (not 20)

Colin may ultimately come into the Works, as there is room for three, after my death.

I conclude the erection of Frank's House in Cwmdu, does not need any further reference in my Will? I wish it to go to my girls ultimately.

I hold two Leaseholds, viz: "All Saints Cottage" @ £9.0.0 a year, and Tyn-y-pant Farm @ £36 a year, and as I have left Frank the stock and crops (say £500) and as Tyn-y-pant is the Home Farm for Glanrhyd House, I think these two leaseholds could be left to Frank.

All Saints Church Trust, I conclude gives powers to Trustees, to appoint others to succeed in case of deaths & I want it clear the patronage remains to my family, as if Charlie goes into the Church, it might suit him.

Howel's name must remain as Trustee & Executor, at any rate until Cecil is of age, in February '97.

The uncle referred to was Richard Carre Lloyd, Arthur's brother-in-law, who had emigrated to Queensland in 1866. Howel initially stayed with his uncle and later married his eldest daughter Harriet May at Blue Gate, Mattaburra.[5]

Arthur Gilbertson to Parrs Banking Co. Ltd., London. 31 Oct. 1895 [2 : 151-2]

My second Son, Arthur Howel has decided on Farming in North Queensland, and I have bought him a Leasehold Farm & stock costing from £2500 to £3000.

I want to realize securities to raise £3000, and I enclose you

Cordoba & Rosario Ry. Co. Ltd. certificates for £900

Cordoba Central Debenture for £346, ditto £231, also London Electric lighting for £750, all of which please sell for me, and I want you to lend me the rest, until February next, against the Bearer Bonds you hold for me, and if not enough, I will send you more "certificates" for sale: but as I shall have some £4000 to pay to my credit, early February next, I dont want to sell out more than needful. I think you will lend me the money @ 3½%? on such absolute security for 3 to 4 months.

I shall ask you kindly to provide me the £3000 at end of second week in November, and the Bank of Australasia, Threadneedle Street (who are acting for me in Australia) will then cable out the £3000 to their Branch in Australia.

Arthur Gilbertson to S. B. Barlow, 31 Oct. 1895 [2 : 149-50]

Frank's proposed marriage

I am a little anxious to know if things are shaping? I think if Mrs. Thomas carries out her idea of "no settlement", i.e. proper "marriage settlement", I must add to the codicil to my Will (about which I write you on another sheet) that all I leave to Frank reverts to my estate or executors, on his death, if there are no children, subject to an annuity of £200 a year to his Widow – it would not do to risk (however remote it may be, or unlikely) Works shares getting under the inspiration for control of Mrs. Thomas.

Mrs. Thomas proposed Deed

Of course Legacy duty has been paid, if she does not alter her late Husband's Will, but if she takes away the Minerals under Loughor Farms, from her two Daughters, she must do so, by a New Will and then I take it, the whole Glanmor Estate must pay Legacy duty again, and as Swansea Town is nearly overrunning it, the increased value for duty, will be very great indeed.

How does Mrs. Thomas secure the £200 per annum allowance to her Daughters? It wd. be unpleasant to have to write for it! and I fancy she lives pretty well up to her means.

The Farms being left by Will of late Iltyd Thomas to his Daughters (2) – the third apparently being left out – of course carry minerals with them, as I believe minerals were not reserved.

Mrs. Mary Dulcibella Thomas (née Eden) was the second wife of Iltyd Thomas (1813-89) who had been a substantial landowner in Swansea, Gower and the Swansea valley. Frank was betrothed to their eldest daughter, Isabel Frances de Winton Thomas.

Arthur Gilbertson to S.B. Barlow. 2 Nov. 1895 [2 : 154-6]

My "Will". Please get on with Codicil, as the Farm for Howel is actually contracted for in his name, and I have arranged to cable out purchase money, middle of this month.

All Saint's Patronage. I observe you will kindly look up.

My Son's Marriage. I conclude you have copy of late Iltyd Thomas's Will? I think we shall want it, when we talk. I will also bring Mrs. Thomas's letters. I am surprised she re-opens the question of my "doing anything" for my Son, this was agreed to be left out as per her own letter, when she altered her promises about Colliery, and I concurred, she also expressed her wish, there should be no settlement.

I think it will advance matters if you will write to R. Smith and say, that Mr. R. Smith's query as to what Mr. Gilbertson intends to do, re-opens everything, which had been settled by Mrs. Thomas's last letter to him, and that under these circumstances Mr. Gilbertson requires a proper marriage settlement with Trustees to be entered into, viz. Mrs. Thomas to allow £200 a year, and confirm ⅓rd. of Personalty under her late Husband's "Will". Mr. Gilbertson Jnr., will insure his life for £4000, and settle Policy. Mr. Gilbertson Snr. will allow £200 a year (like Mrs. Thomas) and will appoint Glanrhyd to his Son: this can all go into the Settlement.

If Mrs. Thomas thinks she has misunderstood matters, she is at liberty to consider the proposed marriage at an end, but I am determined to go no further, without the old Lady being bound, by a proper Settlement.

Please write firmly to Smith, so as to bring it to a point, when I call upon you.

Arthur Gilbertson to John Griffiths, Builder. 16 Nov. 1895 [2 : 168]

I was much disappointed to see the House so slow. I have now paid you £880 on a/c, which with say £150 value of old House & materials is £1030. I cannot go further. You may send me the bills for flooring Board, seasoned Timbers . . . &c., and later, and an account of all the men by name employed this week & I will enable you to pay these. If you do not do this, I must take the completion into my own hands at once.

This letter refers to the building of Cwmdu Lodge for Frank and his bride.

Arthur Gilbertson to John Griffiths. 19 Dec. 1895 [2 : 182]

You faithfully promised me, after last measuring up, that you would keep a pocket book & enter men's names & time daily, upon my work – so that at any time, I could see it and find out what was due to you.

You ought to have done it, and it would have saved you no end of trouble, and saved me worry and annoyance.

It seems useless trying to help you because you wont attend to what I say; so that I am obliged to give out work elsewhere.

I enclose £50 on further a/c. When shall you be out of the House?

What more have you to do to Stables? I do not wish the Hay loft plastered.

Arthur Gilbertson to Bank of Australasia, London. 10 Jan. 1896 [2 : 186]

Thanks for your letter of yesterday. I am almost surprised your Branch did not cable for "power" in first instance, it wld. have saved time & expense, however we know now – please cable immediately to hand over Two thousand pounds on account, and I will ask my Lawyer (S. B. Barlow, 165 Fenchurch Street) to call on you, and draw up "power" for my Son to sign: he will also probably sail himself for Australia at end of this month.

Arthur Gilbertson to S. B. Barlow. 10 Jan. 1896 [2 : 187]

Kindly read enclosed, and call on Bank of Australia & prepare power of attorney for Howel to sign. We should like to send it to the Bank in London, in time to go out next Mail, we think Mail goes on 19th inst. Howel will probably sail on the 30th inst. but the "power" may be convenient before he arrives.

Arthur Gilbertson to S. B. Barlow. 24 Jan. 1896 [2 : 191-2]

. . . Settlement. No doubt your law is better than Robinson Smiths, but he & the old Lady will beat you on matters of fact, if you dont look out!! I wired you "New

House (i.e. Cwmdu Lodge rebuilt, now christened Glynteg) does not go into settlement at all, Frank (my) Tenant at Will, who put this in". You know this house & 15 acres of land is left to my unmarried Daughters in my Will!! and Frank may occupy it until he comes into Glanrhyd. I dont think I can have misunderstood your letter of yesterday & Counsel's opinion? but you seem to propose to give away both my Houses on my death! and where would my family go to?

I suppose the old Lady, who was too ill for business, is at the bottom of this & you now see you have a cunning one to deal with. There has never been a suggestion of settling the New House, and it is expressly left to my Daughters.

As regards other matters I have pencilled on the draft. You see how needful it is, no time should be lost, and details pass out of our minds.

I merely promised to rebuild Cwmdu Lodge for Frank to live in.

I shall be curious to know how this House crept into proposed settlement.

Arthur Gilbertson to S. B. Barlow. 25 Jan. 1896 [2 : 195-6]

I am intensely relieved to find the matter of grabbing both my Houses, did not arise with Robinson Smith & his client. You will, I know, excuse my pointing out to you how important it is, that these matters should be dealt with promptly when instructions are fresh in one's mind. I cant think how it escaped you, seeing you are a party to my "Will".

I should like to have seen these Counsel's points, before you sent them on to R. Smith, and I could then have prevented this awkward mistake going before him.

On 10th Jany you wrote me "before I return &c &c" – I wish this had been done.

I take it you will have written Robinson Smith saying you have discovered serious errors, in your Counsel's opinion, and probably will ask for document to be returned, to be set right, before R. Smith's client is consulted. You will observe other pencil notes of mine, upon which I want your advice please, & therefore wired you this morning "When writing me send Counsel's opinion with my pencil notes for my guidance". I expect sometimes, you, like myself, get almost too much to do, and to carry in one's head, and yet it is difficult to delegate the work to another!

I nearly decided yesterday morning to withdraw my consent!!!

Arthur Gilbertson to S. B. Barlow. 24 Feb. 1896 [2 : 215-6]

I have your letter of yesterday.

Have you not made a slip as to "settling absolutely" the ⅓rd of the Personalty?

I have not copies of R. Smith's letters of 15th & 19th but my recollection is that only £4000 was to be settled & vested in Trustees and that Mrs. Thomas undertook, that on her death Miss Isabel was to have ⅓rd of the Personalty, as it now exists, minus the £4000 – and you were to get a schedule of it.

I think you have worded it, in such a way, as to make the old Lady think you want the ⅓rd handed over to Trustees at once. This was not intended. As regards the

Colliery Frank wishes to give way, that Isabel shld. not have the right of "willing it", as the Thomas's wish to avoid any risk of its going out of their family.

I tell him, I must therefore deal with our Works shares left him in the same way (to keep them in the Gilbertson family) and shall have to leave them to Trustees.

Mrs. Thomas merely placed in March last, her intentions in a more explicit form than she had done in /94. Please state this to R. Smith, and it was not until /95 that I gave formal consent to a time being named.

Arthur Gilbertson to S. B. Barlow. 26 Feb. 1896 [2 : 217-8]

I think I must have a copy of R. Smith's two letters (to keep me current) which you showed me in London. The matter now seems to resolve itself into this – that Mrs. Thomas must hand over the £4000 to the Trustees, and give a list showing what Isabel's ⅓rd. consists of now & must state in the Settlement, that she has the third as it now exists.

The other points Frank wishes to waive.

My recollection is that R. Smith made this suggestion, after Mr. Eden had called on him from Mrs. Thomas & you have Eden's letter on the subject.

If they now try to wriggle out of the third, I simply decline to take any further steps.

Arthur Gilbertson to S. B. Barlow. 7 March 1896 [2 : 220-1]

The contents of R. Smith's letter cause me the greatest surprise. I now recognize the impossibility of binding Mrs. Thomas to anything and I will not further waste the time of yourself, or myself.

It is too late to refuse my assent to the marriage – had the young people flinched in the least degree during these prolonged and painful negotiations, I would have prevented the marriage – they have not done so, on the contrary, they are loyal & devoted to each other, and under these circumstances I do not feel justified in preventing the marriage, altho the promises made as to money are not carried out, by the mother.

I wish you now to write to R. Smith, that I will have nothing to do with any Settlements whatever & that Mrs. Thomas may arrange the marriage, when, & how, she likes.

I absolutely decline any further correspondence on the matter.

My dear Son is a most affectionate & sympathetic companion, and I view his loss, coming on my other losses, almost with consternation. I can only say Miss Thomas is a most fortunate woman. Believe me.

The marriage settlement was finally signed on 23 April 1896, the day before Frank and Isabel were married. It gave Isabel various properties in Bishopston and Loughor and one-third part of her father's personal estate for her sole and separate use, and after her death to be held in trust for her children by Frank Gilbertson.[6]

Arthur Gilbertson to Henry Dever, Auditor. 26 Sept. 1896 [2 : 253-4]

Private

I am glad to see your handwriting again. Reading between the lines you naturally think our business remains much where it was: and possibly that I desire to get rid of some shares "at the low price they might realize". This is not so at all, I would not part with a share, but at a very high premium, which our Balance Sheets would I think warrant.

Being the sole surviving Parent, and the youngest girl only 6 years old, I should like part of my money to be invested for the girls in "Trustee 2¾% investments".

Persons in the Metal Trades must know that the Steel & Sheet branches are in anything but a depressed condition – I expect to make £8000 to £9000 during current six months ending next December, in these Works, and am now adding "Galvanizing" to the business instead of a portion of the Tinplate business. If anything comes of my realizing a certain amount of my holding, it would seem your last suggestion is the only practicable one – Form a new Company, and add "Galvanizing" to our business. I believe there is a good opening for such business (which is undoubtedly migrating to South Wales from Staffordshire).

Do you prima facie think our Works, goodwill, &c would fetch £150,000, judging from our Balance Sheets, myself retaining half my present holding, if a new Company were formed in London?

Arthur Gilbertson to Henry Dever. 3 Oct. 1896 [2 : 256-7]

Steel Works Lease

99 years from 25th March 1890 @ £80 per annum, it is a ground rent – Company may determine every 5 years – Landlord to take at a valuation, or if not company may remove Machinery.

Tin Works Lease

50 years from 25th Decbr. 1885. Rent £270 – Company may determine every 3 years.

Farm Lease – 25 years from 25th Decbr. 1885, rent £80.

Railway Bridge & mill plot of land, freehold of W.Gilbertson & Co. Ltd.

Lease of Land for 8 Houses – 99 years from 25th March 1876 @ £10..10..0 ground rent.

I dont quite know how to apportion the £120,000. The Mills & Tinworks might be £45,000 to £50,000.

Steel Works £45,000 – £50,000 then the Brands & connection are very exceptional & valuable. No doubt the Leases would be renewed, as the machinery is ours.

There may be another £100 a year Rent for a site for further Mills, and a Basic Slag Manure Works which we have in hand.

The Landlord of all is my Brother-in-Law.

Arthur Gilbertson to Henry Dever. **n.d. (c. 6 Oct. 1896) [2 : 258-9]**

Thank you for your explicit letter of yesterday.

I will think carefully over the matter.

I dont quite see how a valuation of the Works alone, would come in, unless they were valued by the light of our "balance sheets".

They are in splendid order & lit by Electric light.

The success of the Works is due to good management & buying & selling carefully, and our markets all over the world & our Brands & reputation.

A mere valuation of an ordinary Steel Works & Tinplate Works would not justify a valuation of the amount, I require.

Arthur Gilbertson to Henry Dever. **n.d. (c. 17 Oct. 1896) [2 : 260-1]**

Thanks for yours of 9th & 10th inst with our Balance Sheets and proforma account. If I understand the latter the Shareholders would receive

	£100,000 less
Expenses &c	8,000
	92,000 & less
present Debs	7,250
	£ 84,750 Total for distribution

and their 700 shares @ £50 each, would remain to them intact?

Altho' we have a sinking fund of £7000, we use this money as floating capital, as our sales, purchases, wages &c. turn over half a million per annum!

I conclude the voting power would remain as at present, as the £100,000 Debentures & Preference Shares would not carry votes? I find for the 8 years ending June 1895, we have declared gross profits (deducting only parochial Taxes*) amounting to £116,359, or an average of £14,545 per annum (*depreciation also deducted) to the Special Income Tax Commissioners. Income Tax on my Salary, now £2000 a year, being paid by myself additional. I am however taking out for you exact particulars for the period you want. We are now expending £1000 out of this half year's profits on a Galvanizing Shop. We have also made a success of two Siemens Basic Furnaces in our Steel Works, and a Yorkshire firm have completed a Works on our Leasehold to grind the slag into manure, and we have a third of the profits & have stipulated that you are to be Auditor – this Slag may yield us £1000 a year as our share of profit.

Arthur Gilbertson to Henry Dever. **19 Oct. 1896 [2 : 262]**

I note what you say about voting power &c, and I shall have to give the scheme more consideration. Having the Works here, and my Sons in them, I must retain my preponderance. I shall probably leave the matter now to the Spring in order to give time for the development of the Basic process, and Galvanizing &c.

I am still anxious to realise a certain amount of my holding. I have had Mr. Barlow here, and among other things told him what I thought of doing and further on I shall ask him to see you.

Arthur Gilbertson to S. B. Barlow. 21 April 1897 [1 : 498]

Would you kindly read enclosed resolution, and tell me, if we ought to pass a similar one? Frank & Cecil are now Directors, and I apportion them such remuneration as I consider right – of course the Company confirm everything I do, as I pay them out their Capital every four or five years, and keep repeating the process!!

Perhaps it is sufficient for us only to pass a resolution, fixing their Salaries, as Assistant Managers or Assistant Managing Directors.

Arthur Gilbertson to S. B. Barlow. 24 April 1897 [2 : 287-8]

. . . In the four Works in which I am Director, I am paid a Salary as "Managing Director", and Fees as "Director" – the former is fixed once for all by a resolution of the Board, the latter (Fees) confirmed annually.

You remember a Works is not like London Coys' Boards – Works entail daily management. Now Frank & Cecil are called "Directors" but they are daily "managers", or whatever they may be called assisting me, and carrying out my orders – it is not advisable to discuss their Salaries every year, and if a Resolution is past apportioning them Salaries, I conclude no further resolution is needed, unless their Salaries are to be altered.

If this is all so, we need not trouble further. I only want to be "in order" – a "Quorum" is only needful once a month in a manufacturing concern, to confirm payments. This is at any rate the usage of such concerns as ours.

You understand I am "Managing Director" with a fixed Salary.

I am inclined to think we need do nothing, and that the resolutions of the Board appointing Frank & Cecil, at Salaries, as assistant Managers, or whatever they may be called, is sufficient.

Kindly return me the printed cutting.

Arthur Gilbertson to S. B. Barlow. 28 April 1897 [2 : 289]

. . . My Salary was fixed by a "minute" before I resigned my position of Sole Director, and is entered in the Minute book.

You no doubt see the difference between a manufacturing concern requiring daily decisions which cannot be deferred, and a London Board of what are called Guinea Pigs!!

The term "Directors" will of course do for my assistants, but it is inconvenient, that their remuneration, does not take the form of fixed Salaries. Of course, if this cannot be done we must be content, and vote their remuneration annually.

My experience is that in manufacturing concerns, this stipulation of the Articles is overlooked, and assistant managers (or whatever they are called) are paid by salaries. Please return the paper cutting.

Arthur Gilbertson to S. B. Barlow. 1 May 1897 [2 : 290-1]

Will. My fourth Son, Colin Richard (not George Noel, who is sixth!) is intended as Exor &c.

Is not last sentence different to my Will & previous Codicils? also pencil words as to £120 arising from Works shares &c.

W. Gilbertson & Co. Ltd. I have known large & good Manufacturing Concerns in South Wales, simply ruined, by a London Board of Directors, not brought up to the trade from their youth, and, of course, not understanding the business. My Sons shall remain designated "Directors", and their remuneration shall be voted, & confirmed, at each annual meeting – This will put that right?

My position & remuneration. Your first sentence – what could arise? and what further is needful than the "resolution" I referred to, passed & entered in our minute book? Of course, we can confirm it annually if needful? No difficulty, in point of fact, could or would arise, as I control ⅔rds. of voting power, and so pleased are our Shareholders at what I have produced for them, that I might place my remuneration at £5000 a year, if I liked. No doubt your friends on their small holdings are, as surprised & pleased, as the Lawrences have expressed themselves, at the results I have obtained.

My remuneration is £2400 a year, and I should have considered myself entitled to more, but as I pay ⅔rds. of it myself, I did not think it worth alteration, and am very glad I have done so well, for my friends.

Arthur Gilbertson to S. B. Barlow. 30 Dec. 1897 [2 : 325-6]

A happy New Year to your Wife & yourself!

"My Will" (You must be tired of it!) Clause 12.

All Saints Church, I have now determined to pay up the £4000 to Trustees, in Colonial Securities, say Francis William, Cecil Frederick, Colin Richard, Harriet Florence, Gilbertson, as Trustees – please draft a document – it can then be omitted from my new Will.

If I live a few years, my Daughters will inherit in cash & shares, some £10,000 apiece. I shall therefore appoint Trustees permanently to protect them in case of marriage (as you before advised), say Francis W., Cecil F., Colin R., & Charles Geoffrey, Gilbertson.

Howel has now settled down in Australia and had better not be an Executor or Trustee.

I also wish to transfer one share in Glynbeudy Works to Mrs. Richardson [Arthur's sister Catherine Anne], and our old Servant, Martha Davies is dead, and both of these can come out of my "Will" (shares No. 7 & 8).

Clause 10. One share to eldest surviving Son, rest [?] divided in No. 11.
Clause 18. I understand gives F.W.G. power to "will" shares to his children, or if none to revert ultimately to his Brothers & Sisters.
I wish to leave especially to Charles G. my large American organ & collection of Sacred & Organ music, collected during some 40 years, with the hope it will be useful to him, if he takes Holy orders in the church, as I hope.

. . . Do you think I allow enough for Charles & George? both young Boys.

Arthur Gilbertson to Capital & Counties Bank Ltd., Neath. 17 Nov. 1898 [1 : 661]

Kindly note Mr. Colin Richard Gilbertson has been appointed a Director of this Company and his signature is at foot.

Arthur Gilbertson to Herbert Lloyd. 17 Nov. 1898 [2 : 368]

I enclose £250.0.0 as loan for Lionel's Indentures – it is understood that this is ultimately to be repaid to me, or my children.

Please sign over this stamp & return letter to me.

Lionel Robert was one of the eleven children of Herbert and Frances Lloyd of Plas Cilybebyll. Herbert was the brother of Arthur's late wife Ellen and a major landowner in the Pontardawe district.

Arthur Gilbertson to S. B. Barlow. 10 Oct. 1904 [4 : 139]

I have agreed with Rice Nicholl he shall change his name to "Dillwyn".

I have agreed that his Mother will settle £5000 on her death & Miss Dillwyn £4000 on her death, Rice Nicholl £1000 Insurance on his life, I settle £1300.0.0 Queensland 3½ Bonds, one twelfth (£1200.0.0) for her Mother (as Cecil's settlement) and 12 shares in W. Gilbertson & Co. Ltd. and I will pay up the balance every year up to £300 a year. I dont want to disclose W.G.G. Ltd. shares, the value, as Messrs. James & Thomas Solicitors represent some Steel Works in Glamorganshire.

I covenant to pay £300 a year. I think we need not go into the value of W. G. & Co. Ltd. shares. I send you a telegram – "I am writing to you this day".

Rice Mansel Nicholl Dillwyn (aged 29) married Arthur's eldest daughter Harriet Florence (aged 26) on 8 December 1904 in All Saints Church. The groom, designated as 'Gentleman' in the marriage register, was the youngest son of John Cole Nicholl of Merthyr Mawr and Mary de la Beche Dillwyn of Swansea. The change of surname had been requested by Rice's aunt, the formidable Amy Dillwyn, who wanted a male heir to continue the Dillwyn family name. He acceded to her request and then joined her as a director of Dillwyn & Company, a spelter works in Llansamlet.[7]

Arthur Gilbertson to S. B. Barlow. **11 Oct. 1904 [4 : 140]**

. . . I enclose the Heads of settlement, but I said to you yesterday, about the value of W. G. & Co. Ltd. shares, since the formation of this private company (about 15 years ago) large extensions have taken place without adding to the Capital & the actual value of the Shares have greatly increased, and I believe now the £50 shares are now worth £200.

The company's Auditors intimated last August that the shares would be valued about £200, but it was not a formal letter. I dont want to disclose to James & Thomas. I covenant to pay the balance up to £300 a year.

Mrs. Nicholl & Miss Dillwyn may live 20 years again, so no Income will come for many years in the Settlement beyond my £300 a year.

Frank Gilbertson to Messrs Dillwyn & Co. Ltd. **27 April 1906 [5 : 253]**

We have to thank you very much for your kind letter of yesterday.

Mr. A. Gilbertson is bearing the sad blow with fortitude.

This letter refers to the death of Arthur's fourth son Colin Richard.

J. Philip Davies to Messrs Barlow, Barlow & Lyde. **17 May 1906 [5 : 265]**

I certify that the five shares in W. Gilbertson & Co. Ltd. held by the late Mr. Colin R. Gilbertson in my opinion, are worth £200 each.

J. P. Davies to Chas. G. Gilbertson, Queen's College, Oxford. **20 May 1906 [5 : 267]**

Kindly furnish us with two copies of your signature on separate slips of paper. These are required to be sent to the Banks in connection with your appointment as a Director of this Company.

J. P. Davies to Capital & Counties Bank Ltd., Neath. **23 May 1906 [5 : 271]**

We beg to advise that Mr. Charles Geoffrey Gilbertson has been appointed a Director of this Company in succession to the late Mr. Colin Richard Gilbertson. We enclose copy of his signature on a separate sheet.

Frank Gilbertson to Sir Alfred Lawrence. **16 April 1908 [5 : 685-6]**

I am sorry to trouble you with enclosed, but we have to alter our Articles & to constitute our Company a "Private Limited Liability Co" in order to escape the obligation to deposit an annual Balance Sheet with the Registrar, where it would be open to inspection by labour leaders!

Would you mind having the proxy signed by Mr. C. L. Lawrence & yourself as Trustees, because we must have a 3/4th majority.

I hope you are better again. We were very sorry not to have seen you again, but the arbitration lasted over the Friday you asked us to lunch. It resulted in splitting the difference as Board of Trade Arbitrations usually do, but it has given us some reduction in wages in one department without the loss & upset of a strike.

Charles Giddings to Shareholders. **27 Sept. 1926 [10 : 616]**

Notice is hereby given that the Forty-first Ordinary General Meeting . . . 5 October 1926 . . . to confirm the appointment of Commander G. N. Gilbertson as a Director.

Addendum by F. W. Gilbertson:

An arrangement we had made for representation in Sheffield and Birmingham having come to an end, we have decided to make use of Commander G. N. Gilbertson to push the sales of our products in those areas; traditional respect has always been shown to officers of H.M. Navy in Sheffield, and we believe this appointment will prove of value to the Company.

As the writer has not been in good health for the past year, we also thought it advisable to add one member to the Board and we have appointed Commander Gilbertson, subject to confirmation at the Annual Meeting at a fee of £250 a year.

NOTES

1. P. F. Drucker, *The Practice of Management* (Heinemann, 1975), 3.
2. F. W Gilbertson entered Charterhouse in the Oration Quarter (Autumn Term) 1886 and left in the Oration Quarter 1888. In the matriculation register of Magdalen College, Oxford, his entry is dated to January 1891 and he was awarded his BA in 1894, taking a Third in Natural Science, specialising in Chemistry.
3. The *Queensland Post Office Directory* for various years shows A. H. Gilbertson as a selector in Muttaburra from 1900 to 1915, and from 1916 at Penlan Station, Longreach. A selector rented a small area of land (a selection) from the Crown for agricultural or grazing purposes. Most types of selections were designed to be converted to freehold tenure after a fixed term provided the selector fulfilled certain conditions. Information from the State Library of Queensland.
4. C. G. Gilbertson matriculated on 20 January 1903 and graduated with a BA Pass degree on 14 June 1906. Information from the Oxford University Archives.
5. After the first World War Howel Gilbertson returned to Britain to farm in Devon. J. Lloyd, *The Lloyds of Plâs Cilybebyll*, (Port Talbot, Andreas Haaf, 1990), 18-19, 77.
6. University of Wales Swansea Library, Iltyd Thomas Papers.
7. D. Painting, *Amy Dillwyn* (Cardiff, University of Wales Press, 1987), 82-8, 97-9.

Chapter 2

TRADE AND EXPANSION 1890-1912

All ten Letter-Books chronicle in considerable detail the responses of Arthur Gilbertson and his sons to a diverse array of issues associated with their primary function of optimising the productive potential of the resources available to them. The selection of letters in this chapter illustrates their personal direction of the Company's technical and commercial activities over twenty-two years of considerable change in the tinplate, steel and galvanizing trades. In 1890 the tinplate industry, centred on West Glamorgan and East Carmarthenshire, was threatened by the anticipated American tariff, but Arthur Gilbertson expanded his tinplate capacity by building the Glynbeudy works in Brynamman and erecting in his Pontardawe works two basic open hearth steel furnaces. Thereafter, he and his sons pursued an expansionist programme, extending the Pontardawe plant as trade increased and selling their output of Siemens steel, mild steel and high carbon billets, tin, terne and blackplates, roofing sheets, steel stampings and galvanised sheets to the home market and through Swansea docks to a world-wide market which included America, the Far East and the Empire. The letters in this chapter provide a commentary on their interaction with local and national industrialists, government departments, employers' associations, solicitors, merchants and agents, and insights into the many problems which confronted them. Included also are copies of letters written by Arthur Gilbertson in 1902 which describe the difficulties which beset his unsuccessful attempt to establish a steelworks on the coast at Port Talbot. In 1907 he suffered a stroke which enforced his withdrawal from the daily management of the company and operational control passed to Frank, with departmental roles and accountability being agreed with his brothers. There are no extant copies of letters written by Arthur Gilbertson after 8 August 1905 and evidence of his continuing role in company decision-making is not available. However, he retained, if only nominally, his executive status as Managing Director until his death on 2 March 1912. The letters in this chapter outline the company's progress to that date, and reflect its transition from a relatively small-scale producer of mild steel bars for tinning to a medium-sized complex employing, in 1911, over 1,600 men and comprising a steelworks with 7 furnaces, 12 sheet mills and a galvanizing works, 8 tinplate and blackplate mills and a slag grinding plant.

Arthur Gilbertson to Messrs Sim & Coventry, Liverpool. 9 Dec. 1890 [1 : 40]

We observe you have registered as a Tin & Terneplate brand the letters "GOM". You are doubtless not aware that these initial letters of our well-known brand "Gilbertson's Old Method" are often used for the brand itself by the Americans. We would therefore feel obliged if you would cancel your registration, and register the letters reversed "MOG" and we would pay for the expense, as you have inadvertently registered a brand likely to deceive & confuse buyers.

Pending your reply we take no action in the matter.

Arthur Gilbertson to Messrs Barlow & James, London. 9 Dec. 1890 [1 : 41]

Is it needful for us to re-register our Trademarks which were registered by "W. Gilbertson & Co." because they handed over everything to the "Limited Co."?

The comptroller has asked us to do so, costing some £30.

A case has just arisen where we may have to take proceedings against a Firm, for imitating our Brand or Trademark.

Arthur Gilbertson to S. B. Barlow. 13 Feb. 1891 [1 : 77-8]

Referring to your letter of 4th November last, we have been able to follow up the matter and have now got a Tin chest with 80 lbs. of Tea in it, this chest made by foreigners. We shall be able now, before long, to make plates similar to those forming this Tin chest, and to send out sheets, for a trial, to Messrs. Geo. Stewart & Co., Colombo. We find therefore Tinplate chests are already in use!

The American trade monopolises our attention until June, as we get such high prices for all Tinplates sent to America before the Tariff on July 1st.

River Plate. We find altho Brugon [?] turned out so badly, he started our Plates in that country and we are now getting much increased business there, which is some compensation for his behaviour!

Arthur Gilbertson to E. Rice Daniel, Cwmfelin Tin Plate Works, Swansea. 6 March 1891 [1 : 90]

. . . My idea was that you & your two friends wished to press me to join the Association* & this I really cannot do. As regards reducing output to prevent ruinous prices, I am quite with you, and have told our men to save their money, so that if I am driven to close the Works rather than sell at a loss, they may have something to fall back on.

**The South Wales, Monmouthshire & Gloucestershire Tinplate Makers' Association.*

(Form 18)

Proposals for { Roofing Plates, Roofing Felt, Pig Tin & Lead.

Philadelphia Pa April 2nd 1886

To Col John M. Wilson,
office of Public Bldngs & Grounds,
Washington D.C.

Sir:

In accordance with your advertisement of March 5. 1886. inviting Proposals for Roofing Plates & Felt, Nails, Pig Tin & Lead, and subject to all the Conditions & requirements thereof, and of yr. Specfns. dated march 5/86. Copies of both of which are hereto attached, and as far as they relate to this proposal are made a part of it, we propose to furnish and deliver at the point of destination all the following Materials at following prices, viz:

One hundred & thirty five (135) boxes I.C 14/20 prime first quality Martin-Siemens Steel Dipped Gilbertsons old method (extra Coated) Roofing Plates, guaranteed to average 120 lbs net per box of 112 sheets @ $6.70 six dollars & seventy cents pr box.

Eight hundred (800) lbs Roofing Felt as per

Proposal to supply GOM roofing plates to the White House, 1886
(National Archives and Records Administration, Washington DC)

Arthur Gilbertson to John Roberts. **7 April 1891 [1 : 94]**

There are rumours that you are ceasing working the Graigola Coal below our Workings. I find our Workings will be exhausted in 8 or 9 months.

Are you disposed to treat with us for the Graigola in question? We should consume most, in our two Tinplate Works.

Arthur Gilbertson to John Roberts. **11 April 1891 [1 : 99]**

. . . I have seen our overman, who has been into the slant. I think we might make something of it for use chiefly at our Boilers, but it is costly to work, or of course you would not have given it up.

We make hardly any profit on present high prices on present taking, if we debited management & office expenses, but it is convenient for our Works.

We think we might try the Coal in question if you would let us the whole place, at a royalty of 6d. per Ton instead of 1s 3d as at present.

Arthur Gilbertson to John Roberts. **1 July 1891 [1 : 120]**

Our Colliery has come to an end, and men had suddenly to be withdrawn yesterday.

We propose now getting rid of all our plant, siding, tips, &c.

Please quote price for Graigola Thro' Coal @ Graigola for about 100 Tons a week & send 20 Tons each day, <u>this week</u> commencing tomorrow.

Arthur Gilbertson to Godfrey Taylor. **19 Sept. 1891 [1 : 154]**

We see a statement in Western Mail that 50 Tinning Machines are waiting shipment at Swansea Harbour for America. We don't credit it but would you kindly ascertain if it is a fact?

Arthur Gilbertson to Messrs Brewer & Son, 33 Chancery Lane, London. **3 Feb. 1893 [1 : 220]**

Please ascertain if Taylor & Struvé's Patent for Tinning Machines has expired?

We wish to protect a process for doubling their Pot, and using 2 plates at a time, instead of 1 plate. Would this be possible? When? The same Machinery &c., only Tinning rolls doubled in length and two cradles alongside each other being used to supply 2 plates.

It may be Taylor & Taylor's Machine & not Taylor & Struvé.

Arthur Gilbertson to C.L. Tormin, Hamburg. **23 June 1894 [1 : 291]**

<u>J. Rech</u>. We are glad to see further enquiries today.

"Perola". We find some plates, which we were instructed to mark thus, were sold by our London Agent to a firm in London called Steadman Crowther & Co. – we will look out for this in future & quote an enhanced price to protect Mr. Rech: it is better to do this, than to decline quoting.

Is it not strange what efforts are made to get our Plates!

Arthur Gilbertson to Messrs Phillips & Hill, 122 Lennox Street, London. **16 Nov. 1894 [2 : 31]**

Are you inclined to sell for us in London at 1% commission? We find it needful to be represented by an active Firm.

Our 4 Mills are first class, and our output some 2,500 Boxes weekly & quality excellent.

Arthur Gilbertson to Messrs Phillips & Hill. **19 Nov. 1894 [2 : 33]**

We have your letter of 17th inst., and quite concur in what you say.

We make "Counter" Coke Tinplates IC 20 x 14 @ 10/6, "Gilder" IC 20 x 14 (Siemens) @ 10/9, all f.o.b. Swansea, less 3% & 1% to yourselves.

Our qualities are distinctly good, and we shall be glad to hear from you.

Please address the Writer, at Pontardawe.

Arthur Gilbertson to E. Rice Daniel. **7 Dec. 1894 [1 : 317]**

Thank you for your letter & circular. I am unable to enter into any "combination" because some Tinplate Makers invariably break thro' it.

Being very much independent of American Trade, I manage to keep going fairly well. As regards a basis price, I think I may say, I am now above any basis you are likely to fix upon. Only a few days ago, I lost a large order for Petroleum Tins, being underbid to the extent of 1/- a box. As a matter of fact, I thought your Firm were the persons who accepted the ruinous price!

Arthur Gilbertson to Richard K. Prichard, Cymmer Colliery, Neath. **26 March 1895 [2 : 73]**

Glynbeudy. You seem to ignore having had 5% on your capital, on an average. You say "I can but wish that our finances were in the same condition at Glynbeudy" – I can't guess what you mean, but I now offer to take your shares in Glynbeudy at par, upon your taking mine at Cymmer Colliery, at par, and I shall have to pay you £200, as your shares at Glynbeudy amount to £1,200, and mine at your Colliery to £1,000.

I entirely object to any business undertaking I am managing, being classed with the Cymmer Co. speculation.

The subscription was "Your affectionate cousin"! Prichard's mother was a member of the Bramah family.

Arthur Gilbertson to G. L. Morris, Ynysmeudw Iron Company. **21 May 1895 [1 : 349]**

I find at times I have surplus "Bars" and could manage to turn them into Tin or Black, if I had more Mills.

It has occurred to me whether your Coy. would care to "rent" us Ynismedw? I might be able to work a couple of Mills, and it would help the people as you know the state of things. I could only pay a small rent, and take working stocks at a valuation, but it might be better for you to take a small rent, than suffer out of pocket expenses there.

Arthur Gilbertson to Richard K. Prichard. **29 May 1895 [2 : 90-1]**

I am sorry you wrote your letter of 20th deliberately as you say.

Insults between you & I, are too absurd to talk of. I don't know what you would call it, if a company in which I was the first named Promoter sent Surveyor over Bryntirion, and cut down your trees, without asking consent! This is what your people did to me.

What you say about your Directorship of the Ry is correct, but you never told me you were the first named Promoter and I did not find this out until I saw the "Bill"!

I have acted for the protection of my property – and have I believe succeeded – by the advice of a first class London Solicitor – a gentleman, and whom Sir Douglas Fox said he liked much. We have only done what is needful to ensure "promises" being carried out, as we have no confidence in the local Solicitors, for several reasons. One of the "insults" you talk of, arose, from your insulting me (to use your word) by your wrongly written letter which you never expressed regret for!

If you will tell me in a plain sentence, what insulting statements I have made, I would gladly withdraw them.

Of course, you know very well you have no interest in making a line up here, beyond getting some money as a Director.

Please let Beatrice read this – she has a good calm judgement.

Beatrice was Richard's sister.

Arthur Gilbertson to John Player, Player's Tin Plate Works, Clydach. **1 Aug. 1895 [1 : 379]**

I am obliged by your letters, but I have quite decided not to sink any more money in Tinplate Works.

I believe a Republican will rule in America next time, and to supply the large amount of capital sunk, and being sunk, in American Tinplate Works, a further duty will be put on, if needful.

Arthur Gilbertson to Herbert Lloyd, Plâs Cilybebyll. 20 Jan. 1896 [1 : 407]

We are now making arrangements to grind Basic Slag. The Works, which will require half acre of land, are to be erected & worked by a Firm from Yorkshire [Swan Bros.]. We think a suitable site would be adjoining the branch canal at the extreme end of our Boundary next old Primrose Wharf.

We find we should want a small portion of land beyond our Boundary on Primrose Wharf, and could pay £10 a year for this.

Would you kindly have the matter looked into.

Arthur Gilbertson to Richard Heathfield, Leadenhall Buildings, London, E.C. 29 Jan. 1896 [2 : 197-8]

Thank you for your letters to myself & my Son, and your frank answers to our questions.

I am anxious to lose no time in going on with the matter, and to arrange a site, for which I shall want to see roughly the Galvanizing department mapped, as well as the Mills, so please kindly put down the Galvanizing plant, to follow the Mills, Annealing & Pickling.

I will enquire about Muriatic Acid.

My Son will be in London about middle of February & will call on you by appointment, but I would like the tracings at once please, and your idea of capital – it looks to me like £10,000? Three Mills, Engine, Boilers, Sheds &c perhaps only putting up 2 Mills at first.

Arthur Gilbertson to Richard Heathfield. 1 Feb. 1896 [2 : 206]

Thank you for yours of 30th ulto & plans, which we are carefully considering. We have ample & suitable space adjoining our sidings, and convenient for our Steel Bars.

We presume Roof over Mills would be Galvanized iron & over Galvanizing House, Timber & Pantiles?

Capital. Kindly give us frankly your views.

Arthur Gilbertson to Francis B. Gilbertson, Liverpool. 7 Feb. 1896 [1 : 408-9]

We return Messrs. The E. P. Wheeler Co's letter of 21st ulto, to Messrs. Humphreys & Skinner with thanks for its perusal. Seeing such good & heavy plates as Gilbertson's Old Method Ternes are shut out of America, by the Tariff, we see no objection to Messrs. Wheeler's suggestion, supposing we can be satisfied that our name will not be injured, and quality fully maintained. For this purpose our Steel should be used for dipping, as it is needful that the quality should seem without a flaw. If Messrs Wheeler's entered into an agreement to pay us one shilling per single box royalty, we would apply it as follows,

1½d. per single box to Mr. F. B. Gilbertson
1½d. " " " Messrs Humphreys & Skinner's
9d " " " ourselves, out of which 9d. we would apply 1½d. to cheapen the cost of our Blackplates, equal to 2/6d. a Ton – so that we could sell at 2/6d. a Ton, under our usual price, which would defeat the American Tariff to that extent.

In case of need, we might supply a man who knows how to coat G.O.M.

Please keep this letter for Mr. F.B.G.'s return.

Arthur Gilbertson to S. B. Barlow. **8 Feb. 1896 [2 : 208-9]**

We have had a wonderfully good six months ending Decr. last, £8,300 for six months, on £35,000 paid up capital!!

I am today signing checks for interim divd. for that period @ 10% for 6 mos. (20% per ann. rate) absorbing £3,500, and we carry forward £4,800.

Now America is rapidly making its own Tinplates & in a year's time, we shall want an outlet for our Steel, instead of part of our present Tinplates. I am making careful enquiries, and I want to put up Sheet Mills & Galvanizing Works.

I think £17,000 outlay needful. I propose to keep the £4,800, and the surplus profits of the current six months in hand (perhaps £4,000) making £8,800, and I want to borrow £7,000 @ 4½% on Debentures. The profits on "Sheets" and "Galvanizing" are more than Tinplates!! and all go to our Colonies, instead of America.

We can beat the Midlands down here, hollow, and they are doing an enormous trade. Would your friends like to subscribe £5,000?

I intend going to Langham Hotel on Thursday next, to see Howel off to Australia, and could see you about Tuesday week.

Arthur Gilbertson to Alfred T. Lawrence. **21 March 1896 [1 : 417]**

Could you spare a few minutes to read the enclosed. We want to register the word "Glory" being a brand on our Tinplates of especial value. That old fool Render Lack, would not admit it. He says it is not descriptive of "quality". We would put any device with it, he likes.

The remark in his letter of 4th inst., as to "already refused" was his refusal to us, before we noticed in the Trades marks Journal, he was passing more doubtful words for other persons! & then we tried thro Brewer & Son.

I daresay you noticed the "Friendly" difference of opinion.

Frank Gilbertson to Richard Heathfield. **24 March 1896 [1 : 420]**

Will you kindly let us know if your "Pots" are heated by Coke, & if there are flues going to a central stack? How are the fumes of this fire & of the Zinc & Flux carried away?

Frank Gilbertson to Richard Heathfield. **26 March, 1896 [1 : 424]**

Will you kindly give us the following information:

How are plates drawn in & out of Annealing Fce? Is the trolly on wheels & does it remain in the Fce? How do the axles &c. not warp?

Should you say Sulphuric acid was more suitable for pickling Steel sheets than Hydrochloric? Which require most water tanks?

We have decided to go on with the works.

Arthur Gilbertson to H. Lloyd, Plâs Cilybebyll. **2 April 1896 [1 : 430]**

Referring to our recent letter as to a Lease of certain land below our Tips for New Mills &c, we are very sorry to say, that after giving the matter very careful consideration during the past month, we have come to the conclusion for several important reasons, that we cannot erect the Works on that site.

We find we could arrange the Slag grinding Works on the site, we first proposed taking a slice of what is called the Primrose Wharf, and we can erect the Mills & Galvanising Works, near our Steel Works, possibly pulling down Ynysderw Cottages, and taking in a small slice of the field adjoining our Works upon which Cottages are building – we find we have rather encroached on the fields below our Tips, opposite Dan-y-graig, in making the sidings needful for our Works, and require some more room there again.

If you can concede these points, we see our way, to erect the Works & to pay you the £110 a year as proposed, our new portions of land not to exceed the Ten acres in all, which we suggested.

The matter, & the present position of our Trade, is causing the Writer rather grave anxiety, as you may imagine. It would appear to be greatly to the interest of your Estate, that these Works should be prosecuted, and if you could visit the spot at an early date, that we may take advantage of Spring weather, we should feel much obliged.

Arthur Gilbertson to R. Heathfield. **8 April 1896 [1 : 433]**

We find it will be a considerable time before we can get up our Sheet Mills, but we could erect a trial Galvanising plant, much quicker. We can now roll sheets up to 5 ft long & 30" wide – Should not this enable us to execute some orders in Galvanised sheets to make a start?

Will you kindly say in what Works your Patent Annealing Fce (of which you sent us plan) is at work?

Do you advise sending Iron sheets hot & dry into Spelter Bath? This is suggested.

Frank Gilbertson to Richard Heathfield & Company. **13 April 1896 [1 : 436]**

. . . We can make plates 6 feet long we find, now, & if there was any trade we could do remuneratively at once, we might erect our Galvanizing shop & begin galvanising before the Sheet Mills are up.

We shall be glad of your advice.

Arthur Gilbertson to D. Jones, Smethwick. **30 April 1896 [1 : 439]**

I think I ought to let you know at once, that I have decided not to go on at present, with the Galvanizing.

I see a new Company just registered at Neath.

Arthur Gilbertson to Messrs Taylor & Farley. **29 May 1896 [1 : 443]**

Thank you for yours of 27th inst. When you say the Eagle Tinplate Co., we think you mean "The Neath Sheet & Galvanizing Co." started by Mr. Eccles of Briton Ferry Steel Works? and we believe they employ a Mr. Hampden to set out the Works? Kindly say?

We are interested to hear what you say.

We have found such a discrepancy among persons experienced in Staffordshire Sheet Mills & Galvanizing Works, that we have rather stood still, are collecting information & may ultimately profit by others experience!

Arthur Gilbertson to R. Heathfield. **20 June 1896 [1 : 452]**

. . . We have decided not to go on with the Sheet Mills & Galvanising Works this Summer. We hear of two Works contemplated in this County, and we are disposed to let them go ahead first, and we may ultimately profit by their experiences.

Arthur Gilbertson to the Editor, *Liverpool Daily Post*. **3 Aug. 1896 [1 : 461-3]**

My attention has been called to your Leader as to Mr. Bryan's candidature, and the Tinplate trade. I understand, as you say, that the United States impose tariff, to produce Revenue – it is not their interest thus to impose such a tariff, as would exclude, say Tinplates, or their Revenue would at once be lost on that article!

I do not think therefore the state of the Welsh Tinplate Maker will be in the future worse than at present – indeed as some of the most unfortunate Works have closed, Tinplate makers may before long be able to stand out for a price which should yield them some small return.

To effect this, Merchants on this side of the water should help the Manufacturers, but unfortunately the competition between the Merchants is so keen, that the weak Tinplate Maker becomes an easy prey!

The stronger Tinplate Maker therefore has to become his own Merchant, or gradually go to the wall.

[signed] Manufacturer

Arthur Gilbertson to Max Waechter, Messrs Bessler, Waechter & Co., Tinplate & Metal Merchants, London. **1 Oct. 1896 [1 : 484]**

Private

I want to tell you for your private information, why we have had to withdraw our prices for Blackplates. We have worked the four Mills at Glynbeudy (about the best & cheapest Works for manufacturing in South Wales) on nothing but Blackplates for four months, as a test, the Tin Works departments being all closed, we have found the actual result of Blackplates, and the Cost is higher than we ever imagined – previously Tinplates & Blackplates were to a certain extent mixed.

It therefore follows that Russians & Italians &c. must pay more for Blackplates, while materials remain as at present. We want £8..5..0 for IC 20/14 112 lbs 108 lbs fob Swansea, to yield a very small profit.

Arthur Gilbertson to Messrs Swan Bros, Middlesbrough. **29 April 1897 [1 : 499]**

You have not acknowledged, or answered, ours of 22nd inst., which is puzzling and annoying.

We have also had needless trouble in getting you to give a plain answer, as to WGI 1,200 Tons Rough Slag: you now say "yes".

Thus we have lost the profit on grinding 2,661 Tons = £532 – we base this on your letter of 20th Novbr 1895, being our third of profits on 10% slag.

You have now clearly admitted your infraction of the agreement, and we decline to be bound by clause 20, and claim to be at liberty to bring the agreement to an end, if we think fit.

We are unable to say more, until we know what you actually intend doing.

Slag from an open hearth charge of basic pig iron and steel scrap was a profitable by-product which, when ground, provided an effective agricultural fertilizer.

Arthur Gilbertson to W. D. Rees, Engineer, Swansea. **14 June 1897 [1 : 510]**

Please read the enclosed & return to us. If you could get our Basic Steel Ingots used by Mannesmann Co., we would give you 1% commission.

We return the sample Tubes you sent us, also a piece of our own Steel, not annealed. You will observe the good quality.

Arthur Gilbertson to Messrs Barlow & Barlow, Solicitors. **15 June 1897 [1 : 512-4]**

We have made every effort to bring matters to a satisfactory issue with Messrs E. W. & H. A. Swan, but they are such "shufflers", we have been unable to do so: they will not give direct replies & avoid altogether answering any questions which place them in a difficulty, they also have no regard for their own reputation as men of business & contradict themselves in the most outrageous manner. We enclose an "agreement" dated March 1/96 into which we entered with them on certain assurances on their part.

We now say they have broken several clauses & not carried out their assurances.

Clause No. 2. They have failed to buy all our Raw Basic Slag at their premises (South Wales Phosphate Co's Works, on W.G. & Co. Ltd's Leasehold at Pontardawe).

Clause 12. We declined to give a lease, seeing their promises & assurances were not being realized.

Clause 15. Stipulates Machinery to "grind all the Basic Slag produced by Vendors" (the Boiler & machinery supplied turned out to be quite inefficient in consequence of Messrs. Swan's "cheese paring" policy in Outlay) and they have only ground up into Basic Meal 719 Tons, out of the 2,942 Tons of rough Slag made by us up to March 1/97. Our yards & sidings became crammed up with rough Slag consequently, and Messrs. Swan have bought 1,200 Tons of Rough Slag, to be shipped away by them, on which we shall lose the ⅓rd of profits stipulated for in Clause 15. The remaining 1,023 Tons Rough Slag has been paid for "on a/c" by Messrs. Swan & remains on our Yard to be ground up.

Clause 18. See our remarks as to Profits & Balance Sheet below.

Clause 20. We say the pecuniary results have not turned out to be somewhat approaching the statement set forth in Purchasers (Swans) letter of 20th Nov. 1895, and also that Purchasers have failed to deal with our output of Rough Slag – we therefore claim the right to cancel the agreement forthwith, and to be paid damages for non-performance.

Clause 22. How does this affect the matter of absolute non-performance? – the facts being we produced 2,942 Tons of Rough Slag, and Purchasers only ground up 719 Tons.

Profits & Balance Sheet. According to Purchasers letter of Nov. 20/95, Profits should have been at least 10/- a Ton – Balance Sheet only shows 6d. a Ton.

Machinery. Purchasers stated in theirs of Feb. 2/97 to Barlow & James they knew every requirement & indeed had machinery at work at their other works so there can be no valid excuse for their non-performance of agreement, by saying their machinery here proved inefficient & even if it did, it is no valid excuse for our suffering loss.

Capital. From the Balance Sheet, it would appear to us, Purchasers from the beginning have been short of Capital, hence the "cheese paring" policy & inefficient machinery, which failed to deal with our Rough Slag. We are convinced if Purchasers had bought proper machinery, they could have ground up to 200 Tons weekly and a profit of 10/- a Ton, would have been realized.

Our stock of Rough Slag is increasing 80 to 100 Tons weekly, and as the Grinding Season only extends over about July to March, we fail to see how Messrs. Swan are going to deal with our output.

We understand at the present moment, they are altering, adding to and replacing machinery at the Phosphate Works, and at the same time writing deliberately to us that the machinery was all sufficient!! The agreement stated Grinding was to begin in August 1896, and they did not start until November, when Season mostly over.

Arthur Gilbertson to W. D. Rees. **17 June 1897 [1 : 515]**

Yours of yesterday with copy to Mannesmann Co., for which we are obliged – we know our Basic is superior to any Siemens Steel made in South Wales, and it requires scientific watching during melting &c. We have to contend with our competitors (W.B. & Co.) on an unequal footing at Landore: we believe they roll the Ingots for the Mannesmann – ours included! We believe we can sustain regular quality.

Our Mr. F. W. Gilbertson is on the Continent for a month & we regret we cannot reply as to analysis, until his return.

If you could get a trial in the Midlands, we shall of course allow you 1%.

We think for Midlands, it would be better to call it "Special Steel" – not Basic.

J. P. Davies, Accountant, to The Editor, *Western Mail*. **31 July 1897 [1 : 545-6]**

Tin Plate Trade

Your London correspondent under yesterday's date refers to Mr. Burrell Prior's utterances. There is a certain amount of truth in what he says, but I almost hope, reading between the lines, that Mr. Prior as a cutting merchant is "cornered" at last, and I sincerely hope he is! No one knows better than him how to get his pound of flesh out of the manufacturer – if the workmen conceded a reduction in wages equal to 3d. a box, it would at once go into the pocket of Mr. Prior & his friends. It would be quite insufficient to meet the protective tariffs of European & American Nations & would not increase the volume of orders one jot. I am inclined to say, let the workmen stick to their guns, and hope some of the cutting merchants will be caught this time.

Yours &c,
Tinplater

Arthur Gilbertson to J. H. R. Ritson, Managing Director, Aberdulais Tinplate Works. **7 Oct. 1897 [2 : 307-8]**

Thank you for your letter & financial statement, practically £1,448..12..1 overdrawn.

I note the loss £876..14..4 ending June 12th last, and I fear the quarter ending 2nd. inst., wont be much better.

Under these circumstances some definite steps must be taken, or we shall eat up our capital, in manufacturing at a loss.

My Doctor & those at Buxton, say I must get rid of some head work & I find Pontardawe, Glynbeudy & Glantawe enough, or too much for me! and I cannot undertake to tackle anything at Aberdulais. I consulted my Brother at Buxton (as I feared the results you now give) and he agreed with me, it would be better for my Sisters, if the Gilbertsons offered their interests in Aberdulais (1/3rd of the whole I think) for sale.

Would you, as so closely interested in Dulais, be inclined to make us an offer? I should not like to offer the shares publicly. The alternative is to shut up the Works, dispose of the stocks & liquidate voluntarily, it is fortunate the Leases come to an end in Decbr/98 & March/99. I think we should give notice on 1st Monday in November to terminate all contracts, Clerks, overmen &c, &c.

I do not know if Mr. Rowland is in a state of mind to be consulted? I am very sorry indeed to come to this decision, but it seems to me, from various reasons, Aberdulais is too antiquated all thro', to sustain the battle.

The brother referred to was Francis Bramah Gilbertson. In his father's will he had been bequeathed 5 shares in Joshua Williams & Co. Ltd., the original owners of Aberdulais Tinplate Works, with the remaining 23 shares being divided among William's other surviving children. Each share had a nominal value of £400 in 1881.

Arthur Gilbertson to J. H. R. Ritson. **9 Oct. 1897 [2 : 309]**

Thank you for your letter of yesterday, by which I understand you are prepared to make an offer for the Gilbertson shares: please say if this is so, and what your idea is?

Will you please send me the last Balance Sheet for the 3 mos. ending June 12th., which I will return to you & will you kindly hurry David on with last 3 mos. a/cs – at Glynbeudy we will get our Balance Sheet out in 10 days!

I know you will understand how sorry I shall be to sever my connection with Dulais – if I were your age, I should buckle to, put a new Cold Roll Engine &c. and with the recent outlay the Works should compete with any, but I am too much occupied & have too many cares to add to them!

I observe you dont answer my letter of 7th inst. fully.

Arthur Gilbertson to J. H. R. Ritson. **18 Oct. 1897 [2 : 313-4]**

Thanks for your letters of 16th & trial balance sheet up to 2nd. inst.

I am glad to see the great loss is stopped. I dont take a hopeless view of trade. I think we are passing thro' the worst time now, and that Tinplates will increase in consumption as time goes on. Aberdulais ought to do as well as any Works a few miles from the Port, and if a general reduction in all Salaries were made for the time of bad trade, you ought to pull on without further loss. The men should be told at once the 15% reduction must date from Llanelly date (1st Novbr.) or that a notice to shut up the Works & terminate all Salaries &c. will be posted first week in November.

Kindly reply definitely if you agree to this? and what the men say. Will you also kindly send me a list of all Salaries & allowances including Managers, Directors, Clerks, Agents &c.

Value of Shares. The £400 were reduced to £225, and I will take upon myself to say that the Gilbertsons would accept £200 for each of their shares.

Mind please, I consider, Dulais ought to be made to pay 5% to 7½% per annum, but I know the extreme difficulty of cutting down expenses in old Works.

I have written to Mr. Rowland telling him I think some steps must be taken.

If we could only stop the loss & reduce expenses, I would stick to & help you all I can – you & I, are too old friends to part easily.

Arthur Gilbertson to J. H. R. Ritson. **20 Oct. 1897 [2 : 315-6]**

Thank you for yours of yesterday with Salaries list.

Men. I am thankful have come to their senses & you may, with economies, manage to get on again.

Output. As you know, help profits greatly, I think it would be well to let your Clerks, Foremen & men know, that I had proposed closing up the Works, but that you & Mr. Rowland had induced me to try on, again.

Salaries. I think we should all take a reduction on a very liberal scale, until things pay again. If Mr. Rowland & I, take 50% less (viz. £50 a year each) I daresay you will also help. I conclude your Salary &c. is equal to £700 a year at least. Then Thos. David, E. Evans, one Pay Clerk & a Boy, should do the work easily. You could then get rid of Hopkins & D. Thomas. David & Evans, should be reduced to £150 & £120 without Houses & Coal, but with half yearly Bonuses according to results. Mill Foreman £130 a year & Tinhouse Foreman £120 & bonus. Then the 12½% & 15% will apply to all the others in your employ.

I am basing all the above upon the new Works you must compete with, which are better placed & lower rentals.

Disagreeable & sad as this is, it must be faced.

Tinhouse Pots at work should be reduced to smallest number, and 8 hour full make got out of them.

Tin Mills on 6 hour shifts & fullest make.
Tin yield form & Mill form, enclosed, will you kindly fill up & return to me, for last week? I believe David spends time, on elaborate "forms" which are quite antiquated & not needful.

I know you will understand the object of my remarks, which are simply to help, as I have experience of modern, small, Works.

Kindly let me see last Mills yields? I expect David runs up a big bill for "Books", Stationery, forms, &c.

Arthur Gilbertson to F. Edwards, Glamorganshire Bank. **30 Dec. 1897 [2 : 323-4]**

Private

You will remember my call upon you, as to Aberdulais & conclude you keep your eye upon it.

Mr. Rowland is unfit for business – I only go (or my Son) to sign checks. Mr. Ritson is responsible for the whole business, and is interested in going on & drawing his large salary, as long as he can. I notice he holds his salary checks instead of cashing them & increasing the debit balance.

Had you not better see him? but I must ask you absolutely to keep my name out of the matter, as if anything arose upon that, I should simply resign my Directorate & that of my Son.

With best wishes for the New Year.

You might suggest to Mr. Ritson, that he & I, should see you, as you cannot allow the overdraft to increase.

Arthur Gilbertson to S. B. Barlow. **21 Jan. 1898 [2 : 332-4]**

You remember Aberdulais Tinplate Works, for which Roberts & Barlow carried out reduction of Capital? It is an old-fashioned Works, badly situated & badly managed, it has never made decent profits and during 1897 made heavy losses. The Managing Director & Secy. draws a large Salary & wants to go on doing so until all is drained out of the Works & then when it is brought to grief, I expect he and his friends would buy it for a song.

He holds ⅓rd, the Gilbertson's another ⅓rd. Mr. Rowland is incapacitated by age & health, the remaining third.

I enclose copies of my letters to Mr. Ritson, the Managing Director & Secy – after putting me off for a week, he gives notice of our monthly Board at Mr. Rowland's private house – Rowland being so ill, that Ritson hopes I cannot broach matters before him. I enclose Articles. Am I right in thinking meeting must be held at Registered Office?

Wire me as to this tomorrow. Then can I take steps to procure a Winding up order, and prevent Works going on exhausting the Capital?

Arthur Gilbertson to J. H. Rowland. 24 Jan. 1898 [2 : 335]

I conclude Mr. Ritson has been to you & I am therefore compelled to trouble you. I wish you would leave matters in my hands?

Aberdulais must be stopped at once – it is our duty to our shareholders.

Mr. Ritson has somehow lost nearly £3,000 in 1897. Glantawe has made over £300 profit, Glynbeudy £1,440 profit, and W. Gilbertson & Co. have done very well indeed. I have reason to complain at Mr. Ritson's want of straightforward and complete answers to my letters. I do not wish to come over tomorrow and cause you worry & excitement, but I advise you to pass this resolution.

"That the Secretary give notice to all Employés of Messrs. Jos. Williams & Co. Ltd. from the Manager downwards to terminate all engagements in one month from February 7th., and also notice to our Tenants" and "that no further contracts be entered into."

If this is done, we shall have time to see what further steps can be taken, but I cannot be a party to further eating up the Shareholders' money in hopeless trading.

Should this course not be adopted, I must take such steps as my London Lawyer advises to stop further eating up of the remaining capital.

Arthur Gilbertson to J. H. R. Ritson. 25 Jan. 1898 [2 : 338]

I am sorry you have acted as you have done with poor old Mr. Rowland.

My suggestion as to leaving Dulais House, was because you said you could not keep it up with less salary & perquisites. You know you are losing £200 a month & you have made no suggestion at all as to what you propose doing.

I am always accustomed to write plainly what I think & mean, and it would have been better had you been equally frank.

Arthur Gilbertson to J. H. R. Ritson. 26 Jan. 1898 [2 : 340-1]

. . . The nominal value of our Shares is £225 each and you ask me to sacrifice £75 per share. I do not care so much for this myself personally but if I go out, my Brother & Sisters must sell also. I know they would not remain Shareholders if I left the concern, and having the capital intact is of importance to my Sister, Mrs. Richardson.

I am prepared (to give you a free hand) to accept your offer of £150 per share for my shares, and my Son Cecil accepts also, but with the proviso that you take also at not less than £150 the remaining shares of the Gilbertson family & Mrs. Richardson, in the latter case if you felt you could give £175 per share I should be glad. If you would send me a letter tomorrow, addressed to me at Bournemouth Villa, Langland Bay, nr. Swansea, I think I could bring the matter to an issue with my family, as I know they would all take my advice.

Arthur Gilbertson to Theodore Gibbins, Melyn Tin Plate & Blackplate Works, Neath. **8 Feb. 1898 [2 : 345]**

I leave my offer open to buy your share for £250 in Glantawe Works for acceptance in a week. I hope you wont sell, and shall be glad to see your annual visit repeated!

Arthur Gilbertson to John Player, Player's Tin Plate Works, Clydach. **10 Feb. 1898 [2 : 347-8]**

I have your letter of yesterday, and note you are preparing transfers of the shares. I dont see what you have to grumble at.

You & Ritson should not have left me in the lurch at our Annual Meeting. ⅔rds. of the Company were represented by proxies.

What we did was strictly in accord with our Articles. Had you attended I should have proposed your re-election, but you had written to offer your Shares for sale before you knew you were not re-elected!!

You evidently had some "arrière pensée" and what I cant guess.

Ritson went out to please himself, as he had bought my Aberdulais shares & yet you grumble at my turning him out!

You have known me since the days of "Bowly & Player", and I think I have cause for disappointment at your recent action.

If you care to come up any day I should be glad to see you & explain why I have gone out of Dulais and anything else you dont see through.

Arthur Gilbertson to Messrs Abercarn Tinplate Co., Mon. **14 May 1898 [1 : 626]**

Your favour of yesterday. We have seen your blue plan and also interviewed our Foreman James. We think his account is satisfactory and with your triple (3 sheet machine) you are probably ahead of Players duplex machine in output. Up to this time "Players duplex" for IC Coke, is the best machine we knew.

We are inclined to try two of your triple machines, one here, and one at Glantawe (½ mile from here, James is foreman) and we would give £150 each, say £300, for the two (2) machines.

We should have to start & settle the labour question and if you get your Patents to work well here, it will be a good start for you.

Mr. Gilbertson leaves on Tuesday night for some weeks & if you accept by return of post he could confirm order, otherwise it may have to wait until July.

We mean your largest machines.

Arthur Gilbertson to Messrs Abercarn Tinplate Co. Ltd. **3 Aug. 1898 [1 : 660]**

As we understand it, we are the only persons in this Valley going to try your Pots and we shall have to fight labour. We understand Dd. Edwards' Pot is somewhat similar, but we have not approached them. We think under the circumstances, you ought to give us the option of up to one dozen of your Pots – in our various Works, at £100 each, including Royalty.

If we make a success of your Pot, you know others will adopt it, and we should then be no better off than now, and have all the outlay & bother.

We have already had to give notice to men at Glantawe Co . . .

Arthur Gilbertson to Messrs Abercarn Tinplate Co. Ltd. **12 Aug. 1898 [1 : 671]**

. . . You would see in Western Mail today that Llanelly people are only making use of you to get their Tinmen to work old Machines, at reduced wages! It is unfortunate your rolls at Glantawe dont take Tin well – no doubt you will get better rolls if we order more Pots?

We dont see we can pay you more than £100 per machine, plus £10 for gearing & reduction of £10 off £100 for quadruple 20 x 10 machine, if your answer to ours of yesterday is satisfactory.

Arthur Gilbertson to Messrs Abercarn Tinplate Co. Ltd. **16 Aug. 1898 [1 : 680]**

Kindly address your letters to the Firm, as Mr. Gilbertson Senr. is not always at business now.

We do not think you should place us in the same position as Mr. Maybery who, if the reports are correct, has tried to make a handle of your Machine to beat down wages on old Machines, instead of buying yours!

Unfortunately we cannot offer you an interview just now, and wired you "Regret cannot give appointment, are writing you".

We are prepared to give you an order for six Machines, if you will say by return how soon you can deliver them, and the very lowest price you will take – we shall understand £10 per set is to be added on to your price for gearing.

Please answer our query of yesterday as to yields & more Tin for better brands.

Arthur Gilbertson to Abercarn Tinplate Co. Ltd. **15 Sept. 1898 [1:711]**

Your letter of yesterday is very unsatisfactory. You have no right to break your promises to us & work "for others". We have given you a tremendous lift. One Pot was due last Monday & one tomorrow. We have pulled out Pots to make room trusting to your promises & we must look to you for damages if you dont deliver. We now beg to specify for 2 more Pots, making up the lot:

viz: one pot for 3 plates
of 21 x 15, or 2 " 31 x 21
rolls nicked for 21 x 15
one pot for 3 plates
41 x 15 or 2 plates 31 x 21
— rolls nicked for 41 x 15
These Pots are due in 7 to 8 weeks.

If you are backward in nicked rolls, shall we try to get them elsewhere? but dont put aside what we have specified.

Arthur Gilbertson to Messrs Barlow & Barlow, London. **7 Oct. 1898 [1 : 719-20]**

We enclose letters from Messrs. Swan, dated 13th & 30th ulto, a proposed agreement from Messrs. Swan, and our pencil notes on same.

We claim the "original agreement" has lapsed, in consequence of Swan not carrying out their pledges. They verbally admit this, by proposing the enclosed draft.

You will observe they are to pay us a higher price for Rough Slag & we cease to participate in the profits of the Slag Meal Works, only getting a Sliding Scale on prices realized for Slag Meal. We have seen enough to feel sure a large profit can be made in Slag Meal Works, but we have been juggled out of our fair share, by the manipulation of the accounts & bad management by Swan's "pupil" placed over the Works.

Unless Swan give us a better price after the period of 3 years from last March, we must get rid of them & buy their plant, or put up our own Slag Meal Works.

We think it may be needful for Mr. S. Barlow, kindly to run down here for a couple of days, when matter has been gone through, before a settlement.

Arthur Gilbertson to Messrs Abercarn Tinplate Co. Ltd. **12 Oct. 1898 [1 : 721]**

We have your letter of yesterday, but we must remind you you have contracted to deliver us certain pots in a certain time & we call upon you to do so. Your reputation is at stake & it is no answer to say, that having induced other Works to order your Pots upon the strength of our having done so (for the correspondence warrants this) that you must delay our deliveries. We must call upon you to deliver as agreed.

Arthur Gilbertson to Mr. D. Smith, Alltwen. **18 Oct. 1898 [1 : 730]**

Mr. Lloyd reminded me a few days ago, we had never had the Lease for the 27 perches land at end of our yard, on which Slag Works stands, altho we pay rent for it, in the £12..0..0 extra. I have therefore sent our Lease to Messrs. Barlow, our Lawyers, to see if it can be endorsed & I have sent them Mr. R. Lloyd's tracing & letter, about this bit of land.

They will communicate with Mr. Lloyd's Lawyer, Mr. Price at Neath, & will you please see to it being carried out.

Arthur Gilbertson to Messrs Abercarn Tinplate Co. Ltd. **5 Nov. 1898 [1 : 741]**

It is really too bad of you to put us off again.

Knowing your family for such a number of years and acting as we did in starting your Pots, we thought we could trust your word. We must insist on having Pots as promised. Our men at Glantawe are on strike. Could you supply a Contractor to work the Two Pots at 2d. a Box (and Boys under him ¾d.) less 10% towards Fireman's wages?

Arthur Gilbertson to Messrs Barlow & Barlow, London. **7 Nov. 1898 [1 : 742-3]**

Please write tomorrow as follows to The Abercarn Tinplate Co. Ltd. (a memo from whom we enclose) saying "Our Clients, Messrs W. Gilbertson & Co. Ltd., by their Managing Director, Mr. Arthur Gilbertson, have requested us to give you notice that in consequence of your repeatedly broken promises as to delivery of your Tinpots bought by them, they will claim damages from you at the rate of saving per Pot, as stated in your letters & circular to them, say £10 per week per Pot, for all periods in which you have made defaults in your promised date for delivery".

Our object is to frighten these people and kindly get the above posted tomorrow.

Arthur Gilbertson to Messrs Barlow & Barlow. **3 Dec. 1898 [1 : 757]**

Abercarn. Are we to understand you, that altho' we hold letters from these people promising to deliver Pots on certain dates (which delivery was of the essence of our purchase) that we cannot claim damages for non-delivery – we must say we dont agree with you. No formal legal contracts as you suggest are usual in our trade – letters are sufficient.

Swans agreement. Is there a clause for either party to terminate agreement at Six months notice? – suppose we ceased to produce Slag!

Arthur Gilbertson to D. Smith, Alltwen. **6 Dec. 1898 [2 : 374-5]**

I was so sorry not to be able to break off to see you this morning.

Mr. Frank at Corston & Mr. Colin away & as the Tinmen are striking & people repudiating contracts because of a falling market, I am pretty well worried.

We have found Mr. Russel Lloyd's figures & plan in pencil on our Big Works plan showing the 10 acres & some perches for which we pay the £120, and there is only to add, the few perches we looked at with Mr. Herbert Lloyd to make access to Sewage Works . . .

Arthur Gilbertson to Messrs Abercarn Tinplate Co. Ltd. **2 Jan. 1899 [1 : 786]**

After a careful trial and much damage to our brand, we have today had a further investigation & have decided we cannot work your Pots with feeder rolls – we must put up with the grievous loss on the 5 Pots at work in the three Works but we have instructed the Glynbeudy Works to return to you the Pot not yet erected, and as we have said we declined to take the two Pots not delivered.

For the sake of peace, if you agree to this, we will put up with the loss, but if not we shall claim damages from you in a Court of Law, and the matter of your Pots will become public property.

Copy of our wire – "Regret obliged to refuse Pot last delivered and am consigning it back to you from Glynbeudy"

Arthur Gilbertson to Colonel J. R. Wright, Phoenix Galvanizing & Corrugating Co. Ltd., Aberavon. **30 Jan. 1899 [2 : 380-1]**

Sometime ago you wrote to me about Glantawe Tin Works. I have before me the Balance Sheet, audited by Deloitte Dever & Griffiths, for the year ending Decbr. 24th last. We paid an interim dividend at rate of 4% per annum, but the balance of profits for the year only show £191 & we thought therefore it was better to carry this small amount forward & declare no further dividend.

I daresay you noticed that Trubshaw & Maybery say they have only made losses for the two last years.

I shall not be able to be present at the Annual Meeting on Monday, as I have been ill & Dr. Griffiths has told me I must take a change at Langland Bay & I hope to go on Wednesday.

Monday's meeting is in fact only formal, but if you would come up here & see me after my return home & discuss the situation & give me your opinion, I should be very glad to see you – also by that time we ought to see what the Spring trade is to be. I bought some people out this year, and gave them "par" value for their shares, and I think I gave too much!

The Gilbertsons hold nearly ⅔rds of the Shares. The Works is compact – on the line – only one Boiler & fitted with best Tinning Patents, but the foolish Workmen struck against the new Thomas Pots & made things worse the last Quarter.

Arthur Gilbertson to Messrs Barlow & Barlow. 24 Feb. 1900 [1 : 956-8]

Swan. Your favor of yesterday, returning analysis.

To keep you current we have to say Mr. Swan called yesterday & saw Mr. F. W. Gilbertson in the absence of the Writer. Mr. F.W.G. told him, he could only hear what Swan had to say & would report to Mr. G. Senr. Mr. Swan first said he wanted Mr. F.W.G. as County Councillor to get the C. C. prosecution withdrawn & Mr. F.W.G. of course said he could not interfere in any way. He then asked us not to load up for the Meal Works, a stock we had of Cold Slag, as he imagined the % age was low and Mr. F.W.G. said he would have it analysed, before loading up. Swan also referred to the fact, that the grinding season was nearly ended.

He then asked some small details as to supply of Trucks, tailings & small steel, quite trifles.

At last he said "Are you going to take up the Slag Works next year?" F.W.G. said it depended partly upon whether we could continue making Basic Steel! Swan had previously said why was there such a difficulty about maintaining the 10%? F.W.G. replied, it (Slag) was a bye product & could not entirely be controlled & that we had great difficulty in getting materials. Swan quite admitted this, & said Wigan & Carlton had had great difficulties. Swan then said possibly he might pick up some Basic Pig & F.W.G. asked him to offer us any.

Swan did not say that they would refuse any Slag under 10%, but when speaking of the County Councillor matter, he said, if this sort of thing (prosecutions) goes on "We shall have to shut up the Mill". He also said, whatever damages we have to pay (as fines in prosecutions) you are liable for – F.W.G. said "he could not discuss that".

Our impression is, that Mr. Swan was very much turned down by the sentence in ours of 17th inst, reminding him, he had only got the Slag Works for about another year. His profits have been very large indeed.

We enclose copy of ours of 22nd inst, which posts you up to date.

Frank Gilbertson to Messrs South Wales Phosphate Co. Ltd. 22 March 1900 [1 : 991]

We heard from your Middlesbrough office that Mr. E. W. Swan intends calling today.

You have no right whatever to retain any of the amount due to us for January deliveries, & we must decline to give Mr. Swan an interview until the balance is paid.

Moreover we intend stopping supplies at once unless you remit the balance, as you have distinctly infringed the Agreement.

Arthur Gilbertson to Herbert Eccles, Managing Director, Briton Ferry Steelworks, Neath. 2 Nov. 1900 [3 : 140-1]

The minutes of Octr. 31st have arrived in Mr. F. W. Gilbertson's absence in Scotland.

As regards Clause 3, whatever the quality of the American Steel may be, we think Steel Manufacturers are quite justified in declining to use Shearings from American Bars. These American Bars are the "surplus" of Carnegies & other Works in America, and are "dumped" upon Great Britain, at prices yielding a loss to the American Steel Maker, but he covers the loss by the high prices he charges American Consumers under the protection of the Tariff, and the American does not contribute 1d. to our Taxation!!

We almost think our working men and their Unions will bring some pressure before long, on this question, on their Parliamentary Representatives.

Meanwhile Steel Makers are justified in boycotting American Steel in every way & the Tinplate Makers who use this Steel.

No Bars should be sold without a contra contract for Shearings, in the proportion of 4 cwt. Shearings to a Ton of Bars.

The introduction of these American Bars by certain Tinplate Makers, has knocked down Tinplate prices hopelessly & done away with any possible advantage in the ridiculous stoppage movement.

Would all Steel Makers agree only to buy Shearings from their own Bars?

Arthur Gilbertson to Alexander Cross, MP, Cross Chemical Company, Falkirk. **5 Jan. 1901 [3 : 174-5]**

Your favor of 3rd inst. Will you kindly say the very best price you could give us for Slag from 8% to 11%. We can then say at once if we can treat with you.

Messrs. Swan want now to form a Limited Co., to take their Works. We dont want to be bothered about it – we would prefer selling our Slag in rough form, out & out, and giving a Lease to the Slag Meal Works.

All depends on what price you will give for various %ges of Slag, we find we must make some 8%.

Our Port Talbot Steel Works are going on rapidly now, and we shall make higher %ges there, we expect.

Best wishes to you for 1901.

Arthur Gilbertson to H. Lloyd, Plâs Cilybebyll. **27 April 1901 [3 : 267]**

We find ourselves cramped in the North corner (near the old Lime kiln) of our Steel Works: we want to get your permission to utilize about an acre of our Sports field, for stocking steel Ingots & putting down some rails. No permanent building will be put on it.

As you gave us the Sports field on special terms, we would be glad to pay an extra rental for this acre, at the rate of £15 per acre per annum.

If you can agree to this as an annual arrangement, we need not trouble the Lawyers about the Lease.

Arthur Gilbertson to Messrs Scrivener & Breffit, Agents. **5 Feb. 1902 [4 : 1]**

Mr Franklen says it may be useful for your Friends to know, that the rental of 21 acres would be £75 an acre if an agreement is come to, with our Steel Works, and that a site for Coke Ovens could be found, connected with the works by Miss Talbot's private railway so that no Railway Rate would be payable.

I am afraid our Steel Works drains would be no use to the Blast Fce Co. I have asked Mr. Franklen if the Landlord (Miss Talbot) would bear the expense of a small trial pit, on proposed site of Blast Fce.

Arthur Gilbertson to Messrs Scrivener & Breffit, Agents. **6 Feb. 1902 [4 : 3-5]**

Thank you for yours of yesterday, with copy of letter of 4th inst from Dupres, I believe.

Sites & Rental. I wrote you yesterday.

Mixer. Is needful for Blast Fce. Co., to maintain "equality", or else constant changes in price & constant analyses of different qualities would be needful. I therefore ask the B. F. Co. to provide the Mixer & maintain & work it. They must meet me in some respects!! I am going to propose to meet them in some other respects.

Basis price. Mr. Massenez does not quite appreciate our suggestion. We added 6/6d. to Basis, representing a Total of 50/9d. for Molten Metal, at which price we can now buy suitable Iron c.i.f. Port Talbot. This actually means an extra price of 1/9d per Ton, for extra quality. Perhaps Mr. Massenez should know that we (Gilbertsons) have been making Basic Steel at our Pontardawe Works for many years & we know all about the needful qualities of materials & have no difficulty in getting them – Canadians have also approached us lately, and are anxious to supply Port Talbot Steel Works, with very suitable Pig Iron – Gilbertsons quality is first class (we make now 600 Tons Basic Steel weekly), accepted by Admiralty & War Office – so there is no question about our getting proper material, the thing is to know how to work it.

Analysis. We quite agree with Mr. Massenez's remarks, we should never think of using such Iron as he describes.

Estimate. We understand applies to 2 Fces [Furnaces], capacity 300 Tons a day for each Fce?

Ore. We understood would be supplied to Blast Fce Co. at cost price! This was stated.

Capital. We understand is proposed as follows

£100,000 Prefce carrying £10,000 ordinary shares
50,000 Debs. carrying 5,000 " "
£150,000 £15,000
15,000 ←
£165,000 capital + £30,000 in ordinary shares
for Mr. Massenez, not to [be] paid for.
Total £195,000 with free shares.

"Preference" would get same profits as ordinary shares besides the position of preference.

Mr. Massenez pays for his Preference shares & takes as remuneration for his information &c. £30,000 worth in ordinary shares free.

This would give him preponderance in voting, and the Steel Co., undoubtedly, under such circumstances, have a right to have an agreement, which will give them substantial advantages, before they give up the option of the site, adjoining their Steel Works. I feel pretty certain Blast Furnaces will be erected by some one, or another.

Arthur Gilbertson to T. M. Franklen, Clerk to Glamorgan County Council. **13 Feb. 1902 [4 : 7-9]**

I got your letter of 11th inst. & enclosures.

We note Mr. Cheston's opinion & the way you suggest to get over the difficulty, seems quite feasible.

Supply of Ore. We only propose to put one Blast Fce. on Basic, the other Fce on Acid (Hematite ore).

Proposed agreement. We note all your suggestions, which are very useful. Frank is writing to Mr. Scrivener, and we shall see Massenez Jnr. when he returns from Germany.

As I am pressing greatly to start our Bertram Thiel Fces at Port Talbot end of April or beginning of May, we are making enquiries for material (Pig Iron). I am sorry to say the Canadian Coy, say they can't supply us at present. I am afraid they are supplying America! did you see enclosed cutting in "The Times"? So we are trying the Germans, but they have put up their Basic Pigs several shillings a Ton. We are negociating with them, and other supplies to which we look. I conclude, as soon as Frank & I, with Colin & Cecil (for we all consult together) think it best to secure Pig Iron for Port Talbot, we have your consent to do so? Finished Steel (Tinplate Bars &c) are rising also in price, and our Port Talbot Bars will help the Tinplate & Sheet trade, because we shall be able to supply the Tonnage which cannot be now got from Germany.

Colonel Estère (from Chestons &c) is here & showing us how to make Steel of high value from cheap material. His "receipt" is so simple, Frank & Colin say, if he had written it on paper & sent it to us, he need not have come personally – it is very much what we have been doing for several years, but there is something in the "prescription" which may help – we are making an Ingot for Woolwich to try. I have had a day in bed, with a chill, but hope to be downstairs tomorrow, much better today.

Excellent news from Mrs. Nicholl & Harrie at Algiers: they are going to start to Tunis – Harrie writing at an open window 7 pm, with scents of Mignionette & sweet flowers coming in. I missed music at night & has got a Pianolo – the Walkyries Ride is wonderful, I have sent for some Bach Fugues.

Arthur Gilbertson to T. M. Franklen. 19 Feb. 1902 [4 : 14]

I got yours of 15th & return the plan.

We would not like the Blast Fce. Co. to supply us molten metal from the 22 acre, or 100 acre sites – too far off – of course it could be done if the Blast Fce. liked to deliver the molten metal to our Works & put up a Mixer there, but we dont think it would work satisfactorily.

Colin came back from staying with Cecil at Aberavon, this morning, and reports everything is going on well & rapidly. Jardine sent me a report this week, thinking we should melt at end of April, but Cecil does not agree. Cecil went to the Foundry at Llanelly, which are keeping back our Furnaces, and he tied them down to dates, but accidents will happen in Foundries.

Altogether we are not getting on badly & if we start in May, it will be a record in building up such a place.

Arthur Gilbertson to T. M. Franklen. 4 April 1902 [4 : 18-20]

Thank you very much for your letter, and I will read it over with Cecil this afternoon, and he shall see Mr. Lipscomb [Resident Land Agent of the Margam Estate].

I would like your opinion on the following. We find it needful to give now quotations to Messrs. Scrivener & Breffit (our Agents) for Steel Tinplate Bars for delivery in June, July, August & September. If we waited until Works started, Buyers might be filled up, therefore we ought, if we sell, to buy some more Russian Pig Iron, if it can be got at a reasonable price, but if we got a certain amount of Stock, we might have to overdraw at Lloyds Bank which is usual in a business like ours, but we should be obliged to inform the Bank of the Debenture Bond, and I rather doubt then, what they would say. When we entered into that Bond, it was understood we were only bound down to expend £70,000 on the site – we shall have expended £110,000, dont you think that would be sufficient guarantee for the £90,000 & possibly now the Debenture Bond might be cancelled, as we have increased our Capital by £30,000 & relieved Miss Talbot of her £3000 shares. I am inclined to think the Debenture Bond will rather hamper us, unless Lloyds Bank have sufficient confidence to give us overdraft at times. It might be possible to stock Pig Iron on neutral ground, say on Docks, and hand the Documents to the Bank, if they advanced us 80% of the amount, until we used the Iron & could pay them in full.

My eldest Sister takes a £50 share & £500 of 6% Preference. I have told Cecil.

Arthur Gilbertson to T. M. Franklen. 10 April 1902 [4 : 21-3]

I received your letter of the 6th inst, but since Frank & our Steel Works Foreman went away, I have been very busy. The reasons why the calculation of Frank & myself, with our Expert advice, are "miscalculations" as Miss Talbot says, cannot naturally, be appreciated by her, but you know the trouble we have taken over the matter – the reasons are, a new process in Great Britain, Electrical & Hydraulic Power, much more than is known in practice in Wales, & indeed in England, except in a few places & the difficulty of the site, from water, it was impossible for us, or our Expert advice, to deal accurately with Cost.

I have done my best & so has Frank and in my case, almost with too much anxiety during the year. Frank & I are not Engineers, and therefore had to employ, as you know, a Constructor & get ideas from Experts – Sir C. Furness' man, said £70,000 for outlay, but Taylor & Farley said "£100,000 none too much".

My Steel Works here cost over £60,000 without floating capital, which gave me an idea for Port Talbot, but I did not sufficiently allow for the Site, Electrical & Hydraulic Power, suitable for Tram rails, girders &c, and for the increased cost of everything the last couple of years.

When we found out our "miscalculations" I provided more money than I intended at first, & now at considerable inconvenience to myself I am allowing my Foreman, who started with me, before Frank left Oxford, to go to Port Talbot, to insure success.

The loss of our Foreman falls upon myself & Colin, we are trying another man, but he must be coached constantly.

I think I may say no one in Wales could have supplied the experience the Gilbertsons bring to Port Talbot, in Basic process. I hope Miss Talbot's heavy stake in Docks & Rys, are already "appreciated" by nearly £50,000 since the Public have noticed the Steel Works. Would you kindly say something to her on these subjects, when you have an opportunity. I expect the Bank will allow a certain amount of overdraft.

Arthur Gilbertson to T. M. Franklen. **14 April 1902 [4 : 28-9]**

Thank you for your letter of 11th inst. I am sensitive about Miss Talbot's opinion and should be thankful if you would explain to her, the reasons for our mis-calculations. I completely concur in your letter of 11th inst., but may I refer to the fact that the £110,000 expended on Miss Talbot's property, makes her mortgage of much more value, than if we had only expended £60,000, of her £90,000, on the Site. I think, the only depreciation of her Security, is the interest of the Preference Shares, viz £1800 a year.

Report in Newspaper. I burnt my letter! Cecil had told our Employés, they should not give information, or allow persons to visit our Works – they said they had given no information at all, but evidently some one had visited the Works & probably got information from the Contractors.

Pig Iron. We have today sent a cheque for Russian Pig Iron to Lloyds Bank London, and we are negociating 4000 Tons for August – we got the Consul at Kerch [Ukrainian seaport] to employ a man to chip off some Iron from the Pigs – the chips arrived today at Pontardawe & our chemist is analysing it, this afternoon. I hope we may not have to accept your very kind offer of guarantee to the Bank – Commercial Banks would allow an overdraft of £10,000 at one time of the month, when our payments are made, and at the other end of the month when our Buyers cheques come in, we should be in credit. Frank is safe, with his men at Gladno – just arrived when I heard.

Arthur Gilbertson to T. M. Franklen. 16 April 1902 [4 : 30]

I think you would like to know, I have a letter from Frank this morning, saying he is quite satisfied with the "process" at Gladno, and that Owen Davies, is astonished, but says (like a Welshman) he can work it better than the Germans! This confirms the impressions Cecil took, when he visited Gladno with Mr. Darby, as to the process & output.

Lysaght is going to Port Talbot today, we could not refuse, but have told Cecil to be reticent – we want Lysaght as a Buyer, not a competitor in Basic process. Russian Iron still negociating – chips prove good.

Arthur Gilbertson to Charles Cheston. 16 April 1902 [4 : 32-3]

. . . The foundations did cost much more than we expected, and delayed our work. We hear from an Expert on Blast Fces that altho' the site will be expensive for erection, it can be overcome.

My eldest Son has gone to Kladno (near Prague in Austria) and taken my head Steel Foreman, whom I intend to allow to go to Port Talbot Steel Works, as he has had experience under us in Basic process for several years, and is a reliable man. We are teaching another man here, who was under our Foreman – and my Son reports today, they are very well pleased with the process at Kladno – the process we have adopted for Port Talbot Steel Wks.

My Son is to meet Mr. Massenez in Germany this week, and if possible to meet Massenez Senior – if that is accomplished, we ought to be able to bring things to a crisis, very soon. Meanwhile we have offers of suitable Ores, from several quarters, and are buying Russian Pig Iron, from Kerch, to start our Steel Works in May, the quality is very good & cheap, but of course we would like a Blast Fce adjoining our Steel Works.

Arthur Gilbertson to T. M. Franklen. 17 July 1902 [4 : 44-6]

We have had a worrying fortnight. Small things breaking down especially in the Electric Machinery, but the men now become more conversant with it – this applies to the Mill. We have now proved that all the Machinery foundations &c are excellent – the Cupolas seem to be right – we had some doubt about them, but the trouble now is, that the Bertram process does not give the output expected, but Owen Davies seems confident that what he saw at Gladno, was genuine work, but he only thinks we shall get an output of 870 Tons per week, when he & the men get accustomed to it.

I endorse statements made out by Cecil & myself, and when the Contractors are paid we shall not have enough floating capital for Stocks & contingencies.

Frank has made a second statement on an output of 2800 Tons per month, instead of 3200 Tons and I think we must ask our Mortgager & Debenture holder, to advance us another £15,000, it will make the property on her Estate a better security, than it is at the present moment – we must have the £15,000 to carry on, commercially, the Works. I shall put off the Contractors as long as I can, but there will be a limit.

Supposing, after a trial of Bertram process for another fortnight, we should adopt the process at Pontardawe, but we should require a third Furnace to be built by degrees, to increase output.

My present opinion is, that the Bertram process will be worth going on with – the quality of Steel Bars is excellent & Byass wants to buy more.

I am very sorry to trouble you – I have had similar experiences in business before, but with energy & application, I have overcome the difficulties.

Cecil is proving a staunch & capable man, and Colin is staying with him to help. I am constantly at the Telephone, and dealing personally with the difficult position.

Oddly enough, I am very well, and able to tackle everything more successfully than I expected.

You will see how "output" affects the position from
Frank's statement on 2800 Tons per month as against
Cecil's statement on 3200 " " "

If Owen is right abt. Bertram, I hope we may get the 3200 Tons.

Arthur Gilbertson to W. Jardine. 18 July 1902 [4 : 47-8]

I have your letter of yesterday. Ask your Father to look over everything as far as he can, giving advice, to Foremen, altho not interfering with them.

I want to compare the number of men at Port Talbot for the production of Steel, with ours at Pontardawe.

Get the Time book for yesterday, day turn of 12 hours, and put down for me, in a neat form, how many men at Cupolas, their rates of pay – Tonnage made – how much their wages come on Ton made, and say what they do. Do the same for all departments Boilers – Gas Producers – Teamers, Ladlemen, Locos, Furnace men, Reheating Fces, Mill – Rollers &c &c, Cranemen, Engineers, add them all up, and divide the money by output of Bars today (not yesterday's output) also put separately all Labourers discharging and loading up Bars, and material to Furnaces & Cupolas.

Do it neatly, you write too "scrawly". If you do this well, it will enable me to judge better the position.

I should be very sorry to get rid of many of our Employés, but it will be of course needful, if things dont improve.

You need not trouble to write to me about breakages, messes, Mr. Colin will do that.

Arthur Gilbertson to Owen Davies. **19 July 1902 [4 : 49]**

My Sons & myself have been talking about the "Cupolas" – we are very anxious to work the Bertram process, all next week, but we agree we should not give unreasonable wages to the unskilled men, practically labourers, on the Cupolas, possibly you & Mr. Rees may be able to arrange about it – I much hope the Cupolas may be worked.

Are these men in any "Union"? if in the Steel Union, that "Union" ought to help you. You know our specifications for Bars are mostly for **A** quality, from Bertram process, but if you cant work Cupola, you should only use German Pig for cold charges.

Arthur Gilbertson to T. M. Franklen. **21 July 1902 [4 : 51-3]**

I am glad to report that the output of the Mill is getting better, the men becoming more accustomed to the new appliances.

We hoped this morning to get the Bertram process going on well, but on Saturday some of the Cupola men refused to work unless we gave them unreasonable wages, we did our best, but Frank & Cecil have just telephoned me that the men wont work so the Cupolas are idle today, but we think the men will give in, after spoiling our work for the week. By degrees we shall find out the nasty men, and shall weed them out – Cecil personally prevented a serious accident to the ladle of molten metal one night last week & dismissed the careless man next morning, and got another. Cecil has been in the Works at night & in the early hours [. . .] about the strain upon him, but he is quite well & plucky – Colin spent last week with him & today Frank has gone over until Wednesday at any rate.

If the fools at the Cupolas can be arranged with, we shall soon see the output of Bertram process. Owen is quite sanguine & he is a cautious man. Contractors are pressing for payment for Machinery & as small things which were troubling, have been satisfactorily dealt with we must find the money to pay them.

We expected, by this time, to have converted more of our Pig Iron into Saleable Bars & Billets, but by the small troubles in the Mill &c, have prevented us realizing as much money, as we expected by this time. We had 2 Messes of Molten Steel in the Pit last week, running into the Pit, about 60 Tons of Molten Steel, but all will be melted up again, with [. . .] Cecil & Owen sacked the man, who we decided was careless & we have engaged another.

1 p.m. Monday. Just got a telephone – the Mill is going splendidly today – Cupola men are still obdurate.

By end of this week, I believe, we shall be able to send a good report.

Arthur Gilbertson to T. M. Franklen. **26 July 1902 [4 : 60-2]**

. . . I went to Port Talbot yesterday to meet Mr. Tonks (Taylor & Farley, Birmingham) to talk about Tramrails &c.

Things are going better, I am thankful to say, Bertram process going better, with experience, Cecil is working splendidly & shows now he has excellent pluck & backbone.

I have decided to get rid of the Jardines next week. They are of no use now.

We have got a Mechanic who was under my employ at Pontardawe for many years, he will support Cecil loyally, and I believe breakages will stop.

We have dismissed several men, and have got others, without a strike!

Mr. Laws (Deloitte & Co.) is at the Office, making Balce. sheet to end of June. Cecil showed him copy of financial statement sent to you, and as far as Mr. Laws was able to go with the figures, he thought it correct. The £15,000 would enable us to go on for Tramrails – Mr. Tonks says Tramrails are the most profitable things to make & I agree with him, and I am now getting all information possible about this business.

I find the private telephone the greatest advantage – Cecil & I, are able to talk continuously, constantly.

I believe next week we shall be able to say the Bertram process is a success – we expected everything to come right, too quickly & forgot the difficulty of starting a foreign process, and more up-to-date Electrical appliances, than any Works in Great Britain have got yet.

When we built Pontardawe Steel Works, the Constructor promised 400 Tons per week from 2 Fces, but I only got 220 Tons! I dismissed him – built further Fces gradually & now I get 1100 Tons, sometimes 1200 Tons, in a week. We must have output up to 1000 Tons a week at Port Talbot.

Arthur Gilbertson to T. M. Franklen. **1 Aug. 1902 [4 : 67-9]**

I wonder if you got two letters from me.

We have gone thro an anxious time, the Bertram Process more difficult to start than we anticipated, but this week is decidedly going better & we believe will soon be quite right – the Cupolas work well, the Mill going better, altho' a small alteration in screwing down gear is being done, the Mill & the Electric appliances are in advance of any other Works, and we must expect some small alterations, which are suggested from time to time, from experience in working. The price of Tinplate Bars has fallen, in consequence of German Bars coming to Wales again.

In June Byass paid £5..5..0, today he offers £4..17..6, with a rebate of 2/- for common Bars, so we must go on with Machinery for Tramrails, requiring an outlay of £6000 to £7000. Tramrails are most profitable & yesterday we had enquiries for 6000 Tons. I fear we should not be able to get the Machine up under 4 months, and to go on with this we must have a further £15,000, the stock of Rolls run into money.

Seeing that we have debentured to our Mortager £40,000, beyond the £90,000 on Mortgage, I think Miss Talbot would probably advance this £15,000, as her Debenture would cover it.

We have proved now the Machinery is splendid, and I feel confidence the Bertram process will come right.

Jardine has left our employ, and we have an old Mechanic who was trained at Pontardawe, who is attached to us & reliable, and more useful than Jardine, for daily work.

If you could arrange the £15,000, we would like to order the Tramrail Machinery at once.

P.S. The alternative might be an increase of the ordinary shares.

Arthur Gilbertson to T. M. Franklen. 5 Aug. 1902 [4 : 70-1]

Could you come to Port Talbot on Friday morning?

In consequence of the stoppage of Machinery and difficulties about the Bertram process we have been unable to convert our Pig Iron into Steel as soon as we expected & therefore as the Pig Iron has to be paid for, we are short of cash – we really want now a guarantee for the Bank for £15,000, until the end of December, reducing every month.

The above amount includes paying off all Contractors for Machinery &c. and interest on mortgage.

The Bertram process seems so uncertain, theoretically we have obtained the right results, but practically difficulties occur daily & prevents our output [. . .] results are not satisfactory this week, that we should give up the Bertram process for the present, until the Patentees can give us some help & we would go on with the process, as at Pontardawe, altho' the output would be small – if so, we ought to have a third Furnace, to increase output.

Mr. Laws is making a balance sheet up to end of June, but I fear it wont be ready under a fortnight.

I think the guarantee for the Bank for £15,000 ought to be provided at once – on the Pontardawe process, we ought to make a decent profit.

I enclose a revised statement – very difficult to be accurate – but I believe it is correct.

Arthur Gilbertson to T. M. Franklen. 6 Aug. 1902 [4 : 72-4]

I am sorry to bother you with another letter, before waiting for your reply to my letter of yesterday, but I want to tell you frankly what occurs daily, that you may consider the position.

I have your letter of yesterday, crossing mine sent to your Cardiff Office.

You will see we are in a fix about money in consequence of Pig Iron paid for & not used up.

We thought it best to buy it, because you kindly said you would arrange about an overdraft at the Bank.

The difficulty is, that every single thing is mortgaged & debentured, amounting nearly to £130,000 for the advance of £90,000, and the land built upon is the property of the Mortgager.

You see we can't pay our Creditors unless some guarantee is given to the Bank, & as the stocks are debentured to Miss Talbot and we [. . .] paid for, on the ground, it seems to me that she, as Debenture holder, might guarantee the £15,000 temporarily.

The question of how to raise further permanent capital to enable us to increase our output and go in for tramrails & girders, can then be gone into.

I feel as I have 12 children (6 girls & 2 boys not started in life) that I cannot risk more than the £19,000 I have paid up. I feel a reconstruction of the Company may be needful, and I must give up the position I have held as holding almost all of the ordinary shares.

To make a success, whether the Bertrand process goes on, or is given up for the present, we ought to make Tramrails, girders &c. for which our fine Machinery was intended for & is suitable, but this business entails stocks of Rolls, & stocks of girders & tramrails, so that the capital would have to be largely increased, this has only recently come to my knowledge, in consequence of the enquiries I have started the last few days in various directions about these businesses.

I have no personal knowledge of manufacture & business, about Tramrails & girders, and we ought to get some one on our Board who has practical experience in that business and I would resign my position and salary if needful, only becoming a Director to make room for an experienced man. At the telephone this morning, Owen Davies does not wish to give up the Bertrand process and one charge this week, has been more satisfactory in a detail, which had been causing trouble.

Frank goes to Port Talbot tomorrow to get "Costs" & "output" and to decide about the Bertrand process, to put before us on Friday.

Arthur Gilbertson to W. B. Laws, 19 Oakfield Street, Roath, Cardiff. **8 Aug. 1902 [4 : 75-6]**

Thank you <u>very much</u> for getting out the rough Balance Sheet, which was most useful today.

In the cost, you added 8/- per Ton to Ingots (£4..8..0). I imagine this 8/- is made up by £5000 a year repayment to Miss Talbot, interest on her mortgage & rent? Kindly say.

In consequence of the difficulties of the Bertrand Process & working new Machinery, a quantity of Iron Pig has been delivered to us, partly paid for, in cash & by bill at short date, in consequence we shall overdraw about £19,000 as you saw on our estimated statement but our stocks will be about £25,000. In which way might we approach our Bankers (Lloyds Ld) giving them a [. . .] overdraft?

Could you make out a statement for us? It would involve you going to Port Talbot next week to define the position.

The Bank have agreed to an ordinary overdraft up to £8000, without lien. The Pig Iron will be used up by degrees.

Pencilled addition: Could you possibly meet Mr. F. W. Gilbertson at Port Talbot on Monday? He has to go there. I am very anxious that you should advise us as to the financial position, & should feel obliged if you would make an effort to meet Mr. F.W.G. – it would not take much time – could you come by 11.24 Port Talbot?

Arthur Gilbertson to T. M. Franklen. 9 Aug. 1902 [4 : 77-8]

I have thought over the position most of last night. I think on consideration your legal knowledge will agree with me that it would not be fair for us as Directors to use the money of overdraft from the Bank in paying Contractors for Machinery to the extent of £12,000, which Plant would at once become the property of the Mortgager. I do beg you to get Miss Talbot to make a further advance of £15,000 on her mortgage for paying for the Plant. Could you kindly see Mr. Cheston on this point? I would then transfer my shares in my own name, and half of the shares I allotted to my eight younger children, to Miss Talbot, or Mr. Cheston, as I cannot provide more cash. Then if Miss Talbot allowed the Company to get a lien from the Bank in October & Novbr. until the abnormal stock of Pig Iron was converted into Steel, the Works could go on, with the Bertrand, or ordinary process, and in a few months, we might show results which would induce more capital for extensions. Unless this is done I see nothing but liquidation, we shall have immediate demands for payment for Plant, and if we hesitate, it will affect our credit.

I feel I cannot (anxious as I am to do my best) go on with financial worry, added to the Works & buying & selling. My Doctor says I shall break down if worry is not reduced, and I know you will allow my first duty is to my small children, with no Mother. I am terribly cut up with non-success of our efforts up to this time. I believe some Steel Works in Germany have cost twice what was intended.

Of course Port Talbot is a place for a Steel Works, and the Margam Estate will gain advantage in the end, because if the present Company collapses, the Works will be taken up by others.

From quotations today our Pig Iron at Port Talbot is 5/- per Ton, under present quotations.

Arthur Gilbertson to T. M. Franklen. 13 Aug. 1902 [4 : 80-1]

Lloyds Bank Ld. have virtually declined to make the advance on lien of stocks, the Manager says he is quite certain the Committee will not do it.

We are overdrawn about £6,000 now, and possibly the Bank wont honour the cheque for wages (£410) on Friday next, if not, what shall we do? You remember we bought Pig Iron (which with the inconvenient Debenture has got us into this trouble) because you told us not to miss a favourable chance of getting Pig Iron, and that if needful you would deposit documents with the Bank up to £10,000 (April 11th 1902) and as you are the Director representing Miss Talbot who is so

949th

[illegible]

My dear Franklen I have thought over the position most
of last night. I think on consideration your
legal knowledge will agree with me that it would
not be fair for us as Directors to use the money
of overdraft from the Bank in paying Contractors
for Machinery to the extent of £12,000, which Plant
would at once become the property of the Mortgagee
I do beg you to get Miss Talbot to make a
further advance of £15,000 on her mortgage for
paying for the Plant. - Could you kindly see Mr.
Chester on this point? I would then transfer
my shares in my own name, and half of
the shares I allotted to my eight younger
children, to Miss Talbot, or Mr Chester, as I
cannot provide more cash - Then if Miss Talbot
allowed the Company to get a lien from the Bank
[illegible] works until the abnormal stock of
Pig Iron was converted into Steel, the works
could go on, with the Bertrand, or ordinary
process, and in a few months, we might
show results which would induce more
capital for extensions - Unless this is done
I can see nothing but liquidation, we. ||

22

Letter from Arthur Gilbertson to T. M. Franklen, 1902

(West Glamorgan Archive Service)

much more interested, directly & indirectly, than any one else in the Company, we bought the Pig Iron – the Bank might stop the Works, any day, but I hardly like to ask you to deposit your documents now, because unless some way is found out of the present difficulty Liquidation is inevitable & in that case the Stocks, that would cover your guarantee would pass into the hands of the Debenture Holder. No doubt the Contractors not paid, would think this unfair, and probably go to a Court to test the matter.

I have carefully thought about the matter & now that the Company have spent £128,000 on the property, instead of £60,000 contemplated on the Mortgage and the Debenture mops up everything, I think Miss Talbot, without disinvesting, might safely give a guarantee up to £30,000 to the Bank, to prevent the venture being wrecked, before properly tried.

If this is not done, what are we to do? Contractor will require to be paid at end of this month, about £12,000, and we have no money for wages or material.

If the wages are not paid, the Works must stop this week, and in that case I should be obliged to send in my resignation, with great sorrow. The loss of our £19,000 would be a heavy one for my large family, but it would be my forfeit, for going into a concern with a new process, without sufficient spare capital. I again say if we could tide over this matter, the Works ought ultimately to be a success.
Pencilled addition: Not Sent.

Arthur Gilbertson to S. B. Barlow. **18 Aug. 1902 [4 : 83, 88-9]**

Frank will write to you from Port Talbot, sending a letter from Mr Franklen & rough draft, which Mr. Franklen thinks Miss Talbot could sign. I conclude this draft practically includes Stocks & Book debts due to the company, as being assigned to the "guaranteeing" Directors? but why is it only for £20,000? I think Frank showed you his "estimated statement of overdraft" and at one period for a short time £33,000 would be overdraft, but reduced quickly by money coming in for Steel sold.

We have spent all our money (capital) on the Works, and have no capital to trade with. If the Company came to a crash at once, we should owe contractors about £12,000, and for Coal, Pig Iron, wages &c., and Bank about £7,000 – and nothing could be paid at all, as Miss Talbot has Debenture & Mortgage.

Would any liability for such a sad position devolve on the Directors? Unfortunately, four are Gilbertsons & the fifth, Mr. Franklen. The form from Lloyds Bk. to Directors to sign has come to Frank today & he will sent it on to you. I understand Mr. Franklen says "joint & several" so that if the overdraft was £33,000 it would mean £26,000 for the four Gilbertsons. Mr. Franklen, you will see, suggests waiver of Stocks to only £20,000.

I dont know what "repayment" means, at the end of the five or six months, we hope to have used up the stocks, to pay contractors &c. Does Mr. Franklen's "waiver" make the Guarantor Directors safe against the Mortgage? It wd. be awkward if Mortgager foreclosed, after Directors gave guarantee to the Bank. We have not paid any of the

£90,000 yet but possibly the endorsement allowing preferential Shares, would protect us?

I am wiring to you to ask if you would kindly come down on Wednesday for the night at Glanrhyd, and possibly you might think it advisable for Frank to go back with you & you might see Mr. Cheston, he is a shareholder and from what Franklen has dropped, I think Cheston would advise Miss Talbot to help us more than Franklen would. Cheston is a large shareholder in the Port Talbot Docks, and [would not?] like the Steel Works stopped, as already the Dock shares have gone up, with the starting of the Steel Works.

To get out of this financial worry, if Cheston & Miss Talbot would undertake to pay creditors, and carry on the Works, I would sacrifice my 60 ordinary shares, and half the shares I allotted to my eight youngest children, to them absolutely. Do the Book debts, viz. amounts due to the Company, for steel sold, belong to the Debenture holder?

Arthur Gilbertson to T. M. Franklen. **18 Aug. 1902 [4 : 90]**

Thank you for your letter of 16th inst with rough draft of Waiver.

I notice the amount is fixed at £20,000. I fear that would not cover us when all Pig Iron is paid for, for a short time in October, how could we meet that?

Could not the Waiver of Debenture on Stocks & Book debts due to us, be without limit? Miss Talbot would still have the £28,000 spent on the Works, beyond her loan, as additional security.

The Bertram process worked better last week & everyone became more experienced in it, but some alterations, not serious, suggest themselves to our men by experience of the week, and now, almost too late, the Patentee is going to send a man to help us, but as we have no time or money to make further experiments at present, we have decided to go on the ordinary Basic process this week in which we have experience ourselves – a report from Sheffield today, says the quality of our Steel Billets is excellent.

Arthur Gilbertson to Owen Roberts. **19 Aug. 1902 [4 : 91]**

By this time, you know all the Machinery – the Engine is too strong for Tin Bars, and should be kept down in power as much as possible.

The breakage of Rolls were no doubt because the Rollermen thought the Engine would take anything thro', but they forgot the Rolls were not so strong.

Now that the output of Steel is only 600 Tons a week, you must get rid of Blacksmiths, Fitters &c, or the Works will make too much loss & will have to be shut up.

I know you will do your best to help Mr. Cecil – economize as far as you can, in Stores, Oil, Tallow &c – mind the Babcock Boilers are blown out regularly, to prevent sediment & corrosion – please make a report for me as to any economies you could suggest.

Arthur Gilbertson to T. M. Franklen. **20 Aug. 1902 [4 : 93-4]**

In my letter replying to yours of the 16th, I pointed out that I did not think £20,000 would meet our requirements. I am most anxious that you & Miss Talbot should quite appreciate the position, and I think the enclosed approximate estimate will explain this, in the best way possible. From this you will see that we anticipate that about the middle of October we may want our Bankers to give us facilities for dealing with from say £26,000 to £28,000 for about a fortnight.

Our Bankers as you know require a joint & several guarantee of the Directors. I and my three Sons are willing to sign such a guarantee, if our joint liability as between ourselves, and the other signatories to the guarantee, can be limited to one half, say £15,000, assuming that the overdraft is not to exceed £30,000, not continue beyond say six months from 1st Septr.

I think I can fairly ask that Miss Talbot and those interested in this undertaking with her should join with us in like basis. If that were agreed to the position would then be that while the actual signatories would all be jointly & severally liable to the Bank for the whole, as between ourselves, the Gilbertson family would be liable for one half, and Miss Talbot and her friends for the other half. I think also this arrangement would avoid any necessity for any formal "waiver" by Miss Talbot. You probably may wish to see Mr. Cheston on the matter – if so, please see him as quickly as possible, for of course we must not incur any further liabilities to trade creditors until we see our way to pay them, so that the end must come one way or another within ten days.

Arthur Gilbertson to T. M. Franklen. **23 Aug. 1902 [4 : 95]**

Cecil tells me that you think the basis of half & half, expressed in my letter of 20th inst., is fair, but Miss Talbot's name must not be brought in.

I would like to explain that our idea was, not that Miss Talbot should join with the Directors in guarantee to the Bank, but that our agreement should be entered into privately between ourselves, Miss Talbot joining with you as to the one half. I thought if she became a party with you between ourselves, there would be no necessity for "Waiver". Will you get letters at St. Hilary on Tuesday morning & shall you see Mr. Cheston on Tuesday afternoon or on Wednesday? Time is so very short.

The quality of our Billets seem excellent & it should help us considerably.

Arthur Gilbertson to S. B. Barlow. **23 Aug. 1902 [4 : 96]**

For your information I enclose the copy letter written by your advice on 20th inst. to Mr. Franklen & copy financial statement. Franklen has not replied, but he saw Cecil at Margam yesterday & I enclose what Cecil remembers of the conversation.

I enclose copy of my letter of today to Mr. Franklen. If Miss Talbot does not become a signatory privately would Gilbertsons be safe, without a "Waiver" of Book

Debts & Stocks, and would it be necessary to have a document saying she would not foreclose the Mortgage during the period of guarantee – if it is absolutely needful (and Franklen is very touchy & we dont want to annoy him) would you draft what is needful at once? Time is so short! Frank thinks you said we should be safe as regards "foreclose" as long as we paid the interest, and no "Waiver" would be needed if Mr. Franklen himself or some other person with him (possibly Mr. Cheston) signed for their half.

Arthur Gilbertson to Messrs Barlow & Barlow. 27 Aug. 1902 [4 : 100-2]

Thank you for your letter of yesterday and notes of interview with Mr. Cheston.

I enclose letter of 26th inst. from Mr. Franklen & copy of my reply, which will answer most of your questions.

I believe if the Coy would issue ordinary shares for £30,000, and if they were taken up by the Mortgager (Miss Talbot) & Debenture holder, the Works would be ultimately a success, or if Miss Talbot, as Debenture holder, would guarantee to the Bank, up to £30,000.

The failure at present is, that the Bertrand Process does not supply what the Patentee said, but fortunately we put our Furnaces in such a position, that a 3rd. Furnace could be built again giving an output up to 1000 Tons a week, without Bertrand Process, but upon a process which we understand ourselves. I understand from you, that Cheston thinks the Bank would allow overdraft on guarantee of the Directors, and the Directors would make an agreement, between themselves, limiting the amount of ½ Gilbertsons & ½ Franklens – if this is so, I would agree to it, and please draft this, as if we sign the Form from the Bank next Wednesday, we should get Franklen's signature at same time, or should Cheston draw it up & submit to you?

As regards Mr Cheston's questions as to £900 a month profit, it would of course depend upon market prices. You see what I say to Franklen in copy of my letter.

I am not quite sure from Franklen's odd letter, enclosed (not replying to many of my points) that Franklen would not ask Miss Talbot to guarantee the overdraft, if he thought the Works would be ultimately successful & in that case no "waiver" would be needful, but possibly endorsement on the Mortgage. The name of Gilbertsons would be seriously affected, if the Works stopped now.

Barlow & Barlow. If it comes to the worst, propose Voluntary liquidation upon terms that all the property, business & assets be transferred to Miss Talbot, she at the same time taking over the liabilities of the Company to the Bank & Trade Creditors.

If this were agreed to, it would involve the loss of all our capital. We believe that with due expenditure the Works can be made successful & if it would be of any assistance to Miss Talbot, Cecil would undertake the management, looking for his remuneration chiefly to results.

The above was drafted by Mr. S. B. Barlow in need.

Arthur Gilbertson to Geo. Barlow. **29 Aug. 1902 [4 : 104-5]**

Thank you for your letter of yesterday with notes of interview with Mr. Cheston. I wired you this morning "We agree to memorandum please instruct Cheston to obtain and prepare necessary documents for Bank for signatures of Directors Gilbertson".

I think it is best for Cheston to get a form (printed) from the Bank and to make it ready for signatures. Will you get it from them tomorrow, look it over for us & send it to us – or Cheston might send it to us, after you have agreed it.

The "form" should state that the guarantee could be brought to an end on three months' notice. I conclude that as there are four Gilbertsons Directors, as against Mr. Franklen (who really is nominated to protect Miss Talbot), the Gilbertsons could carry, at any time, to give 3 months notice to the Bank? even if Franklen voted against it.

Endorsement Policy. We can say nothing until Mr. S. Barlow considers it, with yourself. Document postponing the £5,000 should certainly be executed by Miss Talbot – she is a very delicate woman, and aged – if she died, we should get very little consideration from her representatives!

Memorandum. We conclude 2, 3 & 4 are added by Cheston's as "Lawyers". We should like Cheston to know, that most cheques drawn have been signed by Mr. Franklen, he has been at almost every monthly Directors meeting, and every information has been given to him, in every point & we have given him statements about producing Steel, which we would not have given to any one else. Myself & Sons have suggested that we should receive only half of our very moderate remuneration, to help the Works.

Miss Talbot was aged 62 at this time.

Arthur Gilbertson to T. M. Franklen. **29 Aug. 1902 [4 : 106-7]**

I have your letter of yesterday. I think the guarantee will be entered into. I have received the "memo" from Mr. Barlow this morning.

My reason is, that Miss Talbot should help the Company, is that you invited me to build the Steel Works, I did not respond at once, but on a further letter from you I agreed, and Miss Talbot agreed also. Of course the whole business was to help the Docks and Margam Estate, Miss Talbot a shareholder and a signatory to the Articles, she was protected by Mr Cheston, and as a Solicitor accustomed to Companies & prospectus, he should have said, the issue of ordinary shares were too small, and he should have seen how the Debenture would cripple the Company, but I trusted him completely upon your advice. Now that Miss Talbot is not a shareholder (unfortunately for me, most of her shares have gone to Gilbertsons, to help the company) yourself & Mr Cheston, will not advise her to help the Company.

I have paid up £20,000 & become a guarantee up to £16,000 – I have eight children not started in the World – you imagine what anxiety is caused me.

Even if the selling price of Steel was today the same as two or three months ago, we could have made a good profit, without the Bertrand process.

I never pay attention to anonymous letters, hundreds come to Managers of Works. You may be quite sure that the "Union" wont allow any unfairness to the men! I may say, myself & my Sons, are willing to give up half of our ordinary shares to Miss Talbot if she would protect you in your half of the guarantee.

Arthur Gilbertson to T. M. Franklen. **19 Sept. 1902 [4 : 111]**

There is a report that Bolekun Vaughan & Co. are thinking of a Steel Works in Wales.

I think you know one of the Directors? Would you kindly put before him the Port Talbot Steel Works, layed out for Tramrails & Basic Steel, with powerful Engine & Mill, and Electric appliances intimating we are short of capital & would be glad to amalgamate.

Something of this must be done.

Arthur Gilbertson to C. Cheston. **22 Sept. 1902 [4 : 112-3]**

I have been hoping to hear from you since you saw Miss Talbot, but this morning I have a letter from Mr. Franklen thinking that Colonel Wright might possibly be inclined to join our Company. Will you kindly communicate with Col. Wright at once, about this.

I would like him to have a seat on the Board. To induce any one to come in, I think we must reconstruct the Company, and at the expense of the old Shareholders, must give up something for this object.

I would say the quality of the Steel is excellent, Mr. Byass' complaint was that the Bars did not come to proper weight (one of the reasons for getting rid of Robson) owing to carelessness in the Mill. Our Mill and Engine, are layed out for rolling Big Ingots, into Tramrails & sections, but as I have said, we want certain Mechanics, to finish the Tramrails.

I should be glad if you could communicate with Colonel Wright at once, and you, with your experience in Companies, would know, better than I, how to approach Col. Wright.

Arthur Gilbertson to C. Cheston. **29 Sept. 1902 [4 : 115]**

I hope Col. Wright saw you last week.

We have our monthly meeting at Port Talbot on Thursday. May I ask if it is likely that Col. Wright, or possibly "Baldwins Ltd" (in which Col. Wright is connected) would in any way join us? I hope you were able to tell Miss Talbot about my statement about the whole matter.

This was the last reference to the Steelworks in Letter-Book 4. In February 1903 it was reported that, "Work has been altogether suspended at the works of the Port

Talbot Iron and Steel Company, and about 250 men have been thrown out of employment. The company are not at present in a position to make any statement as to resumption of work" (The Iron and Coal Trades' Review, *6 February 1903, 379). By 20 June 1903 the company was in liquidation and the plant remained idle until Emily Talbot persuaded Col. Sir John R. Wright, chairman of Wright, Butler and Company of Cwmavon and a director of Baldwins Limited, to consider its reopening. The property was purchased in December 1905 and in August 1906 the Port Talbot Steel Company was registered with a capital of £100,000, and owned largely by Baldwins Limited and the Gloucester Carriage and Wagon Company Limited. The plant was immediately modified, the cupolas dismantled and the furnaces reconstructed for straight cold-charged acid and basic open hearth processes, and the first steel was made and rolled in January 1907. In 1915 Messrs. Baldwins Ltd acquired all the shares and increased the capital to £350,000.*

Frank Gilbertson to Ernest Trubshaw, Chairman, Welsh Plate and Sheet Manufacturers' Association. **28 Nov. 1902 [3 : 756]**

Replying to your circular of 25th inst. We have ceased to make Tinplates at these Works for some time.

Our Tinplates are made at the Glynbeudy Tin Works & yesterday the Directors agreed to fall in with the stop weeks arranged by your Association.

It is the only thing to be done, no doubt – & we may possibly have to stop some of our Sheet Mills here, at the end of the year, unless the demand for galvanized sheets improves.

Arthur Gilbertson to Walter Lawrence, Viceroy's Private Secretary, India Office, Whitehall. **29 Dec. 1902 [3 : 767-8]**

Thank you for your letter.

We have not yet heard from Jessop & Co. – could you give me their address? but I hope they are writing to us.

We are successful in producing "Electrical Steel" from which we make sheet and have just got an order from Montreal. No one makes this Steel in Wales, except ourselves.

Would it be useful in India? We are increasing our trade in Japan so much, that my Sons & myself are contemplating a further output, and probably put up a new Engine and two more big Mills.

I expect you are very busy!

Best wishes to you for the New Year.

At end of January we hope to pay Interim dividend, at rate of 20% per annum! Not bad, considering the times.

Frank Gilbertson to Messrs Jaeger Brothers, London. **5 May 1903 [3 : 829]**

Private

We have your wire & are returning the samples of decorated plates.

You have not yet put the particulars of cost & outlay, but, although we feel there should be a future for such plates, we do not think the business would work in with our manufactures here.

We think a separate Co. should be formed to work the decorated stamped plates, & some of our Firm might interest themselves in such a Company.

It might be well to approach the Tinplate Association, as they seem inclined to take up the stamped ceiling & wall plates.

We should like to hear further from you when you decide how to deal with the matter.

Frank Gilbertson to Messrs Jaeger Brothers. **22 May 1903 [3 : 835-6]**

Private

We are obliged by yours of yesterday, re Sinclair's Patent.

We suppose Mr. Sinclair would cease making the stampings at Coalbrookdale, and would hand over all his interest in the Patent to the Company?

How have you arrived at the consumption of the stamped Zinc sheets & where are they used? Can you give us the name of any Firm who use these stampings in London or elsewhere?

Of course the decorated steel sheets would be less permanent in a vicious atmosphere, such as a lavatory, or a ship's cabin, than pure Zinc, & would probably have to be sold much cheaper.

We feel no doubt as to the method of decorating being a good one, but we must consider all the difficulties that would have to be faced, at first, in getting a ready market for them.

We note that Mr. Sinclair's patent claims the production of iridescent colours on the copper deposit. Could not a very slight variation of the method used for depositing the base, evade the patent?

Frank Gilbertson to F. Gordon Miller,
Director of Contracts, Admiralty. **2 June 1903 [3 : 844-5]**

Mr Grant Burls was good enough to give me a private letter of introduction to you and I called on you on Monday the 24th ult.

I desired some information about the Steel you now use for Boiler Tubes. In your absence I was taken to see Mr. Minton, I believe, and explained the matter to him.

He promised to make enquiries and asked me to write a letter detailing my requirements.

The matter is this – My Firm Messrs W. Gilbertson & Co. Ltd. were at one time very successful in supplying Steel to the British Mannesmann Tube Co. Ltd., for Boiler Tubes for Admiralty work – very large quantities of Steel were supplied by us for this purpose in 1899 and 1900, but during the last two years the business has almost disappeared and the British Mannesmann Tube Co. give us to understand that the Admiralty express now a preference for Swedish Steel.

We therefore want to know:–

1. Do you really prefer Swedish Steel?
2. Is there any question about our Steel not standing the required tests?
3. Are you aware none of our steel is now being used for Boiler Tubes?
4. If there is any question of quality, would you investigate our quality again, as your Department did in 1899 when we first commenced the supply?

I hope you will be good enough to consider the question. It seems a pity to have to rely on Sweden and Germany for the raw Steel required for the purpose.

Cecil Gilbertson to John Grey, Brondeg, Glanamman. 3 July 1903 [3 : 860]

We are awaiting your reply to our letter of 2nd inst.

We note all the enquiries and orders sent to us by you, are addressed to the Raven Tinplate Co.

We understand from you that the Raven Company are stopping their finishing Departments entirely and cannot deal with these enquiries and that these sheets are only produced by your patent? which is your property. If this is correct please telephone or wire us tomorrow saying "Correct". We could then enter:

A. C. Leslie & Co's orders at the prices stated.

The 25 boxes of special polish for J. Williams & Co. @ £15..0..0 per ton but we dont make ordinary Canadas

and Messrs Samuel & Co's order

We understand you agree to what we said in our letter of the 2nd inst.

Arthur Gilbertson to Messrs Wm Menzies & Co., London. 20 July 1903 [3 : 873-4]

Thank you very much for your confidential letter of 16th inst.

We quoted you the lowest price we could take – we know some other Works are able to sell at a lower price, because they are able to make <u>heavy sheets</u> more cheaply than we can do, at present, but the position in two months will be altered, our New Mills, being built now, we hope will start in Septr, and they will be the most modern Mills in this District, and will enable us to reduce our price for heavy gauges; by that time I think you will get a reply from Australia, about the Mutual brand &c., and then we will try seriously to get into that market.

We make our <u>own Steel</u>, and it is of exceptional good quality. The Pagoda brand is made of Steel not made in their Works, and is often made of Sheets, bought, also, it is difficult to get uniform quality. In the lighter gauges we are able to compete with any one, but our Brands enable us to get a premium price.

Frank Gilbertson to John Grey. **7 Aug. 1903 [3 : 878]**

We are in receipt of yours of 5th inst., this morning. We are much surprised at what you write, as we understood that you arranged with our Mr. Philip Davies, as far back as July 2nd, that you should give us any information that would assist us in making the blue plates, in return for 1% on the orders booked by us, & 6d. a ton royalty on your oiling process, & on this basis you sent us various orders.

We think that whether the Raven Co. start their finishing departments, or not, the arrangement between us should stand; as the Raven Co. are not so interested in your bluing or oiling processes.

We have distributed samples & quoted various friends & wish to push the business & establish a good connection, which we are in a good position to do, with our Agents abroad.

Arthur Gilbertson to Messrs Wm. Menzies & Co., London. **12 Aug. 1903 [3 : 882-3]**

We thank you for your letter of 9th inst, which we treat as "private". We have considered the prices stated and have come to the conclusion that the competitors who quote such extraordinary low prices, are only going in for trade of the <u>lowest quality</u>, and their Brand cannot be known in Australia, they do not make their own steel & buy sheets to galvanize, so the quality must be irregular. We, ourselves, go in only for very best quality and you would be surprised the prices we get for our Brands "Comet Best" in Australia.

We must say at once & definitely, that we cannot compete with Sellers of cheap sheets, our prices would be as at foot.

Patent flattened Australian Sheets:

72" x 36" & 30" x 24" WG .... £14..5..0 per ton
72" x 36" & 30" x 26" WG .... £15..2..6 " "
72" x 36" & 30" x 28" WG .... £15.15.0 " "

in 10 cwt. felt-lined cases delivered London, 5/- per ton less delivered Bristol.

We are now entering orders at the above prices from other friends, but we would reduce say 5/- a ton to make a start, for a 50 ton lot.

Colin Gilbertson to Messrs Phillips & Hill, London. **17 Aug. 1903 [3 : 886-7]**

Some months ago we advised you that Messrs William Menzies & Co. had approached us with regard to pushing our Galvanized sheets in Australia which they told us they were in an exceptionally good position to undertake.

This proposal was that we should send out consignments under a joint brand with them, but after a good deal of correspondence, they say that the prices we quote them are quite hopeless, & they have sent us quotations from other well known Firms, 22/6 under us on 28 WG, 30/- under on 26WG & 42/6 under on 24WG. We gave them equal prices to what we are now obtaining from Messrs. Harries Scarfe, Briscoe & others.

We notice that we enter now, through you, about 50 to 60 tons a month on an average at very good prices, but with our new mills approaching completion, we would like to increase this considerably. We would be glad of your opinion as to whether we could effect this by meeting the competition of Neath, Baldwins & Lysaghts (we understand that the latter Firm quote quite as cheap a price as the former for "good Australian quality").

We would be glad if you would ascertain for us what Messrs Lysaght quote for their "Orb" brand in Patent flattened sheets.

Do you think our present business with Messrs Harries Scarfe & others is likely to increase?

Messrs. Menzies wish us to meet the competition & promise us a large volume of business if we do, & we would be glad of your opinion with regard to the advisability of our entering into any such connection with them.

42 x 36 JAPAN FLATS. We hear that Messrs. Franklin Saunders at Llanelly are working very heavily on these & are just putting down another Pot to work them entirely. It would appear that we are still above the competition on this order?

P.S. Messrs Menzies wished us to agree that when the business had assumed large proportions, we should protect them in price against other London merchants.

Arthur Gilbertson to Messrs Wm. Menzies & Co., London. **20 Aug. 1903 [3 : 890]**

Thank you for your letter of 15th inst. We have considered the matter seriously, and we are very sorry to say that we cannot entertain such prices, we only go in for best quality, and we expect a good price.

Arthur Gilbertson to the Editor of *The Western Mail.* **n.d. c. 9 Oct. 1903 [4 : 128-30]**

Dumped Steel – Some convincing Facts about Newport importation

In your issue of 31st ulto. you published an article about the above idea. Will you kindly allow me to reply?

"Dumping" Steel from America, Germany & Belgium

The word of "dumping" means that Foreign Countries, protected by high tariffs, are able to make a very large profit in their own Country, and the "surplus" is dumped on a Free Trade Country regardless of "cost" and "loss". This was predicted by Mr. Carnegie, in a letter to the Pall Mall Gazette some years ago, saying "Great Britain will know, before very long, what the 'Law of Surplus' means!"

Who uses it? (as your article says) the "dumped" Steel – well, people who have not expended their money in Steel Works, and very few Firms are able to use it, as the specifications for Tinplates are difficult and so various in weights. Of course, Messrs. Lysaght are glad to get the "dumped" Steel, and are enabled to undersell their competitors, who have Steel Works, and the increase, for Messrs. Lysaght, in profits is large, but can we say this is good for our Country. Certainly ¾ths. of the Trade are obliged to use Welsh Steel Bars – supposing this "dumped" Steel increases in quantity, the Competitors of Messrs. Lysaght must shut up their Steel Works – what would happen if War took place?
We buy what we want. Yes, but is it fair, and profitable for Great Britain, in consequence of a very few Firms, by using "dumped" Steel which does not pay ½d. to our Rates & Taxes and will ruin our South Wales Steel Works.
Effect upon the Workers – "Dumping" Steel will ruin the Workmen in Steel Works, Collieries, Foundries, &c &c, but if this foreign Steel paid a protective Tariff, at a reasonable rate, all Galvanizing Works & Tinplate Works would be on a fair basis.

Arthur Gilbertson to W. Griffiths, Slag Works Manager. **27 Oct. 1903 [3 : 916-7]**

We have gone over the position of the Slag works –
256 Tons Basic Meal, were only sent out in two weeks including Octr. 24th.
The output same period was only 110 Tons.
This is expensive – small output.
We have rough slag (WG &Co) – 4,000 Tons
Wigan slag ———————— 1,000 "
Basic Meal ———————— 1,800 "
and nearly 3,000 Tons will be due from Wigan contract.
You know the financial position.
We have come to the conclusion, that outlay in
labour &c., must be stopped at once. We fear this Season
will be a very bad one unless things get better in a few
weeks, we shall try to sell some of Wigan slag in export.
You said the overdraft would be reduced – instead, it is increasing.
You must get in money overdue.

Arthur Gilbertson to C. L. Tormin, Hamburg. **12 Nov. 1903 [3 : 920]**

We are not satisfied about payment from Messrs. Simon Evers & Co. They provided a cheque on Monday last – today we get a letter from them saying we shall be paid by The Union Discount Company of London for £2,170..8..5. They omit the big Invoice of Oct 23rd. £2,006..5..0, and we have sent them a telegram, they must pay at once.

We expect Mr. Tormin Senr., to attend to this at once.

Arthur Gilbertson to W. Griffiths. **18 Dec. 1903 [3 : 940]**

Let me know the overdraft in the Bank, and how you think it will be reduced every week?

The Slag Works eat up much money now!

Arthur Gilbertson to S. B. Barlow. **3 Jan. 1904 [3 : 947]**

We have found out the name of the man who was in our Works, our Foreman told him to go out at once, the man refused, and offered to give "a drink" to our Foreman, but our Foreman refused, and took him out. He gave wrong name & wrong address, but fortunately some of our men knew the man – he was certainly employed by the Raven Company, to find out our Works. We believe the man is an employé of the Raven Company. Can we not attach the man beyond "trespass"?
Name of man: Daniel Jones.

Frank Gilbertson to W. Griffiths. **11 Jan. 1904 [3 : 948]**

Seeing the overdraft at the Slag department is high & the stocks of meal high also, we have decided it will be better to stop grinding at the end of this month.

Arthur Gilbertson to W. Griffiths. **22 Jan. 1904 [3 : 955]**

Your letter of 20th inst. We must stop grinding at the end of this month. It is very disappointing.

We will give work for Seddon, and Davies, in our Works, but the rest, including the Clerk, must be paid off.

Let me know how much Tonnage was sold last Season, and roughly state how many Tons were sold to our Agents & big Buyers, stating Tonnage to each & say how much we have sold this Season, to the same people.

Arthur Gilbertson to W. Griffiths. **26 Jan. 1904 [3 : 960]**

We are sorry to give you notice to terminate your agreement with us at the end of three months.

Frank Gilbertson to Messrs R. & C. B. Jenkins. **2 Feb. 1904 [3 : 970]**

Referring to our request to you to issue a Summons for trespass against Daniel Jones of Glanamman.

We find a mistake was made & the man we want is David Jones – his address is not known, but he is a Fitter & Millwright at the Raven Works Glanamman so there should be no difficulty in finding him.

Will you have the Summons served as soon as possible please?

Can no offence beyond ordinary trespass be passed?

He was in the Works solely to learn the details of our process which the Raven Co. are about to adopt.

P. Davies to J. Griffiths, Neath. **28 March 1904 [3 : 991]**

Referring to our insurance No. 1653241. We have now pulled down the old Copperas house building No. 31, and have erected a new Copperas plant on another site which we wish to insure for £500. We have also erected a new boiler and boiler house which we wish to cover at £100.

The Mill house No. 12, 13 & 14 has also been extended and two mills & Engine have been erected therein – we wish to increase amount against Nos. 12, 13 & 14 to £350. We enclose policy for this alteration – perhaps you will send over to take fuller particulars.

Colin Gilbertson to Messrs John Summers & Co., Stalybridge. **31 March 1905 [5 : 104]**

We are obliged for your wire reading: "Neath wire they are in full agreement. Have no reply yet from Raven & Franklin".

On looking through the list of Firms present at the dinner, we notice that The Monmouthshire Steel & Tinplate Co. were not represented. They are fairly large Makers, we believe, & they have been cutting prices very much lately in the light gauges. We hope they will fall in.

What is the minimum price to be quoted for Canadian specification, say 96 x 30 x 28 WG. According to the list received from Mr. Wenham the price for this specification should be £13/2/6, in skeleton felt lined cases, allowing 12/6 for working up quality. This seems too low. We have been quoting £13/15/0 & obtained it a few days ago.

Arthur Gilbertson to Henry Summers, Stalybridge. **15 June 1905 [5 : 140]**

I am in receipt of your letter of yesterday & regret my present state of health does not admit of my attending the meeting. I have always been opposed to the Association as likely to increase competition in the future, but yielded to the wishes of my sons who desired to fall in with other Makers as far as possible.

I have instructed them that if other Makers decide to carry on the Combination, we will stay on if our percentage of output is not reduced.

P.S. We have reduced every week our reasonable output.

Typewritten and copy unsigned.

Colin Gilbertson to Messrs the Monmouthshire Galvanizing Co. **10 July 1905 [5 : 146]**

Galvanized Iron Association. We are sorry you have not seen your way to join the Association, & your decision affects us more than others, owing to our being engaged in the same class of business, we are writing to ask if you will not reconsider your position.

You will understand that it is not to our interest to remain in the Association, if there is one Firm making thin sheets, & able to underquote us, & if we fall out, other South Wales Makers will join us, & the result will be that thin gauges will be left out of the business altogether, & Associated Makers will be able to dump these at any price they like.

This will not be satisfactory to any of us, & we will be glad to hear if you will give the matter your favourable consideration.

The Galvanized Iron Trade Association was formed in 1883 to regulate competition and fix prices in the trade. It lasted until 1900 and was succeeded in 1905 by the National Galvanized Sheet Association which was formally terminated in 1910 and re-established in 1913 "on a broader and stronger basis" (Carr, A History of the British Steel Industry, *260).*

Frank Gilbertson to Sir Walter Lawrence, 22 Sloane Gardens, London. SW **17 July 1905 [5 : 150-1]**

I am enclosing a letter explaining a difficulty that you might perhaps be able to help us over.

We have quite recently started a business in high carbon steel billets, & have been most successful in producing a better quality than our competitors.

Messrs W. Griffiths & Sons took a sample charge of 15 tons & on the strength of the results secured a 300 ton order for Indian Railway Springs, we understand.

We are now asked to furnish references from Railway Companies who use our steel for springs. This we cannot do as we have only started the business & have not manufactured for 9 months yet.

Surely the tests being found satisfactory should enable Messrs Randal & Robertson to pass our steel.

Although this class of business is new our steel generally must be well known by some of the government departments. We have supplied thousands of tons for Navy boiler tubes & during the South African War we made a lot of high carbon steel for gas bottles for the balloon services.

We started this high carbon billet trade 9 months ago, sending samples to Sheffield where the steel is rolled into springs, &c, and we have now 5,000 tons on order. This shows how the quality has been liked by some 300 Sheffield firms who tried the samples & have given us regular orders.

Is it fair to ask you to put in a word at the India Office?

Cecil Gilbertson to Sir Walter Lawrence. 18 July 1905 [5 : 152]

Thank you very much for your telephone of today.

We are very much obliged to you for giving the matter such prompt attention, and are very glad to see that you have been able to get Sir Alex Randal [i.e. Rendel] to withdraw his objection to using our Steel.

Frank Gilbertson to Messrs Wenham Bros. & Co. 11 Sept. 1905 [5 : 171]

Galv. Iron Association

Following ours of Saturday, we beg to enclose return of Home & Export trade for 5 mos. ending Aug. 31/05. We conclude these are all the particulars you require. Your circular of 24th Aug. appears to have been mislaid with us.

	Home	**Export**	**Total**
Apl. 1905	27. 3.2.26	1,733.19.1.19	1,761. 3.0.17
May "	40. 2.2.12	1,976.12.1. 5	2,016.14.3.17
June "	53. 6.3.15	1,591. 8.1.27	1,644.15.1.14
July "	40. 7.0.25	1,369. 8.3.11	1,409.16.0. 8
Aug "	77.17.0.19	1,720.17.2. 8	1,798.14.2.27
	238.17.2.13	8,392. 6.2.14	8,631. 4.0.27

The figures are expressed in Tons, Hundredweights, Quarters & Pounds.

Frank Gilbertson to the Slag Department. 12 Oct. 1905 [5 : 188]

In order to assist you to obtain orders for Basic Meal & so to use up the high priced Wigan slag, we have decided to charge our rough slag to you at 2/6 a ton, this season.

This will enable you to reduce your price for meal & compete better with the high grades of Slag.

We hope you will make every effort to increase your sales at the reduced prices.

Frank Gilbertson to Henry Summers. 10 May 1906 [5 : 263-4]

We regret it will be impossible for us to attend the next meeting of the Association, which we regret particularly as the first year's results will come up for discussion. We may say we are entirely pleased with the working of the Association.

The state of affairs in the East, where we find our chief market, has prevented our getting quite our full share of orders, & probably this was accentuated by the Raven Co. starting on the same trade quite a short time before the Association was formed, but we are quite satisfied during most of the year, the Association alone allowed business to be carried on profitably.

We also wish to point out that in spite of our small output we have done what was expected of us, & have bought heavily from the three blacksheet makers here, whom it is to our interest to keep out of galvanizing, although it has entailed our stopping some of our Mills & working "black plate" in others.

We hope to be able to attend succeeding meetings of the Association.

P.S. We are still very short of orders & our output is miserable, but we are booking better for forward delivery.

Frank Gilbertson to S. R. Lysaght, Bristol. **22 May 1906 [5 : 269]**

Private

We thank you for your favour of yesterday suggesting a presentation to our Chairman. We entirely concur in the suggestion as it stands in your letter.

Extraordinary tact & ability have been required to bring the Association to a permanent success, & we feel personally indebted to Mr. Summers for his work.

Frank Gilbertson to Messrs Wenham Brothers & Co. **24 July 1906 [5 : 322]**

Our total output of tinplate bars for the 3 years ended June 30th 1906 has been 144,099 Tons – 3 cwts – 3 qrs.

This gives an average of 923¼ tons per week.

Since December 31st 1904 we have also been making billets, & our output of tinplate bars for the 18 months succeeding that date has been 71,955 Tons 10 cwts, giving an average of 922½ tons per week.

We consider we are entitled to an allotment based on these figures, as before we made billets we used to sell ingots & we claim on the actual total of tinplate bars made, only.

Frank Gilbertson to Henry Summers. **5 Feb. 1907 [5 : 438-9]**

Thank you for your letter of 31st ulto. I agree with you that, considering the rise of spelter since the Assn. started work, & the relatively large quantity of spelter that 30 gauge iron requires, the rise of price for this gauge has not meant a rise of profit equivalent to that on 24 gauge. And as you say, the output of 30 gauge is only half of 24 gauge.

At the same time we are opposed to increasing extras & we think our neighbours will be too.

The reasons principally are:

(1) Present prices being far more remunerative than Tinplate making, we fear any further advance tempting one or two Tinplate Makers who have made all inquiries needed for starting galvanizing but have not yet made the plunge.

(2) We also hear very definitely that the Japanese are going to make tinplates, & if they try to galvanize, or are tempted to try, a high price for their specification will tell against us.

Although competition in 24 gauge has been removed, in Staffordshire, the Tinplate Maker remains as a possible menace to our trade. So far we have been saved by the temporary improvement in Tinplates, but we dont know if it will last, & we must remember the Steel Makers in South Wales will have money to invest at the end of the year.

Frank Gilbertson to Henry Summers. 13 March 1907 [5 : 453]

. . . If it was possible to make any arrangement with the Americans, I quite agree that the time to do it will have passed when they become short of work at home.

I think you may count on our co-operation in any scheme that may occur to you.

Frank Gilbertson to Messrs. R. & C. B. Jenkins. 2 May 1907 [5 : 471-2]

We have a Patent Greasing Machine for use in Tin & Sheet Mills. The patent is in the names of Mr. David Jenkins & ourselves & is No. 10456/05.

We allow the Glynbeudy Tinplate Co. Ld, which concern we largely own, to use the machine.

In other directions we charge £10 per annum, per Mill, for its use.

Some 2 months ago Ernest Madge, Foreman at the Avondale Tinplate Co, Pontnewydd, Nr. Newport, was found in the Glynbeudy Works, at night, in company with two local men.

Our Manager demanded an apology in writing, but only 1 of the 2 local men replied. Our Manager, therefore, felt some suspicion as to the cause of their visit to the Works, especially as he heard they had spent some time by the patent Greaser.

He therefore got a man to go up from Newport & see what the Avondale Company was doing & the man says they have copied the greaser exactly & are using it in 2 or more Mills.

We wish therefore to proceed against the Avondale Co.

What steps are necessary? We presume they will have to give us an opportunity of viewing the machine if they contend it is not the same as we have protected?

Frank Gilbertson to Messrs Barlow, Barlow & Lyde. 11 Oct. 1907 [5 : 553-6]

In 1886 we made an agreement with the Midland Railway Co. Our copy of the Agreement has been lost for years, but in consequence of a dispute with the Co. a copy of one clause has been shown us by them & we enclose it.

This clause is certainly the chief purpose of the Agreement.

It is evident from this clause that a preference in the consigning of the traffic that then passed in & out of these Works was a sufficient consideration for the Railway Co. doing their part of the agreement, which we believe included the construction of a bridge as well as its maintenance & the repairs of the sidings upon it.

Since that time the Works has changed its character, a Steel Works, not then contemplated, has been built, & the amount of traffic enormously increased.

At certain times, owing to the increase of traffic, the Railway Co. does not give proper facilities for dealing with the discharge of our cargoes at Swansea & we then retaliate by consigning through traffic by GWR, which it is often convenient to do.

This always brings them to reason, but lately they have been so troublesome that we have persisted in this diversion of traffic to GWR & have stated our intention of continuing to do so unless they undertake in future to supply empty wagons for all our cargoes at Swansea, or themselves to pay the extra cost involved by the non-supply of wagons.

They now suggest that under our agreement of 1886 we are not at liberty to pursue this policy.

Our view is, that however much traffic we send by GWR we are still sending, & cannot avoid sending, by MR, a very much larger quantity than was contemplated in 1886, & formed a sufficient consideration for the Railway Co's part of the agreement & that therefore the Company could not use the agreement against us.

Could you advise us whether we are wrong in this view?

It is possible that within the next few years other railways will be constructed and connections with our Works made, & we think the time has come for our Agreement of 1886 to be brought to an end & a new one entered into.

We hardly think it wise to disclose that our copy of the Agreement is lost & its terms unknown to us, at present; but we presume that when we have settled our present difficulty you could apply for a copy of the Agreement, & see what clauses exist for terminating it?

Frank Gilbertson to Messrs Brewer & Co., Patent Agents. **28 Feb. 1908 [5 : 649]**

You will remember you registered our brand "Comet" in Japan.

Will you please make it your business to maintain this brand for us?

Some alteration in Japanese law might affect it without our knowledge, but the brand has become so important that we cannot risk any loss of our rights, & perhaps for a yearly fee you would perform this service

Frank Gilbertson to Messrs Phillips & Hill. **2 May 1908 [5 : 705-6]**

Private

We thank you for your favour of yesterday & regret that the writer should so nearly have placed you & your informant in a difficult position.

We sent your letter to Mr. Henry Summers for his personal information, explaining that if you were successful in obtaining leave to make use of the information, we would write him again.

He appears however to have made use of our information which was not discreet.

We felt that it was desirable to give him personally the earliest news of such a transaction, as he acts for the Association in negotiating with America. For your private information we may say that we have a hard & fast bargain with America, whereby we take steel bars against their undertaking to maintain prices. As a new bargain was in course of settlement we thought Summers should know at once that America was not keeping faith.

If you can get permission for us to report the sale officially to Mr. Summers so that he can communicate with Mr. Farrell, it may be the means of checking this undesirable development. We enclose you Mr. Summers's letter to us.

Frank Gilbertson to Henry Summers. 5 May 1908 [5 : 710-1]

We have obtained permission to give you certain figures given below, in connection with the sales by America to Japan of 6' x 3' x 56 sheets. Messrs. Mitsui wish their names to be kept entirely out of any use you may see fit to make of the information.

200	Tons	Booked	April 4th	@ 255	pence	per piece
200	"	"	"	252	"	" "
200	"	"	"	252	"	" "
100	"	"	April 2nd	255	"	" "
200	"	"	April 6th	253	"	" "
100	"	"	9th	253	"	" "
150	"	"	10th	253	"	" "

all C.I.F. & including 1% which the American House add to sellers' prices when advising Japan of their purchases.

The corresponding price of "Comet" today is, they say, 257d. per piece. We make the C & F only price to be 254d. per piece & then there is the 1% that the London or New York House adds to our price before advising Japan.

We should be glad if you would take every precaution to avoid Messrs. Mitsui's name getting out, & we suggest that in writing Mr. Farrell you only refer to the total quantity of 1,150 tons that have undoubtedly been sold to Japan at below agreed prices, & omit such details as would suggest that Mitsui's themselves had disclosed the business.

We understand that no question of commission by the U.S. Co. arises & that Mitsui have refused to act as Agents for some members in this country.

I was glad to get your letter of 30th ulto.

Frank Gilbertson to Messrs John Lysaght & Sons Ltd. 12 May 1908 [5 : 714]

Private

We are much obliged by your wire.

But we really cannot believe Mr. Farrell's assurances in this matter!

Our informants gave us details of 1,100 tons sold to their New York House, & they had no reason for misleading us, their object being to stop the underselling in New

York as they naturally prefer the business going through the London House. We had very exact details given us. However we are very glad to hear that the matter has been discussed by Mr. Lysaght & Mr. Farrell, & have no doubt that the result will be the exercise of a little more supervision in New York.

Frank Gilbertson to Messrs Phillips & Hill. 29 May 1908 [5 : 733]

We enclose copy of a letter that Mr. Summers has received from Mr. Lysaght. I shall be in London on Wednesday & shall discuss the matter with Mr. Summers then, but we should be glad if you would consider whether anything can be done to convict Mr. Farrell more conclusively.

Mr. Lysaght is always too ready to believe this very astute gentleman. Could you obtain the dates of shipment & watch the deliveries into Japan from the U.S.?

Frank Gilbertson to Sydney Lysaght, Bristol. 4 June 1908 [5 : 743-4]

I saw Mr. Hill yesterday, and showed him the copies of correspondence that have passed between the New York and Japanese houses, of the firm who purchased the 1,150 tons of 30 gauge sheets from the United States Co., and he promised to let you know that he had seen these.

He quite agreed with me that these documents were a conclusive proof of the Americans having sold, in April, 1,150 tons of 6' x 3' x 30 G. Galvd. sheets to Japan, at about 3/- to 7/- below the agreed price.

The information that Mr. Farrell gave you, according to your letter to Mr. Summers, with reference to a sale in London was also incorrect, as the quantity was not 100 tons but 200 tons, and was sold to Messrs. Strachan.

These large totals, in the present state of Japanese business, affect the Welsh Members of the Association in a most serious manner, and I hope that you will draw Mr. Farrell's immediate attention to the confirmation of the reports that we have now received, and do all in your power to stop these sales in future.

We are sorry to upset your confidence in this gentleman, but it is no good making bar contracts with him, if we do not get the consideration, to which we are entitled.

Frank Gilbertson to John Lysaght, Bristol. 6 June 1908 [5 : 746-7]

. . . As regards the improbability of the Japanese market in its present condition buying so largely, I may say that we ourselves had a 900 ton order in April from one house & a 500 ton order from another, so there is no reason to doubt the American sale from the point of view of size alone . . . I think you may tell Mr. Farrell that we are the people who complain, that at equal prices we could have had the business . . . We have now shipped almost our last order for Japan, & immediate prospects in our market are most gloomy.

Frank Gilbertson to John Lysaght. 10 June 1908 [5 : 749-50]

We are sorry to trouble you, but it is wise in our opinion, to take into consideration every report of irregularity now that business is so bad.

Americans.

You will remember we wrote you about Thos. Robertson & Co. booking an order with them at below Assn. prices for 28 gauge & heavier, ordinary Canadian flats, best quality. These people have now bought 500 tons from the Americans – They always used to give us a good share of their business.

Shanghai Market.

Messrs. Tuppers representative reports that the Americans are quoting 7' x 3' & 7' x 10/3" 41, 42 & even 43 sheets per case at the agreed price for 40 sheets.

These reports are most exasperating.

We have no orders on our books, some mills are idle & others working into stock, & here we find the Americans taking orders in Shanghai & Canada, both markets in which we have always had a fair share of the trade.

Shipments from Avonmouth.

A customer of ours in Canada, J. Watterson, is buying no iron from us this year & claims to have placed 500 tons already this season at £15..17..6 f.o.b. Avonmouth.

Is it worth your making enquiries at this port to ascertain who has miscalculated the price?

Frank Gilbertson to N. K. Turnbull, 3 July 1908 [5 : 770-1]
42 Birch Lane, Longsight, Manchester.

We must express our regret at the long delay in our reply to your proposal.

We have given the matter very careful consideration, & we have decided against any development in the direction of wire rods.

We feel that you have placed before us a most tempting proposal, but all our interests are here in land & labour, & we decide to spend our money here.

We are therefore going to increase our tinplate trade & build a new Tin works, which will enable us to use up most of our soft steel although we quite believe the profit will be much less than the adoption of your proposals would have meant.

We are sorry to have troubled you, & we beg to thank you very much for the clear way you presented your project which enabled us to decide definitely. If it had been possible to manufacture wire rods here we should probably have gone into the trade, but the reasons you gave for locating the works near Manchester appeared to us to be conclusive.

Frank Gilbertson to Messrs. J. & H. Summers. 27 July 1908 [5 : 810-11]

Thank you for your letter of 25th.

Lead Coated Sheets. I believe Smith & Co. are right in saying some have actually gone to Rangoon.

I also think it might be serious competition for galvanized sheets if Members were allowed to encourage it. They can be made at much lower cost, with only some 3% of coating & they stand weather well, according to our old experience in small terne plates.

Mr. Farrell. I really cannot form an opinion. The letter was apparently straightforward, but nothing could have been clearer than the proofs Mitsui gave us.

I am not letting the matter drop but will let you know when I get anything more definite. It is not impossible that the actual contracts may be forthcoming.

Stradey. I heard from Mr. Spence on Saturday complaining of "Comet" sheets being sold to Japan at 7/6 below price. I told him it was not true, & offered to show him contracts & invoices for any lot that he required, to be able to refute the allegations of his Agent [Franklin Saunders].

We have also heard rumours of underselling, but as they all originate in Hamburg, I think it is part of a plot to set us all "by the ears".

I hope your issue of preference shares will be a great success, as no doubt it will, seeing what proofs of good management are shown in the prospectus.

Frank Gilbertson to Messrs J. & H. Summers. 2 Jan. 1909 [5 : 927]

I am very much obliged to you for your letter of 30th ulto. with copies of letters from Japan.

They are very interesting indeed to us & it is kind of you to have sent them.

The demand from Japan is always very irregular, but no doubt your friends have correct information when they look for constant expansion on the whole. We notice that they consider Apollo sheets to be cheaper than the Association minimum, & also that they make no mention of internal Japanese competition, the latter being a satisfactory feature of their report.

We hope that this year will prove the correctness of their estimate.

Thanking you for your good wishes which we heartily reciprocate.

Frank Gilbertson to A. H. Cooper, Dorman Long & Co. 23 Jan. 1909 [5 : 947-8]

I am obliged by your favour of 21st which reached us this morning.

You say Steel Peech & Tozer have the order at £5..2..6, but we have a telegram from Fox saying that they are taking it at £5..1..3 & asking for our consent, adding that the others have given theirs.

You must excuse my saying that under these circumstances my firm can no longer be a party to the arrangement.

We were first told to take not less than £5..5..0, & then without our knowledge £5..2..6 was agreed to, & now that one firm has a definite offer a further reduction is suggested.

We were not quoting less than the suggested official prices, before any understanding was attempted, & it appears to us that the manner in which the official price has been varied is ridiculous & shows the greatest weakness on the part of the manufacturers.

We also do not see why a Sheffield House should be given exceptional opportunities to take a West Coast order.

We regret therefore that we cannot continue the arrangement, which could only prove a satisfactory one if all the manufacturers stuck to it rigidly.

Frank Gilbertson to Messrs Wenham Bros. Co. Ld. **20 Feb. 1909 [5 : 976-8]**

Your favour of yesterday with enclosure from Messrs Lysaght.

Has the American letter gone to Baldwins & Monmouthshire Co?

We hardly know how to treat it. The facts are that the Americans took all last year's business at about £14..10..0, & I have not heard that they have put their prices up to 20/- above Baldwins this season, & really doubt it.

Baldwins are most interested & we would agree to follow them, but the Americans have gone astray in thinking Baldwins have two brands with a difference of 35/- a ton in price.

We should like to know what Baldwins say, & would then write you fully our views.

Frank Gilbertson to Messrs J. & H. Summers. **22 Feb. 1909 [5 : 980]**

. . . Apparently the Americans want 10,000 tons a month. Would it not be reasonable to offer to contract for 2 months only at the last price? The only excuse for a higher price would be the possibility of improving prices during the 6 months covered by the contract.

We should not be in favour of breaking with the Americans under any circumstances.

Frank Gilbertson to Basil Wenham. **23 April 1909 [7 : 11]**

The general impression seems to be that the Raven Co. have increased their output & are now working 3 Pots.

If they had occasion to start 3 Pots their output must be more than 200 tons weekly, & 3 Pots should make 320 tons weekly, of 30 gauge & heavier, mixed. I don't think their allotment gives them more than 140 tons weekly, so it does look as if an investigation was wanted. I should like to see the Pay Book checked with the invoices.

Perhaps you will consult the Chairman.

P.S. I have seen <u>their</u> <u>own</u> weight lists for 7' x 3' flats for China, recently & they are not observing the Rules.

Frank Gilbertson to Messrs George Adams & Sons Ltd. **26 April 1909 [7 : 16-7]**

Private

Some time ago you asked me if we had appointed Messrs John Duthie our Agents in New Zealand, & I replied no.

They have now applied to be appointed our Agents & I want to know if you will agree.

Mr. Walker says he believes you will not object, & as far as we are concerned we should like to enter into the arrangement.

We are very sorry that we were forced into taking any business that offered itself to us. The New Zealand trade does not suit us well, but so many makers have gone into the 30 gauge trade, since the Association started, that we cannot keep our Works going without enlarging our markets.

In olden days we did nothing but 30 gauge but by degrees, Summers & Walkers & the Birmingham Corrugated Co. all came into the trade, & just when the Association started the Raven Co. followed & later on the Stradey & the Willfield Cos.

Our position was getting very difficult as we were losing our 30 gauge business so largely, & were from 1,000 to 2,000 tons short of our allotment each year, so that when Messrs. John Duthie said they were looking for a new supplier, & if we did not take up the business they would go to someone else, we could not refuse the chance.

Frank Gilbertson to Messrs James Bros, Morriston Silica Brick Works. **4 May 1909 [7 : 24]**

We are in receipt of yours of yesterday & as promised we enclose you a cheque for £250 in payment of bricks which you will deliver as we require them.

Please keep a stock for us, but do not send them on faster than we want them.

Please think over our proposal to start Works here, or to move your present ones.

Are your kilns any good for ordinary bricks or fire bricks? Could you not make them at Morriston & start Silica Bricks here?

Perhaps your landlord could let your ground for building & would be willing to cancel your lease? Please think over all these questions.

Frank Gilbertson to Sydney R. Lysaght, Bristol. **25 May 1909 [7 : 41-2]**

I enclose copy of a letter we have written to Wenham, & as you are chiefly interested in the New Zealand market I thought an explanation due to you.

Messrs John Duthie approached us some time ago & said that as Messrs. Adams would not sell at the minimum Association rates they had ceased to act for them & were going to buy their sheets from any manufacturer in the open market, & they offered us business.

26 gauge sheets do not suit us, & we should not have cared for the business had we been able to get our old share of the 30 gauge trade, but since the start of the Association we have had so much new competition in the 30 gauge market, that we have, nearly all through, been short of our tonnage. Raven Co, Stradey, Alyn, & Wellfield have all cut into our market & Summers & B'ham Corrugated Co. have greatly increased their business in light sheets.

We therefore could not refuse to throw away any new business that was offered to us.

Since then Messrs John Duthie have offered to represent us as Agents & we have ascertained that Messrs. Adams do not object.

Frank Gilbertson to Deloitte, Plender & Griffiths. 8 June 1909 [7 : 69-70]

With reference to the account you are preparing for the Income Tax Authorities, of our payments into & receipts from the Galvanizing Association for the year ended March 31st 1908.

We find we have made a small mistake in the return we gave the Surveyor.

We returned £1,470..13..6 as our contributions to the Galvanizing Association, which was arrived at by deducting our loss on the American Bar Contract which we placed at £1,875..10..4, from the total payment to the Association of £3,346..3..10. The actual loss was £1,526..10..0, so that we must add £313..0..4 to the amount we returned to the Surveyor.

The loss arose in this way. We bought 2,500 tons of American bars through the Association at £5 a ton & we did not use them but sold them to other members of the Association at £4..7..6 a ton, losing 12/6 a ton on the transaction.

We used the machinery of the Association to effect the transaction so that our loss was contained in the payment made to the Association.

For the preceding two years there had been no transactions in American Bars through the Association & our returns to the Surveyor for those years are the actual amounts, in toto, that we paid in.

Frank Gilbertson to Messrs Braby & Co. Ltd., London. 9 June 1909 [7 : 72-3]

Private

We hear that our Glasgow house is selling 72 x 36 x 30 gauge black sheets in large quantities & at low prices.

We think you should know that these black sheets are all galvanized somewhere & so enter into competition with the Association, indirectly.

No one at present produces them outside of the Association & I think it is worth while considering carefully what is being done.

With these sheets at £7..15..0 less 4% fob Liverpool there must be a great temptation to the Japanese to galvanize.

Further, a Belgian Works has to our knowledge sold 200 tons of 72 x 36 x 30 gauge galvanized sheets to Japan & further orders will be given them if the quality is approved of.

The black sheets needed for this order are coming from this country.

You will see that the difference between £7..15..0 less 4% (which is far below the cost of production in Wales), & the selling price of this specification, galvanized, must tempt foreign galvanizers to an unprecedented extent.

May I suggest that you give this matter your careful consideration?

We ought to have no difficulty in stamping out the Belgium competition if we act in concert.

Frank Gilbertson to Pilliner. **9 June 1909 [7 : 92-3]**

For your own guidance entirely, the Association meets next Tuesday, & I expect that a very drastic course will be followed & probably open prices declared.

Our object will be to work as fully as possible in order to reduce our costs, as prices will certainly fall to point of absolute cost.

I think it would be well for us to deal generously with any contracts on our books not shipped.

Summers will have a shot at the Japanese trade & you will probably find that our prices must follow his.

If the first slump is very bad it will probably be followed by a moderate rise in a couple of months, so we should not desire to enter far ahead but we should like to see a full order book for prompt delivery.

I have no idea where prices will go, but I expect more than 40/- drop in 30 gauge, & please understand that our policy will be full work at competitors' prices so that you will have an absolute free hand to take any order, unless we are full up.

I shall be unable to attend on Tuesday but after the decision is come to, I will let you know what has led to this.

In July 1909 the Association abandoned price control and prices dropped to £11..10..0 by the end of the year (c.f. a maximum of £13..17..6 in 1907).

P. Davies to Messrs Beor & Plant, Solicitors, Swansea. **12 July 1909 [7 : 95]**

Referring to the documents which our Mr. F. W. Gilbertson has handed you for completion, we give you at foot copy of a minute passed at a meeting of our Directors, held on Saturday morning last.

We now await return of the documents duly completed.

"It was resolved to confirm attachment of the Seal of the Company to Power of "Attorney granted in favour of Mr. Walter Augustus de Havilland, Tokyo, Japan

"(Thro' Messrs Brewer & Son) in connection with the registration of Trade Mark 'Comet'
"in Japan, and in addition to signatures of Francis W. Gilbertson, Director, and
"Philip Davies, Secretary, were duly authorized, and confirmed."

Frank Gilbertson to Messrs. J. & H. Summers. 29 July 1909 [7 : 115-6]

I understand that we have all "to try & keep to existing sheetages", but that we are not bound to, if others break them.

We have been offered a very large order of 30 gauge if we would sell sheets that ought to weigh 20 tons as T 18 – 12 – 0 – 0.

We could roll this sheetage, & the price was acceptable, but we have refused the order, as we don't wish to be the first to break rules. My view is that we were at liberty to take it, as our Agent was shown invoices that prove others have been selling this sheetage recently, or rather invoicing at the actual weight of 18 – 12 – 0 – 0 instead of the nominal weight of 20 – 0 – 0 – 0. It is disgusting to find how dishonest some of our friends have been & I hope they will now get a dose that they wont forget, but I should like to know if you think we are at liberty to follow competition if we get clear proof that the rules as to sheetages have been broken.

Frank Gilbertson to Edw. J. Gibbins. 9 Aug. 1909 [7 : 125-6]

Excuse my making this proposal to you privately, before writing it to your firm. As I told you we recognise that the only chance now of our avoiding loss is to greatly increase our output.

We have a good hold on the market & can book orders for as many sheets as we can galvanize if we can secure the black sheets.

I cannot conceive that Stradey can cover cost at today's prices & so I asked them if they cared to sell the sheets they had bought from you, at a figure. They reply that they are short of orders, but expect to book some soon, & will not therefore sacrifice their black sheets.

I understood from you that you were not disposed to sell us more of your output than we have already bought because of your contract with Stradey.

Our contracts with you are for 1,000 tons & we hope you will be able to deliver nearly 100 tons a week in September & say 50 tons a week after, but the earliest delivery you can give us of the whole contract will be very convenient to us.

Supposing after delivery of above quantities to us, you reserve a weekly quantity for Stradey which they don't specify, will you sell us that quantity week by week?

We could fix a price for these balances, & take on just what Stradey failed to take. This would keep you fully going & would enable us to improve our output & we would take 36", 29" & 22½" wide, as suited you.

P.S. I don't suggest cancelling any sheets that Stradey don't take, but if you give them latitude in specifying, my proposal will fill [?] you with specifications when they don't [?].

Frank Gilbertson to Messrs Ash & Lacy Ltd. 3 Sept. 1909 [7 : 140]

Private

Your enquiry of yesterday for sheets.

We regret our Mills are quite full.

Do you care to buy from "The Bryngwyn Steel Co. Ld, Gorseinon"?

I have written to Mr. Summers to ask his opinion, but I should be inclined to say it would be wise to give Bryngwyn & Upper Forest some black sheet business, as it would hinder their entry into the galvanizing trade.

Bryngwyn are going to start rolling next month, but they have no galvanizing plant fixed yet.

The order was for 500 tons of black sheets which prompted FWG to write to Summers [7:139] for his opinion on the position of associated members buying from non-associated mills, suggesting that "it might be to our interest that Bryngwyn and Upper Forest should have some orders for black sheets, which would delay their entry into the galvanizing trade".

Frank Gilbertson to Sydney R. Lysaght, Bristol. 23 Oct. 1909 [7 : 151]

Our Agent in Canada writes "I am informed that both Summers & Baldwins are taking orders for next year".

I should be glad to know what you think, & when the restriction will be removed.

We shall follow your lead, but we are rather sorry to miss a share of the orders that are placed with makers of the same class of sheet as we manufacture ourselves.

Frank Gilbertson to Messrs J. & H. Summers. 30 Oct. 1909 [7 : 156]

It was stated at the meeting that extras as well as sheetages should be adhered to. It did not strike me at the time, but surely it is impossible to maintain extras. Thirty gauge prices have so completely broken up that it is impossible to maintain any relation between the prices of 24 & 30 gauge. Ever since the break up of prices the extra for the Rangoon specification over the Japanese has gone by the board, & in our opinion it is hopeless to keep to any extras except those for long lengths.

Frank Gilbertson to Messrs the Capital & Counties Bank Ltd. 8 Feb. 1910 [7 : 198]

We desire to open an account for our new Tinplate Department.

It will be worked in the same way as our Slag Department account.

Please open the a/c. & if any resolution is needed by our Board, please send us a draft of it.

Frank Gilbertson to the Executors of the late G. Lawrence. **15 Feb. 1910 [7 : 202]**

To enable you to decide upon enclosed circular, we should mention that the total Debenture debt is £14,000 & that we have just spent over £40,000, out of profits, on a new 6 Mill Tinplate Works.

Frank Gilbertson to Messrs Phillips & Hill, London Agents. **19 Feb. 1910 [7 : 209]**

Tinplate Department

We are conducting all buying & selling from this office, but we intend all questions of delivery & all invoicing whether of Glynbeudy plates or our own, to be dealt with by the new Tinplate Works office.

Would you therefore, in your correspondence, kindly use separate sheets for matters that will be dealt with by the new office, & would it be quite convenient for you to pay in all amounts you collect against tinplate invoices at a branch of the Capital & Counties Bank?

We enclose a list of their branches & a book of slips.

Frank Gilbertson to Messrs Brewer & Son. **1 March 1910 [7 : 217]**

. . . As far as we understand it, we agree with your action.

At the same time we feel we are entirely in your hands, & beg you will not forget that the security of Comet brand as concerning Galvanized Sheets in Japan is of absolutely vital importance to our trade.

Frank Gilbertson to The Secretary of State for Foreign Affairs, London. **5 April 1910 [7 : 254-5]**

We desire to bring to your notice a proposed change in the Customs duties of Japan that will seriously affect an important industry.

It is intended to raise the duties on Galvanized Flat and Corrugated Sheets from 74,1 yen per pcl (1/5 per 133⅓ lbs) to 2,0 yen per pcl (4/- per 133⅓ lbs), sometime during 1911.

Our own business in this article is very large as we are exporting to Japan at present about 1,500 tons per month of an approximate value of £22,000. The amount of wages we pay ourselves in the manufacture of these Sheets for Japan (from the Pig Iron on to the finished Sheet) is about £65,000 per annum.

The proposed increase of duty amounts to about 14% of the value of the goods, and if the proposal passes into law it is likely to damage this industry in South Wales most seriously.

The sheets are used in Japan as a cheap building material, and for the manufacture of buckets and small articles, and any considerable increase in the cost is certain to affect the consumption.

This particular trade with Japan has for many years formed so large a proportion of our manufacture, that any large reduction in it must affect the state of employment here, and we hope you may be able to exercise some influence in the direction of modifying the proposed increase of duty.

Frank Gilbertston to Theodore Gibbins. 13 April 1910 [7 : 257-8]

. . . We should be glad to be rid of Glynbeudy as I told you & I decided last week to make some enquiries.

A Mr. Peregrine had several times approached our Mr. Philip Davies to know if we wanted to clear out, & I told Philip to let Mr. Peregrine know our ideas, which he did yesterday. Our idea is that if we could clear out, without loss, we would do so, & I thought that the best way to do so would be for the whole place to be transferred, to the newcomers.

As we (i.e. my family & a few friends) only hold 42 shares out of 62, this concern would entail our getting the consent of the other 20 shareholders & I had prepared a circular to ascertain their views.

I will now send this circular out & by the time I get the replies I shall know whether Peregrine is prepared to offer the sum we have indicated to him.

The Works have cost £19,000 odd & approximately we would (as far as our interests are concerned) accept £12,500 which with the Stocks and book debts would return our capital £18,600 intact.

If you care to discuss it further with me & to inspect the Works please suggest an afternoon this week.

Frank Gilbertson to Frederick Edwards, Capital & Counties Bank. 30 April 1910 [7 : 265]

I thought I would send you a line to say that now we have our new Tinplate Works in full operation, we have decided to concentrate our interests here.

My family have therefore disposed of their interest in Glynbeudy, & as the other shareholders were agreeable, the whole Company has been transferred.

The newcomers are Mr. Theo Gibbins, the Melyn Co. & friends, so that the Works has got into good hands, who will make them "pay" if anyone can.

My brother Charles & myself remain Directors until all the arrangements are complete, perhaps for another couple of weeks.

Cecil Gilbertson to H. Summers. 30 May 1910 [7 : 321-2]

About a year ago we were offered an order for some 6' x 9/3" Galvanized Sheets 268s. to the ton. We refused the order on account of the sheetage being lighter than the Rules of the Association permitted. Our Agent was then given occular proof that the buyer was getting this sheetage from another maker. We placed the matter before you and accepted the order with this sheetage, as you will remember.

We wish to report to you that the same thing exactly has occurred this year over the same order and although for some time we refused to quote, our Agent was shown the quotation of our competitors including this light sheetage, and we have therefore again accepted it.

We do not know what you think about it, but we are tired of the constant breaches of the Rules, and whenever we get actual evidence of our other friends quoting for prohibited counts we feel disposed to compete for the business.

We hear of several members regularly quoting for improper counts now.

Cecil Gilbertson to Messrs Wenham Bros & Co. 3 June 1910 [7 : 328-9]

. . . We have based our calculations upon the cost of manufacture in our own works and on the assumption that the exports would be 30 G. The total exports of Galvanized sheets to Japan from this Country in the year 1908 amounted to 26,559 tons representing a total money value of £401,268. During the year 1909 the total exports amounted to 25,769 tons representing a value of £380,137. Taking an average for the two years the exports would amount to 25,164 tons, annually.

To manufacture this quantity of Galvanized sheets 26,500 tons of steel bars would be used which would represent in wages £13,898. The spelter used to coat the sheets would be 3,848 tons most of which would probably be smelted in this Country and would represent in wages £10,400.

The actual labour in the Galvanizing Works would represent in wages a sum of £65,412.

The total amount of wages therefore paid in the manufacture of Galvanized sheets exported to Japan during the two past years is approximately £89,710 annually.

Our Mr. F. W. Gilbertson's wish was merely to bring to the notice of the Committee the amount of labour that this trade provides which would conceivably be greatly reduced should the proposed new Tariff come into force.

Frank Gilbertson to The General Manager, Midland Railway, Derby. 2 Aug. 1910 [7 : 369-70]

Mr. Loney & Mr. Tatlow have explained to the Writer the suggested new line, intended to give better access for the valley traffic to the Swansea Docks.

We wish to express our view that this improvement is a necessary one.

At present we know that the traffic has become more than the present line can deal with, without delay & inconvenience to traders, & we are sure that your staff have great difficulties in giving the facilities you do.

We have felt some apprehension as to the future, because the increased trade of the Valley can only add to the difficulties until the point is reached when serious delays cannot be avoided.

We have just built 6 new Mills, Glanrhyd Works are building 4, & several new ones are contemplated in the Valley.

We are building a new Steel furnace which will turn out 25,000 tons yearly, & we know of many new Colliery enterprises.

We feel sure that there will be large developments in the Valley in the Anthracite trade, & altogether we feel that the traffic problem will become an impossible one soon, unless some new Railway work is undertaken.

Frank Gilbertson to The Secretary of State for Foreign Affairs. **24 Aug. 1910 [7 : 388-9]**

We beg to refer to our letter of 5th April last upon the question of the New Japanese Tariff in which we showed the serious results that might follow the increased duties on Galvanized sheets to ourselves and our Workpeople.

Will you be good enough to assist us further under the following circumstances, viz:-

If the tariff as proposed comes into effect it will seriously cripple the galvanized sheet industry in this country, and will encourage the manufacture of Galvanized sheets in Japan. We are by far the largest Manufacturers interested in the Japanese Market, and we have to consider how to keep our position in that market and how to avoid a great part of this Works being thrown idle.

The obvious course for us to follow is to erect a Galvanizing Works in Japan, and under such circumstances it might be possible for us to retain our hold on the Market and to keep the vast majority of our Workpeople employed, by rolling the Steel sheets here and sending them to Japan to galvanize in our new Factory there. If we proceed on these lines however and make enquiries for a site etc. in Japan, it will come to the knowledge of their Government, and will greatly strengthen their determination to resist your appeals for a reduction in the tariff.

We do not therefore desire to start any enquiries until we hear from you that you do not expect to be able to effect any reduction in the proposed tariff.

We should be very much obliged if you could give us your advice upon this matter as soon as you are able to.

We regret to trouble you, but the fact that more than half the production of this large Works finds a market in Japan must be our excuse.

P. Davies to Arthur Gilbertson. **28 Sept. 1910 [7 : 414-5]**

. . . The Directors report that the new six Mill Tinplate Works has been completed and is now fully at work, and it is hoped that by the end of this year this extension will contribute to the profits of the Company.

Considerable extension to the Steel Works are in course of erection but will necessitate no addition to the Capital of the Company.

Frank Gilbertson to E. Llewelyn Davies. **28 Nov. 1910 [7 : 452-3]**

We have further considered the question of casting the Rolls.
There are two alternatives open to us.

(1) To build a foundry able to supply our needs for Rolls, Ingot Moulds & general work.
(2) To make as small & cheap a building as possible, simply to carry your experiments on, but in such a form as to be capable of development if the experiments are ultimately successful.

We have come to the conclusion that the general foundry trade is unprofitable, & we have enough on our hands at present, & that the second alternative is the wisest. Under these circumstances we do not think we should take the man you mentioned. Could one of his under hands be obtained, with a promise to the head man to consider him if the results of the experiments justified proceeding on a large scale?
Would he, for a fee, provide you with advice & plans of an air furnace? We take it that an air furnace & not a cupola would be the best, as we should not go in for ordinary foundry work at first.

Llewelyn Davies of neighbouring Clydach had invented a process for welding chilled iron to steel. His experiments were successful in producing a compound roll where a chilled surface of cast iron was welded to a steel core to produce a roll which would "save this Company £5,000 a year by eliminating Rolls breaking" [7 : 742-4], a persistent problem which was costly and invariably halted production while the roll was changed. It was further envisaged that the process could be adjusted to produce armoured plate [7 : 786]. The patent and its protection thus become major priorities.

Frank Gilbertson to W. J. Percy Player, Player's Tin Plate Works, Clydach. **30 Nov. 1910 [7 : 457-8]**

We have been carrying out some experiments in a certain direction, which show considerable promise of success.
If anything ultimately comes of it, it will affect the interests of Roll Makers very much.
We want to discuss the matter with you, with a view to your joining in the completion of the experiments.
We should not ask you to join in the cost, but either the co-operation of a Roll Maker, or else the erection of a Foundry here is essential to the final proof of the process.
We should much like to go into the matter with you, but no time is to be lost, as the provisional protection will expire in the Spring. We look upon the matter as of

very great importance & we should like to discuss it with Mr. John Player & yourselves.

Is there any chance of Mr. John Player being down shortly?

It would be more convenient to meet at your office, but if Mr. John Player cannot come down we would be prepared to go to see him.

We think his experience would enable him to say whether the samples we would show promise sufficient success to be worth some trouble.

If you went in with us, we should bear the cost but for your co-operation we would suggest your having a share of the profits if there ever are any.

Charles Gilbertson to Ashton M. Heath, Whitehall Gardens, London. **20 Jan. 1911 [7 : 479-80]**

We have just received a telegram from a firm in Birmingham, regular customers of ours, stating that they have been stopped making drawbar springs, because we are not on Colonial Office lists.

We are extremely sorry to hear this, as Messrs Simpson & Co. (the firm referred to above) are very good customers.

We supply steel in large quantities to other firms for making springs, for government Railways in India, and our steel invariably stands the tests required for such work, viz. Sir Rendall's Test.

We feel confident that, if a test of this nature is required, that our steel will give every satisfaction.

We hope that something can be done to remove the objection raised to our steel.

Charles Gilbertson to Sir Walter Lawrence. **20 Jan. 1911 [7 : 481-2]**

We have received from a Birmingham firm, Messrs Simpson & Co, a telegram reading as follows, "Ashton M. Heath, Whitehall Gardens, London, Chief Inspecting Engineer to Crown Agents for the Colonies, has stopped us making drawbar springs because you are not on their lists for this Class of Steel".

You may possibly remember that some difficulty of a similar kind arose some years ago, in connection with the India Office, & you kindly assisted then to put the matter right.

We understand that with Messrs. Simpson & Co, this particular business is a new one, & likely to extend. We are anxious therefore to assist them, as they are good Customers of ours & do not want to lose this business.

I wonder if you could advise us as to the best course to adopt. In the case of the India Office, our steel has to undergo "Rendall's Test". Do you happen to know if a similar test is required by the Colonial Office. If so, there can be no doubt that our steel would be suitable, & would pass the required test.

I am writing to Mr. Heath, explaining to him, but fear that it will not have much effect.

If you can assist us to remove the objection to our steel, we shall be extremely grateful.

Frank Gilbertson to The Secretary of State for Foreign Affairs. **30 Jan. 1911 [7 : 484-5]**

Referring to our recent correspondence on the matter of the Japanese Tariff and its likely effect upon the South Wales trade in Galvanized Sheets.

Would you kindly let us know whether you have any further information to give us yet, as the business is being much dislocated by the doubt that appears to exist among the merchants in the trade as to the final outcome of the negotiations?

We have seen it stated in the press that the existing Treaties between Japan and America do not terminate until a year after the Treaties between Japan and this Country. The United States of America are our chief competitors in the Japanese market in Galvanized Iron, and if it were the fact that the new duties could be levied against us for a year before they were levied against the United States, the result would be very disastrous, several important Works in this Country would be entirely closed.

Any information you can give us on these matters would be of real value to us in arranging our business for the near future.

P.S. If there was any information that you could give, which you did not desire to be made public, we would treat it as confidential.
We are by far the largest exporters to Japan, & the matter is of the most urgent concern to us.

Frank Gilbertson to Ogilvy Spence, Aberpergwm. **7 March 1911 [7 : 506-7]**

<u>Private</u>

I am writing a line about Stradey Co. I reported at the last meeting that they had quoted for 60 x 30 & 34 x 23 in excess of the permitted sheetage, & that they had denied it to me in correspondence. The quotation was made by Messrs Williams & George.

The Secretaries were instructed to follow it up.

They have done so & asked 2 categorised questions.

(1) Have your Agents quoted for more than 35 bundles to the ton of 34 x 23?
(2) Ditto 28 bundles of 60 x 30?

To both of these the Stradey Co. say <u>no</u>.

Now the matter is really very unsatisfactory because I have myself seen the original quotation!!

I am not at liberty to mention any names, & I beg you will make enquiries without mentioning my name, but if necessary I must finally disclose my knowledge.

Excuse my saying it, but do you consider Thomas an honest man?

P. Davies to Geo Rowe, Hotel Victoria, London. 16 March 1911 [7 : 512-4]

We are instructed by our Mr. F. W. Gilbertson to send you enclosed statement of his views with regard to the proposed new Railway as it affects Pontardawe.

He says this is a rough suggestion for you to add to your evidence if you care to do so. With regard to the Pontardawe district, there are three Works there (belonging to Members of our Association) – the Glanrhyd Tinplate Co. Ltd., with 4 mills at work and 5 mills building), Ynismeudw with 5 mills, and W. Gilbertson & Co. Ltd., with 20 Sheet and Tinplate mills and a large Steel Works.

I will give some details of the latter Works as it is the largest of the three.

Messrs W. Gilbertson & Co. Ltd., employ some 1,600 men and their plant consists of a Steel Works with 6 furnaces producing 1,400 tons of Steel weekly, and a seventh furnace nearly completed having an estimated production of 450 tons weekly.

They have 12 Sheet Mills and a Galvanizing Works with a total capacity of 650 tons of Galvanized Sheets weekly.

They have 8 Tinplate & Blackplate Mills with an output of over 6,000 boxes weekly.

They have also a Slag grinding plant which is being enlarged so as to grind 10,000 tons of Basic Slag per annum.

For such a large Works their situation is not favourable, being 8 miles from the Port of Swansea, but this is set off to some extent by their proximity to the Anthracite coal field.

In times past they have used Anthracite Coal for Steel melting and although they do not use this coal for this purpose now, it might again suit them to do so at some future time.

They actually use very large quantities of Anthracite Coal in their boilers and the Coal which the proposed Railway will develop in the Cwmgorse & Egel Valleys will be of a particularly suitable quality for this purpose.

The Egel Valley is within a mile of the Pontardawe Works and if this Coal could be carried at a reasonable rate, their proximity to the coalfield would largely compensate them for their distance from the shipping port. Their consumption of steam coal is at present 400/500 tons per week, but if the Great Western Company are permitted to carry out their proposals without amendment the coal from the Cwmgorse & Egel Valleys will be of no service to W. Gilbertson Co. whatever, although the trains will actually run within a stone's throw of the Works.

The Railway Company propose no junction with the Midland Railway with whose lines W. Gilbertson & Co. are connected, nor do they propose to provide access to the Works themselves.

Under the powers they now ask for, even if they arranged for a connection with this Works they would be entitled to a toll of 9d a ton upon coal worked within a mile of the Works, which would not permit the collieries to compete with those in the Swansea Valley for the trade of this Works.

If the powers they ask for are granted in their entirety, coal which W. Gilbertson

& Co. would like to use will actually pass within 100 yards of their sidings and will incur a toll of 9d a ton before it is handed to the Midland Railway to be conveyed back to these Works.

The result will be that this new Coalfield will be of no use at all to the Works that are practically situated in its midst.

Frank Gilbertson to Henry Summers. **20 March 1911 [7 : 516-7]**

I thank you for your letter of the 18th inst. I have also heard that the Grovesend Co have had enough and have given 28 days notice, but whether this is a fact or not I shall know tomorrow. Whitford Co have started 2 mills and I don't envy them their prospects, I shall also be able to hear tomorrow whether there is truth in the report you have heard with regard to their labour troubles. Upper Forest are working almost entirely on 30 G, and I know as a fact that they are thoroughly disgusted with their venture.

It is a great pity all these people did not realise what was in store for them before they erected plant, which must be a menace to the trade for several years.

With regard to 30 G counts, I used to be of your opinion, but the American imports into Japan have increased so heavily that I felt and still feel we were right in meeting their competition fully. We have had a case of "Apollo" Sheets returned which was found to contain 58 sheets and to weigh 5 cwts 0 qrs 12 lbs. Are you able to convict anybody in particular of exceeding even the new count? We have heard of some business being booked for 70" x 7/3" x 320 sheets to the ton but we have not been able to ascertain who the sellers are, and apart from that we have not recently heard of any breaches of our rules.

I am having a correspondence with Mr. Spence about a very glaring case which I reported to the last meeting, although I have had the original quotation of their agents in my possession they steadfastly deny ever having quoted for the sheetage I accused them of. I hope the matter will be brought to a head before the next meeting because I think it is a case for exemplary punishment.

I must say on the whole the prospects of ever limiting counts and prices in such a way that some of our competitors will not evade them, seems to me more and more discouraging, and should you at some future time consider that joint action is again desirable to render our trade remunerative, I am very much disposed to think Mr. Gibbins's suggestion the best, of having no fixed minimum price but a heavy fine for over production and a generous payment for under production.

Not only is the trade now unremunerative but it has an unpleasant character on account of the dishonesty of some of our members.

We are rapidly reducing our output of Galvanized Sheets rather than accept the prices that are now ruling, and I am afraid the condition of our trade will be still worse whenever the Tariff with Japan has finally been settled.

No doubt you know that the Whitford Co have 6 mills erected, and the Wellfield Co. have ordered an engine to drive 6 mills which will be erected when they have secured the necessary capital.

Frank Gilbertson to Geo Rowe. 23 March 1911 [7 : 521]

. . . I think you have made the best bargain possible under the circumstances. I am sorry the Midland Co. failed to get running powers in the first House.

Frank Gilbertson to Ogilvy Spence. 1 April 1911 [7 : 535]

It is not true to say that the Association is dissolved or that the Rules are habitually broken. We are carrying on our business, at a reduced scale certainly, but still at the rate of 500 tons weekly, every ton of which is sold strictly under the regulations.

However it is a fact that a proposal will be made to wind up, but whether it will be passed or not depends upon the voting at the next meeting.

We are still adhering to every rule.

The Aberlash Works are in the hands of Messrs J. M. Leader & Son for dismantling, so please apply to them.

Charles Gilbertson to Sir Walter Lawrence. 3 April 1911 [7 : 529]

. . . Since I wrote to you, an Inspector has been down here from the Crown Agents for the Colonies to inspect our plant, etc.

He took full particulars, & gave us the impression that he was satisfied with what he saw.

We also received a form which we filled in, applying to be put on the list of suppliers to the Colonies.

We have heard nothing more as yet. We think that nothing but good could come of a personal visit from you to Mr. Heath, & if you could see your way to do this, we should be extremely obliged to you.

Your influence would, no doubt, be of great value & would bring things to a head.

Charles Gilbertson to Sir Walter Lawrence. 10 April 1911 [7 : 533]

. . . We are glad to see that a considerable reduction in the Statutory tariff has been arranged under the Anglo Japanese Treaty. As the United States of America export a large quantity of galvanized sheets to Japan, it will be of great interest to us, as the largest manufacturers for this market, to know whether the reduced rates will equally apply to America. May we ask you to kindly give us this information?

Frank Gilbertson to Messrs Abel & Imray. 19 April 1911 [7 : 543-5]

Mr. E. Llewelyn Davies consents to our writing to you about his Roll Patent.

We are paying the expenses of the experimental rolls & Mr. Davies & ourselves are working in unison in the matter . . .

. . . If the result is finally successful there is no doubt all Rolls will eventually be made by this method.

You will see therefore that it is of great importance that Mr. Davies' invention should be properly protected in countries where many Rolls are used, & at the same time that no unnecessary expense be incurred. We understand you are completing the Patent as far as Gt. Britain is concerned, & we should like to know how long you can safely delay the disclosure of the process & how long you can wait before applying for protection in Foreign Countries?

The two most important Foreign Countries are United States & Germany.

After these Russia, France, Spain, Italy, Austria, Japan & Belgium are important. Could you give us the cost of applying for Patents for all these countries?

Charles Gilbertson to Sir Walter Lawrence. **20 April 1911 [7 : 546]**

. . . We are very disappointed to see that the United States will be able to share the concessions gained by this Country under the Japanese Tariff, whereas we understand the United States do not themselves put the same construction upon the most favoured nation clause, and do not propose to give us the benefit of the reduced tariff proposed to be granted to Canada under the reciprocity treaty.

Frank Gilbertson to H. C. Ferron, Amsterdam. **15 May 1911 [7 : 562]**

I wish to convey my thanks to Mr. Verwer for his kind reception and the very interesting visit I paid to his Works.

We are very interested in the question of the aluminium-coated plates, and we beg you will approach Mr. Verwer at once and ask him to name his terms (for preference upon a royalty basis). We should like to know quite approximately what the cost of a plant might be, and we should also like to know whether it is possible to protect the process by patent.

I will write to you in the course of the next 2/3 days upon the other matters that transpired at our meeting, but I do not wish any delay to take place in negotiating this matter with Mr. Verwer.

Frank Gilbertson to H. C. Ferron. **19 May 1911 [7 : 564-6]**

I have at last time to write & thank you for all your hospitality. You made our visit to Amsterdam most interesting & I hope that our business together will increase.

Aluminium coated plates. We consider this matter to be most important & we hope you will soon be able to give us Mr. Verwer's terms. Please do not delay the matter as we think we could find some customers who are urgently requiring some such article, & we should not like to be forestalled by someone else.

Verwer's blackplates. I am very sorry to find a mistake was made & our blackplate that I inspected had not been delivered.

I think Mr. Verwer will find it suitable for his work.

Special blackplate. You remember the coloured sheet he showed us. Our men say they can produce this finish regularly. If Mr. Verwer likes to try a sample, say 10 cwts, we should be glad to send them at 2/6 a ton extra.

Please refer to this quality as "Rainbow blackplate".

Once cold rolled plates. After my visit I am inclined to think this quality will not suit Mr. Verwer so we are only sending 1 box as sample.

Wood boxes. We are already taking steps to change our suppliers.

Tels Co Ld. There seems to be some recollection in our office of the curt treatment Mr. Goldschmitt received at a time when we knew nothing of Messrs Tels! However we think the gentleman accepted our apologies & that business between us may now be encouraged.

We would propose the following arrangement. Every year, starting say on June 1st, we will reckon up the total deliveries to Messrs. Tels & will pay them an extra discount upon the turnover as follows –

Over 250	tons in the	year	⅓rd	per cent
" 500	"	"	⅔rd	"
" 750	"	"	1	"

It is hardly worth suggesting more as if we did so, it would mean a temptation to us to increase our quotations, as business in galvanized sheets cannot bear more than 5%, between the buyer & the Agent, really.

Frank Gilbertson to H. C. Ferron. 22 May 1911 [7 : 568-9]

Private

. . . I am obliged to you for dealing with the matter so promptly & hope that we may soon be able to come to terms.

I wired our Patent Agents today for a copy of Messrs Paton & Calvert's specification [for coating plates with Aluminium] which I will forward to you when I receive it.

Terms. We consider these not unreasonable, but we shall make some counter proposals when the matter of the Patent is cleared up, with the object of reducing the Royalty to Mr. Verwer on larger quantities than the initial output you name.

Output. Do I understand that the plant will produce 600 boxes of 28 x 20 x 112 sheets in a week, working day only, & a correspondingly larger output if worked by night also?

How many printing machines are required for an output of 600 boxes? It would appear to us that 6 men would not be required for a single unit of 1 Machine & 1 oven.

Manufacture. I gather the figures you give are applicable to the new plant I saw, which is not yet at work, & that if any difficulty occurred with the chain in the oven, that the old type of oven could be utilized.

Samples. As soon as ever we settle terms we should like to send some blackplate to be coated which we could submit to some of our customers as samples.

We are much obliged to Mr. Verwer for putting the matter before us & for the confidence he shows in us.

Frank Gilbertson to H. C. Ferron. **6 June 1911 [7 : 585-6]**

Private

Aluminium Coated Sheets

We feel that this is such an important matter that we must proceed carefully, & before going further into terms, it is necessary to clear up the question of Patent.

We have instructed our Patent Agents to make careful search & they now send us enclosed No. 20, 669 AD 1910.

We are afraid that it looks as though Messrs. Verwer's competitors in Krommenie had discovered Verwer's process & patented it themselves? If so, immediate action should be taken to upset the Patent on the grounds that Verwer had already invented & used the process. We think this could be done, but we do not know for certain.

The Writer will be in Brussels the first week in July, & if things have progressed sufficiently, would return by Amsterdam.

We have plenty of space in which to put the buildings, & if we had come to a definite arrangement, our Engineer should visit Verwer's Works at the same time.

Please give us your views upon the Patent very fully.

Frank Gilbertson to H. C. Ferron. **24 June 1911 [7 : 608-9]**

Private

Thank you for your letter of 31st inst. I am very sorry to see from it that I entirely misunderstood the purport of your letter of the 9th inst, as I had formed the opinion that Woud's patent would have covered the process invented by Mr. Verwer, and that the secret had probably been stolen from Mr. Verwer's Works. I am very glad to understand now that the process is essentially different. My letter of the 17th inst was therefore based upon an entirely incorrect notion of the facts . . .

You may be quite sure that we are keeping this matter absolutely private, and the friends to whom we have mentioned the possibility of our being able to supply a suitable material or certain work, have no idea of what the material really consists.

Frank Gilbertson to Messrs Phillips & Hill. **20 July 1911 [7 : 628-30]**

Private

. . . Mr. Earle has telephoned to the Writer today after looking more fully into the matter. For our private guidance, he has quoted Massey £14..2..6 for 36 x 24 – 22 – 39 & Massey replies, "I regret I have to go to London without dealing with your quotation which however appears to me to be somewhat too high to bring business".

Mr. Earle's reading of this is that Massey would no doubt pay £14..0..0 & according to our costs this should mean £14..2..6 or £14..5..0 for 34 x 23 x 22 x 45 bundles.

The Writer has told Mr. Earle that if we take anything less than these figures we will let him know.

Mr. Earle is more or less of a private friend & can be absolutely relied on.

It is quite obvious that our last contract with Parker was 10/- a ton below what he paid Mr. Earle, & we are bound to say it has a little shaken our confidence in Mr. Vermont's statements.

Mr. Earle says that this time last year he was bombarded with enquiries for Ternes & that everyone told him his prices were 20/- out; but that eventually his prices were paid for all he could manufacture.

We note what you say as to quality. We believe Ystalyfera Ternes are made through Resin & ours, like W. H. Edwards, are made through Palm Oil. Our mixture is too rich in Tin at present, but next week we shall have it right. This will increase the quantity of the coating, but reduce the cost.

If Mr. Pilliner was able to spare a day & spend a couple of nights with the Writer it would give him great pleasure, & might be of mutual advantage for you to see the actual manufacture.

Frank Gilbertson to W. N. Earle, Ystalyfera Tinplate Co. **16 Aug. 1911 [7 : 647-8]**

<u>Private</u>

As we have now made a considerable sale of Ternes, I think I should let you know.

We have sold 2,250 tons 34" x 23" x 45" and or 36" x 24" x 39" at the following prices.

750 tons £13..12..6 f.o.b. Swansea
1,500 " £13..15..0

We understand the whole will be specified in 34 x 23 x 45, & as we can make this size fairly well, we believe it only costs us some 10d a ton more than the 36 x 24. I felt at liberty to take this price for this size, as you did not sell it yourself, & I was shown a contract with Glan Ebbw for a large quantity at £13..10..0, & have information that they intend putting another pot on.

We shall not now be in the market again for delivery this side of June.

Frank Gilbertson to H. C. Ferron. **22 Aug. 1911 [7 : 652]**

. . . We should like to come to an understanding about the price of the compound.

On May 17th you give the approximate cost of coating; we should like to know upon what price this cost was based, & something in the nature of a sliding scale might be arranged, contingent upon the cost of Aluminium. On thinking further over your suggestion as to the use of "Gloria" for a brand, we do not think it would be to our interests to agree to a brand in which we had no interest. If the brand was registered in Great Britain as our joint property, and in Holland as Mr. Verwer's property, we should be quite satisfied but we consider we should have some definite interest in the brand in England.

We have started our building.

P. Davies to Ashton M. Heath, Whitehall Gardens, London. **25 Aug. 1911 [7 : 655]**

We beg to acknowledge with thanks your favour of the 21st inst. acquainting us that our name has been placed on the Office List of Subcontractors for the supply of Steel for the Manufacture of springs.

Frank Gilbertson to Messrs Barlow, Barlow & Lyde. **29 Aug. 1911 [7 : 657]**

. . . We are afraid we know nothing of Messrs. Carl Lund's business beyond their being makers of butter tins for consumption in Denmark. We doubt the wisdom of our making enquiries through our Agent there, as they are not a trustworthy race.

We hope you will make all enquiries you can, & we will see if any of the Trade Societies we subscribe to can give us information.

We suppose Tinplates waiting for shipment for Messrs Carl Lunds would not do, as they would not have been paid for, & we should get into difficulties with the Tinplate Maker who was shipping them.

Frank Gilbertson to Messrs Barlow, Barlow & Lyde. **7 Sept. 1911 [7 : 665]**

. . . Suppose Carl Lunds had a credit in the hands of a London Bank, could we recover the debt from the Bank?

Frank Gilbertson to J. C. Woods, Messrs Collins & Woods. **5 Oct. 1911 [7 : 692-3]**

I think it would be well for Messrs J. M. Leeder & Son to be instructed to prepare a complete inventory of the plant at Aberlash, so as to be in a position to start selling immediately we are able to do so.

I suggest you write Mr. Jones again to say we must have his reply to your last offer by the end of next week, after which it will not be open.

Will you please let me know at what date we can exercise our option to purchase, & when the purchase money should be handed over?

Could you also tell me if the Colliery Co. have any rights over the sidings. I am under the impression that they are using the sidings, & if they have not the right of doing so, Messrs. J. M. Leeder might be asked to ascertain to what extent they are being used.

Frank Gilbertson to Thomas Russel, Traffic Mgr. 9 Oct. 1911 [7 : 697]

The GWR complain they are only getting one third of the traffic we gave them last year.

Keep this matter private, but understand our Water supply is endangered if we do not greatly increase the traffic we give them.

It is really a very important matter, & you must at all costs give them enough traffic to satisfy them.

Frank Gilbertson to Messrs Brooker Dore & Co. 16 Nov. 1911 [7 : 719]

. . . We have acquired the sole rights to manufacture Aluminium plates in Gt. Britain by one of the processes in use, & have completed the building & are now waiting for the machines.

We think that it would be highly desirable for us to meet & see if it is possible for us to act together & not be competitors.

The Writer has engagements in London on Dec. 1st & probably on Nov. 27th or Dec. 4th. Would you kindly say what date would suit you best?

Frank Gilbertson to Messrs Brooker Dore & Co. 5 Dec. 1911 [7 : 748-51]

We are obliged to you for giving the Writer an interview upon the Aluminium coating of Black Sheets.

We gather that your arrangement with your Patentee is that you have the exclusive rights of manufacture in Gt. Britain, & pay him a royalty, but no lump sum. We gather this from the amount of Capital you suggested.

Our arrangements with our Patentee are similar. We are inclined to think your process will make a plate that will be the more popular in England, & that our process will be the more popular on the Continent.

Would you be good enough to send us a small sample of your manufacture? If you will call on our Agents Messrs Phillips & Hill, you will be able to see Tins made from the plates we are going to manufacture.

On the whole we are inclined to think that there is a future for both processes, & that if they were in the same hands a profitable business should result.

If however we were competitors, the price would probably be forced much lower than necessary.

We see no great difficulty in forming a new Company in which yourselves & ourselves were jointly interested. The new Company to take over the Agreements with both Patentees, to take a lease of the buildings we have already erected & enter into Agreements for Electric Power, Light, Shunting &c with us.

Provided we could each arrange with our Patentees to assign their Agreements with each of us to the new Company, something on these lines might be possible, & might save you a considerable proportion of the Capital you intend to expend in Sidings, Boiler power &c.

P.S. If you send us a sample of your sheet we will undertake not to send it abroad, or to let it out of our office till you give us permission.

Frank Gilbertson to Messrs Phillips & Hill. 7 Feb. 1912 [7 : 841]

Have you any means of ascertaining privately upon what London bank or branch of a foreign bank, Messrs Carl Lunds Fabriker of Copenhagen draw cheques for payment for tinplates &c purchased in this country?

We have obtained judgement against them for about £450, but cannot enforce this judgement unless we can "garnishee" any funds they may hold in England.

Chapter 3

GROWTH AND DECLINE 1912-1929

The seventeen years covered by the letters in this chapter were momentous ones for W. Gilbertson & Company. Despite Britain's relative decline as an iron and steel producing nation, the high level of industrial activity which had characterized the last years of the nineteenth century and from 1905 to 1913 brought employment and prosperity to the South Wales coalfield and a renewed vitality to the tinplate and steel industries. The company and Pontardawe benefited from these years of economic growth and anticipated their continuance. A measure of Frank Gilbertson's optimism was his ambitious, if speculative, decision to form the Roumanian Sheet & Galvanizing Company in partnership with Bessler, Waechter & Co., six months before the outbreak of the Great War. Several of the letters express the concerns of the Gilbertson brothers over the slow progress of their newly erected plant in distant Galatz, an inland port on the lower Danube. Start-up problems, inexperienced labour and high manufacturing costs were exacerbated by the war which made communications, access and control more difficult and ultimately impossible.

On the home front, steel production from 1914 was geared to war demand and the letters convey a broad array of associated issues and problems, such as the status of pre-war contracts with German firms, the shortage of coal and bricks, the allocation of steel orders, the limited profits of controlled establishments, labour shortages and military service, and the torpedoeing of the *s.s. Dixiana* en route from Savannah to Swansea with its cargo of basic iron for the Pontardawe works.

Post-war expectations of continued industrial growth were to be dashed. By the end of 1920 the slump in Britain's staple industries was the prelude to fifteen years of industrial stagnation, severe unemployment and corrosive poverty. The selection ends with Frank Gilbertson's last letters in 1928 when the steel industry was mired in the depression and struggling to survive.

Frank Gilbertson to Sir Walter Lawrence. 18 May 1912 [7 : 924-4a]

. . . I am very glad that Sir A. Rendel now knows the position.

If we can do any business now that everybody's eyes are open, we shall be glad, but if not we cannot regret it.

I will tell the Spring bar makers that when they tender for our Steel, they must be prepared to give a certificate from us as to the nature of Raw Material & the method of manufacture, which we will provide when required.

I should like to add that Sir A. Rendel is not quite correct in thinking that carelessness on the part of our men could affect the quality, for this reason. Every charge is completely analysed before the ingots are taken from the Pit.

If the charge had not been properly worked the Phosphorus & Sulphur would most certainly exceed ·035% . . .

The only loophole would be if we added Carbon in the ladle, because in that case we could "doctor" the charge.

We are prepared to give any guarantee that Carbon has never been added in the Ladle in our Works & never will be.

I hope Sir A. Rendel has convinced himself that the Steel we have hitherto supplied has been as good in results as any Steel he has used.

Frank Gilbertson to Messrs Barlow, Barlow & Lyde. **8 July 1912 [7 : 952-3]**

About ten years ago you acted for us in some negotiations with Messrs Hallams who were acting on behalf of Messrs Swan Bros, Middlesborough, which resulted in our purchasing Swan's grinding Plant here. A couple of months ago we were induced by our Slag Agent in Liverpool to issue a writ against The Western Counties Co-operative Association. As all our sales of Slag are conducted in Liverpool, and as we understood there was very little probability of the case actually coming into Court, we allowed our Agent to employ his Solicitors in Liverpool, Messrs Alsop, Stevens, Crooks & Co. It now appears that we shall be involved in an expensive Suit, and the Writer is desirous of reading through the correspondence that took place with Messrs Swan Brothers during a period prior to 1902. Would you kindly let us know if you have this correspondence or any copies of it?

We mention the above facts to explain why you are not acting for us, as you would have done if we had known the consequences of our threatening proceedings.

Frank Gilbertson to Messrs Barlow, Barlow & Lyde. **10 July 1912 [7 : 9551]**

We are obliged by yours of yesterday & have safely received the parcel of letters.

We omitted to say that the explanation of our Liverpool Agent that the party we sued would climb down, without a trial, was quite sound, had it not been that the whole of the Basic Slag "Ring" has taken this opportunity of backing him in the hopes of extinguishing us!

Frank Gilbertson to Messrs Barlow, Barlow & Lyde. **19 July 1912 [7 : 985]**

A gentleman from the Continent is now in Birmingham hawking a process for coating plates with Aluminium, we believe, representing a Mr. A. Bastian of Hagen. He has written to us inviting an interview. We think this strengthens our idea that we should not go in with Baldwins, unless they can get the clause as to exports amended in the way we suggested. Would you hand this news on to Messrs. Pinsent?

Frank Gilbertson to H. C. Ferron. **22 July 1912 [7 : 970-1]**

. . . First with regard to Woud's Patent. I wrote Messrs Brookes on 20th inst, asking them not to communicate Mr. Waters' opinion on Woud's Patent to Amsterdam, as I wished to tell you of it personally to ask you to keep it private.

If it becomes known that Woud's Patent is weak we might have competition springing up immediately. This is most important, & please do all you can to prevent this being known.

Messrs. Baldwins have obtained an opinion that Woud's Patent is a good one, & therefore we must consider it is open to doubt. So long as it is known that Baldwins & ourselves have an interest in Woud's Patent outsiders are not likely to attack us, as we are a strong combination, but it is most important for Mr. Verwer's interests that no impression should get abroad that Woud's Patent can be ignored.

I think that the sooner we have a discussion the better.

I shall be away from business from August 3rd to August 10th, but at any other time I would meet you.

It would however be desirable for you to come to Pontardawe so that we could meet Mr. J. C. Davies of Baldwins at the same time.

Frank Gilbertson to Messrs Tubes Ltd, Birmingham. **26 July 1912 [7 : 978-81]**

Private and Confidential

We are obliged by your favour of yesterday, and we are replying as fully as we can, but you will understand that some portions of the letter are of a private nature and please treat it as such.

First of all with regard to our Plant. We are really ashamed to offer any further explanations, but the fact is the whole Plant is now completed and has been for a couple of months – Boilers, Pushing Furnace, Gantry, Saw, Cooling Banks, etc. But one vital machine to discharge the furnace is already about 6 months overdue from the makers Messrs Broadbent and is not likely to be here until the first week of next month, after which erection must take a fortnight. You will understand that we have not neglected to press these people when we tell you that we have over 4,000 tons of ingots waiting to be rolled, and all our customers are in a state of irritation over our delays.

Now with regard to quality. Until we have arrived at a satisfactory explanation of the extraordinary differences in the suitability of different charges for Tube making, we are not disposed to grumble so much at the delay in completion of the Plant. Our only means of ascertaining what the quality of the different charges may be, is the testing undertaken by the Mannesmann of a sample ingot from each charge we make, and the probability of their test affording us the means of ascertaining whether the Steel would be suitable for you or not, seems to be confirmed by the fact that one of the Ingots we originally sent you (rolled roughly into rounds) and of which all 8 bars were reported by you as being defective, was an ingot out of a charge that the Mannesmann had accepted but had reported upon as being rather unsuitable for their work.

We have had a good many charges rejected by the Mannesmann in recent months and have kept our manufacture within very small limits because of this uncertainty. The Manager of these Works promised some time ago to obtain answers to a long series of questions that we compiled when he visited certain Continental Works that regularly produced the right quality. He originally intended visiting these Works in April but has not gone yet, but we understand he is shortly arranging to do so. If we obtain answers to these questions we believe our path will be made very much easier, but until then we cannot feel any confidence in the suitability of any particular charge that we have tapped for Tube making, and we are bound to say that for the particular fault Mr. Rheinhart's hints did not prove to be of any use. We have kept a number of Ingots back intending to roll them for you as samples as soon as our new re-heating furnace is working, and we hope you will allow us to wait until that time before delivering you any further samples.

Generally speaking we appreciate the importance and the prospects of the business in a very high degree, and we are anxious to take the opportunity you offer us of learning this trade, but until we can increase our knowledge from one source or another we cannot support you as we should desire to do.

We understand that the only Steel coming into our neighbours' Works that is really suitable for Cold Drawn Admiralty Work is Swedish Steel and a quality specially made by Messrs. Krupp. Messrs. Krupp's have apparently no facilities for making this Steel that are not common to other Steel makers in this Country, and it would be a very important thing to obtain some knowledge of how Messrs. Krupp's carry out this particular manufacture. We presume you have no opportunities in this direction?

The whole difficulty is one of reducing the blow holes in the charge and placing such as remain in a certain position in the section of the Ingot, and we have quite certainly proved that no additions of any material in the ladle can of themselves produce this correct distribution of the blow holes. The mechanical properties of the Steel offer no difficulty whatever.

Frank Gilbertson to Messrs Barlow, Barlow & Lyde. **30 July 1912 [7 : 986]**

. . . It really does appear to us that a Licence that does not permit exportation to the only market immediately available is worthless.

After having seen Mr. Walters' opinion we do not quite understand why Messrs. Baldwins should be prepared to negotiate any further. However if they do enter into an Agreement we prefer for commercial reasons to join, but it must be with the free right to export to countries in which Woud has a Patent.

Please say we are not prepared to join in the purchase without the right of exportation that we mentioned at our interview.

Frank Gilbertson to The Manager, London & South Western Bank Ld. **20 Nov. 1912 [8 : 95]**

Private

In reply to your enquiry re Mr. J. Vermont. We have no means of knowing what his resources are, but we can speak very highly of him as a business man.

He represents a very big house in Roumania, & has done a very large business with us for this house, & on his own account, during recent years, probably over £100,000 a year.

Although Roumania is a most difficult market we have not received a single complaint, or had any trouble at all over this business, & we consider that these facts speak well for Mr. Vermont's capacity.

He was then a member of Messrs J. R. H. Parker Co. Ld, but he was responsible for all this Roumanian trade.

Frank Gilbertson to Messrs Parrs Bank Ltd. **30 Dec. 1912 [8 : 136]**

Owing to the financial position of the Balkan States, we have to hold very large stocks of goods for those markets, & it is possible that our Banking a/c may have to be overdrawn. It is not at all certain, but we should like to know what your ideas would be should we require an overdraft.

Frank Gilbertson to H. C. Bond, Messrs Richard Thomas & Co. Ltd, Eastcheap. **30 Jan. 1913 [8 : 173-4]**

At the Executive meeting of the Tinplate Association last Tuesday there was a very general feeling that the output should be reduced, but there were various objections raised to the methods proposed. My own opinion is, & I think the balance of opinion at the meeting tended the same way, that a stop week for all Works is the only method that can command a majority.

It is also the only method that could be compulsorily put into force if a sufficient majority voted for it.

Is it worth your while approaching Cwmfelin & Mr. Paton to ascertain if, in the event of your scheme failing to pass, they would fall in with a stop week?

If Easter week was chosen the increase of cost would be somewhat minimised.

The reports we get from people who have bought our products for the Balkan market are gloomy in the extreme.

Frank Gilbertson to Pilliner, Phillips & Hill. 15 March 1913 [8 : 191-2]

We are very much obliged by your favour of yesterday.

On the whole we think the prospects are sufficiently favourable to make the matter one for careful investigation.

I have decided to go out to Galatz, probably next month, to form an opinion on the spot with the help of the British Consul.

I should rather like Mr. Vermont to know that we are contemplating the erection of a galvanizing plant so as to secure his advice, & to delay Messrs. Goldenberg's order for machinery.

If we decide to undertake the venture it would probably be necessary to form a Company in which we held all the shares – I think it is well worth considering if it would not be advisable to give Mr. Goldenberg & perhaps Mr. Vermont some interest in the undertaking to secure their interest instead of their hostility & to minimise local difficulties.

Evidently the matter is very important & requires the most careful consideration & our best judgement of the situation that is likely to arise during coming years. If you talk over the matter with Mr. Vermont I might go up to London for a day shortly to discuss it further with you.

Frank Gilbertson to Pilliner. 18 March 1913 [8 : 193-4]

Thank you for your letter. I think the point you make of interesting other distributors of Sheets a very important one.

No doubt if the project comes off, we should endeavour to keep prices in Galatz as high as possible & some British sheets would find a sale still, in addition to which I expect British makers would still do the Bulgarian, Servian & Macedonian trade. It would therefore seem very important, judging from our experience since we abandoned direct trading, to enlist the co-operation of big houses such as Bessler, Krogsdal, &c.

Possibly we might acquire an interest of not less than 55% & if possible more, in a new Company, & offer to divide the rest among the Merchants. Please consider this & what Firms we ought eventually to invite to join.

My idea is to take my holiday when I go out, & to take my wife & daughter. I am making my plans now, but approximately I propose starting about April 24th & travelling to Trieste, thence to Ragusa for a couple of days, then to Yablanice for a week & then to the nearest point on the Danube where I would take the steamer to Galatz. This would bring me to Galatz about the middle of May or a little earlier.

I should be very glad indeed if Mr. Vermont was able to be at Galatz then.

Will you please tell him of my proposal & ask him to criticise it, & I can then make a definite time table.

Frank Gilbertson to Joseph Vermont. 20 March 1913 [8 : 198-200]

Mr. Pilliner has handed me your letter of yesterday. I am sorry to say it will not be convenient for me to travel out till the latter part of April and as I want a holiday I would rather travel out slowly enjoying the Country on my way.

I suggest that you go out, as you propose, immediately after Easter, and discuss the matter with Mr. Goldenberg in the light of what I write below, and that then, if you can possibly spare the time, that you should go out again (at our expense) to assist me in the final arrangements in the middle of May.

The following points should be considered carefully by Mr. Goldenberg:

(1) We are inclined to seriously consider the advisability of erecting coating Works in Braila or Galatz, but if Mr. Goldenberg starts galvanizing himself we shall consider the advisability of competing with him with all the resources at our command.

(2) If Mr. Goldenberg will hold his hands till I visit the country in the middle of May, we will consider how we can co-operate with him and perhaps one or two more of the important Merchants who might otherwise become competitors. There is no hurry for Mr. Goldenberg to start himself, as he has plenty of Sheets bought from us, and if he started manufacturing without specifying for the Sheets he has bought, he would be putting himself hopelessly in the wrong, and we could enforce our contracts.

(3) We are by far the largest and best galvanizers of thin Sheets and no one else can hope to command the skill and experience our Workmen have acquired.

(4) If we are driven to compete with Mr. Goldenberg, as well as Mr. Auschnitt, the fact that we make our own Steel and roll our own Sheets will place us in a position against which he could not possibly compete.

(5) A plant bought "ready made" from Messrs. Thompson could not possibly compete against our plant. We have various details that we manufacture ourselves that will assure us of a lower cost.

(6) When Mr. Auschnitt started, Stradey and Franklin Saunders were giving up galvanizing, and there were Workmen available. This is not the case today and we believe that we have the facilities for producing sheets better and cheaper than anyone else and certainly better than Stradey, Wellfield, Franklin Saunders, and such firms.

If you go out next week to discuss the whole matter with Mr. Goldenberg it would be well for you to acquire information as to the cost of Electrical Power, Coke, Land in suitable position for manufacturing and for receiving and delivering Sheets, the nature of taxation, the usual cost of unskilled labour, and anything else that would in your opinion affect our decision.

If Mr. Goldenberg would see it, our idea might be a means of the development of a large business in which a combination of ourselves, himself, & one or two other Merchant Firms, might hold the trade against Mr. Auschnitt or any other competitor.

Frank Gilbertson to J. Vermont. **10 June 1913 [8 : 236]**

. . . We shall have details & proposals of various forms of power when we next meet. My only object in letting you know about the Diesel Engines was that Mr. Auschnitt should not think we were going blindly into the matter, & the fact that Mr. Herrmann spoke of very large horsepowers indicated that he knew more than we did at that time.

Will you please endeavour to obtain the following information:

(1) The price of bituminous slack coal delivered Danube ports from the Donetz coalfield. The shipping ports are probably Rostov on Don, Taganrog & Marinpol – perhaps also Khercon & Nicolaieff.
(2) The duties on coal entering Roumania.

Two days later [8 : 239] Frank wrote to Barlow requesting him to write to the Roumanian Consul for information on duties charged on coal and whether steel sheet bars for rolling into sheets would be admitted into Roumania.

Frank Gilbertson to Messrs Barlow, Barlow & Lyde. **18 June 1913 [8 : 242-3]**

We are much obliged by yours of yesterday. We certainly contemplate taking one or more Roumanians into partnership with us in the new project.

The conditions as to labourers & capital are easily met.

The raw material matter is one of very great importance & we can hardly believe that the Vice Consul has correct information. When I was at Braila I saw imported steel billets being rolled into rods & shapes & these billets paid 3 francs per ton duty although they were the raw material for a fair sized Works.

We presume nothing more definite can be obtained till we submit a complete scheme, which we may be able to do about the end of this month.

On 30 June Cecil Gilbertson wrote to Max Auschnitt [8 : 272] with a sketch of the proposed site, requested an accurate survey and the names of manufacturers of oil fired boilers.

Frank Gilbertson to Messrs Barlow, Barlow & Lyde. 2 July 1913 [8 : 274]

. . . On the whole we think we had better base our estimates upon the worst conditions we may have to meet, & then see what can be done to obtain better terms.

Probably Messrs. Besslers & Messrs. Auschnitt will be in the best position to approach the corrupt government of Roumania, & that we had better leave it to them.

Roumania remained neutral in the first Balkan War when the Balkan League attacked and defeated Turkey in October 1912, but in the second Balkan War in June 1913 Roumania joined Serbia and Greece and by the Treaty of Bucharest (August 1913) gained southern Dobrudja from defeated Bulgaria, with most of Macedonia going to Serbia and the rest to Greece.

Frank Gilbertson to Messrs Barlow, Barlow & Lyde. 20 Aug. 1913 [8 : 317-8]

Port Talbot Steel Co – Slag Contract

We are having some difficulty over the above & although our relations with the Co are very friendly & there is no likelihood of a rupture, we want to know our exact legal position so as to frame our correspondence.

We enclose copy of the contract & the correspondence leading to it.

The position of the Pig Iron & scrap markets have changed in a very unexpected way since the contract was made, & as a consequence the PT Co are making much more of the 7 to 9 percent grade & much less of the 9-10 percent.

The former is useless to us & we sell it in the rough state for export.

There are 2 difficulties:

(1) Too much of the 7 to 9 grade is made now for the market to absorb, & we cannot sell it as fast as the PT Co make it.

(2) We are not getting as much of the 9-10 grade as we require for grinding into manure to meet our trade.

We enclose copy of a recent letter in which the PT Co promise to try & help us to dispose of some of the low grade, but they admit no liability in respect of their output varying so tremendously from the estimate made when the contract was entered into.

We want you please to give your most careful consideration to the matter.

Frank Gilbertson to Theodore Gibbins, Melyn Tin Works, Neath. 6 Sept. 1913 [8 : 328-9]

Thank you for your private lines.

The position is not an easy one. People are running down their galvanized sheets worse even than tinplates.

At the present moment we have bought all the blackplates we can't roll, to fill our orders, but we had one very large enquiry this week which we know will be severely cut for & for which we quoted a price that has not brought business.

We will follow this up now & endeavour to obtain an offer.

If you will name the lowest price you would take for 200 tons of S/0 sheets monthly, Nov – Dec – Jan we will have our cost ready if we succeed in obtaining an offer for the galvanized sheets, & we should be prepared to do the business at a nominal profit to help keep standing charges down.

You would have to base your figures upon Bars at £4-16-3 d/d shearings arising at 50/- f.o.t.

Sheet & Tinplate bars are, & have always been, priced the same by the Association.

Frank Gilbertson to J. Vermont. **27 Sept. 1913 [8 : 353-4]**

Private

Thank you for your letter of 25th inst. I am much obliged to you for expressing yourself so fully.

I am however driven to the conclusion that a parcel of Ternes would assist your business just now by enabling you to discount a bill when you receive it from your buyer.

I don't feel that I am justified as a Director of this Company, & therefore to an extent a Trustee for the shareholders, in incurring any risk of a bad debt.

I have every confidence in your personal honour & in your exceptional business abilities, but events might prove too strong for you.

We have already shown our desire to help you in our mutual business by giving you 100 tons of ternes upon easy terms, & I reluctantly came to the conclusion that I should not do more.

Our correspondence will be kept strictly private, but I think you may not be unwise if you disclose it to Mr. Pilliner on his return, in case there is any more to be said.

Cecil Gilbertson to Messrs Abel & Imray. **6 Oct. 1913 [8 : 359]**

We enclose you a short description of an invention that we wish you to protect in the name of Messrs Francis William Gilbertson of Glynteg, Pontardawe, and Cecil Frederic Gilbertson of Abercrave House, Abercrave.

If the description is sufficient we should like to have it protected at once and we will then put the machine into work and see if it will answer its purpose.

Letter 8 : 360-1 describes details of 'An Invention for the Mechanical Boshing of Iron or Steel Bars'.

Frank Gilbertson to Messrs Richard Johnson, Clapham & Morris Ltd. **30 Oct. 1913 [8 : 377-8]**

Aluminium coated plates for France

We are sorry to say that there is a real hitch here.

For your private information we may say our process is not the same as Messrs Baldwins, but to avoid fighting, as we are on very friendly terms with them, we mutually agreed to accept a licence from them. To all intents & purposes therefore we must consider we have no rights beyond their licence.

It appears that the original inventor of Messrs Baldwins process, Alutol, reserved his rights in France as he sold his French Patent to somebody else.

If any party in France threatens you with proceedings it is probably because he has now acquired the French Patent, & we have to decide whether to ignore him & risk an action for infringement against yourselves & us.

After careful consideration we decide that we should not fight, & therefore we must abandon the French business. We are very sorry indeed to have caused you so much trouble, & we regret that we did not warn you at first. It should have been in our mind when you proposed the business, but it was not.

We are writing to our Continental friends who introduced the process to us, & if we have anything more to say on hearing from them we will write to you again.

Frank Gilbertson to W. Isaac Williams. **28 Nov. 1913 [8 : 398-9]**

Thank you for your letter of yesterday. The object of the meeting is to give Mr. Frank Thomas & the others an opportunity for a general discussion upon the work & methods of the Tinplate Association, with a view to their joining if they are satisfied. They will probably put forward some suggestions which the Trustees will have to consider & convey to the Executive Committee.

I believe it will not be difficult to meet Mr. Frank Thomas's views & in that case I think Mr. Paton will follow, & I know Messrs R. T. & Co's outside Works will.

Melingriffith is likely to follow their lead, & you will then be the only important Firm whose decision will be awaited.

If the meeting resulted in all these Firms joining the Association it would mean an addition of over 100 Mills, & would put the Association in a very strong position.

In my own view there are many directions in which the cost of tinplates could be reduced if the Association was able to negotiate with the Workmen's Unions with the knowledge that practically the whole trade was behind it.

P.S. Mr. Paton, Frank Thomas, Beaumont Thomas, F. W. Gibbins, Major Lewis & myself will attend & probably Mr. Spence Thomas.

Frank Gilbertson to H. C. Bond. **3 Jan. 1914 [8 : 461-3]**

Thank you for your letter. I think you are to be congratulated on your day's work.

I was rather doubtful about Byass, & his example will influence others.

I have seen Theodore Gibbins & have submitted to the full torrent of his eloquence for 2 hours.

He will make up his mind next Wednesday after meeting his Directors, but I shall be very surprised if he does not then agree to join, subject to approval of details. He strongly desires some later date than "a day in March" to be fixed for the commencement of the pool, as he has sold ahead very fully.

I notice in Wenham's Minutes received today that it is recorded as a resolution passed that the 6 months ended Dec 20th 1913 to be the period taken for basing allotment.

I was certainly under the impression that the basis of allotment would receive further consideration at the hands of the Committee, & I think it should.

We don't want more claims than necessary to go to the Arbitrator.

Several people suggested that the option of taking 1913 or 1912 would meet the case.

I am sure it would be wise to get Byass on the Committee.

I will urge Theo Gibbins to make up his mind on Wednesday so as to attend the Committee meeting on Thursday.

I would rather that an older man took the post of Vice Chairman & one with a larger stake in the trade, but I would not refuse if no one else would take it on.

Frank Gilbertson to Messrs Bessler, Waechter & Co. Ltd, Tinplate & Metal Merchants, London. **17 Jan. 1914 [8 : 443-4]**

We are much obliged by your letter of yesterday signed by Mr. Stükken.

We suggest that we may now carry on the correspondence as between our two firms. All our letters are opened by quite confidential Clerks.

We entirely approve of the arrangement you have made for one of your Staff to join the staff of the new Company & thank you.

We shall be glad to show him all we can here, but unfortunately we expect a strike in our galvanizing department on Monday, & as we do not intend to give way at all the plant may be idle for a short time.

With regard to spelter, probably your own judgement will be based on better information than we possess here. Our habit is to buy just to cover orders.

On the whole we should recommend buying all the spelter likely to be required for the new Company to the end of April.

We should also suggest covering in Blackplate, as we find a better tone down here & Pig Iron has advanced. A very little push is required to put Blackplate, Tinplates & Steel Bars to a higher level.

Frank Gilbertson to Messrs Bessler, Waechter & Co. Ltd. **19 Jan. 1914 [9 : 2]**

In reply to your favour of 17th inst, we agree to the alteration in the name of the new Company.

We regret that on this occasion it will not suit us to quote for the Blackplate required.

We do not agree that it would be prejudicial to the interests of the new Company for us to know the prices of our competitors, unless experience showed that we took the orders so often that outsiders gave up quoting competitive prices. This is not likely to be the case.

Cecil Gilbertson to Messrs Bessler, Waechter & Co. Ltd. **9 Feb. 1914 [9 : 12]**

Roumanian Sheet & Galvanizing Co. Ltd.

With reference to your letter of the 6th inst.
The two Directors we appoint to be above Company are
Mr. Francis William Gilbertson, of Glynteg, Pontardawe, Glamorgan, Steel Works Manager
and, Mr. Cecil Frederic Gilbertson, of Abercrave House, Abercrave, Breconshire, Steel Works Manager

The Roumanian Sheet & Galvanizing Company was registered on 5 February 1914 with a nominal capital of £75,000 divided into 7,500 shares of £10 each. The Register of Directors listed Sir Ralph C. Forster, Sir Harry Waechter, Osias and Max Auschnitt and Frank and Cecil Gilbertson. The Return of Share Allotments showed Bessler, Waechter & Co. holding 711 shares, R. C. Forster and H. Waechter taking 60 each, Osias and Max Auschnitt with 733 and 100 shares respectively, whilst H. M. Forster and A. Stükken held one share each. The Gilbertson holding totalled 833 shares. The Company was voluntarily wound up by special resolution on 2 July 1923 with the final winding up meeting on 11 June 1924 (P.R.O. BT 31 22041/133791).

Cecil Gilbertson to Messrs Bessler, Waechter & Co. Ltd. **21 Feb. 1914 [9 : 26-9]**

Galv. Company of Roumania

New Gal. Pot – We have received three quotations for this plant, viz.

Mr John Thompson	£350 f.o.b. Swansea
Messrs. Thompson Bros.	£210 f.o.b. Liverpool
The Lliw Forge Works	£350 f.o.b. Swansea.

We enclose you Messrs Thompson Bros' quotation which we advise the new Company to accept subject to the conditions we specify on attached sheet.

We get the best pots from this firm and they are the cheapest. They however do not include "furnace plates" in their quotation and they must be added.

Will you send them the official order for this plant please?

For Mr. Auschnitt's information we give the amount it would cost us to erect such a plant in our works here.

Foundations	Excavations	£0..10..0
	Concrete	£2.. 0.. 0
	Masonry	£2.. 8.. 0
	Mason's Labour	£1.. 2.. 0
Gal.Bath.	Masonry	£2.. 0.. 0
	Mason's Labour	£2.. 4.. 0
Dryer & Carrier	Masonry	£4..16..0
	Mason's Labour	£3.. 6.. 0
Fitters & B'smiths	Labour	£14..0..0
		£32..6..0

("Masonry" includes Bricks, Mortar & Clay)

The overhead driving gear, and its erection are not included, and will be extra, this depends upon the relative position of Mr. Auschnitt's Engine and shafting, to the position of the new pot. It could only be a matter of a few pounds in any case.

The total cost of this addition should therefore be,

	£. s. d.
Messrs. Thompson Bros. for Plant	210..0..0
Cost of erection in Roumania (say)	40..0..0
Cost of & erection of overhead gear (say)	10..0..0
	£260..0..0

Add Freight, insurance & cost of transit dock to works.
Add cost of furnace plates if not included by Thompson Bros.

In sending formal order please specify

1. The Pot is to be of same quality as those supplied to Messrs W. Gilbertson & Co. Ltd, and is to be made of plates 1¼" thick.
2. Furnace plates are to be included as shown on drawing.

Cecil Gilbertson to Messrs Bessler, Waechter & Co. Ltd. **25 Feb. 1914 [9 : 31]**

We are in receipt of your letter of the 23rd inst, enclosing letter from Mr. Osias Auschnitt which we return.

We gather from this letter that Mr. Goldenberg is willing to sign an agreement not to interest himself in any other Galvanizing business if we buy his plant at the price of £700 without any stipulation as to our allowing him a preference. That this agreement should be in force for 3 years at the end of which time should the Mills not be erected a fresh agreement would have to be entered into, and if the Mills are erected the question of preference in price would have to be dealt with.

We do not think there is anything unreasonable in this proposal and so far as we are concerned we would agree to it

Cecil Gilbertson to Messrs Bessler, Waechter & Co. Ltd. **26 Feb. 1914 [9 : 33]**

With reference to your letter of the 17th inst.

Will you kindly register our 833 shares in the names of

Mr. Francis William Gilbertson	60 shares
Mr. Cecil Frederic Gilbertson	60 "
Mr. Charles Geoffrey Gilbertson	30 "
Messrs W. Gilbertson & Co. Ltd.	683 "

Cecil Gilbertson to Messrs Bessler, Waechter & Co. Ltd. **5 March 1914 [8 : 521-2]**

We thank you for your letter of the 4th inst.

Thompson Bros. We note they are prepared to supply the plates at the price of £12/10/0 per ton f.o.b. Liverpool, and we would advise your accepting this.

Stocks. On looking through them we have compared the prices at which we would be prepared to sell Galvanized sheets c.i.f. Galatz for some of the principal lines.

2,088 bd's 60" x 30" x 12s x 40 bld per ton
Priced on Inventory at . . . . £18..17..0 per ton nett
Our price would be . . . . £16..10..0 " " "

6,190 bd's 34" x 23" x 22s x 40 bld per ton
Priced on Inventory at . . . . . £20.. 0..0 " " "
Our price would be . . . . £17.. 5..0 " " "

5,722 bd's 34" x 23" x 22s x 35 b1d per ton
Priced on Inventory at . . . . . £18..10.0 " " "
Our price would be . . . . £16.. 0..0 " " "

As Messrs Auschnitt's have guaranteed that their prices shall be at least 1 free[?] per bundle less than the price obtainable and we are only to pay 80% on account no doubt the prices on the Inventory are all right, but the difference is very large and we have based our prices on a basis that would give us a decent profit.

Frank Gilbertson to Henry Holford, Capital & Counties Bank. **10 March 1914 [8 : 524]**

In reply to your favour of 28th ulto. I have not yet had a chance to pay you the visit you suggest, & today my firm is asked to pay up in full for the shares allotted us by the Galvanizing Company of Roumania Ld.

We are therefore drawing a cheque on your Bank for £5,030.

Our overdraft will be round about this figure for a short time probably, until some of the Stocks accumulated during the strike are sent out & paid for.

As our investment a/c stood at about £28,000 before this investment in the Roumanian Co., we have no doubt you will make no difficulty about the overdraft & we thank you for the accommodation. The strike is now over, & successfully.

Cecil Gilbertson to Messrs Bessler, Waechter & Co. Ltd. **10 March 1914 [9 : 44]**

. . . cheque value £8,030 in full payment for 683 + 60 x 2. CGG will send his cheque direct.

Cecil Gilbertson to Joseph Vermont. **12 March 1914 [9 : 45-6]**

We are in receipt of your letter of the 7th inst and account.

No doubt you are aware that the proposed Rolling Mills in Roumania have been abandoned, at all events for the present and will not in any case be erected in Braila.

The actual work that you did for the proposed Company consisted of a day and a half at Pontardawe, & just the levelling of the site at Braila and the preparation of the plan for proposed Workmen's Cottages, which are not being proceeded with. Had these cottages been built & you given the supervision of their erection you would have been entitled to a commission, but for merely providing us with one copy of the plan (without any specification or detailed drawings) and for the levelling of the site and the short time you spent at these works we would suggest that £20 would be a reasonable remuneration and enclose you our cheque for this amount.

Frank Gilbertson to Arthur Stükken, Director, Messrs Bessler, Waechter & Co. Ltd. **17 March 1914 [9 : 48]**

. . . The reports of working in the new Works are not unsatisfactory, but the output is not as high as we were led to expect.

. . . We will supply a small quantity of the mixture we use in our Pots for Evans the Foreman to try & report on.

Frank Gilbertson to A. Stükken. 19 March 1914 [9 : 53]

We thank you for your letter of the 18th inst. and are glad you have caught Messrs. Goldenberg out. It certainly is very disgusting especially considering the liberal way in which the new Company have treated them.

Frank Gilbertson to A. Edwards, per Messrs Phillips & Hill, London. 23 March 1914 [8 : 538]

We beg to confirm the arrangement we mutually made at our interview last week. In consideration of your working in Japan, Manchuria & Korea in our interests, and using your best efforts to increase the sale of Comet Galvanized Sheets, we agree to pay you Two hundred and fifty a year, and fifty pounds for every 1,000 tons of Galvanized Sheets that we manufacture for that market in excess of 8,000 tons in any year. This arrangement to last for one year certain and afterwards either party to be able to terminate it without notice, but we may say we think the arrangement should suit us and that we should not be likely to bring it to an end unless we were both satisfied that it was no longer to our interest to continue it. It is understood that your activities will be confined to stimulating the demand for our brand and giving us information, and that you do not enter actual orders for Galvanized Sheets yourself.

Frank Gilbertson to A. Stükken. 27 March 1914 [9 : 56-7]

. . . The report is of course bad.

We think Mr. Böhringer should be told that from the point of manufacturing cost, nothing is so important as regular work & full outputs.

We quite understand the difficulty in this particular case, but knowing the very vague, dilatory & unpunctual character of the Roumanian nature, we think Mr. Böhringer should be warned to combat it as much as he can.

It is most certainly more economical to work one full week than two half weeks. We should like to know when the second Pot bought from Goldenberg's will start. Our experience is that the small sizes pay better than 60 x 30 & such sizes, & certainly there is better demand for them. Mr. Auschnitt seemed to us to be rather keener on big sizes than our experience of the market indicated.

We hope every possible effort will be made to look ahead in the matter of raw material requirements, so as to avoid as far as possible all stoppages of output.

We are glad to hear some decent sales have been made.

Goldenberg's are specifying 150 tons monthly at the moment, from us. Next year of course this business will go to the new Company.

Frank Gilbertson to S. Stükken. **7 April 1914 [9 : 61-2]**

We enclose an enquiry received today from Messrs Brooker Dore & Co.

We still get enquiries for decent lots of Galvanized Sheets for Roumania, & we should like to know if it is worth referring buyers to the Roumanian Galvanizing Co. Ld, at your address, for you to deal with.

Possibly some of them might have business to place & might be prepared to buy f.o.t. Galatz from the new Company. If you took this view, & if the new Company was unable to deal with all the business booked by it, we should at any time be willing to make a shipment to them, at a price that would yield them a Merchant's profit, & be glad to do so.

Cecil Gilbertson to Messrs. Bessler, Waechter & Co. Ltd. **15 April 1914 [8 : 567-8]**

With reference to your letter of the 14th inst and enclosures from Galatz.

Allowances of Spelter. 35 grammes per square foot is the allowance we suggested.

Store room. Without seeing the sketches we cannot give a definite opinion on the alterations Mr. Auschnitt suggests, but we think this may safely be left to Mr. Auschnitt to whom we explained fully our plans for the future extension. No doubt 4 metres is sufficient height for a store room, but would not be high enough for a satisfactory Pickling and Galvanizing shop. Mr. Auschnitt however is better able to judge the cost of increasing the height of this Building later on if required than we are. While the room is being used as a store room a galvanized sheet roof would not be unsatisfactory, but it would never last if it was placed in contact with pickling fumes.

Report for week March 30/April 14. We note the loss in spelter for this week. Certainly we get losses in some of our Pots some weeks which it is difficult to account for, but we would say that the Dippers have as much to do with the yield of a pot as anything else and if the Rolls were in good order and the sheets of good quality and the pickling satisfactory, it was probably due to bad workmanship on the part of the Dippers.

We do not weigh our stock of spelter weekly, it would be impossible, we weigh all spelter as it comes in and also as it is delivered to the Pots and if a careful account is kept of such weighings we always know exactly the stock we have.

We make out our yields every week for each Pot and think Mr. Böhringer would do well to do so and for the present at all events to forward us copies.

Dross. We note your remarks and agree that it would be hardly worthwhile bringing it back to Antwerp.

Frank Gilbertson to Theodore Gibbins. **17 April 1914 [8 : 564-6]**

In reply to yours of yesterday, I am not the Vice Chairman of the Galvanizers Conference and have no official position in it. I will however pass your remarks on to Mr. Summers.

As I read your letter I imagine you think your position is not commonly shared by other Manufacturers, but as a matter of fact I should say others were worse off than you.

Putting our Steel Works and Sheet Mills together we have actually lost money during the past six months upon the quantity of Steel consumed in those mills.

Today we have 6 mills idle in our works and shall have 6 idle next week again.

As you know, we are sometimes buyers and sometimes sellers of 6' x 3' black sheets, and we may tell you that we are sellers today, but we are absolutely unable to obtain a single order, as the business has gone to America.

In this line of trade you cannot justly blame any Galvanizer in Great Britain for the position of things.

With regard to Roumanian Roofers, we are also unable to obtain any orders but we do not for a moment believe they are going to Galvanized Sheet Makers.

They are being cut for by the big Tin Mills in our opinion, and the demand is also below the supply.

We may tell you for your own satisfaction that so far the Roumanian Galvanizing Co, in which we are interested, has not taken a single black sheet from us. The Company found plenty of Tinplate Works to quote prices that we did not care to touch. With regard to your proposal to put down Sheet Mills & Galvanizing plant, we think that if you saw our books for the past 12 months the project would not appeal to you, but in any case I am personally of opinion that any move on the part of a Tinplate Maker to Galvanize would break up both "Conferences", and would spell disaster to both trades for a very long period.

There is no doubt in both trades there are too many Mills built and it is only by everyone sacrificing his ambitions and reducing his output that we can live quietly through the difficult period we are in.

I know of my own knowledge that the Galvanizers have generally reduced their output and stopped Mills wholesale, but I will mention your complaint at the next meeting on May 20th, and if you have any definite information you would like Mr. Summers or myself to convey to any particular works I am sure we should be glad to do so. To give you an idea of what the 30 Gauge Galvanize Trade is like today I may tell you that while our normal output when working fully, is 700 tons a week, we have entered less than 400 tons of new business since January 1st.

In our view the intrinsic position of this trade cannot possibly be worse and it is only the existence of a Conference with the promise of better things as a result of its checking overproduction that could permit us to regard the future with any peace of mind at all.

Frank Gilbertson to Messrs. Roumanian Sheet & Galvanizing Co. Ltd, London. **20 April 1914 [9 : 65-6]**

We regret engagements will prevent our attending the Statutory Meeting on 24th. No doubt you will be able to arrange for a quorum?

Are any orders for Blackplate now being placed for the Galatz Works?

We should like to have the refusal of the next parcel.

The Writer will be in London between May 18 & 20 & would like to have a talk with Mr. Stükken over the present situation of the Works.

If you are not in possession of the information, perhaps you would ask for a report from the Works giving the dates upon which they hope to increase their output, & the prospects of the market.

We have frequent enquiries for Galvanized Sheets against which we do not quote but we think that unless the new Works can secure the bulk of the trade & can then cope with the demand, there is no valid reason why all the open orders should fall into other hands than ours!

Frank Gilbertson to Messrs Bessler, Waechter & Co. Ltd. **4 May 1914 [9 : 77-8]**

Referring to your letter of 1st inst. signed by Mr. Stükken. We are much obliged for the same.

We are acting now on the principle that if any Roumanian business comes to us at £14..10..0 basis, or over, from English Houses, we shall feel entitled for the present to take it.

We confess we do not expect much, if any business, but we shall now feel that you have no cause for grumbling!

We do not like seeing Mr. Edwards &c quite busy on these sheets, when our interest is confined to a third of the profit of 1 Pot in Galatz, our old trade having been the output of 3 Pots here!

We are glad to hear the second Pot will be at work at Galatz in say 3 weeks. It would seem to us that some avoidable delay had taken place . . .

Cecil Gilbertson to B. J. Ackerley. **25 May 1914 [8 : 627-8]**

Private

You may have heard that a new Company has been formed to take over and re-start the Aberdulais Works (Joshua Williams & Co.), and we as a firm have taken a small interest in this concern. Our interest is taken more from the point of view of a Bar Maker, than from any hopes of obtaining a good return on our investment, but of course having some interest in the concern now we are anxious to help in any way we can to make it a success.

You asked me when I saw you in Liverpool whether I knew what was likely to happen to the place, and at that time I had no idea, this move has entirely come about since that date. I gathered from you that the company at one time did a considerable business through you in Blackplate and that for some time their deliveries gave every satisfaction, but that of late promises had been broken and you had had a good deal of trouble getting their Contracts attended to.

The new Company is composed of entirely different people and we [expect?] that the Works will be capably managed.

Considerable alterations will be undertaken in the Boiler plant and Machinery before the Works will be restarted, but quite as a guess they may probably start work again in the Autumn.

The new Company will have to consider what class of trade it will suit them best to compete for, and it is really to ask your advice upon this matter that I am writing to you. In the past I understand they have gone in for very thin plates and the workmen are accustomed to such specifications and are quite capable of turning out good makes and good work in light orders.

I should greatly appreciate any information you could give me about the quality of the work turned out by the Aberdulais Works in late years and whether in your opinion they have any brands that hold a good reputation in the market, and also whether the name of "Joshua Williams and Co." is one that would be likely to influence any business.

Frank Gilbertson to J. H. Strick, — 2 June 1914 [8 : 638-9]
Messrs. Cardonnel Tinplate Co. Ltd., Skewen, Neath.

<u>Tinplate Conference</u>*

I had a talk with Sir Thomas Ratcliffe Ellis who pointed out to me that he had no power to give any allotment to anyone who was not a Member of the Conference, & was not in a position to make a bargain.

He said it would be necessary for your Firm to join the Conference before he could make any allotment or take any official note of any figures.

He told me unofficially that he would give your Firm a gross allotment equal to 775 boxes per Mill per week on the figures I mentioned to him, but this is private & please regard it as such.

Are you willing to take my word on it & to apply for membership in the ordinary way? I am afraid I can't go further, but you may rely upon it that if you apply for membership you will receive the allotment I have named.

I am sure you will appreciate his position & see that he cannot act differently to any Firm to the way he treated the original members – who had to join unconditionally.

**A scheme to counteract falling prices by regulating output through pooling and allocating orders.*

Frank Gilbertson to Sir Walter Lawrence Bt. 5 June 1914 [8 : 647-50]

Business in Galvanized Sheets and Tinplates is so extraordinary bad that we have decided to seek some other outlets for part of our production.

Ten or twelve years ago we used to make a good deal of Steel for electrical purposes – the steel was rolled into sheets and we stamped the sheets into Armature Discs, and various special shapes for the Electrical Works. The number of patterns became so large that the business was not profitable because the largest users did their own stamping, and the requirements of the smaller makers were all different.

We then abandoned the manufacture entirely, but the experience of some two or three years work was that we could supply the very special quality of steel required for this work with ease and regularity.

I am now very anxious to re-enter the trade, and to supply the large works with Sheets, not Stampings.

At present the business is almost, if not entirely, confined to Sankeys of Bilston, and Lysaght of Newport, and I have reason to believe that the production being so restricted, the prices are very high, and very profitable.

I think it is obviously to the interest of the big Electrical Firms that an additional competitor should enter the market, and your connection with Messrs. Siemens gives us the opportunity for asking for information from them if they consider it to be to their interest to give it us.

We have approached some of the big makers, and we are shortly going to send round some samples of our electrical sheets for them to test, but we are not able to get from them all the general information we require to make our plans.

We want to know the following points:

No. 1. The approximate quantity used in one year, separated into the different gauges, by one big Firm.

No. 2. The present selling price.

No. 3. The extreme limits of dimension for each gauge separately.

No. 4. A sample of the sheets that now give satisfaction, in two different gauges. The lightest in use whether 30, 31 or 32, and an averagely heavy sheet such as 24 or 26 gauge.

We particularly want some samples so as to ascertain what change in composition of the steel if any, has been found to suit the Manufacturers since the time we did the business ten or twelve years ago.

We also want to know the price because we believe the business has been kept in very few hands, and that quite a fancy price is obtainable.

Our idea would be that if our quality suited the works, we might enter a quantity of sheets at about 5/- a ton less than they are at present paying, in return for the assistance given us at the start.

If the business developed the consumers would have a constant advantage in the addition of a large maker to their present sources of supply, and prices would of course tend to be reduced by the competition.

We have to feel our way a little cautiously because the electrical steel of the quality we used to make is very soft indeed, and very soft steel in large sizes is not easily rolled into very thin plates because such soft steel tends to stick when the plates are rolled in packs in the Mills.

Perhaps you would be disposed to discuss the matter with your Colleagues, and if you thought there was any prospect of Messrs. Siemens benefiting from our entry into the trade, one of our Staff might be permitted to visit your Works if you think the information could be best obtained that way.

Personally I look upon the matter as an important one from our point of view, and should like to take our Chemist to the Works at Stafford, myself.

On 4 August 1914 Britain declared war on Germany.

Frank Gilbertson to Messrs Parrs Bank Ltd. — 10 Aug. 1914 [8 : 750-1]

Referring to yours of 8th inst. We had better explain & you will understand.

We take it that our duty is to provide employment for our Workmen as much as possible.

Today we are very heavily stocked & have £25,000 worth of goods awaiting shipment & payment at Ports.

We see the possibility of running considerably into stock & getting no money in.

At present the balance at our Banks is small, & if the need of overdrawing should become pressing we should overdraw at the Bank which provides us with cash for our wages.

It will therefore save trouble if you hand our securities to the Capital & Counties Bank & for them to forward to their Neath branch for safe custody for us – very likely no deposit of securities will be wanted by them, but in the present state of affairs we should prefer that they should hold them, & we are sending them those we keep here.

P. Davies to Henry Holford, Messrs Capital & Counties Bank Ltd, Neath. — 12 Aug. 1914 [8 : 753]

We enclose herewith the undermentioned securities for safe custody on our account, as arranged with our Principal. Please acknowledge receipt.

£2,350 – Alexandra (Newport & South Wales) Docks & Railway Co. 4½% Preferred Consolidated "B" Stock
£2,000 – Rhymney Railway Preferred Ordinary Stock

£1,518 – Ordinary Shares of £1 each (fully paid) Vickers Ltd.
£300 – 30 of 6% Preference Shares of £10 each (fully paid) Pockett's Bristol Channel Steam Packet Co. Ltd.
£8,030 – 803 Ordinary Shares of £10 each (fully paid) Roumanian Sheet & Galvanizing Co. Ltd.
£2,395 – Ordinary Shares of £1 each (fully paid) J. & C. Holcroft Ltd.
£1,000 – 100 Shares of £10 each (fully paid) Aberdulais Tinplate Co. Ltd.

P. Davies to Henry Holford, Neath **13 Aug. 1914 [8 : 753]**

We are informed by Messrs. Parrs Bank Ltd, that they have handed the undermentioned securities to The Capital & Counties Bank Ltd., London, to be forwarded to your branch at Neath, for safe custody on our account.

Kindly let us have your receipt for same.

£5,000 Stock Receipt, Natal 3½% 1934/44
£3,000 Cape of Good Hope 4% Debentures
£3,000 Queensland 4% Debentures
£5,000 Buenos Ayres & Pacific Railway First Debenture Stock
£2,500 Canada 3½% 1930/50 Stock

Frank Gilbertson to Messrs Barlow, Barlow & Lyde, Solicitors. **15 Aug. 1914 [8 : 757]**

What is the position in regard to Contracts entered into before the war with German Firms?

We have bought Pig Iron & have sold Galvanized Sheets.

Are the contracts necessarily cancelled?

Can either party demand cancellation when the war is over & trade resumed?

The probability is that at the end of the war present contracts will be in favour of British buyers of German Pig Iron & against sellers of British Galvanized Iron.

Frank Gilbertson to Messrs Bessler, Waechter & Co. Ltd. **25 Aug. 1914 [8 : 761-2]**

Private

In reply to your favour of the 22nd inst. re. the R. S. & G. Co. The position is undoubtedly a very difficult one. Our opinion is that unless buyers are able to take up the Sheets by the time delivery is due, or within a reasonable time afterwards, they can justly refuse to permit an extension, and can cancel such portions as have not been taken up.

It is of course within all our knowledge that where the situation is reversed buyers invariably retain the right to cancel undelivered balances, unless non-delivery was caused by strikes, accidents, or other causes within the particular clauses of the contract – financial difficulties and shipping difficulties such as now confront the trade are not contemplated by the strike and accident clause. Our position is that our finances will be strained for the next 6/8 weeks, as we are getting very few payments in and are making our normal payments out, having also to receive and pay for large supplies of American Iron, but it would seem to us to be good business to take up some of these Sheets when we can conveniently do so, and we will open the matter with you later on when our problem is clearer.

We suggest that you protest as far as you can against the cancellation of any of these Sheets, and at any rate only permit such quantities to be cancelled as cannot be avoided. It would not be unreasonable to insist on August deliveries being taken in September, and running September into October and so on.

The prices at which you purchased are very considerably below cost; you will of course understand the Sheets would be of no use to us, and if we took any of these up, we should have to store them until the R. S. & G. Co. were in a position to re-purchase them from us at prices to be arranged upon an equitable basis. We cannot yet say for certain that we can adopt such a course, as it will depend upon how we are able to get money in during the next 6 weeks.

Frank Gilbertson to Henry Holford, Capital & Counties Bank, Neath. **27 Aug. 1914 [8 : 763-4]**

Personal

I have had a rough estimate made of our financial position.

I find after paying our debts on Sept 1st & receiving the payments then due to us, our accounts with you will be overdrawn about £5,000.

During September we shall pay out for wages & some material £7,000 & shall receive only about £5,000 to £7,000 in.

It is however quite probable that we shall be able to arrange for shipment of a large boat of American Pig Iron due to us at a very low price.

If we succeed in getting this boat we may require a further £11,000 to pay for it before the end of September.

In those circumstances our accounts may be overdrawn £15,000 to £17,000 at the end of September, but on Oct 1st we are due to receive £20,000 for Steel rolled this month, & shall only be paying perhaps £10,000 out, reducing our overdraft to £5,000 to £7,000. By Nov 1st very heavy payments will be due to us for Steel & our accounts should show a considerable credit.

If at any time some of our foreign debts were paid, or if any of our galvanized iron now locked up at Ports was shipped, there should be an improvement in our estimate of the position.

As you hold a considerable total of Stock for us & as we do not overdraw at Parr's Bank, I presume you will be able to give us the accommodation outlined?

We are very heavily stocked with material that has all been paid for in cash & we are working it up now at a very satisfactory rate.

Cecil Gilbertson to Messrs Bessler, Waechter & Co. Ltd. **2 Sept. 1914 [9 : 107-8]**

We thank you for your letter of the 1st inst. enclosing copies of Reports from the R. S. G. Co. & also of Mr. Bohringer's letter of Aug. 23/5.
Registration Fees. We think you have done all it is necessary to do in way of protest re above, & we agree to the claim being passed.
Yields. We note Mr. Bohringer's explanations. No doubt the inexperience of the workmen is the principal factor. At the present time it is impossible to send any of our men out there, but we certainly think it would be advisable to send one of our Foremen out as soon as it is possible to do so, in order that we may be satisfied there is no blame due to the method of working, beyond the inexperience of the men.

Of course such things as leaky Pots, and dial stoppages are necessarily bad for the Yield and these should be tackled at once. We note the Bath is to be changed. We should like Mr. Auschnitt to be pressed to consider some scheme for driving our plant independently of his own. We are so much in the dark here it is most difficult for us to make recommendations, but there must be some way of providing a constant supply of power sufficient for our small requirements.

Frank Gilbertson to Messrs Barlow, Barlow & Lyde. **30 Oct. 1914 [8 : 802]**

Messrs Carl Lunds are trying to obtain tinplates for ultimate use by the German Army.

It is therefore probable that they have established Bank Credits in this country.

Have you any means of ascertaining if they have funds at the Credit Lyonnaise against which you could use the garnishee order?

It is probable that there are Tinplates destined for them at Swansea stopped by the Customs Authorities, but we should not imagine these plates would be paid for until shipping documents were obtained, & therefore that they would not yet actually belong to Carl Lunds.

W. G. & Co. had traded with Carl Lunds Fabriker of Copenhagen "for 20 or 30 years till a dispute brought it to an end" [8 : 808], with Gilbertson being owed a substantial amount by Lunds for delivered orders. See Chap. 2 [7 : 841] dated 7 February 1912.

Frank Gilbertson to A. Hethey. **2 Nov. 1914 [8 : 804]**
Messrs British Mannesmann Tube Co., Ltd.

We have been considering the question of steel supplies & we can see that if we are eventually to cope with your requirements without keeping our own Mills idle, we shall have to build an entirely new Furnace.

We are quite prepared to do this if means could be found of ensuring for us a continuance of your orders under all conditions at some sliding scale arrangement of prices.

At the same time we feel that with your extensions at Newport it might be in our mutual interests to consider joining hands & putting down a couple of furnaces at a convenient spot together.

We think we have shown you that we are most anxious for closer relations & we should be glad to talk either of these matters over with you if you care to do so.

Charles Gilbertson to Messrs Bessler, Waechter & Co. Ltd. **2 Nov. 1914 [9 : 109-11]**

. . . With regard to Mr. Böhringer's letter of Sept 15/28.

We notice in the last paragraph he says that the Works will probably have to be closed and the Englishmen sent home. Does he mean that the men will be discharged, or that they will be sent home on leave as it were, still in receipt of wages?

In any case kindly ask Mr. Böhringer to advise us at once when the men leave for England as we wish to see the English Foreman, and go through a number of points with him.

We shall be able, by means of a personal interview with the Foreman, to arrive at a very much better knowledge of the state of things out there than we can by correspondence.

Charles Gilbertson to Messrs Bessler, Waechter & Co. Ltd. **18 Nov. 1914 [9 : 114-5]**

. . . We think that the men Lawrence and Williams are entitled to their expenses home, and from what you say in your letter the amount they ask is not excessive.

With regard to Evans, we think that he should be instructed to call on us as soon as he returns home. We shall endeavour to find him some work though the rate of wages we should be able to pay him would be considerably less than what he has been earning in Roumania.

We think that the Roumanian Company should make some arrangements to make good a portion of the balance so as to provide Evans with the wage which he is prepared to accept in order to keep him in the services of the Roumanian Company.

We consider it very important that the Roumanian Company should not lose Evans' services.

With regard to the Dippers Lawrence and Williams who have returned home, it is quite possible that they will be able to obtain employment in this country for the time being and they would very likely be willing to return to Roumania when the Works restarted.

Charles Gilbertson to Messrs Roumanian Sheet & Galvanizing Co. Ltd. **1 Jan. 1915 [9 : 123-6]**

In reply to your letter dated Dec 24th 1914, experience of six months work in Roumania has established the fact that the cost of manufacturing Galv. sheets in Roumania is so much higher than the cost of manufacturing in England, that the present duty on Galv. sheets is not sufficient to protect the native industry.

The extra cost arises from the following causes –

1. Fuel costs are much higher in Roumania.
2. Duty on all articles used in manufacture.
3. Freight charges.
4. Native labour is not yet used to industrial pursuits – is less efficient.
5. Many more men are required in Galatz than England.
6. A certain number of skilled English workmen have to be employed, who will not work in a foreign country unless they are paid higher wages than they are accustomed to earn at home.

As regards the actual extra cost –

It has been ascertained by six months' work that the extra cost of manufacturing in Galatz over the cost of manufacturing similar sheets in our works here, in Wales, is as follows:-

Extra cost of the Blackplate used for making one ton of Galvanized sheets		£3. 1. 3
(N.B. This is occasioned by freight on Welsh Blackplate to Galatz	£1. 1. 0	
Insurance and Dock dues	7. 6)	
Extra cost of Wages		10. 0
" " " Spelter (due to freight & duty)		1. 0.11
" " " Ammonium Chloride		9
" " " Coke		2.11
" " " Rents, Taxes & general charges		7. 4
" " " Engines & Machinery (1.2 cost of		
" " " Motive power – repairs, renewals)		5. 0
" " " Sulphuric Acid		2. 5
		£5.10. 7

Against this extra cost of manufacturing Galv. sheets in Galatz we have protection in the Import Duty equal to £3-6-8 per ton, & the cost of conveying Galv. Sheets from Swansea to Galatz, freight, Insurance, & Dock dues, amounting to, say, £1-8-6.

Total – £4-15-2

Difference – £0-15-5

Therefore, unless the Import Duty into Roumania on Galv. sheets is included, the English Galv. sheet can always be delivered into Galatz 15/5 a ton cheaper than the Roumanian Galv. sheet can be manufactured in Galatz, & the native Industry cannot increase & is in danger of being discontinued.

Charles Gilbertson to Messrs Roumanian Sheet & Galvanizing Co. Ltd. **1 Jan. 1915 [9 : 127]**

With regard to your letter of Dec 24/1914 we have dealt with the question of Galv. sheets in another letter.

From our experience of manufacturing in Roumania, we have come to the conclusion that the manufacturing of black plate would be undesirable, in fact almost impossible. Serious extra costs have to be faced in manufacturing a Galvanized sheet, which is comparatively simple.

These extra costs would be considerably magnified in manufacturing Black plate, & the difficulty of labour would be almost insurmountable. We consider therefore that, at any rate for the present, no extra duty should be imposed on imported blackplate, so as not to increase the cost of the Galv. sheet.

Charles Gilbertson to Messrs Bessler, Waechter & Co. Ltd. **1 Jan. 1915 [9 : 128]**

In reply to yours of the 28th ult. we enclose a reply to the letter from the R. S. G. & Co. Ltd.

Will you kindly pass it on. You will note that we reply separately with regard to Galv. sheets & blackplates, because we consider that whereas it would be advisable to get an increased duty on Galv. sheets, it would be unwise to get an increased duty on blackplate.

The difficulties that have come to light in manufacturing Galv. sheets, which is a comparatively simple process, lead us to the decision that to manufacture black plate in Roumania would present such difficulties as to make the manufacture of them undesirable, if not impossible.

Frank Gilbertson to Messrs Barlow, Barlow & Lyde. **5 March 1915 [8 : 871]**

Referring to the enclosed cutting, we are sending you herewith copies of three invoices for Galvanized Sheets shipped before the outbreak of War on account of German firms, and for which we are still awaiting payment. Will you kindly present our claim for these amounts to the proper Authorities at the Colonial Office, and do all you can to protect us in the matter? You will see that the latest date for receiving claims is March 31st, and we are under the impression that these German houses have their branch business houses in British West Africa.

Frank Gilbertson to Herbert Eccles. **29 March 1915 [8 : 896-7]**

It seems possible that the little Silica Brick Works owned by Mr. James in Morriston can be bought from the Bank for about £1,250 – The quality of brick we always found to be very good.

I should be rather disposed to go into the matter if your Company cared to join. I am sorry for James, & Lloyd, who has been carrying on the commercial management & who has lost money in the concern, & if people like you & I got control we might do the fair thing by James & Lloyd & give them some interest in a new Company & retain their services.

If it is merely sold by the Bank to the highest bidder no money would be shown to James & Lloyd & the place would fall into the hands of the Silica Brick Combine. I think an early decision is necessary, & if you thought anything of it we might look at the Works together.

Frank Gilbertson to General Meehan, Woolwich Arsenal. **15 April 1915 [8 : 902]**

Mr. Hethey of the British Mannesmann Tube Co., has kindly given me your name, as I wished to communicate a matter to someone who would know if it was of any interest or not.

A young man, Mr. Owen, of this village has designed a type of shell that he believes might be useful in attacking Air Ships, & a model has been made here & is sent you with this (per parcel post).

It is suggested that the Arms will spring apart on leaving the gun, & that on piercing the envelope they will give the necessary pull to fire an explosive or an inflammatory charge.

The model explains itself & perhaps you would be so kind as to examine it?

Frank Gilbertson to L. Byass, Mansel Works, Port Talbot. **30 April 1915 [8 : 909-10]**

I hope you wont mind my writing to urge you all I can to reconsider your decision to retire from the Tinplate Conference.

If you would only remain in until the end of the year, at any rate, it would be such a useful lead to some who are wavering.

I feel as sure as I can be that the Tinplate trade has benefited by the conference methods, since January, to quite a large extent. Your trade will I suppose not return in its old volume during the War, & perhaps it will be no actual sacrifice to you to remain in for a time, & it certainly may influence others.

Apart from prices, we must remember we have to deal with a very hot headed man in Beaumont Thomas & I am very much afraid that if the Conference breaks down, his annoyance will lead him to do something rash in the Tinplate Association, & it would be a disaster if the end of the War found us Employers again divided in our dealings with the men.

Apart from yourself 31 Mills I believe have given notice, & some of them say it was only a precautionary measure.

You know more about business than I do, & I can't produce any arguments that you have not already considered, but personally I do beg you will try it again if you can.

P. Davies to Messrs Abel & Imray, London. **3 May 1915 [8 : 911]**

Referring to your notice of 26th April regarding Luxembourg Patent 9035/11, we have decided that in view of the present conditions of affairs on the Continent not to renew this Patent in Luxembourg, kindly note.

Frank Gilbertson to W. N. Jones, Hotel Cecil, Strand, London. **10 May 1915 [8 : 916]**

Raglan Collieries

I am obliged by your favour of 8th enclosing copy of letter from The Treasury dated 7th.

It would appear that The Treasury does not at all appreciate the bearing of our proposals on the gravity of the present situation in South Wales.

When the Raglan Colliery [at Heol-y-cyw, near Bridgend] stopped at the commencement of the War, there was only enough Gas Coal to just go round the South Wales Steel Works, and after the stoppage there was a serious shortage, which was accentuated as Steel Works resumed normal operations.

The four Steel Works who are behind the new Raglan Co. believe that the reopening of the Colliery is essential to their trade.

I can only speak of my own Firm, and I can say that my output of certain forms of special steel, required by the War Departments is limited by the quantity of good Gas Coal I can obtain. We are unable to obtain enough Gas Coal and have to import inferior qualities from the Forest of Dean to keep our Steel furnaces going.

This quality of coal will not permit of our making Steel for Shells, Boiler Tubes, Gas bottles, Steam pipes, and various gun parts, for which purposes we are supplying many of the chief firms with our material, and all are crying out for increased deliveries. Our output of deep stamping tinplates is also curtailed from want of the proper quality of Gas Coal.

No doubt when the Treasury learn these facts, and are made aware the proposed new Company makes no public issues, but simply consists of four large Steel Works, providing for their own requirements of a necessary raw material, they will reconsider their objection.

I should be glad if you would hand this letter to the proper authorities.

P. Davies to W. N. Jones, Dyffryn House, Ammanford. **22 May 1915 [8 : 924]**

We beg to enclose cheque value £4,000 drawn in favour of the British Wagon Co. Ltd., being balance of present amount due from us as our share of the purchase price for the Raglan Collieries.

Frank Gilbertson to H. C. Bond, Wargrave Court, Berks. **22 May 1915 [8 : 925-8]**

I write to you as I do not know Mr. Beaumont Thomas's present address. Perhaps you could send this on to him.

We met at Cwmfelin Office yesterday afternoon & considered the offer Mr. W. N. Jones brought us, as a result of his interview with Mr. Hirsch.

We were offered 38,500 20/- shares in the Coytrahen Park Colliery [near Tondu, Bridgend] at a price of £55,000.

Mr. Hirsch makes a condition that we should buy Mr. Eller's shares, which number 1250 at the same rate if the latter wishes to sell.

We accepted the offer on certain conditions which carry out the promises made by Mr. Hirsch at the interview & which include his undertaking to obtain due transference & registration of the shares, the appointment of our nominees on the Board before his group retires, & the undertaking that no forward sales of coal be made without our concurrence.

Practically the output is free from July 1st.

Since yesterday we have decided to meet again on Tuesday at 10.30 am at Cwmfelin to consider the question of the other shares held by neutral parties, 6250 in number, which we are likely to have offered to us at the same rate.

It appears that £17,500 has been paid on the wagons & that we shall have the benefit of the profits that have accrued in recent months which is stated to be over £2000 a month on the old selling prices.

It appears that 23/- to 24/- is likely to be the price of gas coal for the next quarter, & we are of opinion that the larger interest we can acquire in the concern the better.

The area is 1500 acres, not 1000 as I told you.

The Cwmfelin Co. & ourselves will put in £25,000 each & Messrs Lewis & Sons probably £10,000. I said that your Firm would consider increasing your holding to £15,000.

As a matter of form it may be necessary for us all to put our quota into the two undertakings Raglan & Coytrahen separately, as it appears unlikely that we shall be allowed to form the Raglan Co., with a substantial capital – The Treasury have again refused their sanction.

We have handed Mr. W. N. Jones £12,000, between us, to complete the purchase of Raglan, & if registration is long delayed he will have to work the Colliery as our Trustee.

Seeing that the concern is now assuming a different shape, & that the output is going to be very large if the combined undertakings & the Share Capital is not quickly held, we are all of the opinion that the clause dealing with disposal of profits should be altered, so that after the various allocations decided from year to year by the Board, &c, the balance be divided as to 3 parts to the ordinary shareholders, & as to 1 part to the consuming shareholders in proportion to the coal they consumed.

This I think will appeal to you as a fair arrangement?

We are of opinion that in the present circumstances there is no need to invite any other party to join us. If we get the control of Coytrahen the immediate profits of the fully going concern will be large, & will provide cash for future contingencies.

Frank Gilbertson to The Manager, Capital & Counties Bank, Neath. **24 May 1915 [8 : 929]**

. . . We like our Bankers to know what we are doing & we may say that our object in selling securities is to have a large sum free to invest in certain coal undertakings to ensure our due supplies.

Without such provision we consider the future position of our Works to be rather difficult & we believe the steps we are taking will make our position quite secure.

Charles Gilbertson to Messrs The Roumanian Sheet &Galvanizing Co. Ltd. **31 May 1915 [8:933]**

We are in receipt of your letter of 28th inst.

We are glad to note that the blackplates are being sold at good prices.

We will get Evans, the foreman, before he returns to Roumania, to call here & go fully into the process of manufacturing Sulphate of Iron.

We will also provide him with a plan, showing a suitable plant for a couple of Galv. pots.

Frank Gilbertson to Blackett. **1 June 1915 [8 : 934-6]**

Mr. W. N. Jones has had interviews with you in regard to application for permission to register a new Company to be known as "The Raglan Collieries Ltd".

I think it may be desirable for me to add certain information.

My Firm manufactures Steel, Galvanized Sheets & Tinplates.

The Galvanized Sheet branch is practically idle owing to the market conditions, but the Steel Works is pressed on all sides for its full output.

We make a special matter of certain qualities of Steel that are being used by the British Mannesmann Tube Co. & by various Sheffield & Midland consumers for urgent War Office & Admiralty work.

These qualities of Steel can not be made by us unless the furnaces are working at their very best, & that condition is unobtainable unless we have sufficient Gas coal of the best quality.

At present the output of Gas coal is not sufficient for South Wales.

For the month of April we had to use over 20% of our total requirements in second rate qualities from the Forest of Dean, & when using that coal we were unable to produce the special steels required for War purposes.

Our output at present is approximately as follows, per week:

A	British Mannesmann Tube Co. Steel Ingots	250 tons
B	High Carbon Billets & Ingots for Sheffield &c.	500 "
C	Tinplates	200 "
D	Sheets, Black, Painted or Galvanized	200 "
E	Tinplate Bars & Sheet Bars	600 "

Against the 250 tons sent to the British Mannesmann Tube Co. we have urgent calls from them for up to 700 tons, & all our Sheffield buyers are calling on more of our Special Carbon & Alloy Steels. If we had full supplies of the best gas coal we could increase the manufacture of Classes A & B at the expense of E, which would certainly assist the War Departments.

Please place these facts before Lord St. Aldwyn's Committee & ask for a reconsideration of the case.

Frank Gilbertson to Messrs Barlow, Barlow & Lyde. **3 June 1915 [8 : 939-40]**

We have noticed an occasional reference in the Newspapers to a proposal to satisfy enemy debts in this country by distributing enemy property.

Would you watch developments for us & note that the following sums are owed us by enemy firms, chiefly Hamburg Agents & Merchants for Tinplates & Galvanized Sheets duly delivered & shipped, but not paid for.

Particulars of amounts owing by German Houses

Bromberg & Co	Hamburg	980.19. 2
ACL Fraeb	do	248. 8. 9
Oetling Gebrüder	do	291. 4. 1
Nelson & Moritz	do	136. 2. 1
Westphalen & Co	do	64.16. 0
G.L. Gaiser	do	345. 0. 0
Gustav Güntzel	do	371.10. 8
Riensch & Held	do	44. 3. 0
Behrens & Wehner	do	36.14. 4
Augustuso de Freitas	do	18. 8. 9

P. Davies to Messrs The Capital & Counties Bank Ltd., Swansea. **3 June 1915 [8 : 941]**

s.s. "Dixiana"

We confirm 'phonic conversation, and will send remittance to lift these documents as soon as we have received the official proof of the loss of the boat. We have asked The United States Steel Products Co., to let us have this.

Charles Gilbertson to W. Evans, Llaneurwg, Copper Works Rd, Llanelly. **17 June 1915 [9 : 144-5]**

We have been in correspondence with our friends in London, with regard to what salary or retaining fee should be paid to you until you return to Roumania.

Seeing that the works are at a stand-still, they are loath to pay out in wages more than is absolutely necessary.

If it was possible for you to find some temporary work, that would be the best way of dealing with the question.

But we quite realise that, as the galvanizing trade is almost dead at the moment, you will not be able to find any work likely to suit you. We must therefore pay you such a wage as will enable you to live until you are able to return to Roumania.

You realise that we value your services in Roumania, and are anxious to retain your services, to return there as soon as the works restarts. Would you consider 30/- to 35/- per week a reasonable amount?

You will understand that we are not in a position to suggest as liberal an amount as we might wish to do under ordinary circumstances, as owing to the war, the Roumanian works are at a stand-still. You must let us know, quite frankly, what your position is, and how our suggestion attracts you.

Possibly you could supplement it to some extent, by picking up a temporary job from time to time.

Whatever amount is agreed upon, will be sent you by cheque, monthly.

Frank Gilbertson to T. E. Argile, Swansea. **26 June 1915 [8 : 977]**

I beg you will excuse my interference in a matter that concerns our neighbours the Glanrhyd Tinplate Co. Ltd. I do so because their Managing Director is an old Secretary of my Firm's, and as I am at present acting Chairman of the Tinplate Manufacturers Association I think the interests of our members concern me.

I understand your Company have summoned the Glanrhyd Tinplate Co. Ltd., for wrong declaration of weights of tinplates consigned to Swansea.

I understand the Company has no defence and that the incorrect weights are admitted and are so glaring and far removed from any probable weight of the consignments in question that any suggestion of deliberate cheating on the Company's part is quite out of the question.

It appears to be a case of a most incompetent and foolish servant, and insufficient supervision.

I want to be allowed to suggest that to take such a case into Court brings undeserved odium on the Company and its Directors, and that the matter might quite properly be met by an adjustment of the accounts and a payment of the actual expenses incurred in eliciting the facts. Although the Company is responsible for its servant's actions, there is no proportion between its responsibility in such a matter and the damage to its reputation that a public action would entail.

If the facts you hold are the same as have been put before me it would appear that the incorrect consignments were so glaring that a challenge at any time would have shown the Management what was going on.

Would you kindly put my communication before the proper authority?

Frank Gilbertson to H. J. Munro, 84 Grantham Road, Stockwell, London. **5 July 1915 [8 : 1002-3]**

. . . We confirm our offer of the post of Engineer of all these Works to you at a salary of £500 a year.

We suggest that the engagement be subject to one month's notice on either side until you have been here some little time, when if both parties are agreeable an agreement for a period might be arranged.

We wish to have you here at the earliest possible moment.

At present we are almost entirely engaged in Government work, & we have been ordered to undertake at once the manufacture of round bars for high explosive shells, so that you can consider your services will be used at once for the most important Government work. Much of our work is directly for the British or Allied governments, & most of the rest is indirectly for them.

P. Davies to Messrs Barlow, Barlow & Lyde, London. **12 July 1915 [10 : 6-8]**

We are sending you herewith particulars of loss suffered by us in consequence of the s.s. "Dixiana", being torpedoed by a German Submarine, as per copy of Certified Protest herewith.

Our Principal asks if you would kindly send in our claim in regards to the "Dixiana" to the Claim Department of the Foreign Office, as he observed from the reply given in the House of Commons to a question bearing upon such losses sustained by Traders, it is possible that the Government might decide to assist Traders who have suffered heavily from the operations of the enemy submarines.

Kindly follow up this matter on our behalf.

<u>Particulars of Claim by W. Gilbertson & Co., Limited</u>
4,500 Tons . . . Basic Iron sold to W. Gilbertson & Co. Ltd.
for delivery c.i.f. Swansea, by the –
United States Steel Products Co.,
36-38 New Bond Street,
London. E.C.
Their Invoice April 17th 1915 – No. 17320
Basic Iron shipped per "Dixiana" 7,751. 9.11
Cost of Insurance, War Risk only, Policy No.
1665994, with Maritime Insurance Company –
Savannah to Swansea

Premium £35% on £8,526	£149. 3. 9	
Policy Stamp	14. 4	
	£149. 18. 1	
Less 10%	14. 19.10	134. 18. 3
Cost of Agency collecting claim, paid Messrs L. G. Jeffreys & Co., Swansea		10. 10. 0
Add discharging expenses at Swansea and Railway rate on Pig Iron to Pontardawe 2,500 tons @ 1/6d.		187.10. 0
		£ 8,084. 8. 2
Amount received from The Maritime Insurance Co. on loss of "Dixiana" with Pig Iron, copy of Certified Protest herewith		£ 8,525. 0. 0
To replace the Pig Iron lost in "Dixiana" we were compelled to buy 2,500 Basic Iron from North Lincolnshire Iron Co. Ltd. @ 15/- per ton f.o.s. Scunthorpe, Contracts June 2nd and June 8th, 1915.		£ 9,375. 0. 0
Add Carriage to Pontardawe @ 12/- per ton		£ 1,500. 0. 0
		£10,875. 0. 0

Cost of replace lot is £2,350 above amount recovered from the Insurance Co., and this represents nett loss to W. Gilbertson & Co. Ltd.

Frank Gilbertson to Messrs Barlow, Barlow & Lyde, London. **10 Aug. 1915 [10 : 25]**

In reply to your favour of yesterday, perhaps we had not made our claim quite as clear as we might. What we intended it to be was a claim for the difference between the insured value of the cargo and the market price at the date of the loss, and this difference was £2,350. The figures given on our statement will make it clear to you how this nett loss was arrived at.

We think it is well to lodge a claim although we are not at all sanguine that anything will be recovered from the German Government.

P. Davies to Messrs Barlow, Barlow & Lyde, London. **2 Sept. 1915 [10 : 40]**

s.s. "Dixiana"

We have your favour of yesterday, and thank you for copy of letter from the Foreign Claims Branch of the Foreign Office. It appears to us from the copy of letter in question that our chance of recovering anything is extremely remote, as you say, and under the circumstances we agree to allow the matter to drop.

Frank Gilbertson to Colonel W. Charles Wright, Room 305, Armament Buildings, Whitechapel, 5W. **20 Sept. 1915 [10 : 45-6]**

I attended a Meeting of Steel Makers on the 10th inst. in London, and I have seen the copies of some letters that have since passed between the Committee of Steel Makers and your Department. I hope you will not mind my writing these private lines to you to convey one aspect of the matter that has forced itself on my attention rightly or wrongly. I thought that the Committee put their proposals before the Steel Makers generally in rather a cut and dried fashion, and I certainly received the impression that the Committee largely expected to control the allocation of orders for Shell Steel. As one of the Board of Management of a National Shell Factory I have had a little experience in the use of Shell Steel and I have seen and heard of results at other Factories, and I feel quite sure that a very great deal of difference exists between the qualities manufactured at different Works. I have seen Steel giving 90 or even 100% of Waste Shells, and I think it will be a mistake if your Department placed the allocation of orders in the hands of the Steel Committee without retaining ample powers for distributing the orders in the manner your Department found best. No doubt the matter is fully before you but I daresay you will not mind my mentioning my impressions to you.

Frank Gilbertson to Messrs Bessler, Waechter & Co. Ltd., London. **4 Oct. 1915 [9 : 157]**

We are obliged by your favour of the 29th ulto. We are bound to say that until an enormous change takes place in the relative cost of fuel in the two Countries, it is quite impossible to think of extending the manufacture to include the rolling of Sheets, and still more impossible to consider the manufacture of Steel. Rolling Sheet bars and the smelting of the Steel could not be performed on a commercial scale with an output of less than 1500/2000 tons per week, and the Capital outlay to produce this output would be about £150,000 in this Country, and of course very much more in Roumania. We feel quite sure that unless conditions change materially it is very much wiser to confine ourselves to the costing of imported Black Sheets. If Mr. Auschnitt should press the matter further, we will take the trouble to prepare figures to show him how speculative and unpromising such a large venture would be but we do not take it that at present he requires us to do this.

Frank Gilbertson to Owen Davies, Steel Works Manager. **25 Oct. 1915 [10 : 62]**

I have decided to make an alteration in your Bonus arrangement.

It is much more important now for us to get a big output of Special steel than a big output of ordinary steel.

I therefore propose to pay you

(1) ½d. per ton on output of Melting Shop instead of 1d.
(2) 2d. per ton on all specials
(3) 2d. per ton additional upon all Shell bars invoiced out
(4) No other bonus
(5) The present 10% increase on your standing salary

This arrangement to start from today & the bonuses to be paid you quarterly.

The Returns to the Special Commissioners dated 30 June 1916 show Owen Davies's salary for 1915-16 to be £324..10..0 plus a bonus of £417.

Frank Gilbertson to Stanley Davies, Analytical Chemist. **25 Oct. 1915 [10 : 63]**

The Shell Steel will give you much extra work & worry & I propose that in addition to your 2d. per ton on Specials you should have 2d. per ton upon all Shell bars that are invoiced out.

His salary for 1915-16 was £210 plus a bonus of £339.

Frank Gilbertson to Colonel W. Charles Wright. **28 Oct. 1915 [10 : 68-9]**

I am sorry to trouble you, but if you could give me advice and perhaps help me in the following circumstances, I should be very grateful.

My Firm had notice yesterday of the Ministers' intention to declare our Works a Controlled Establishment.

If all other Steel Works engaged in the Tin Bar and Billet trades are declared Controlled Establishments, I am content, and have no grievance. If, however, that is not the case, my Firm will be most seriously affected.

Tin Bars can show today 30/- a ton profit at a rate when manufactured half in acid and half in basic furnaces as we do here and there seems every reason to anticipate similar conditions throughout next year.

If a neighbour of mine, not controlled, is able to make 30/- a ton on his output, subject only to excess profits tax, is it not hard that our profits should be limited to a very small sum, the standard years being bad ones in our concern? Is it not hard that this blow should fall on <u>us</u>, who have done so much since the War started to produce higher grades of Steel and to help the Country in many ways, while competitors of ours who have not lifted a finger are left alone and allowed to enjoy the profits fortune and not enterprise has placed in their way?

The direction in which I believe we shall suffer is, that such Firms will be able, out of their own large 1916 profits, to improve and extend their Works for better competition in the future, while my firm will be restricted to making small profits only sufficient for ordinary dividends and depreciation.

Is this not rather an unfair return for the trouble and hard work I have put into the job since the start?

Please remember I have no complaint if all Steel Works are controlled, and in any event, I have said I am prepared to manufacture exactly what the Director of Materials orders us to do.

Charles Gilbertson to Messrs Bessler, Waechter & Co., Ltd. **4 Dec. 1915 [9 : 162]**

We are in receipt of yr. letter of the 3rd inst. enclosing a/c re Mr. W. Böhringer, up to March 1915. We presume that, up to that date, he was working for us, in which case his salary is due to him. Since March we imagine that he has left Galatz and returned to Germany.

Is this so?

If this is the case, no further payment will be made to him, of course.

Charles Gilbertson to W. Evans, Llanelly **6 Dec. 1915 [9 : 163]**

As arranged with you this morning, our retaining fee of 35/- per week will cease from today, seeing that you have secured suitable employment, temporarily, which will provide you with an amount in excess of 35/- per week. We were glad to hear that you are able to give up the work at any time, with one week's notice, so as to enable you to return to Roumania whenever we may require your services there again, according to our agreement – which, however, we fear may not be for some considerable time.

In the meantime, we trust that you will find your present post of Insurance Agent*, congenial & lucrative.

**with the Refuge Assurance Company [9 : 167]*

Frank Gilbertson to Messrs Bessler, Waechter & Co. Ltd. **31 Dec. 1915 [9 : 164-5]**

. . . With regard to the financial position, we will approve of any course that commends itself to you.

With regard to the question of the Works, we shall be quite prepared to submit details of what would be entailed at a suitable time, but it is hardly that today.

We received a letter from the Bd of Trade a couple of days ago, saying they were informed that we had an Agent in Galatz of Enemy nationality, & requesting us to substitute a neutral. We do not know what they referred to, unless it was the case of Mr Böhringer, but have asked for further information.

At the present time when Roumania's attitude is uncertain, we think it would not be wise to correspond about the erection of Steel Works.

Frank Gilbertson to Messrs R. & C. B. Jenkins. 1 Feb. 1916 [10 : 119]

A Craneman, W. Shephard, has twice recently come to his work drunk.

The occupation is important & the result of a drunken man handling a Crane may be disastrous.

We wish to prosecute him in the Munitions Court as an example and a warning to him.

Would you please make the necessary arrangements with Mr. Thorpe?

Our Mr. Owen Davies, Steel Works Manager, knows the facts.

Charles Gilbertson to Messrs Bessler, Waechter & Co. Ltd. 3 March 1916 [9 : 168-9]

We are in receipt of your letter of the 22nd ult. We are pleased to note that the R.S. & G. Co. has done well during the last year.

With regard to the Blackplates. We agree with you as to the advisability of not selling them all, but we are inclined to go further, and suggest that it is worth while considering the advisability of keeping the whole stock unsold. Owing to the probability of a shortage of labour immediately following the close of the War, and the general disorganisation, it is quite possible that it might take us or any other Firm considerable time to replace the Black Sheets now in stock, whereas if the present stock is kept in hand there will be something ready, in the event of the R. S. & G. Co. calling for Black Sheets for galvanizing before the Works in this Country are able to supply as quickly as required.

We consider that the present day price for the 34 x 23 x 44 x 24 lbs would be about £21, and between now and the end of the War, this price may be even higher.

We shall be glad to have your further view upon the matter.

P. Davies to Messrs Bessler, Waechter & Co. 8 May 1916 [9 : 170]

We beg to confirm your telegram received today as follows:

" Roumanian Government issuing Consols bearing
" Five per cent interest at 84 R.S.C. Suggest
" investing One hundred thousand Lei but we
" propose investing about twelve thousand pounds
" representing Half amount outstanding, wire
" confirming. Bessler."

Our Mr. Gilbertson is away from the office for a few days, and we would suggest your communicating with him direct at the Grand Hotel, London, where he will be staying until Thursday.

Charles Gilbertson to Messrs Bessler, Waechter & Co., Ltd. **10 May 1916 [9 : 171]**

In reply to your letter of the 8th inst, we think that you will be wise in selling the 4 tons of the 36" x 24" Sheets, for the price which you have been able to obtain, viz. £18, and, if possible, the further 20 tons, if the sample lot is approved of.

We do not see any prospect of your being able to do better anywhere in the near future.

Possibly, once you have got rid of this lot, you will be able to get rid of the balance.

This was the last letter to Gilbertson's partners recorded in the Letter-Books. Roumania had maintained a precarious neutrality until 27 August 1916 when, persuaded by the Allies, she declared war on Austria. By the end of November, Roumania had been overrun by the Germans and Austrians and had ceded her vast oil and wheat resources to the Central Powers. The Peace Settlement resulted in Roumania doubling its size by the acquisition of neighbouring territories. There is no reference in any Letter-Book to a resumption of trade in Roumania by the partnership, although Frank and Cecil were still registered as directors in 1919 and their share allotment in October 1920 was unchanged from that in 1914.

Frank Gilbertson to Messrs The Cwmfelin Steel Co. Ltd., Swansea. **17 Oct. 1916 [10 : 240-1]**

I met the partners of the Tawe Clay Company at Messrs. Ingledew & Phillips office last evening.

I arranged to purchase the Works for £9,000 as from October 14th 1916, including all stocks, materials, bricks, stones, etc, with the exception of 1 Kiln of burnt bricks now being discharged, subject to Mr. Phillips' approval of lease.

The Lease is for 35 years from March 1905 at £20 per annum, the Vendors to assign any rights they possess with regard to supplies of stone and to covenant not to engage in Silica Brick manufacture in Brecon, Carmarthen or Glamorgan for ten years.

There are no rights over Silica [. . ?] that cannot be determined at short notice, and so Mr. White is to immediately negotiate a lease for the stone in the River beds from Lord Tredegar and Lord Dynevor.

The present output of the Works is 17,000 [bricks] weekly capable of being increased to over 25,000 with adequate supply of labour.

Mr. White's sister will continue to manage the office and Mr. White will supervise at a commission to be arranged.

My Book-Keeper will go down shortly and make an Inventory of the material and plant.

It was arranged that the sale be made to Mr. F. T. Thomas and myself, who can enter into an Agreement with our respective Companies to hold the place for them.

Mr. Phillips advises that we should not at present form a Limited Company.
The whole matter was left to Mr. Phillips to complete.
I hope these arrangements meet with Mr. Thomas's approval.

An agreement was drawn up with the Cwmfelin Co. for the joint management of the Works and the equal division of bricks and all profits and losses [10 : 254].

Frank Gilbertson to His Worship the Mayor of Swansea. **18 Jan. 1917 [10 : 282]**

As I gathered from your remarks at the Meeting you addressed at the Metal Exchange that it was your wish that Firms in the Swansea district should make their applications for the new War Loan through Swansea Banks, we have decided to apply through two Swansea Banks for £100,000 worth.

I hope very much and fully believe that the appeal you so effectively made last Tuesday will meet with a very generous response in the district.

Frank Gilbertson to A. L. White. **20 Jan. 1917 [10 : 285]**

Silica Brick Works

I have returned to work & have had an opportunity of seeing the accounts you have sent us.

I am exceedingly disappointed to see the output only averages about 12,000 a week. When we purchased the place I fully understood we should have an output of 18,000 & a profit of some £3,000 per annum. Will you kindly write me a full report of what is wrong.

With regard to your commission I considered 2/- per 1,000 was fair.

If you are prepared to split the difference & say 2/6 we shall agree.

Frank Gilbertson to Messrs The Capital & Counties Bank, Swansea. **29 Jan. 1917 [10 : 294]**

We enclose Application for £90,000 5% War Loan, and cheque for £4,500.

As arranged, please advance us the balance, and open a new account for us at your Swansea Branch.

We are asking Parr's Bank to forward you £50,000 Treasury Bills, and please credit the account with the proceeds when received.

We understand you will charge us 5% upon the outstanding overdraft on this account.

The charge was 1% below bank rate.

Frank Gilbertson to Messrs The London City & Midland Bank, Swansea. **29 Jan. 1917 [10 : 295]**

War Loan

We enclose

(1) Application for £5,000
(2) Cheque for £250

Kindly also let us have two Conversion Forms for the conversion of £5,000 and £3,270 4½ per cent War Stock 1925-1945 to the 5% War Loan 1929-1947.

Frank Gilbertson to Owen H. Smith, Ministry of Munitions of War, Northumberland Avenue, London. **14 Feb. 1917 [10 : 309-10]**

Following your letter of [n.d.] asking us to prepare detailed Trading Accounts, we requested Messrs Deloitte Plender & Griffiths to undertake the work as they did on the last occasion when an analysis of our accounts was made in this way, our staff being very short at present.

They replied that it is unpracticable for them to undertake this work at present, but we shall go into the matter further and let you know shortly what we can do.

Meanwhile, is it any use our drawing your attention to the fact that it does seem absurd at the present time, when all sorts of accounting and auditing work are being vastly increased, as a result of the Munition Act, and the recent Finance Acts, the staffs of the larger Accountants are continually being drawn upon for Military Service when there are heaps of men in the country who could be spared without any National loss.

I passed through Neath last Saturday evening and witnessed a queue of fully 1,000 able bodied young men waiting their turn to witness a boxing match, the greater proportion of these probably being colliers in the Neath Valley, working Anthracite Coal and employed perhaps two days per week.

It would seem that Workmen's organisations sufficiently powerful to wield political influence, are able to protect their members from Military Service by some wire pulling or another, while other interests that may be much more valuable to the Country, but lacking means of presenting their case, are called upon to do more than their share.

At any rate, it creates a very bad impression to see thousands of Colliers, particularly, but not only, in the Anthracite Districts, employed 1, 2 & 3 days a week, owing to shortage of tonnage for export, idling their time, and sometimes even begging for a few days labour, and yet immune from Military Service.

Charles Gilbertson to E. A. John, Labour Exchange, Swansea. **19 Feb. 1917 [10 : 315]**

A. Ll. Jones

Please note that we intend to train this man to take the place of

Humphreys, Edward J., electric Crane Driver,

Alltwen Hill, Pontardawe.

We consider that Jones should be able to take over the job in about 3 or 4 weeks.

We therefore leave the calling up of Humphreys in your hands, or if you prefer, you may take another name from our Register, from using the Electric Crane drivers that can be spared in exchange for a substitute.

Charles Gilbertson to Capt. Bevan, Recruiting Office, Swansea. **27 Feb. 1917 [10 : 316]**

We enclose names of three young men, to whom you are free to send calling up notices, for any day after Wednesday, 7 March.

In the case of John and Thompson, we hope you will not fail to do so, as they have both expressed themselves as being anxious to join, so the sooner you have them the better.

By the 7th March, we shall have been able to find men to replace them. In the case of Humphreys, the matter is, of course, entirely in your hands, because he has not expressed a desire to join, but we have accepted from the Labour Exchange, a substitute for him, so that, so far as we are concerned, we shall be able to release him, any time after the date mentioned.

We are very much obliged to you for having returned John and Thompson to us, to remain at their work until we have their substitutes ready.

E.J. Humphreys was called up and served as a Private in the Army. A total of 287 employees of W. Gilbertson & Co. Ltd. served in the armed forces and 34 of these gave their lives. The names of all, and the departments in which they were employed, are commemorated on a plaque in the Public Hall & Institute.

Frank Gilbertson to Piercey, c/o Owen H. Smith, Ministry of Munitions. **27 April 1917 [10 : 331]**

You were good enough to interest yourself in the matter of contributions to the Swansea Technical College Scheme, and to obtain the Minister's consent to two-fifths of the contributions made by certain Controlled Establishments in this District, being treated as a working expense.

Might I ask you whether it is not possible to get the Board of Inland Revenue to agree to the two-fifths being treated as a working expense in the accounts of the Controlled Firms, as rendered for Income Tax and Excess Profits Duty.

It is very confusing, and it might conceivably defeat the object, if this sum is to be a working expense, so far as the Munition levy is concerned, but not in the case of Income-tax and Excess profits.

Messrs. Baldwins made a very handsome contribution, but the Surveyor of Taxes refuses to allow any portion of their contribution to be charged against Revenue.

Frank Gilbertson was a co-opted member of the Technical College Sub-Committee which was appointed by the Local Education Authority in March 1916 to act as the governing body of the College. In the same year it was proposed to the Haldane Commission that the Technical College should become a new University College.

Frank Gilbertson to Messrs The Cwmfelin Steel & Tinplate Co. Ltd., Swansea. **13 July 1917 [10 : 372]**

re. Morriston Silica Brick Works

We have had to spend some money there, in building a new Kiln, and buying a second-hand Crane, in order to facilitate the loading of Silica Stone up the River.

The £9,000 that we originally provided jointly was absorbed in the purchase, and left nothing over for working capital and stocks.

We have paid in a further £500 as a loan, some time ago, and another £500 is needed to finance the concern.

After that, the outlay will be finished, and we shall be benefiting from the profits we are making.

The first six months showed something over £400, but it will no doubt improve as the place gets into order and the output increases.

Would you be disposed to pay in £500, so that the loan will be equally divided between our two concerns.

Frank Gilbertson to C. H. Eden, Vivian & Sons, Landore. **22 Jan. 1918 [10 : 500]**

Thank you for your letter.

F.B.I. [Federation of British Industries]

One of the Associations, of which I am a Member, has considered the F.B.I. proposals, and has decided to give general approval, subject to details, and to a deliberate decision being come to as to whether, and to what extent, the proposed benefits should be part of a State scheme.

I think it is very wise for the F.B.I. to negotiate with Labour, but I am not yet sure whether it is wise to make a definite proposal for a bargain between Employers' Associations and Trades Unions, or whether it would be better to indicate the extent to which the support of Employers could be promised to new legislation on the broad lines of the Committee's recommendations.

In your letter, you raise one important point, and I am not sure that I agree with you.

If some form of industrial super-tax was ear-marked for the benefit of the working class alone, would there not be a temptation for the working man to exercise his vote always in the direction of increased super-tax, as it would benefit his class, and his class only.

What I have always hoped might be one of the results of the War would be that the State should recognise its responsibility for furthering and developing industry in every way possible, and to recognise that almost its principal duty was to ensure profitable and growing industry, and that, as a return, industry should be prepared to recognise that the State had a call upon surplus profits, when made, i.e. that some form of excess profits duty should be a permanent policy of the State, and that the Revenue thereby obtained should be applied to the benefit of the State as a whole, including further provision for sickness, unemployment benefits, etc., but that such Revenue should not be ear-marked for that particular purpose.

Of course, it would be necessary, and probably quite easy, to devise proper means of arriving at what were really excess profits, i.e., the profits remaining over, after proper provision has been made for depreciation, obsolescence, fair return on the actual capital employed, etc., with proper provision for average.

I think Hichens is a very clever man, with a very fertile brain, and his opinion is always worth considering, but we have to remember that his whole training has been, first, a schoolmaster, and second, a Civil Servant, and that, as Chairman of Cammell Laird, he is not really in touch with manufacturing difficulties, difficulties of competition, etc.

I think, on the whole, Labour is not prepared to back any scheme for definite sharing in profits. It prefers remaining in the position of wage earning, and would be quite satisfied for the State to take charge of surplus profits, or a portion of them, and I think a great deal of the mis-conception that arises, is due to high rates of dividend paid by many Companies on a nominal capital, much below the actual capital involved, and I fancy we shall all be wise in the future, if we capitalize such share of our profits as we put back into our business from time to time.

There is no doubt all these questions will become of practical interest in the next few years, and I think it is all to the good that Employers are beginning to discuss them together, and to see the need, in the future, of stating their case to the Public, which they have never done in the past.

Frank Gilbertson to John Hall, Controller of Iron & Steel Production, Ministry of Munitions, Whitehall, London, S.W.1. **25 Feb. 1918 [10 : 524]**

With reference to the work of Mr. J. C. Davies and myself in allocating Tin Bars, and in distributing information and instructions from yourself to the Tinplate Trade, we had incurred expenses from January 1917 to December 1st, 1917 of £319:11:4.

At the time you asked us to undertake this work, you indicated that Messrs Baldwins Ltd., and W. Gilbertson & Co. Ltd., would have to bear any expense.

I should be glad if you would drop a line to my firm, telling them that they will be in order in charging £139:15:8 in their accounts as a working expense.

From December 1st last, the expenses of the Office will be borne by the Ministry as the South Wales area Steel Department.

Frank Gilbertson to Frederick Edwards, Capital & Counties Bank Ltd., Swansea. **25 Feb. 1918 [10 : 525]**

Private

I am obliged by your letter of the 14th inst, which I am afraid I have neglected to reply to for a little time.

We are enclosing cheque for the interest due on this account, and with regard to the overdraft of £31,000, we should like an expression of opinion from you on the following points.

We have just been instructed to commence an Extension of our Works, which will prove a new industry for the District of rather an important nature.

We expect to spend £85,000 upon plant, upon which we shall be able to write down out of excess profits, say 33½%.

There will probably be some £15,000 of working capital absorbed in the business as well.

Our Steel Works has largely increased its production during the War, probably by 80%, and, with the increased value of material, the working capital required to carry on operations will have to be larger after the War than it was before.

It is probable, therefore, that we shall require to borrow against our £100,000 of War Loan, up to its full value, and before we decide to pay off the £31,000 on this special account we shall be glad to know if you can assure us that we can, at any time, obtain advances against the War Loans that we hold.

Frank Gilbertson to Rhys Bevan, Steel Works Manager. **10 March 1925 [10 : 605-6]**

I have seen my brother's letter of 12th to you. I have been very little at business for a long time, but I have been aware of the difficulties that face us.

In the present state of trade it seems to me really to be doubtful if we can go on making steel. At any rate the time has come for very drastic measures.

When you came here you effected great economies & put right many of the bad factors that had grown up in the War & under Lister.

But with reducing trade you have failed to maintain your costs.

In the comparisons given you it would seem that it is costing us £3..14..4 to convert material into Bars.

I know of a works converting at £2..15..0.

Advertisement for W. Gilbertson & Co. Ltd., in *The Times Trade Supplement*, Industrial Wales Section, 29 October 1921 *(Clive Reed)*

I must try & make you believe that our position has grown to be serious, & beg you to undertake a very careful survey & in addition to doing all you can day by day to improve things, to draw up a detailed report, sparing no one, but clearly showing us how it is possible for you to right the position. Mr. Kift has had a lot of experience reorganizing Dyffryn. Would you care to ask him privately to come up & go over your figures when you are clear about details, & give you some help? Grovesend costs are not included in the comparisons given you.

In making comparisons strike out

A. Works Ingot yield } they are not
B. Works Bar yield } reliable

Get Charlie Giddings to help you with any figures in forming your conclusions for your report.

R.P. Bevan ended his employment on 9 July 1925 [10 : 608].

Cecil Gilbertson to Sir Walter Lawrence. **29 June 1927 [10 : 621]**

Thank you very much for your letter of the 27th and I am so grateful to you for the trouble you have taken in interviewing the High Commissioner for India on our behalf. I hope we shall now get a share of the orders that are placed direct in addition to any passing through Messrs. Rendle Patman & Tritton's hands.

Orders are very scarce and prices for Tinplates & Galvanized Sheets reduced considerably.

Frank Gilbertson to Sir Walter Lawrence. **21 Aug. 1928 [10 : 625-6]**

Thank you for your letter. I am afraid it wont be possible to hold our annual meeting before Sept 3rd.

However, I can bring the balance sheet to show you on your return from Aix. If we hold it about Sept 10th to 15th, which I expect, is it worth coming to London this time?

Let me know if you agree to the arrangement it is proposed to make with the Bank over the Cwmguinea Colliery losses, as set out in my letter to Lord Trevethin & yourself? Things down here in coal are worse than ever – Our trades are holding their own, but a serious development in Sheet Rolling in Belgium has occurred. The wage equivalents on the Continent are so far below ours that enormous profits are being made with selling prices that leave little or no profit to English makers.

What is to be the end of this wage disparity? In this case of Sheet Rolling no question of better plant, cheaper coal, or railway rates are involved – It is simply & solely a difference in the direct wages paid the Sheet Rollers & Galvanizers.

Probably Cwmgwineu Colliery, which was a small level that worked the Rock Fawr (No. 2 Rhondda) seam and was located near Bryn, Port Talbot. It operated between 1922 and 1927.

Frank Gilbertson to Ivor Harris. **23 Aug. 1928 [10 : 627]**

I am writing to say that W. Gilbertson & Co. Ltd. are prepared to seriously consider making an offer for the Glantawe Works, if your Colleagues on the Board of The Glanrhyd Tinplate Co. would care for us to do so, provided they will allow us to inspect the Works and to examine the accounts, and to obtain such information as is necessary to enable us to assess the value of the works and the exact financial position of the Company.

As soon as we hear that the Board is willing to provide such facilities we will see no time is lost in making our enquiries and putting forward an offer.

In October 1928 W. Gilbertson & Co. Ltd. repurchased the Glanrhyd Tinplate Works. This was the last of Frank Gilbertson's letters to be copied in the Letter-Book.

The last letter [10 : 630] to be recorded was dated 7 October 1929, the day before Frank Gilbertson died, and merely records the despatch of the annual return and summary of share capital. The penultimate entry [10 : 629] was undated but presumed to be May 1929 and is a tax return of salaries, wages, bonuses and commissions, and this is reproduced at the close of the next chapter.

Chapter 4

FINANCIAL PERFORMANCE

W. Gilbertson and Company was registered as a limited company in November 1885 with £35,000 capital. The share list of 1891 showed that there were 700 shares of £50 issued, of which 462 (66%) were owned by Arthur Gilbertson and 210 (30%) by George Lawrence of Cheltenham. The remaining 28 shares were distributed among family and associates. In addition there was long term debt financing through the issue of 5% debentures, also restricted to family and associates. The letters confirm that the share capital was increased to £175,000 in April 1914 and the debentures were exchanged for 6% preference shares. In March 1918 a further capital reorganisation increasing the share capital to £469,000 was agreed and 5,880 additional shares at £50 were issued.

Interpretation of the company's financial position and its capacity for sustainable growth is limited by the adequacy of the data which are available in the Letter-Books. Unfortunately, there were no copies of the balance sheets, which would have provided a clear picture of the company's assets and liabilities, nor of the profit and loss accounts detailing the company's trading record. However, the Letter-Books do contain the company's returns to the Surveyor of Taxes from 1892 to 1907 which provide a year on year statement of profits and additional information from which it is possible to calculate the company's earnings before interest and tax, net earnings and the earnings per share as a percentage of its nominal value (Table 1). Moreover, the tax returns were accompanied by a list of employees, their designations and gross annual salaries, including those of Arthur Gilbertson and his sons, and these lists continue to 1929. Additionally, the company secretary's notices of the annual Ordinary General Meetings from 1891 to 1925 specified the dividends payable (Table 2) and occasionally referred to the factors which influenced the total dividend distribution and provided a comment on the state of the trade. The framework of company returns and notices is supplemented by a selection of letters, mainly to bank managers, solicitors, equity holders, creditors and employees, which together provide insights into the company's financial performance over nearly four decades.

Arthur Gilbertson to Messrs The Glamorganshire Banking Co. Ltd., Neath. **14 Aug. 1890 [1 : 14]**

We object to the charge of 7%, 6% & 5% on occasional small overdrafts for three or four days, when our account is in credit a good many thousand pounds, for the greater part of the month & we submit the commission should cover this.

Arthur Gilbertson to The Glamorganshire Banking Co. **16 Aug. 1890 [1 : 5]**

Your favour of yesterday to hand & we are quite prepared to wait your Manager's return but we must press our request. Very frequently there was no overdraft at all, even in first week of the month, and afterwards a good credit.

Today you have £2,500 to our credit, yesterday it was nearly £4,000 & will increased to £8,000 or more, as month goes on.

Arthur Gilbertson to George Lawrence, Cheltenham. **13 Feb. 1891 [1 : 76]**

Turn up the check for £1,050..0..0 first! Dividend 10% for six months (equal to 20% per annum).

166 old shares –	£ 8,300
46 new shares –	£ 2,300
212	£10,600

at 10% = £1,060..0..0, check enclosed. The Steel Works are going fairly well.

J. P. Davies to George Aplin, Surveyor of Taxes, Swansea. **8 July 1891 [1 : 125-6]**

Private

We enclose statement as usual for Special Commissioners.

The profits, if any, of our small Colliery (now abandoned) are merged into Tinplate account.

March 1890-91. Payable for year ending 5 April 1892

	Profits	Losses	Rate	Amounts
Llangavelach				
Year ending March 1889	13,380			
" " " 1890	17,992			
" " " 1891	24,526			
Divided by 3	) 55,898			
	18,633			
Less Union Assessment of Works	1,520			
	17,113			
add Interest on Debentures £10,250 @ 5%	512			
	£17,625			

Hamlet of Ynisymond			
(Parish of Cadoxton)			
Royalty – Howel Jeffreys	£ 7	6d	3..6
Wayleave – Duke of Beaufort	57		
Howel Jeffreys	52		
Mrs. Ellen E. Gwyn	92		
	201	6d	5.. 0..6
			£445..16..6

Royalty	Howel Jeffreys		
May 1890	5.. 7..3		
Mch 1891	1.. 9..3		
	6.16..6		
Wayleave	Duke of Beaufort	Howel Jeffreys	Mrs. Gwyn
June 1890	14 .. 2..6	13..0..0	65 .. 9 .. 0
Sept "	14 .. 2..6	13..0..0	14..19..10
Dec "	14 .. 2..6	13..0..0	6 .. 0 .. 4
Mch 1891	14 .. 2..6	13..0..0	5..10 .. 2
	56..10..0	52..0..0	91..19 .. 4

Extracted from Books
Jno. P. Davies

J. P. Davies to Arthur Gilbertson, Esq., Glanrhyd. 16 July 1891 [1 : 128]

Notice is hereby given that the Sixth Ordinary General Meeting of the proprietors of W. Gilbertson & Co. Limited will be held at the registered office of the Company, Pontardawe, near Swansea, on Tuesday, 25th day of July 1891 and that at such meeting the Sole Director recommends that a final dividend of 20% on the paid up Capital of £35,000 be declared & other business proceeded with.

Arthur Gilbertson to George Lawrence. 25 July 1891 [1 : 131]

I hope enclosed for £2,100..0..0 will please you. I also send £10 each for Lillian & Arthur.

We have also paid for our Steel Works and put £2,000 to Debenture sinking fund, leaving £8,000 in Debentures to be extinguished year by year if possible.

All is going well here & Steel Works a grand success.

Arthur Gilbertson to Messrs Barlow & James, London. 27 Jan. 1892 [1 : 168]

Your favour of yesterday with Debentures Nos. 65 & 66 safely to hand.

You know we are very anxious to keep our Debentures in sight, which is best done by having them registered.

The Writer would prefer buying up the above himself, than having them unregistered. He would pay "par" value and interest @ 5% from date of last coupon.

P.S. We find that Mr. J. B. Barlow holds five, with cancelled Registration, and Mr. George Barlow three. We would prefer buying these also. The fact of no registration had escaped us.

Arthur Gilbertson to Messrs Barlow & James. 30 Jan. 1892 [1 : 169]

. . . We note what you are good enough to say as to character of our Debentures as an investment. Apparently you dont fear McKinley! Seeing what you say as to your keeping the Debentures under your eye & control, we will of course cancel registration of Nos 65 & 66, and will complete this on Monday.

Kindly correct enclosed to £125 (not £155).

Arthur Gilbertson to George Lawrence. 9 Feb. 1892 [1 : 174]

I am glad to say the interim dividend is better than I expected and I enclose checks for £1,837..10..0 yourself
8..15..0 Lillian
8..15..0 Arthur

Sign receipt for same.

Everything is very depressed now, but I think bottom must be touched.

Arthur Gilbertson to Alfred T. Lawrence. 25 July 1892 [1 : 185]

You no doubt got formal notice of our "Meeting" and of the dividend I proposed to pay.

I was fortunate enough to get Mr. S. B. Barlow to attend, and showed him everything – we could not divide all our profits, or we should have to overdraw too much out of our Bank, as our "capital" is small, for our largely increased operations.

We are doing exceedingly well, in spite of the state of trade generally. My first assize begins next week. I wish you were "Judge"! I am very nervous about it.

With kind regards to you all.

Arthur Gilbertson was sworn in as High Sheriff of Glamorganshire in 1892.

J. P. Davies to George Aplin, Surveyor of Taxes, Swansea. **26 July 1892 [1 : 196-9]**

<u>Private</u>

We enclose return of Special Commissioners. The Colliery was abandoned nearly a year ago. We also enclosed List of Employés . . .

Arthur Gilbertson	Sole Director	Glanrhyd Pontardawe	1,600..0..0
Jno. P. Davies	Accountant	Herbert St do	220..0..0
Oliver Adams	do	Bak Villa do	150..0..0
William Evans	Foreman	Herbert St. do	195..0..0
Rees Edwards	do	High St. do	156..0..0
Llewelyn Jones	do	Thomas St. do	156..0..0
William Roberts	Mechanic	Swansea Rd do	156..0..0
Owen Davies	Sample Passer	High St. do	240..0..0
John Henry	do	Brecon Rd. do	240..0..0
Oliver John	Melter	James St. do	176..0..0
Harris Thomas	do	do do	180..0..0
Thomas Meyrick	Teamer	Graig Rd. do	156..0..0
Daniel Evans	Melter	Ynismeudwy Swansea Valley	160..0..0
Thomas Evans	Bar Roller	Swansea Rd. Pontardawe	208..0..0
Philip Davies	do	do do	186..0..0
David Evans	do	Orchard St. do	192..0..0
Llewelyn Davies	do	Trebanos Swansea Valley	155..0..0
Robert Thomas	do	James St. Pontardawe	153..0..0
Richard Francis	Melter	Trebanos Swansea Valley	168..0..0
James Wilcox	do	Ynisderw Pontardawe	175..0..0

Pencilled bracket down right side with comment 'Claim abatement'.

Arthur Gilbertson to Glamorganshire Bank, Neath. **19 Jan. 1893 [1 : 214]**

We find you have charged us abt. £54..10..7 for commission & £8..0..0 for interest for 6 months ending Decbr. 31st. We really cannot afford this. We have very seldom been overdrawn, and the greater part of each month largely in credit – at end of Decbr. just £7,000.

We are going to ask you to make no charge for commission in future, or we shall be compelled to reduce our a/c. which we should greatly regret.

Arthur Gilbertson to T. Estall, National Provincial Bank, London. **28 Jan. 1893 [1 : 217]**

We think of concentrating our Banking account with yourselves, only keeping sufficient cash in Wales to pay workmen's wages.

Our turnover is about £150,000 per annum, we give no acceptances & pay everything in cash monthly.

Our checks at end of each month amount to about £9,000 or £10,000. We pay good dividends half yearly and at that time, if stocks exceed £20,000, we sometimes have to overdraw from £1,000 to £3,000, at the beginning of the month, and at the beginning of several months, until profits wipe it off.

Our Auditors are Deloitte, Dever & Griffiths, our Solicitors Barlow & James, 49 Lime Street.

We would pay 5% on the overdraft, during the time it exists.

Would you undertake this account, and if needful, we would ask Mr. Barlow to call on you.

Arthur Gilbertson to The Glamorganshire Banking Co., Neath. **15 Feb. 1893 [1 : 222]**

Thanks for your letter of 13th inst. & enclosure. I should like to make a few remarks on it please.

Credit balances. I dont think you are quite correct in your remark? Your a/c shows £4,300 in Octr., £5,000 in Novbr., £7,000 in December. For the previous three months it was more often in Debit.

Overdraft. I imagined an overdraft of a few thousands with a Firm like ours, 5% with money @ 2½ to Depositors was rather fine business. However we will try to avoid overdrafts, and in this event must ask you not to charge any commission. Mr. Edwards has agreed to this for Glynbeudy.

Pontardawe Branch. You seem to forget serves three Tinplate Works, a large Chemical Works, Foundry & Fitting Shop, Primrose Coal Co. and Brewery, Public without end, and a thriving district of some 3,000 people, and covers the ground for you.

Glamorganshire Bank. I have quite a reservation for this old concern, and declined a seat on the Board of the Swansea Bank Ltd. when first started, for no other reason.

Arthur Gilbertson to D. J. Rhys, Glamorganshire Bank. **27 Feb. 1893 [1 : 224]**

. . . It would not answer our purpose to let £2,500 remain idle, at your Bank.

We are not prepared to pay you any commission, but will pay 5% on any overdraft.

Should you not see your way to continue our account on these terms, we must then make other arrangements & find out if any Bank would like to undertake our account, and deliver our pay at Pontardawe, or open a Room fortnightly in this Village.

A considerable amount of the monthly payments between our circle of Workers, is merely the exchange of paper, no cash having to be found by you.

P.S. I find you keep Bank here once a week. Why is this as we only use it twice a month?

Arthur Gilbertson to D. J. Rhys. **3 March 1893 [1 : 226]**

Kindly reply to ours of 27th ult. Five minutes would enable you to do so.

Arthur Gilbertson to E. Edwards, Glamorganshire Bank. **2 July 1894 [1 : 296]**

I have your letter of 30th ulto. Would you kindly say at what periods & how long we were overdrawn during past half year? You remember checks to & from Glynbeudu & Glantawe are only book transfers.

We cannot agree that we should pay for your Branch up here. You receive cash at it from the Trades of this District & another Bank would gladly open here for our account.

We think our "average trade" in your hands should pay you.

Arthur Gilbertson to The Glamorganshire Bank, Swansea. **18 July 1894 [1 : 297]**

Can you find out for us if we can safely give credit to the Ynismedwy Tinplate Co. for £1,000? Their Bankers are "Capital & Counties Bank".

Arthur Gilbertson to Surveyor of Taxes. **15 Sept. 1894 [1 : 305]**

Yours of yesterday. We have been rather short handed in our Office, and only just able to get our returns ready for Special Commissioners which we now enclose. When sending out forms for Income Tax to our Workers (whose names are scrupulously returned to you) please send your demands thro the post, or by the local Collector, and not by us, as on last occasion. In the latter event the men think we personally assess them which of course is not the case.

We hope other Works are equally careful in giving you returns for their Workmen – it used not to be so.

J. P. Davies to George Lawrence. **6 Feb. 1895 [1 : 330]**

We enclose cheque £525 for interim dividend for half year ending 5th ult. at rate of 10% per annum.

Seeing that our Debentures have to be paid off in June next, and the depressed state of Trade the Sole Director thinks it not advisable to declare a larger interim dividend.

P.S. We also enclose two cheques for £2..10..0 each in favor of Miss Lawrence & Mr. Arthur Lawrence respectively.

Arthur Gilbertson to Alfred T. Lawrence, Cheltenham. **2 March 1896 [2 : 222-3]**

I am very sorry to hear of your Father-in-law's illness.

You are a better Lawyer than a Financier! You fortunate people have had 20% per annum not 10%, i.e. the dividend for 6 months was at rate of 20% per annum!! a simply phenomenal result, in these times. I believe Mr. Lawrence paid in £6,000 to this concern, and I have been paying him over £2,000 a year for it! I might have charged any sum I liked for my personal remuneration.

Trusting the old gentleman is almost "non compos" I will write him anything you like to soothe him: it must be very trying to you all.

Our success is greatly owing to certain results from our Steel Works recently and for this, we have in a great measure, to thank Frank, for his special scientific knowledge.

Arthur Gilbertson to S. B. Barlow. **5 March 1896 [1 : 412-3]**

Debentures

I have had some correspondence with Mrs. Alfred Lawrence, and her Husband will take £1,000, out of my £2,000. She wrote to ask if any "shares" were to be had. I said, no, and offered the Debentures.

I have had to find

£3,000	for	Howell's Farm
2,000	"	Frank's House &c.
1,200	"	my Church
£6,200		

which has rather eaten up ready cash for the present, so that £1,000 would suit me better than £2,000 – if you can place the £5,000.

I am hard at work getting all particulars about the Sheet Steel Mills & Galvanizing, and feel as certain as it is possible to be that we shall have a good profitable trade.

Mr. Lloyd agrees to take a surrender of Ten acres of our Farm Lease (Ynisderw) and to give us a new Lease for Works of this 10 acres. I conclude on same terms as our present Steel Works Lease at a rent of £10 a year. Will you kindly refer to this, and see if you suggest any alterations – I think term 45 years.

Please note all this to W. G. & Co. Ltd.

Arthur Gilbertson to Edward Lawrence, Tredegar Chambers, Newport. **25 March 1896[1 : 421-2]**

In reply to your letter of yesterday, our shares are £50, fully paid, and your Father has 210 shares. The only case which has arisen as to actual value of these shares for probate, was the one share left by my dear Wife, and I declared that at £100, which is I believe a fair valuation. The present, and increasingly difficult position in which the Tinplate Trade is placed, owing to the growth of "protected" Works in America, might possibly make an Outsider doubtful, as to giving £100, for one of our £50 shares, but seeing our Reserve fund, and our position generally, I certainly think £100 a fair value for probate.

I note your instructions as to Executors & future dividends, and conclude we shall in due course receive the needful documents to enter in our Minute Book, and the "transfer" to issue new shares in exchange for the old ones, in names of the Executors. I conclude the Debentures will all be similarly dealt with.

J. P. Davies to S. B. Barlow. **13 April 1896 [1 : 435]**

Our Mr. A. Gilbertson has instructed us to say, that we are now prepared to receive the £1,200 as a loan at 4½%, bearing interest from 25th of March last. And that you may, please, pay this amount to our a/c at National Provincial Bank of England, Bishopsgate St, or send us your cheque. When remitting kindly say what notice for repayment or withdrawal you would like, perhaps one month?

It is understood you are to receive a Debenture for this amount, when they are issued for prosecuting the proposed new works.

Arthur Gilbertson to Miss Lilian Lawrence, Kensington. **6 Aug. 1896 [1 : 467]**

Your father transferred one share to you some years ago, but took the dividend himself. The dividend upon this share will now be payable to you, and I enclose £10..0..0 for the final half of our financial year. We have been very fortunate in Trade. This is a business letter only!

Arthur Gilbertson to Arthur Lawrence, 3 Pembroke Terrace, Cardiff. **10 Aug. 1896 [1 : 469]**

. . . The shares are £50 each (not £100) and fully paid, so that you hold three (not two) at £50. Debentures £250.

The value of the shares is no doubt much more than the nominal £50 each. We have been very lucky and doing well now, but everybody is trying to get at our "connection"! and spoiling our prices.

Arthur Gilbertson to G. H. Richard, The Lindens, Prestbury RSO, Gloucestershire. **4 Sept. 1896 [2 : 251-2]**

I have your letter of yesterday. Of course I cannot undertake to enquire about the security and shall require a formal letter from Dick & his Wife, and also a report from his Solicitor, asking and advising myself & my co-Trustee, to accept the mortgage instead of Consols. You may imagine the amount of business I have to deal with, and

I prefer my Trusts to remain in Consols: it is so difficult to remember and attend to other securities & the responsibility upon myself or my Exors would be great.

Minute **6 Aug. 1897 [1 : 553]**

Proposed by Mr. A. Gilbertson & seconded by Mr. F. W. Gilbertson that Messrs. Deloitte & Co. be offered the appointment as Auditors at a fee of 20 guineas, as paid the late Henry Dever whose loss, by death, we deplore.

Arthur Gilbertson to S. B. Barlow. **8 Dec. 1897 [2 : 320]**

I wrote you hurriedly yesterday, after receipt of Frank's telegram. I am above all things glad, that our reputation as Tinplate makers of the highest standard has been sustained, and I dont agree with the Judge's remarks, I think I know my business – I dont split straws with Rogues, and it is quite worth while paying costs, to have sustained our reputation. After my first letter or so, to Wallis Cox & Co., it became apparent to me, that they, or their Principals, were going to try for a reduction in price – possibly 1/- a box would have satisfied them – but then our reputation would have been lost and you can hardly imagine how our high repute for quality has carried us through bad times.

Deloitte Dever & Griffiths. I have been corresponded with, as to rearrangement of W. Gilbertson & Co. Ltd., and enclose you my letters to them of 22nd ulto, and their reply, also our last Balance Sheet, which you see gives a wonderful result, and it seems absurd to allow our Capital to remain at £35,000.

But upon thinking the matter over, I dont like the idea of the £50,000 Debentures – it would injure our credit as Buyers of material and with the Bank, and I think therefore we should satisfy ourselves by rearranging our Capital, so as to represent its real [?] value, every £50 share is fully worth £100. I would let our present Debentures £7,250 remain, and would further borrow £7,500 (which shld. include Miss Barlow's £1,200) @ 4% or 4½% and this new issue would provide for the Sheet Mills & galvanizing extensions.

Do you think you could place the balance of the £7,500 minus Miss Barlow's £1,200?

Please see Deloitte & Co., after you have thought this over.

Arthur Gilbertson to S. B. Barlow. **30 Dec. 1897 [2 : 322]**

Thank you for your letter of yesterday.

1st plan. I dislike Dissolution & reconstruction.

2nd. Do you & Dever & Co. think it incumbent upon us to revalue? or may our Capital a/c &c. continue to stand as it does on Balance sheet? If it may, I think then your

3rd plan is best, viz. to borrow £7,500, including Miss Barlow's £1,200, and if you concur in this, we should like the money, early, in next year, as we are now laying out our Galvanizing Works & Sheet Mill.

Arthur Gilbertson to Messrs Deloitte Dever Griffiths & Co. **1 July 1898 [1 : 648]**

Your favor of yesterday. We would remind you, you were appointed Auditors for the Year, at the same fee as before & we understood you accepted it.

The Writer is so conversant with his own business after so many years of close attention, that he is in no uneasiness as regards the accounts, and your experience as our Auditors over a great number of years, has shown you the absolute accuracy of our accounts (the results of which have possibly somewhat surprised you, seeing the failures of P. S. Phillips & Morewood & Co.) but at the same time, we will agree to pay you £35 per annum, for an increased audit, as you appear to wish it so.

Your letter of acceptance is dated August 10/97 for 20 guineas.

J. P. Davies to Arthur Gilbertson. **25 July 1898 [1 : 657]**

Notice is hereby given that the Thirteenth Ordinary General Meeting of the proprietors of W. Gilbertson & Co. Ltd. will be held at the registered office of the company, Pontardawe, on Tuesday the 2nd day of August 1898 at 11 a.m. and that at such meeting the Directors recommend that a final dividend at the rate of 10% [10% deleted and 15% pencilled in] per annum on the paid up capital of £35,000 be declared, making together with the interim dividend paid in March last, a total distribution of 12½% [10%] for the year.

The Directors desire to call attention to the fact that the Coal Strike having increased the cost of the 1,000 Tons Coal consumed weekly in these works by 2/- a Ton, as such a serious item, that they do not feel justified in declaring a larger final dividend than they have done.

Arthur Gilbertson to S. B. Barlow. **17 Feb. 1899 [2 : 382-3]**

. . . I came home last night, and am certainly better, but may have to start again soon for Bath, they say massage would be good for me.

The Engine is off again and my Sons working well. The last half year W. G. & Co. Ltd. only made about £2,700 profits, and we have to hold such increased stocks, with spelter &c. for Galvanizing process (which is a success) that I dont feel we ought to declare an <u>interim</u> dividend as usual. I believe this Quarter we are making profits on galvanized sheets, steel sheets & Steel Works, and should show a good result. Would it be well to wait until end of this Quarter (Balance sheet about 3rd. week in April) before deciding whether to pay an interim dividend or not?

If we paid an interim dividend now, it causes too much Bank overdraft.

I enclose Leases of Ynisderw Farm & Tin Works. You have the Steel Works.

Arthur Gilbertson to Messrs Pontifex Hewitt & Pitt,Andrew St., London. **27 March 1899 [1 : 817]**

We rather regret getting your wire thru' a small village office here! and had to reply "Yes, a small one".

We expect to declare an interim dividend at rate of 5% per annum, at our Directors meeting on 29th inst.

Notice of the Fourteenth Ordinary General Meeting, 15 August 1899. **1 Aug. 1899 [1 : 880]**

. . . The Directors recommend that a final dividend at the rate of 15% per annum . . . be declared, making, together with the interim dividend paid in April last, a total distribution of 10% for the year.

The Directors desire to call attention to the fact, that a sum that would yield a larger dividend has been earned during the last six months but in consequence of a large Steel Furnace having to be built to enable us to compete better in the markets the Directors think it advisable to carry forward a proportion of the profits earned last half year to meet the outlay now going on.

Arthur Gilbertson to S. B. Barlow. **14 Nov. 1899 [1 : 924]**

Would it be possible for us to pay our Income Tax in London? We make our return to the Special Commissioners at Somerset House, but they send the amount payable to an Official at Swansea, to whom we have to hand our cheque. We believe the amount has sometimes leaked out!

Arthur Gilbertson to J. W. Symonds, Inland Revenue, Swansea. **5 March 1900 [1 : 964]**

Your note to Mr. F. W. Gilbertson has been handed to us. Be good enough to address the Firm, & why did you not in a proper manner write to the Firm reminding them that their cheque was due? We very much object to the tone of your letter.

The Writer is one of the oldest Commissioners in the Valley, and worked at it for many years.

We enclose cheque £247..2..8.

Arthur Gilbertson to Messrs Barlow & Barlow, London. **8 March 1900 [1 : 969-70]**

Issue of 5% Debentures to take up Debentures falling due in June & the unsecured Loans.

We wish to give three months notice to holders, and as the Writer is leaving home for some time on Tuesday morning next, we would like to settle the matter.

We propose sending out the enclosed letter & would like your opinion or any suggestions.

Proposed letter Say March 26th 1900

Dear Sir (or Madam)
We wish to give notice that your Loan (or Debenture) of £ ____ will be repaid you on 30th June next but we are issuing Debentures for Ten years, but terminable at any time by ourselves giving the holders, three years notice, the Debentures will bear interest @ 5% per annum, paid half yearly. Kindly say if you would like to take up Debentures to the amount of your present loan or holding. Our complete & sole issue of Debentures will then amount to £15,125 – each Debenture will be for £125..0..0.

Frank Gilbertson to Arthur Gilbertson. 6 April 1900 [1 : 998]

Please take notice that your Loan (or Debenture) of £4,750 will be repaid you at the National Provincial Bank of England Ld. London on the 31st May next.

We take the opportunity of informing you that we intend to make a fresh issue of Debentures on that date for £15,125, the same amount as Loans or Debentures now existing, for 10 years, but terminable at our option at any time upon our giving the Holders of all or part not less than one year's notice.

Each Debenture will be for £125, and will bear interest at 5 per cent per annum paid half yearly.

If you would like to take such Debentures to the amount of your present loan or holding and will so inform us not later than 1st day of May next, we will endeavour to meet your wishes as far as possible.

Upon the first issue of £15,125 Debentures being made the same will constitute a first floating charge on all our assets and no further charge will be made except subject to such Issue.

Arthur Gilbertson to Messrs Barlow & Barlow, London. 4 May 1900 [3 :18]

. . . We find we can allot your group £4,875..0..0 in the new Debentures, and will send you a cheque for £75, balance between old Debentures & loans, and new Debentures.

We conclude you will send us the old Debentures & we will send you the new ones.

The complete issue will be 112 Debs. @ £125..0..0 = £14,000.

Will you kindly get them printed.

On 23 May 1900 he offered the group an allotment worth £5,000 with debentures priced @ £100 [3 : 32].

Arthur Gilbertson to Messrs National Provincial Bank of England. **24 May 1900 [3 : 33]**

Your favor of yesterday re Bonds.

The following will be paid off, viz:

Miss Gilbertson		– Debs.	29 to 34	–	£750..0..0
Mr.	T. E. D. Philpott	"	41 to 46	–	£750..0..0
"	H. P. Gwynne James	"	54 & 55	–	£250..0..0
					£1,750..0..0

upon their depositing with you the original Debentures, and please place this amount to our debit, as also £181..15..0 less Tax, being last coupons due 1st proxo.

The remaining Debenture holders £5,500, are taking New Debentures, which will be issued by our Solicitors, Messrs Barlow & Barlow, 165 Fenchurch St, London, who we will ask to call on you.

Frank Gilbertson to Arthur Gilbertson. **7 June 1900 [3 :53]**

Referring to your letter of April 17th last, we now beg to enclose

Fortyseven £100 New Debentures Nos 1/47 inclusive –	£4,700
Cheque	50
	£4,750
in lieu of	
Twenty-two £125 Old Debentures	2,750
Loan	2,000
	£4,750

Kindly acknowledge receipt & return the Old Debentures.

With amendments, a similar letter was sent to Frank Gilbertson (10 debentures), F.B. Gilbertson (5), and to Arthur's daughters Ellen, Madelina and Maude, each holding 4 debentures [3 : 54, 57-60].

Notice of the Fifteenth O.G.M., 7 August 1900. **30 July 1900 [3 : 88]**

. . . The Directors recommend that a final dividend at the rate of 40% per annum . . . be declared for the 6 months ending June 16th last, making together with the interim dividend at the rate of 20% per annum paid for the 6 months ending December last, a total distribution of 30% for the year.

The Directors desire to call attention to the fact that the sum that would yield a larger dividend has been earned during the last year, but in consequence of further developments having to be made, to enable us to compete better in the markets, the Directors think it advisable to carry forward a proportion of the profits last year to meet the outlay now going on.

The "further developments" possibly referred to the steelworks being built in Port Talbot.

J. P. Davies to J. W. Symons, Surveyor of Taxes, Swansea. **6 Dec. 1900 [3 : 152]**

Income Tax Assessment

We notice you have assessed us for £9,745. Our return was for £9,130.

Kindly explain how you arrive at your amount.

J. P. Davies to J. W. Symons. **17 Dec. 1900 [3 : 159]**

. . . We agree with same with the exception of Schedule A assessment. We paid as follows under Schedule A:

No. of assessment			
1013	-	Tinplate Works	1,699
1041	-	Steel Works	666
1187	–	New Sheet Mill	135
			2,500

So deduct this amount from £11,672 leaves £9,172. Please correct.

Arthur Gilbertson to National Provincial Bank &Capital & Counties Bank, Neath. **18 Dec. 1900 [3 : 161-2]**

Mr. Jno. P. Davies will cease to be our Secretary from tomorrow – he has with our consent, accepted a better appointment.

Mr. Philip Davies, whose signature is at foot, will be our new Secretary.

P. Davies to J. W. Symons, Swansea. **28 Dec. 1900 [3 : 167]**

. . . The only difference between us now is the item of Tinplate Works – Assessment No. 1013 – Sch A as we paid Income Tax on £1,699 for the year 1899-1900 – we believe this is the correct figure for deduction from our return.

We presume that the Tinplate Works will be assessed at £1,125 Sch A for years 1900-1901 & this amount will be deducted from our next return.

Arthur Gilbertson to Messrs Parrs Banking Co. Ltd. **4 Jan. 1901 [3 : 173]**

If we transferred our London account to yourselves, what interest would you allow us on our weekly current balances?

Our London agents pay in about £12,000 to £13,000 monthly to our credit & we draw it out monthly by cheques to persons supplying us materials.

Arthur Gilbertson to J. W. Symons. **7 Jan. 1901 [3 : 178]**

What is your idea for percentage for depreciation on capital value of Plant & Machinery? Of course in Steel Works, Furnaces wear out rapidly – not so in Tinplate Works & Sheet Mills, which last longer.

I think there should be two % ages.
I will enquire elsewhere & please give me your idea.

Arthur Gilbertson to G. Hethey, Mannesmann Tube Co. Ltd. **15 Jan. 1901 [3 : 183]**

I have now a reply from a friend in the Midlands as to the custom there, regarding "Depreciation". I find there is no rule, but "appeals" constantly take place, annually – it seems admitted that Steel Furnaces, which are frequently wearing out, should be allowed a large allowance, and I think that 5% or 6% would not be too much on such plant.

Arthur Gilbertson to F. E. Edwards, Capital & Counties Bank Ltd., Swansea. **5 Feb. 1901 [3 : 201]**

We give credit to the Ynismedwy Tinplate & Galvanizing Co., because you told us, Mr. Richards would not buy anything he could not pay for, so we did not trouble further about the matter.

They owe us some £230 odd. We are told your Bank hold Debentures for more than the value of the Works!!

Your Bank will no doubt see our £230 is paid us.

The Ynismedwy Co. sold at ridiculous prices, the last 2 or three weeks.

Arthur Gilbertson to F. E. Edwards. **8 Feb. 1901 [3 : 204-5]**

I have your letter of yesterday. I cant quite agree with you.

You told me you considered Mr. Richards would not order anything he could not pay for, but you did not tell me your Bank held Debentures for more than the value of the Works & why did you not make Richards & Aeron Thomas sign an agreement about the guarantee of overdraft, like you made me for old Mr. White?

I understand Richards & Thomas wriggled out of their guarantee & therefore we are asked to lose £230..0..0 odd.

I will not consent to this & if needful a legal investigation must take place. I conclude Richards & Thomas deceived you – the printed Balance Sheet of September 1900, is not audited & is, on the face of it, an absurd Statement.

A man named Haines is supposed to be a creditor for £1,439 for "Shearings". The Works never used any Shearings!!

Your Bank made me pay up very promptly for Mr. White, and unless the Bank pays us the £230..0..0 I shall place the whole matter before our London Solicitor, at once.

I am very sorry this has arisen after so many years. I should be sorry to remove our account.

Arthur Gilbertson to F. E. Edwards. **13 Feb. 1901 [3 : 216]**

Your letter of yesterday. You do not reply to several of my statements & what you say about Debentures, in no way answers my remark, you should have told me your Bank held all the Debentures!! or you should have given no information to me at all.

You know what Aeron Thomas & Richards did about withdrawing their guarantee for overdraft.

Haines should be a Debtor, for Shearings, not a Creditor.

I have never come across such an unsatisfactory business.

P. Davies to Messrs The Capital & Counties Bank Ltd, Neath. **27 Feb. 1901 [3 : 233]**

We shall be glad if you will kindly tell us in confidence whether you consider the firms named at foot are safe for their engagements and if you would advise giving £1,000 credit to each of them?

Messrs The Morriston Tinplate Co. Ltd.	Morriston
" " Phoenix Tinplate Co. Ltd.	Lower Cwmtwrch
" " Gyrnos Tinplate Co. Ltd.	"
" " Beaufort Tinplate Co.	Morriston

Arthur Gilbertson to Messrs Barlow & Barlow, London. **18 April 1901 [3 : 254]**

Ynismedw Tinplate Co. Ltd.

Will you please give notice to the Capital & Counties Bank, Swansea, that as they did not disclose to us, when professing to give us such information as to enable us to give credit to the Coy, that they (the Bank) had got Debentures to a very large amount, that we hold them responsible for the money due to us from Ynismedw Co.

Arthur Gilbertson to Messrs Capital & Counties Bank, Neath. **20 April 1901 [3 : 256]**

Your favor of the 18th inst re interest allowed us and debited us – we really think you make a very nice little business on this. We do not agree to several of your dates, but will let this pass. As regards the 1/16th charged for commission, we do not want to take up your time needlessly to talk the matter over, we are going to ask you to cease making this charge please.

Our London Bankers are much more liberal to us, and allow us interest without notice, on all our credit balance over £1,000.

Arthur Gilbertson to Barlow & Barlow. **9 May 1901 [3 : 275-6]**

Your favor of 7th inst. We think the behaviour of the Bank, very shabby.

They gave us information about the Ynismedw Co, and withheld the important fact, that the whole of their property was pawned to the Bank.

The "contra a/cs" are not worth going into. What would be the legal procedure to take against the Bank and what might be the expense?

We think their mode of procedure ought to be exposed?

Can you not let them know Mr. Gilbertson is inclined to take the opinion of a Court of Law.

P. Davies to J. W. Symons, Inland Revenue, Swansea. **24 May 1901 [3 : 281-2]**

Return of Salaries for year ending April 1901

Arthur Gilbertson	Glanrhyd	Pontardawe	Managing Director	2,500	-	-
F. W. Gilbertson	Glynteg	do	Director	1,150	-	-
C. F. Gilbertson	Glanrhyd	do	do	200	-	-
C. R. Gilbertson	do	do	do	225	7	-
John P. Davies	Gwynfe	do	Secretary	237	10	-
Philip Davies	Danygraig	do	do	300	-	-
Owen Davies	High St.	do	Steel Works Manager	358	-	-
James Wilcox	Francis St.	do	Steel Smelter	322	-	-
David Morton	Railway Terrace Alltwen	do	do	322	-	-
William Jones	Primrose Row	Pontardawe	Pitman	193	-	-
Robert Bodycombe	Francis St.	do	Teamer	208	-	-
George Bowen	Coed Fryn House Brecon Rd.	Pontardawe	do	202	-	-
Evan Williams	Brecon Road	Pontardawe	Steel Smelter	244	-	-
Rees Jones	do	do	do	229	10	-
David Joseph	Graig Glynmeirch	Trebanos	do	188	10	-
Evan Davies	Ynisderw Road	Pontardawe	do	239	-	-
Evan Williams	Grove Road	do	do	267	10	-
Robert Henry	Swansea Road	do	do	289	-	-
John Lewis	Church St.	do	do	217	10	-
William Rapsey	George St.	do	do	165	-	-
Gwilym Williams	Swansea Road	do	do	191	-	-
Tom Aldridge	Church St.	do	do	200	-	-
Thomas Rees	High St.	do	do	179	10	-
Thomas Davies	Orchard St.	do	do	231	-	-
Robert Thomas	Railway Terrace	Alltwen	Bar Roller	160	-	-
David Evans	c/o Mrs Thomas Orchard St, Pontardawe		do	176	10	-
David M. Davies	Brecon Road	Pontardawe	Tinplate Roller	171	-	-

T. R. Williams	Ynismeudwy	Pontardawe	do	175 - -
William Hopkin	Gwyn St, Alltwen	do	do	171 - -
Evan J. Evans	Banwen, do	do	do	164 - -
Edward Griffiths	Vardre,	Cwm Clydach	do	166 - -
Andrew Little	Herbert St,	Pontardawe	Head Mechanic	245 - -

The amount paid to Arthur Gilbertson "includes a special bonus of £500 . . . which will not be repeated this year". Frank's salary had been increased from £600 p.a. to £800 on 1 January. The extras making up £1,150 in total "will not be likely to recur again" [3 : 284-5].

Arthur Gilbertson to Capital & Counties Bank, Neath. **27 June 1901 [3 : 313]**

Your favor of yesterday. We have been Clients of your Bank for sixty years (Father & Son) and should be very sorry indeed to sever our connection with you, but we feel very sore at the treatment we have had from Mr. Edwards at Swansea.

We can only think he was deceived by persons he put trust in, or he would have warned the Writer.

We accept your suggestion of yesterday as to our account.

P. Davies to J. W. Symons, Surveyor of Taxes, Swansea. **3 July 1902 [3 : 671-2]**

We enclose return for special commissioners – you will observe that we put Schedule A Assessment at £2,258, as all the rents and profits from our houses and lands in Llangyfelach and Llanguicke Parishes are included in our statement of profits for last year.

March 1900-1902 – Payable for year ending April 5th 1903

	1899	**1900**	**1901**
Profits	19,248	14,125	10,089
Debenture Interest	362	615	700
Interest on Loans	355	89	–
Wayleave (Marquis of Worcester)	56	56	56
Income Tax – Sch A	90	107	138
do Sch D	267	487	770
Ground Rent	137	137	490
	20,495	15,616	13,045

1899	–	20,495
1900	–	15,616
1901	–	13,045
	3)	49,156
Average		16,385
Less Sch.A Assessment		2,258
Taxable Profit		14,127

July 3rd 1902

Extracted from books
Philip Davies

Arthur Gilbertson to J. W. Symons. **7 July 1902 [3 : 674]**

I am somewhat surprised at your enquiry of 5th inst., asking why my salary is reduced.

I state that my salary is £2,000 for the year in question.

You may be quite satisfied that returns from my Office are correct & carefully made out.

P. Davies to J. W. Symons, Dynevor Place, Swansea. **7 July 1902 [3 : 676]**

Private

We have your form of 5th inst regarding salaries returned by us for last year – we would refer you to our letter of the 24th May 1901 which will explain the difference referred to in the case of Mr. Arthur Gilbertson. Other amounts were reduced from various causes chiefly in account of a slack period which we experienced within the last year.

We will do our best to help you in obtaining returns from the Company's officials, but we cannot undertake to send in claims of abatement from the office.

P. Davies to W. A. Ford, Swansea. **7 July 1902 [3 : 680]**

Following on ours of the 4th inst. we return form duly completed – estimated wages for each department over next year will be as follows:

Steel Wks	£28,000
Tin Works	33,000
Galvanizing Wks.	9,000
Clerks &c.	1,260
	£71,260

Arthur Gilbertson to John Griffiths, Capital & Counties Bank. **25 Aug. 1902 [3 : 711]**

We are likely to do more business with the Mannesman Tube Co. at Landore. Could you kindly find out their financial position & would you make a note to let us know if you, at any time, hear anything about them.

P. Davies to F. Edwards, Capital & Counties Bank, Neath. **4 Sept. 1902 [3 : 717]**

Private

Kindly tell us in confidence if you consider the Aberlash Tinplate Co. Ltd., Ammanford, safe for £2,000 in the way of business. We would be obliged for any further information you could give regarding their financial position.

Arthur Gilbertson to the National Provincial Bank, London. **30 Jan. 1903 [3 : 785]**

Private

Would you kindly tell us the character & financial position of Messrs William Menzies & Co, 16 Mark Lane, EC.

Their Bankers are Bank of Scotland. Messrs Wm M. & Co. desire to represent us in Australia.

Arthur Gilbertson to Messrs Taylor Sons & Humbert, Grays Inn, London WC. **1 July 1903 [3 : 857]**

Your favour of yesterday. Would you kindly say what we should "endorse" on the Probate? and we understand you will send us a transfer, and we shall cancel the certificate, and issue a new one.

We are a small private Company and dont quite know what to do. Kindly instruct fully.

This letter referred to the estate of H. P. Gwynne James who had held 4 shares in the Company [3 : 854].

Arthur Gilbertson to the Capital & Counties Bank, Neath. **28 Aug. 1903 [3 : 893]**

We find our Slag Department will be overdrawn about £2,000, in consequence of "Stock" and outlay for enlargement, but our other a/c. will be in considerable credit? We conclude, under those circumstances, you will not charge anything, for overdraft on Slag Department, and you will allow us on credit balance?

Arthur Gilbertson to the Capital & Counties Bank, Swansea. **16 Nov. 1903 [3 : 921]**

Please read the enclosed, the cheques are always signed by myself or my Sons – all my Sons were away on that date, so I wrote a letter to the Bank to provide money for the wages. I am surprised at the conduct of the Bank.

This must not happen again, or we shall have to make arrangements which I would be sorry to do, as we have been good clients to your Bank over 40 years.

Frank Gilbertson to Messrs Pontifex Hewitt & Pitt. **26 Jan. 1904 [3 : 956]**

Replying to your favour of 20th inst, we estimate that in 1890 the value of each £50 share in our Company was £75, and the £125 debentures were worth £125 each.

Frank Gilbertson to The Surveyor of Taxes, Swansea. **10 Sept. 1904 [5 : 71-2]**

Referring to your letter of 6th inst.

We hardly think you wrote advisedly, & we object to the tone of your letter & also to the careless way it is written & worded.

We are unable to read even your signature.

For the last 40 years the Writer's Grandfather, Father, & now the writer himself, have taken an active part in the work as Income Tax Commissioners, & we are not likely to put any difficulty in your way.

The returns, which we make to the Special Commissioners, will be sent, as usual, at the earliest opportunity, but as our Audited Balance Sheet is seldom in our hands until the middle of August, & our Secretary takes his holiday immediately after, it is not possible to send the returns before the end of the month, or early September.

We do not understand your reference to "several applications".

Notice of the Twentieth O.G.M., 28 July 1905. **20 July 1905 [5 : 154]**

. . . The Directors recommend that a final dividend at the rate of 60% per annum . . . be declared for the six months ending June 5th last, making together with the interim dividend at the rate of 30% per annum paid for the six months ending December last, a total distribution of 45% for the year.

Frank Gilbertson to F. G. Baker, Surveyor of Taxes. **16 Nov. 1905 [5 : 200-2]**

Referring to our interview –

We have gone carefully into the question & enclose a list of the plant on which we claim an allowance for depreciation.

The older Mills & engines we put at a little over half their original value & all values are exclusive of buildings, roofs, rolls (in case of Mills), chimneys &c.

You must bear in mind we have two big Steel Mills, while no other works in the district has more than one, & also our Sheet Mills are far larger than any this side of Newport. Their value cannot be at all compared with that of tinplate Mills.

Our steel furnaces also are basic which cost more than acid, & depreciate much quicker.

	£
Cost of No. 12 – 14 Mills	10,117
do No. 10 & 11 "	5,574
Value of Nine other "	
@ £2,500	22,500
	38,191 including Engines but exclusive of Roofs, Chimneys & Rolls.
T. Galloway Boilers	4,500
6 Babcock do	4,800
2 Locos	2,500
4 Cranes	3,000
Pickling M'ches	2,000
Annealing F'ces	2,000
Electric Plant & Motors	3,000
Slag Works Machinery	2,500 (exclusive of Buildings)
Galvanizing M'ches,	
presses, engines &c.	1,000
Fitting Shop M'ches	600
2 Steel Mills	20,000
Cold Rolls Plant	1,500
Railways	5,000
	£90,591 @ 3% = £2,717
Steel Furnaces	
6 Steel Furnaces	£30,000 – estimated value today
5 Balling F'ces &	
Gas Producers	5,000
	£35,000 @ 5% = 1,750

Depreciation claimed £4,467

Frank Gilbertson to F. G. Baker. 27 Nov. 1905 [5 : 205-6]

Your favour of 23rd inst., to which the writer has been prevented, by illness, from replying before.

The amounts deducted for depreciation in the years you name are

1902	£3,500
1903	£5,000
1904	£5,000

The locos have been renewed by capital expenditure, out of profits, & cost was not charged to revenue.

Constant repairs to railways take place & are charged to revenue, but at times we relay large portions of our sidings & charge to capital. The last time we did this (about 4 years ago) we spent nearly £2,000 out of profits on relaying & improving one section of our railways & we think £5,000, an amount far below the cost of construction, is a fair value on which to allow depreciation.

Frank Gilbertson to Messrs Pontifex Hewitt & Pitt. 14 Dec. 1905 [5 : 213]

. . . In our opinion the 210 shares in this Company, held by Mr. George Lawrence's Executors on 29th November last, are worth £200 each, & the 7 £100 Debentures are worth £100 each.

Frank Gilbertson to Messrs Parrs Bank Ltd. 28 May 1906 [5 : 276]

Will you be good enough to let us know the terms upon which you would take our Banking a/c. in London?

At present the National Provincial does our work but if your terms were as favourable we should wish to transfer to you.

We give below a statement of our year's turnover, & weekly balances, to give you an idea of the nature of the account.

Most of the cash is paid in by our London Agents from the large Exporting Houses in the City.

Our regular pay day is the last day of the month after which our balance is at its lowest.

We have another a/c. with the Capital & Counties Bank at Neath, Glamorgan, with whom we do an equally large business but of a more local character, & this account we do not propose to change.

The National Provincial Bank charges us 10/- per annum for postage but makes no other charge, & pays us 2½% interest on our balance when over £1,000.

Will you please also send us a copy of your Balance Sheet.

We may say the payments into, & out of, our London a/c. are mostly in large sums.

Frank Gilbertson to Parrs Bank, Lombard St, EC. 1 June 1906 [5 : 283-4]

. . . We are glad you are able to meet us with regard to terms, & that our Firm will in future bank with you. The Writer's Great Grandfather kept his a/c with Messrs Fuller Banbury Nix & Co, & there has been no break in the connection since.

P. Davies to F. G. Baker, Surveyor of Taxes, Swansea. 31 Aug. 1906 [5 : 338]

Your favour of yesterday and we return form filled up.

In arriving at the amount of profit for last year, we deducted 3% depreciation upon £87,874 and 5% depreciation upon £33,250 – you will get these figures by deducting depreciation in previous year from value of our plant as given in ours of 16 November /05 – we also deducted 3% depreciation upon our amount of £3,000 since outlayed in our Sheet Mills, making a total amount of £4,388 allowance claimed for depreciation.

We are not in a position to give numbers of various assessments for Schedule A.

Frank Gilbertson to Parrs Bank, London. 15 Nov. 1906 [5 : 385]

. . . The Debenture holders are not many in number & are friends or relations of our Directors, & they have all been advised of the change [to Parrs Bank].

Frank Gilbertson to The Clerk to Pontardawe District Council. 19 Nov. 1906 [5 : 387]

We have a letter from Messrs Hedley Mason & Hedley informing us that they have been instructed to make a valuation of our Steel Works for your Committee. The Writer understood from his conversation with you that an arrangement might be come to with your Committee on the lines in force in the Swansea Union, viz. a tonnage rate upon our returns of output.

We should prefer this, & would rather not have the Valuers in our Works. Will you please instruct them, if your Committee agree?

We shall be pleased to discuss a tonnage rate with you at any time.

Frank Gilbertson to The Clerk to Pontardawe District Council. 3 Dec. 1906 [3 : 395]

We hear again from Messrs Hedley that they propose starting their valuation of our Steel Works this week.

We presume therefore that your Committee does not see its way to accept our proposal to be assessed upon a tonnage return?

Frank Gilbertson to The Clerk to Pontardawe District Council. 27 Feb. 1907[5 : 446]

We are obliged by your favour of 23 inst & we will attend at the Board Room on March 28th at 2.30 to state our objections to the valuation of our Steel Works.

Frank Gilbertson to Messrs The Briton Ferry Steel Co. Ld. **27 Feb. 1907 [5 : 448]**

The Pontardawe District Council has had our Steel Works (only) professionally valued for rating purposes.

The valuation has been notified to us as £5,000 gross & £2,000 rateable.

Upon our average output for past 3 years £2,000 represents 8¼d. a ton on ingots. We understand the Swansea Union Assessment is based on 4¼d. a ton on ingots.

Are you disposed to kindly give us any information with respect to your valuation that we could use in objecting before the Assessment Committee?

We are writing a similar letter to the other members of the Assn.

From the above the approx. average output would have been 58,180 ingot tons per year, which at 4¼d would have reduced the rateable value to £1,030, a reduction of £970.

Frank Gilbertson to The Clerk to Pontardawe District Council. **14 June 1907 [5 : 484]**

We have today received the demand note for Poor rate & Sanitary rate. We notice our Steel Works is assessed at £1,143.

We had hoped after the Committee had heard our objections that our Works would have been assessed upon the same basis as the rest of the South Wales Steel Trade.

We regret therefore we must make further objection, & appeal if needful. Meanwhile we pay 3/4ths of the rate, in respect of this item on the list, on account.

Frank Gilbertson to The Clerk to Pontardawe District Council. **27 June 1907 [5 : 488]**

. . . note that the Assessment Committee agree to our Steel Works being assessed on the basis of the Swansea Union.

Notice of Twenty-second O.G.M., 27 July 1907. **19 July 1907 [5 : 498]**

. . . The Directors recommend that a final dividend at the rate of 150% per annum . . . be declared for the six months ending June 8th last, making together with the interim dividend at the rate of 100% per annum paid up for the six months ending December last, a total distribution of 125% for the year.

Obviously an excellent investment, with dividends exceeding the nominal share value. Even at a probate value of £200 per share [see 5 : 213, 14 December 1905] the previous 2 years had produced an average annual yield of 26·8%.

For Special Commissioners. **7 Aug. 1907 [5 : 510]**

March 1906-1907 Payable year ending April 5th 1907

	1904	1905	1906
Profits	28,577	38,912	66,414
Debenture Interest	700	700	700
Wayleave (Marquis of Worcester)	56	56	56
Income Tax – Schedule A	126	135	144
do do B	990	1,193	1,278
Ground Rent	490	490	490
	30,939	41,486	69,082

1904	30,939
1905	41,486
1906	69,082
	3) 141,507
Average	47,169
Less Schedule A Assesst.	2,881
	44,288
Less Wear & Tear	4,235
Taxable Profit	£40,053

Frank Gilbertson to F. G. Baker. **13 Aug. 1907 [5 : 513]**

Your favour of 10th inst to hand today. We are not aware of any reason why we should depart from our old custom with regard to our return of profits. In any case we should object to make a detailed return, but if you pressed us, which we hardly expect you to do, we will put you in communication with our Auditors who could furnish a certificate as to the correctness of our return.

With regard to payments made to Associations existing for the purpose of increasing profits, we regret we take a different view to yourself & must decline to furnish particulars.

Frank Gilbertson to Messrs Barlow, Barlow & Lyde. **27 Dec. 1907 [5 : 605]**

We wish to invest a considerable sum as a reserve fund, apart from our own business.

We presume there is nothing in the constitution of our Company that would prohibit our investing in any class of security?

Frank Gilbertson to Parrs Bank Ltd. **27 Dec. 1907 [5 : 606]**

We wish to invest some £20,000 to £30,000 to hold as a reserve fund. Will you kindly recommend us suitable securities? We presume that in the present conditions it is possible to select securities that will yield fully 4% & yet be sufficiently safe for the purpose of a reserve fund.

Frank Gilbertson to Parrs Bank Ltd. — 21 Jan. 1908 [5 : 627]

We regret not having replied to your letters re. investments. We shall write upon this matter shortly. We notice in a recent case in the Law Courts that Bankers give information to the representatives of well accredited Trade Protection Societies.

Which are the best of such societies in your opinion?

We have never found them much use & when P. Macfadyen failed, owing us £5,700, we had in our possession 2 excellent financial reports not 14 days old.

We should appreciate your confidential advice.

P. Davies to Messrs Wenham Bros. & Co., Birmingham. — 3 March 1908 [5 : 651]

. . . the amount of wages paid by us in the Sheet Rolling and Galvanizing departments only, for the year ending 31st. December 1907 are as follows:–

Sheet Rolling	£42,101..3.. 6
Galvanizing	£14,782..6..10

Frank Gilbertson to Parrs Bank Ltd. — 26 March 1908 [5 : 667]

. . . Please purchase for us

about	£3,000	Cape of Good Hope 4% 10 year Bonds
"	£3,000	Queensland 4% 1915 Bonds
"	£3,000	Argentine 5% 1886
"	£3,000	Chinese 5% Gold 1896
"	£3,000	Japan 4½% 1st Series
"	£5,000	Canadian Pacific Ry 4% Pref. Stock
"	£5,000	Buenos Ayres & Pacific 4% 1st Debentures.

The amounts represent actual cost of stock not nominal value. You will use ample discretion in fixing the actual amounts but the total must be £25,000 as near as possible.

Notice of the Twenty-third O.G.M., 31 July 1908. — 23 July 1908 [5 : 805]

. . . The Directors recommend that a final dividend at the rate of 50% per annum . . . be declared for the six months ending June 6th last making together with the interim dividend at the rate of 100% per annum paid for the six months ending December last, a total distribution of 75% for the year.

The Directors have decided to recommend this reduced rate of interest on account of the depressed condition of the Steel trade, and also in view of the very considerable addition to the Works which they propose to undertake without increasing the Capital or debt of the Company.

Frank Gilbertson to Sir Alfred Lawrence. **23 July 1908 [5 : 806]**

. . . The addition we contemplate to the Works is 6 tinplate mills & a new tinplate department complete. The old trade is in a better state again.

P. Davies to F. G. Baker, Swansea. **16 Nov. 1908 [5 : 880-3]**

Referring to yours of the 2nd inst we now enclose copies of our Balance Sheets for the last three years – in comparing these with the returns of profits sent you we find that we have been adding Debenture Interest to these profits under a misapprehension – we have not placed Debenture Interest as a charge against our working costs, and as you will see from copies of Balance Sheets our profits have been given to include the £700 interest yearly, and it is therefore incorrect to add this amount yearly to our profits as we have been doing in our returns to you – you will therefore see that we are entitled to a refund of the amounts charged for Income Tax upon same. Please amend accordingly.

We also append further particulars asked for of amounts paid into and received from Associations –

Year ending April 1906 –	
Levies upon Galvanized Sheets & other contributions	1,057.. 8.. 4
Less received from Association and included in our returns of profit	537..16.. 3
	£519..12.. 1
Year ending April 1907 –	
Levies upon Galvanized Sheets & other contributions	1,292.. 1.. 4
Contributions to Steel Association	158..12.. 1
	1,450..13.. 5
Less received from Associations & included in our returns of profits	479.. 8..10
	£971.. 4.. 7

We also enclose a separate sheet giving particulars of profits for different periods in each year, and which will enable you to compare Balance Sheets with our previous returns.

Profit as returned by W. G. & Co. Ld.		**Profits as per Balance Sheet**
		Year ending June 9/06
	£	£
9 Mos. ending Mch 17/06	32,588	41,506
3 " " June 9/06	8,918	41,506
		Year ending June 8/07
	£	£
9 Mos. ending Mch 16/07	57,496	78,453
3 " " June 8/07	20,956	78,452
		Year ending June 6/08
	£	£
9 Mos. ending Mch 14/08	38,959	52,183
3 " " June 6/08	13,224	52,183

Frank Gilbertson to Messrs Parrs Bank Ld, London. **27 Nov. 1908 [5 : 899]**

As it will be some time before we shall need a large part of our cash reserves for our new works, now in course of erection, we propose to invest another £25,000.

Would you kindly recommend us suitable investments & give us a good list.

P. Davies to Messrs Parrs Bank Ld., **30 Nov. 1908 [5 : 901]**

We are obliged by Mr. Carnegie's letter addressed to our Mr. F. W. Gilbertson and shall be glad if you will purchase for us £5,000 each of the following

Natal 3½% (new) @ £96
Canada 4% Debenture Redeemable 1912 £102
Egyptian Unified 4% Bonds @ £102
Japan 4½% 1st Series @ £94
Burma Railways new £10 shares @ 10½

You will understand that actual cost is to be about £25,000 in all.

Frank Gilbertson to F. G. Baker. **21 Dec. 1908 [5 : 921-3]**

Your favour of 17th inst. We think it may be desirable for the Writer to have another interview with you, but we will reply to your letter as far as we can.

We note that the Commissioners instruct you that the proper method of Assessment is to take the 3 years ended June 1907.

Under the circumstances this would be a most unfair time to make such a change as it would mean including the year of exceptional prosperity in 4 assessments instead of 3.

We cannot believe the Commissioners would allow us to suffer this injustice & we should certainly oppose it, as they have never before raised any question as to the period covered by each assessment, & there is no doubt that the system we have always adopted of taking March to March was originally started in consultation with the Supervisor at that time.

The Writer's Father & Grandfather were always active & valuable Commissioners, & acted in concert with the Surveyor at all times.

Replying to the other points.

For the year ended June 1905 no payments were made to any Association.

As regards Profit & Loss a/c. – These are drawn up in the manner that Deloitte Plender & Griffiths are accustomed to & show the actual profit & loss, & they include any interest received from investments and Bank interest. As a matter of fact it is only the latter that has hitherto appeared in our books, as until recently & since the return, we have never held any investments.

We cannot supply any other trading account, & now that we have agreed to return the Association payments we think any demand of the sort would be simply vexatious. Are not the Commissioners satisfied that, in comparing our profits with other similar Works, our returns represent a reasonable parity?

As regards Plant & Machinery, we do not follow you – of course renewals so far as they are needed to keep existing plant efficient are charged to revenue here & at every properly managed factory in the country.

Rents of cottages are credited the trading a/c.

Frank Gilbertson to Messrs Seyd & Co. Ld. **6 Jan. 1909 [5 : 930]**

Private

We return the form you sent us which is correct so far as it goes.

Ours is a private Company & we do not care to give anyone details of our trading, but we may say for your own information only, that our reserves amount to many times our total capital.

Frank Gilbertson to Messrs Parrs Bank Ld. **8 Jan. 1909 [5 : 935]**

Yours of yesterday re. the Natal Stock & the London & Westminster Bank.

We do not know what a Certificate of Incorporation is, & can only suggest that you apply to our Solicitors, Messrs Barlow, Barlow & Lyde, 165 Fenchurch St. who attended to the formation of this Company – we have no patience with this red tape & if there is any further difficulty please sell the stock & advise us of something that will give less trouble.

P. Davies to F. G. Baker. **25 Jan. 1909 [5 : 951-2]**

Referring to your favour of the 31st ulto. the amount of our profit for the year ending June '05 was £30,377.

With regard to the new method of assessment proposed by the Commissioners, the abnormal profits for the year 1906-07 have already been taken into account once in an average for three years, which has already borne assessment, whereas the alteration proposed would involve the inclusion of these exceptional profits in further three returns swelling the average for four returns altogether.

Our accounts are made up quarterly, and a proper balance is made every quarter. We cannot see that you are correct in stating that the three months' profit is not one fourth of the year's profit – if you will again refer to our return you will find that in two cases out of three the quarter's profit exceeds the quarterly average of the year.

Rent of Cottages. This is a small matter and as we are given credit for Schedule 'A' Assessment in our return we will waive any difference which is slightly against us.

Our Mr. F. W. Gilbertson wishes to say he is sorry that he has not been able to call upon you, but hopes that with the explanations given in this letter, it may not be necessary for him now to do so.

P. Davies to F. G. Baker. **27 Jan. 1909 [5 : 963]**

We have your favour of y'day, with notice of Assessment, and we observe your explanatory note. We accordingly beg to give notice of appeal against the Assessment which exceeds our return of profits, and does not provide for refund of amounts paid on Debenture Interest incorrectly added to our profits for some years past.

In the meantime, we are sending Cheque £2,000 on account of the assessment.

Frank Gilbertson to W. B. Laws, Auditor, Cardiff. **13 Feb. 1909 [5 : 973]**

The Special Commissioners now demand accounts of all sums spent on Repairs, Renewals & Replacements.

It is so necessary to spend money, that might come under these headings, in order to keep a plant running, let alone running efficiently, that we hardly know where to begin.

Do you know of any Association that really understands this work & that you could advise us to call in to our assistance?

Frank Gilbertson to R. Whitaker Evans, Llanelly Steel Co. Ld. **13 Feb. 1909 [5 : 974]**

We are having trouble with the Income Tax Officers, & the Special Commissioners demand accounts of all sums spent in Repairs & Renewals & Replacements.

Would it be within the province of the Association to enquire of each member whether he has had any trouble, & whether any one knows of a Professional man or an Association that has experience in Steel Works & has been of assistance in arranging these questions?

P. Davies to Messrs The Machinery Users' Association. **8 March 1909 [5 : 984]**

The Special Commissioners for Income Tax have assessed us under Schedule D at a higher rate than our return of profits.

We have appealed and they have written demanding an account of all sums paid under the heads of Repairs, Renewals & Replacements and whether charged to Revenue or Capital.

We understand none of our fellow Manufacturers has had a similar demand and it opens a very difficult question in a Steel Works. Are you in a position to help us and if necessary to fight the appeal for us, and if so what are your approximate charges?

Frank Gilbertson to The Special Commissioners of Income Tax. **10 March 1909 [5 : 987-9]**

In reply to your letter of 6th inst SC 360/1909. We had replied on 8th inst, but our reply was put in the wrong envelope, & a letter to the Machinery Users' Association sent you instead, which you have kindly returned.

The position is this. You ask us for certain accounts which we have never been asked for before, nor can we find that any of our Competitors in our trades are asked for them.

It will also be impossible to prepare such accounts from our books.

We therefore seek the assistance of some Association, or some professional man who can act for us with the necessary experience. Broadly speaking, in a Steel & Sheet Works like ours a body of men, Masons, Smiths, Fitters &c. have to be daily employed in repairs, & renewals have to be daily made to keep the plant running, & no separate account is kept of this work.

When we extend our Works, as we constantly do, we devote a portion of our profits, on which tax has been paid, to the purpose. As a matter of fact we do not pay in dividends a third part of our profits on which we pay tax, the remaining ⅔rds going to increase & improve our Works.

Our accounts are audited by Deloitte Plender & Griffiths & we always return our gross profits, & then deduct an agreed percentage on our Capital value of plant. For the first time we have been asked to show our Audited Balance Sheets, & we at once gave the local Surveyor all the Balance Sheets for past years that he required.

We do not see why we, who have always been most careful in our returns, should be singled out, & given exceptional trouble in this matter.

No doubt you are aware that the amount of £2,000 has been paid by this Company on account of the Income Tax Assessment, & if, pending the result of our appeal, you require a further payment on account, we are willing to make one up to the amount of the Tax on our return of profit.

P. Davies to Messrs Humphreys Davies & Co., London. **18 May 1909 [7 : 31,34]**

Re: Income Tax Assessment

Referring to your favour of the 13th inst. we are now sending you a detailed list of loose plant and rolling stock at our Works – we have also attached an estimate of the present value.

No.		£	s	d
2	Locomotives	2,500	..	..
40	Railway Wagons	600	..	..
15	" Iron do	300	..	..
4	Steam Cranes	3,000	..	..
2	Mortar Mills	50	..	..
6	Steel Ladles	2,100	..	..
300	Ingot Moulds	1,875	..	..
12	Bogies	60	..	..
9	Portable Weighing Machines	90	..	..
20	Pulley Blocks	120	..	..
48	Barrows	24	..	..
28	Rail Trolleys	140	..	..
59	Hand Trolleys	295	..	..
11	Hot Bar Trolleys	110	..	..
6	Trams for carrying Ashes	24	..	..
15	Hydraulic Jacks	120	..	..
3	[?] legs with [?] blocks	120	..	..
1	Merryweather's Fire Engine	20	..	..
15	Benches for Openers	7	10	..
3	Annealing Carriages	30	..	..
15	Large Annealing "	450	..	..
19	do do Stands	380	..	..
55	Small Annealing Pots	110	..	..
54	do do Stands	25	..	..
7	Rope	17	10	..
	Hand Tools	500	..	..
		£13,068	..	..

Frank Gilbertson to Messrs Seyd & Co. Ltd. **3 Jan. 1910 [7 : 181]**

We return the form you sent us, but we do not like to disclose the dividend we pay. We may say our Works represent a value of at least four times our Capital & Debentures, & that we hold £50,000 worth of stocks & have investments to a similar amount, so that we think our Financial Status is better than you give us credit for in your lists.

Frank Gilbertson to Messrs Barlow, Barlow & Lyde, London. **31 Jan. 1910 [7 : 192]**

Our Debentures, £14,000, mature next June. We are prepared to pay them off, but in view of our extensions of plant, we think it may be desirable to renew the Debentures in any case where the holder wishes to retain them. Will you kindly send us a draft of a notice to be sent to each holder, asking his wishes, & giving March 31st as the last day we shall receive applications for a renewal of the Debentures.

When we know how many desire to renew we will settle the amount of the new issue.

Can the existing Debentures be renewed, or must a fresh issue be made? We want to do it in the least expensive & public manner.

Frank Gilbertson to Messrs Barlow, Barlow & Lyde. **4 Feb. 1910 [7 : 197]**

. . . We shall require about 16 Notices, and the names and addresses of the present holders are known to us except for the £5,000 which was allotted through yourselves – perhaps you will kindly furnish us with the list of names and addresses for this amount.

Frank Gilbertson to Messrs Capital & Counties Bank, Neath. **17 Feb. 1910 [7 : 204]**

With reference to our Tinplate a/c.

Our London Agents, Messrs Phillips & Hill, 122 Cannon Street, are in the habit of collecting large amounts of money in London & paying straight into our a/c at Parrs Bank.

By this means some time is saved, & as in the Galvanizing trade the sums are often very large, some risk is also saved.

We should like to carry on the same method of collecting debts in London for our Tinplate department, & we wish to know if such amounts as are collected in London can be paid into one of your City branches, & then transferred by yourselves to Neath?

Philip Davies to Messrs Barlow, Barlow & Lyde, London. **[7 : 247-8] 31 March 1910**

. . . We shall be glad if you will prepare agreements and have new coupons printed against debentures given on attached list . . .

Debenture Holders – additional to list submitted by Messrs Barlow, Barlow & Lyde.

	Amount	Numbers
Arthur Gilbertson	£4,700	1-47
Chas Lewis Lawrence Sir Alfred Tristram Lawrence execs of late George Lawrence	£ 700	48-54
Sir Alfred T. Lawrence	£ 700	55-61
Arthur Lawrence	£ 200	62-63
Francis William Gilbertson	£1,000	64-73
Francis Bramah Gilbertson	£ 500	74-78
Miss Ellen Louise Gilbertson	£ 400	79-82
" Madelina Gilbertson	£ 400	83-86
" Emily Maude Gilbertson	£ 400	87-90

P. Davies to Messrs Humphreys Davies Co. Ltd. 31 March 1910 [7 : 250]

Income Tax Assessment 1908-9

	£	£
Assessed Profits 1905-6	41,486	
Less Debenture Interest	700	40,786
Assessed Profits 1906-7	69,082	
Less Debentures Interest	700	68,382
Profits for 1907-8		62,643
	3)	171,811
		57,270
Deduct Schedule 'A' Assessment		2,881
		£ 54,389

Frank Gilbertson to Messrs Parrs Bank Ltd. 1 April 1910 [7 : 252]

We are obliged by yours of yesterday with list of securities you hold for us.
Will you please sell the following & credit our account with the proceeds.

£2,750 Chinese Govt 5% 1896 Gold Loan
£8,300 Japanese 4½% 1 Series
£5,000 Egyptian Unified 4%
£5,000 Burma Railway Co. Ld.

P. Davies to F. G. Baker **n.d. c. 12 May 1910 [7 : 297-8]**

Income Tax Assessment 1909-1910

	Profit per certified Accounts for the Year ending	Deduct Profit for Quarter ending	Add Profit for Quarter ending	Profit for 12 months ending
	5 June 1909	5 June 1909	6 June 1908	13 Mch 1909
Steel Bars	9,646	1,224	3,039	11,461
Billets	5,397	1,231	1,169	5,335
Galvanized Sheets	45,000	8,671	8,720	45,049
Tin Plates	207	52	93	248
Blackplate Sale	768	823	Less 283	Less 338
Slag Wks Department	163	40	57	180
Interest & Dividends	2,193	766	485	1,912
	63,374	12,807	13,280	63,847
Less Dividends from which tax was deducted	1,409	352		1,057
	£61,965	12,455	13,280	62,790

	Year to Mch 1907	Year to Mch 1908	Year to Mch 1909
Profits per Accounts	66,414	59,915	62,790
Additions			
Wayleaves	56	56	56
Income Tax Schedule 'A'	144	144	148
do " 'D'	1,278	2,038	2,000
Ground Rents	490	490	533
Subscriptions	52	250	702
	68,434	62,893	66,229
Less Schedule 'A' Assessment on Works	2,881	2,881	2,942
	65,553	60,012	63,287
			65,553
			60,012
			3) 188,852
Average for 3 years			£ 62,950

Notice of Twenty-fifth O.G.M., 7 October 1910. **28 Sept. 1910 [7 : 414]**

(i) To confirm final dividend at the rate of 50% per annum on the paid up Capital of £35,000 paid on the fourth August last . . .

The Directors report that the new six Mill Tinplate Works has been completed and is now fully at work, and it is hoped that by the end of this year this extension will contribute to the profits of the Company.

Considerable extensions to the Steel Works are in course of erection but will necessitate no addition to the Capital of the Company.

Frank Gilbertson to F. Atterbury, Somerset House, London. **4 March 1912 [7 : 853]**

. . . We regret to note we have not made the return [of the Debenture issue] that was required.

Before asking you for the form, we wish to say it is almost certain we shall pay off the whole of the Debenture issue before the end of this year.

If we undertake to make the return in 6 months time, provided our intentions are not carried out, can the matter stand over for that period?

There is no practical issue at stake, seeing that we have a reserve fund of £200,000!

Frank Gilbertson to Messrs Deloitte Plender & Griffiths **9 March 1912 [7 : 856]**

We desire to rearrange our Capital. Would you kindly instruct your South Wales Manager to arrange a meeting with the Writer?

After we have given him our ideas we should like you to discuss the proposals with our Solicitors, Messrs Barlow, Barlow & Lyde, 165, Fenchurch St.

Arthur Gilbertson had died on 2 March 1912.

Philip Davies to Barlow, Barlow & Lyde, London. **16 March 1912 [7 : 861]**

re Arthur Gilbertson deceased

I have been requested to give you my idea of the present value of a £50 ordinary share in this Company. I consider that a fair price for this share today would be £200.

Philip Davies to W. B. Aldriff, Messrs Parrs Bank Ld, London. **16 March 1912 [7 : 862]**

re Arthur Gilbertson deceased

. . . I consider that a fair price for the £4,700 5% debentures would be par value.

Frank Gilbertson to Frank W. Higgison, Deloitte Plender Griffiths & Co. **2 April 1912 [7 : 873]**

Referring to your favour of the 29th ulto, the particulars of the manner in which the balance standing to the credit of Profit & Loss Account as at 3rd June 1911 has been dealt with, are as follows:

For a Final Dividend at rate of 50% per annum	£ 8,750 – 0 – 0
To Reserve	£20,122 – 4 – 6
To Suspense a/c. for Workmen's Compensation a/c.	£ 1,000 – 0 – 0
To Electric Stations & Motor Plants for depreciation	£ 3,000 – 0 – 0
To Slag Grinding Plant & Works for depreciation	£ 2,000 – 0 – 0
To Investment a/c for depreciation	£ 31 – 6 – 2
and balance to be carried into current year's account viz:-	£ 91,064 –18 – 6
	£125,968 – 9 – 2

P. Davies to Frederick Edwards, Capital & Counties Bank. **31 May 1912 [7 : 939]**

Mr. F. W. Gilbertson before leaving for the Continent last week advised me that he had sent you cheque in readiness to meet purchase of shares held by Mr. W. Fred. Richards in the Samlet Colliery Ltd., and he also intimated at the same time that his brother-in-law, Mr. Rice Mansel Dillwyn would be ready to send you a similar amount should Mr. W. Fred. Richards decide to sell.

I have today heard from Mr. Richards that he is prepared to sell his shares for £1,050, and that Mr. J. Aeron Thomas will receive the money for him.

Will you kindly arrange to complete the transaction on behalf of Mr. Gilbertson, and the shares are to be transferred to Mr. Rice Mansel Dillwyn, Graig-y-mor, Mumbles.

The nominal value of the shares is £1,000.

Frank Gilbertson to Messrs Barlow, Barlow & Lyde. **31 Aug. 1912 [8 : 13-17]**

Your favour of yesterday re value of Ordinary Shares in this Company.

Please communicate with Messrs Deloitte as you suggest.

I may say Mr. Fitchie, the junior of the 2 gentlemen who came here from Deloitte & Co, told me he thought £200 a proper value.

Mr. Higgison, the new Manager of their South Wales business however told me unofficially that he thought £300 could be sustained.

From my point of view the following considerations affect the value.

(1) No good will can properly be considered an asset in such a competitive business as this.
The business entirely depends upon the successful or unsuccessful management.

(2) The department that used to provide the best profits has been spoilt by competition & last year the Galvanizing resulted in a heavy loss.
The new concerns in the galvanizing trade are much better equipped with plant & machinery than we are. We have all worked at a loss since they commenced manufacturing.

(3) The Steel trade we do is in competition with Germany, Belgium & America & is the lowest priced steel business in the Country & most liable to fluctuations.
(4) In our Balance Sheet the large reserve is because we have not wiped off any sums for depreciation.
(5) The dividends we have paid are the maximum consistent with the maintenance of our power to compete with new & modern Works.
(6) The value of £200 means putting the concern on a 12½% basis. In South Wales no one would dream of investing in a Steel Works, Tinplate Works or Galvanized Sheet Works that did not yield 12½% to 20% upon the purchase price.
The market price of Briton Ferry Steel Co. shares which are dealt in largely return 13% at present rate of dividends.
When we sold the Glynbeudy Works at a time of great prosperity in the Tinplate trade we only got Par value for the Shares & had to give away the whole of the Reserve Fund.
(7) There is an instability in these South Wales trades owing to foreign competition that really does not exist in any other industries in this country, & the Works that make profits make them as a result of good management, & good buying & selling & not as a result of the value of the plant engaged.

How to prove it I dont know but it is a certain fact that if our shares were in the market in South Wales the maximum price they would fetch would be a figure that would yield between 10% & 15% upon the recent dividends paid.

Notice of Twenty-eighth O.G.M., 29 July 1913. **18 July 1913 [8 : 298-9]**

. . . total distribution of 50% for year.

. . . The Directors desire to report that the past year's trading has been very profitable but they do not recommend the declaration of a larger dividend because the prospects of the raw Steel Trade, the Galvanizing and Tinplate Trades for the immediate future are exceedingly bad.

These trades appear likely to pass through a more difficult period than has been experienced for many years . . .

Frank Gilbertson to S. B. Barlow. **28 March 1914 [8 : 543-4]**

We have during recent years spent large sums out of the profits of the Company upon improving and enlarging the works.

Although the trades in which we are engaged are at present in a very depressed condition, we expect when conditions improve to reap the benefit of this expenditure.

The value of the Works is, therefore, now out of all proportion to the nominal Capital of the Company, and there are reasons why it is desirable to increase the

Capital so that dividends will represent a lower percentage of the nominal Capital than is now the case.

We have taken the advice of our Solicitors and Auditors and recommend that £105,000 of the sum at present standing to the credit of our Profit and Loss account be distributed as a bonus declaration of profits in the form of one £50 6% Preference Share and two £50 Ordinary Shares to the holders of each of the present £50 Ordinary Shares.

We also propose exchanging 6% Preference Shares for the existing Debentures, amounting to £14,000, so far as the holders are willing to exchange.

The issued Capital of the Company after this bonus distribution, provided Debenture holders agree to the proposals, will be –

£105,000 Ordinary Shares
£ 49,000 6% Preference Shares

We take this opportunity of proposing certain alterations in our Articles of Association that were recommended by our Solicitors and Auditors.

Pencilled footnote 'Copy of this letter sent to all other shareholders'.

Frank Gilbertson to Debenture Holders. **29 April 1914 [8 : 581]**

Extraordinary General Meetings of this Company have recently been held and resolutions passed increasing the Capital of the Company to £175,000.

Power has been taken to issue 980 6% Cumulative Preference Shares of £50 each.

It is our wish to exchange 2 £50 6% Preference Shares for each £100 5% Debenture, which amount altogether to £14,000.

We wish to clear the Company of all Debenture debt, and in the event of any Debenture holders being unable or unwilling to accept an equivalent amount of Preference shares we should be very glad if they would allow the Debentures they hold to be paid off for cash.

The resolutions dealing with this matter are No's 1 and 4 passed at the Extraordinary General Meeting on April 27th 1914 and we enclose copies of them.

Please let us have your decision as soon as possible.

Holders of nearly half the present Debentures have already signified their willingness to accept Preference Shares in exchange.

P. Davies to Messrs Parrs Bank, London. **27 July 1914 [8 : 706]**

List of Debentures to be exchanged for an equivalent value of Preference Shares

	£	s	d		
Francis W. Gilbertson	600			Certificate indicates Bonus Share	
Chas. G. Gilbertson	300			do	do
George N. Gilbertson	1,000			do	do
Mrs. Harriet F. Dillwyn	1,000			do	do
Francis W. Gilbertson Cecil F. Gilbertson Campbell W. Giffard }	400			do	do
C. L. & Sir A.T. Lawrence	700			Certificate includes Bonus Share	
Arthur Lawrence	200			do	do
Sir Alfred Lawrence	700			do	do
Francis W. Gilbertson Cecil F. Gilbertson Chas. G. Gilbertson }	2,000				
Francis Bramah Gilbertson	500				
Miss Ellen L. Gilbertson	400				
Miss Madelina Gilbertson	400				
Miss E. Maude Gilbertson	400				
Miss Helen I. Barlow	1,100				
Miss Lydia C. Barlow Miss Cecilia C. Barlow }	2,000				
Lieut Colonel S. Babington George E. J. H. Barlow }	1,000				
Stephen B. Barlow George E. J. H. Barlow Lieut Colonel S. Babington }	500				
Stephen B. Barlow Mrs. Helen Barlow }	400				
Mrs Isabel de Winton Gilbertson	400				
	£14,000				

Frank Gilbertson to Messrs Parrs Bank. **27 July 1914 [8 : 708]**

Referring to my Company's letter of this date re Debenture Exchange.

You hold my Debentures. Will you please take note that I require £400 of the Preference Shares, corresponding, to be in my wife's name, although I shall be paying the whole £1,000 in respect of them.

With regard to the Trust represented by

F. W. Gilbertson
Cecil F. Gilbertson
Campbell W. Giffard }

The Trustees have no Banking Account. Could you open one just for this transaction & allow me to use one of my own cheques?

Frank Gilbertson to Messrs Barlow, Barlow & Lyde, London. **4 Dec. 1914 [8 : 833]**

In reply to your letter of the 2nd, Mr. Francis Bramah Gilbertson is the only survivor of the three Trustees. His address is The Royal Hotel, Hoylake.

There is no actual knowledge of the death of Mr. W. F. Richardson, but I think his death has been presumed by the courts some time ago.

He disappeared, and is believed to have been dead, I think, for more than twenty years.

It may be desirable for the short deed of conveyance to be drawn up and executed by Mr. F. B. Gilbertson as soon as possible.

F.W. Gilbertson to Messrs Seyd & Co. Ld. **18 Jan. 1915 [8 : 863]**

Since our last return we have carried out an alteration in our Capital & the figures now are as under.

You must excuse our giving information as to our profits & dividends.

. . . Capital Authorised £175,000 in £50 Pref & Ord Shares
Issued £105,000 Ord £49,000 Pref.

Debentures }
Mortgages } Nil
Loans }

Reserve Fund £200,000

P. Davies to D. Thomas, Messrs The Capital & Counties Bank Ltd, Neath. **n.d. June 1915 [8 : 943]**

Securities held for safe keeping

We have your favour of yesterday, and thank you for return of receipts Nos. 525 and 531, the securities sold deleted therefrom.

We note you retain receipt No. 550, having sold all these shares.

We thank you for Contract for the £450 Alexandra (Newport & South Wales) Docks & Railway Consolidated "B" Stock sold on our behalf.

Your remarks regarding placing of the proceeds of the £3,000 Cape of Good Hope 4% 10 year Debs. 1917 to the credit of the Steel Department Current Account are in order.

Frank Gilbertson to F. Edwards, Capital & Counties Bank, Neath. **28 June 1915 [8 : 987]**

I thought I had better open this matter with you personally.

We have to pay a cheque for £7,000 today from our Tinplate account into our Steel account.

If we pay it in at Parrs there are no charges. If we pay it into our a/c with you at Neath there will be £3-10-0 charges, although both the Tinplate & Steel departments have their a/cs at your Neath branch.

In view of the terms arranged for Raglan it suggests itself to me that you should give us as good terms.

As things stand today we are of course tempted to keep larger sums at Parrs than with the C. & C. Bank.

P. Davies to Messrs Lloyd & Ward, London. **29 June 1915 [8 : 992]**

We are in receipt of your favour of y'day addressed to our Mr. F. W. Gilbertson & note for what purpose the information is required.

The old £50 Shares were valued for probate on the decease of the late Mr. Arthur Gilbertson @ £275.

In May 1914 the Capital of this Company was increased by the distribution out of accumulated profits, which were before the Somerset House Authorities when they agreed the valuation, of 2 Ordinary £50 Shares & one 6% Cumulative Preference Share of £50 to the holders of every original £50 Ordinary Share.

Thus 3 Ordinary Shares & 1 Preference Share could today be valued @ £275 in our opinion – taking the Preference Share at par this leaves £75 as the value of each £50 Ord Share today.

You will know whether it is the original £50 share you have to value or the shares since the increase of Capital.

Frank Gilbertson to Messrs Brydges, Mellersh & Melhuish, Cheltenham. **22 July 1915 [10 : 19-20]**

. . . We were dealing with the late Arthur Gilbertson's interests in the Firm which amounted to practically ⅔rds of the shares of the Co. . . .

. . . We have no objection to telling you at once the Dividends paid the last 3 years & give them at foot. You will note the change that occurred after the nominal capital was increased.

		Dividends
Year ended June 1st 1912	–	50% on old Capital
" " May 31st 1913	–	50% " " "
" " May 30th 1914	–	40% " " "
Half year ended Dec 12th 1914	–	12½% on new Capital

Frank Gilbertson to Messrs Brydges, Mellersh & Melhuish. **10 Aug. 1915 [10 : 27-8]**

. . . Previous to 1914 the Capital of the Company was as follows:–

	£
700 Ordinary Shares of £50 ea.	35,000
120 Debentures of £100 ea.	12,000

but in April 1914 the Authorized Capital was increased to £175,000 . . . consequently the Capital is as follows:–

	£
Authorized – 2,520 Ordinary Shares of £50 ea.	126,000
980 Preference do of £50 ea.	49,000
	£175,000

Issued:-	£
700 Ordinary Shares of £50 ea. fully paid	35,000
1,400 do allotted July 29/14 & credited as fully paid in satisfaction of bonus	70,000
700 Preference Shares of £50 each allotted July 29/14 & credited as fully paid in satisfaction of bonus	35,000
280 Preference Shares of £50 each issued for cash & allotted July 29/14	14,000
	£154,000

We trust the foregoing information will clearly explain our position to you.

You will take note that the Inland Revenue seem to refer to the Authorised Capital as the Capital of the Company but only a proportion is actually issued.

P. Davies to A. Howel Gilbertson. **30 Nov. 1915 [10 : 82]**

I have your favor of y'day. I am of opinion that our ordinary shares of £50 each can fairly be considered to be worth £75 each and our Preference Shares of £50 each may be regarded as of par value – your holding in this company will therefore give

26 Preference Shares		@ £50 each	£1,300
78 Ordinary	do	@ £75 "	£5,850
			£7,150

Mr. Frank is in accord with this estimate of value of Shares. I trust you are now settled down comfortably in your new home.

P. Davies to Messrs Parrs Bank Ltd. 29 March 1916 [10 : 152]

We beg to enclose herewith Certificate No. 43 for ten preference shares, issued to Lieut. George Noel Gilbertson, in this Company, for safe custody.

Cecil Gilbertson to Messrs Parrs Bank Ltd, London. 12 May 1916 [10 : 171]

We are carrying out large extensions to our Works, which will considerably increase our business in the near future, and, in view of this, we are forced to make some alteration in our office, which will necessitate the opening of a fresh Account at your Bank, which we desire to be called No. 2 Account.

The only transactions which will pass through this Account will be of a very private nature, relating more especially to Dividends, Interest, etc.

Will you kindly prepare a special Cheque Book accordingly, as we wish the change to take place at the end of our financial year on May 27th.

On 18 October and 14 November 1916 Cecil Gilbertson asked Parrs Bank to transfer £30,000 & £35,000 respectively from the No. 1 a/c. to the No. 2 a/c. [10 : 243,268]

Philip Davies to Surveyor of Taxes, Swansea. 6 July 1917 [10 : 365-6]

Salaries & Wages year ended April 5, 1917

					Bonus
Francis W. Gilbertson	Managing Director	Glynteg,	Pontardawe	1,500	9,562
Cecil F. Gilbertson	Director	Abercrave House	Ystradgynlais, Brecon	1,500	9,562
Chas. G. Gilbertson	do	Gellygron,	Pontardawe	900	9,562
Philip Davies	Secretary	Danygraig,	do	477..10	3,297
Chas. Giddings	Accountant	Bronygraig	do	358	2,438
Thomas B. George	do	Brolon, Rhydyfro	do	238..18	100
J. J. Emmanuel	do	Glynhelyg, Brecon Road	do	155	80
David J. Bowen	do	Frondeg, Alltwen	do	358	1,204
H. J. Munro	Chief Engineer	Lyndhurst, Uplands	do	500	350
Alfred Palmer	Accountant	Heathfield Road	do	120	55
Wm. R. Jones	do	Dyffryn Road, Alltwen	do	113	55
Edgar Jenkins	do	Francis St,	do	130	40
David Davies	do	20 Grove Road	do	107	55
David J. Davies	do	2 Ynysymond Road, Alltwen	do	114	55
C. A. Hardy	Mill Manager	St. Dunstan's, Brecon Rd.	do	400	–
Stanley R. Davies	Analytical Chemist	Erwig, Uplands	do	247..16	704

Owen Davies	Steel Works Manager	Bryneithin, do	do	372..19	737
Stephen Davies	Mills Superintendent	Bettwsycoed, do	do	234	149
Joshua Davies	do	Old Road, Ynysmeudw		220..15	–
John Roberts	Foreman Mechanic	2 Vine Villa, Brecon Rd.	do	310	–
Prosser Thomas	Traffic Foreman	Graig Road, Trebanos		186..16	5
William R. Williams	Foreman Mason	4 Derw Rd.	do	239..16	–
Wilfred D. Williams	Draughtsman	High St.	do	238..17	5
Elias Morgan	Foreman Bricklayer	10 Grove Rd.	do	334	–
David Davies	Galvanizing Foreman	37 Swansea Road	do	186.. 9	5
David Rees	Foreman Engineer	Bristol House, High St.	do	155	5
Morgan Jones	Demurrage Clerk	Uplands	do	124..8	10
David Morgan	Tinplate Manager	Goedwig, Uplands	do	274..10	1,185
Chas. M. Jenkins	Accountant	Alltwen Hill	do	149	55
Thos. J. Richards	Mills Superintendent	Danycoed, Dyffryn Rd.	do	253..18	55
George Webb	Tinhouse do	Mador View, Uplands	do	201..19	30
William Evans	Annealing Foreman	Ynysderw Rd.	do	201..19	–
Dd. C. Jones	Cold Mills Superintendent	Arthur St.	do	174..15	–
Ivor G. Harries	Metal Coating Manager	Brynbedw, Uplands	do	50	–

P. Davies to Messrs Parrs Bank Ltd., London. **28 July 1916 [10 : 204]**

We should like your expression of opinion on the following subject.

We wish to invest £25,000 in either Exchequer Bonds or Treasury Bills for a few months, or until we are asked to pay over the amount due from us for excess Profits Duty to the Treasury.

Will you kindly advise us which of these securities would under the circumstances be best to take up.

P. Davies to Messrs Parrs Bank Ltd. **29 Jan. 1917 [10 : 293]**

Referring to Certificates for £50,000 Treasury Bills which you hold for us, kindly transfer these on our behalf to Messrs The Capital & Counties Bank Ltd, Swansea, and let us know when you have sent them forward.

Frank Gilbertson to F. W. Higgison, Messrs Deloitte Plender Griffiths & Co., Cardiff. **22 Aug. 1917 [10 : 405]**

I have, for some time, been contemplating that we ought again to increase our capital to a figure that will fairly represent what is involved in the business.

I should like to increase it to as large a figure as possible.

As far as our prospects are concerned, there would seem no reason why we should not expect to maintain, and even increase, our present distribution of profit, and I think it would be much better if that sum only represented 6½ or 7½% per annum.

One reason why I should like to bring our capital up to its true value today is that I am seriously considering a scheme to put before our workmen to encourage them to become ordinary shareholders in the concern, now that a good many have investments in the War Loan, and, therefore, cash savings that could be transferred into the business.

If any such scheme could be worked out, it might be a small contribution to the solution of the serious industrial problems that face us after the War, and the workmen could be let in on such terms that would give them the full advantage of any increase in our prosperity, but should not enable them to participate in the accumulated increment of our Company's property, which really belongs to the shareholders of the past.

I should be very glad if you would think this matter over, and perhaps Sir William Plender would give his advice too, because there are many reasons why I think it may be an important and useful move.

If it was necessary to obtain Treasury sanction to a considerable increase of capital, it would probably be viewed in a more favourable light if it was part of the scheme for admitting our workmen into partnership with us.

To Messrs W. B. Peat & Co., 11 Ironmonger Lane, London, EC2. **23 Nov. 1917 [10 : 465]**

<u>Federation of British Industries</u>

We are in receipt of your favour of the 21st inst, and the particulars you ask for are as follows:

Amount of Sales of Steel	£685,620
Amount of wages paid to workmen	£126,185
Amount of dividends in sterling actually paid to shareholders	£ 16,450

The Return relates to the production of semi-manufactured Steel and also to the further manufacture of a considerable proportion into Tinplates and Galvanized Sheets.

Frank Gilbertson to F. W. Higgison, Deloitte & Co. **15 Jan. 1918 [10 : 491-2]**

Thank you for your letters of 14th & 9th inst. We are very much indebted to you for the trouble you have taken & the clear statements you send us.

New Capital

At first sight we like the proposal to give two ordinary and one preference share in respect of each one ordinary share now held.

There is no hurry, but if as a result of further enquiry you can satisfy yourself that no question of Income Tax or Super Tax would arise on the Bonus distribution, we would suggest your discussing the proposal with our Solicitors before very long.

Inland Revenue

We should be glad if you would give formal notice of Appeal, which would permit of some further consideration of the figures, but broadly speaking we do not suppose there is much to quarrel about. I think that as the amount to be allowed on a/c. of Directors' commissions is at the discretion of the Board the decision to base the standard on the last pre-war year might be questioned. The amount of extra work & responsibility incurred by the Board has been very large, & the last pre-war year does stand out as an exceptionally unfortunate one to form the standard.

Frank Gilbertson to Messrs Barlow, Barlow & Lyde. **19 Jan. 1918 [10 : 496]**

We enclose a statement prepared by Mr. Higgison of Deloittes.

We want to again increase our Capital & without delay.

We are not sure as to the position that may be taken up by Inland Revenue. One of our friends has been advised that a bonus distribution of shares makes the Shareholders liable to super tax upon the value of the increased capital.

This matter is of course of great importance & we could not proceed without official assurance that no claims would be made.

We should value your opinions.

P. Davies to Surveyor of Taxes, Swansea. **21 Feb. 1918 [10 : 519]**

Private & Confidential

I duly received your favour of the 7th inst, and have also yours of the 20th inst.

The profits of our Company for the year ended 26th May 1917 have not yet been adjusted for Income Tax purposes, but as desired by you we have gone into the matter carefully with the view of forming an estimate of the amount of profit retained by us after allowances have been made for Excess Profits Duty and Munitions Levy payable for the period in question.

The estimate we have made, without any engagement on our part, is as follows:–

Profit for year ending 26th May 1917
after deducting Excess Profits Duty & Munitions Levy – £99,803

According to our figures this would give an average of £78,373 for the three years on which the 1918-19 assessment will be based. It is understood that this estimate will be used solely for statistical purposes.

P. Davies to F. W. Higgison. **2 March 1918 [10 : 537, 540-1]**

Reorganisation of Capital

Mr. Gilbertson has decided to proceed with the scheme as recommended at the Meeting in London, and, having received Counsel's Opinion, which is quite favourable to the course outlined by us being taken, we have today sent Notice convening an Extraordinary General Meeting of the Company, copy of which is enclosed herewith for your information.

* * *

NOTICE IS HEREBY GIVEN that an Extraordinary General Meeting of W. Gilbertson & Co. Limited will be held . . . on the 11th day of March 1918 . . . when the subjoined resolutions will be proposed.

RESOLUTIONS

1. THAT the capital of the Company be increased to £469,000 by the creation of 5,880 additional shares of £50 each.
2. THAT the said additional shares shall be ordinary shares and shall in all respects rank pari passu with the existing ordinary shares of the Company.
3. THAT it is desirable to capitalise the sum of £315,000 (being as to £220,000 part of the undivided profits of the Company standing to the credit of the Company's reserve fund and as to the balance of £95,000 part of the amount standing to the credit of the Company's profit and loss account) and with a view . . . to declare a bonus of £150 per share free of income tax on each of the 2,100 issued Ordinary shares of the Company and to satisfy such bonus by allotment and distribution amongst the holders of the said issued Ordinary shares rateably of the 6,300 unissued Ordinary shares of the Company of £50 each (including the said 5,880 additional shares) credited as fully paid up making 3 new shares of an aggregate nominal value of £150 for each issued share and that the Directors be and they are hereby authorised and requested pursuant to Article 108 (15A) to give effect to and carry out the said capitalisation of profits bonus and distribution of unissued shares as fully paid up as aforesaid.

Philip Davies to Special Commissioners of Taxes, Swansea. **13 June 1918 [10 : 553-4]**

Salaries & Wages year ended April 5, 1918

					Bonus
Francis W. Gilbertson	Managing Director	Glynteg,	Pontardawe	1,500	7,318
Cecil F. Gilbertson	Director	Abercrave House	Ystradgynlais	1,500	7,318
Chas. G. Gilbertson	do	Gellygron,	Pontardawe	900	7,318
Philip Davies	Secretary	Danygraig,	do	560	2,525
Chas. Giddings	Accountant	Bronygraig	do	420	1,866
David J. Bowen	do	Frondeg, Alltwen,	do	420	923
Thomas George	do	Brolon, Rhydyfro	do	490	68..15
J. J. Emmanuel	do	Glynhelyg, Brecon Road	do	299..5	55
Alfred Palmer	do	Heathfield Road	do	252	37..16
Wm. R. Jones	do	Dyffryn Road, Alltwen	do	248	37..16
David Davies	do	20 Grove Road	do	232	37..16
Edgar Jenkins	do	Francis St	do	240	27..10
David Jno. Davies	do	2 Ynysymond Road, Alltwen	do	248	37..16
David Lewis	do	Pantglas, Alltwen	do	195	24
Thomas Jenkins	do	Alador View, Uplands	do	178..15	15..5
Edward Hudson	do	Graig, Trebanos	do	142	11..16
(Mrs.) E. Tarling	do	Uplands,	do	153	–
David Morgan	Tinplate Manager	Goedwig, Uplands	do	353..3	580..19
Chas. M. Jenkins	Accountant	Alltwen Hill	do	300..10	37..16
Harry Jenkins	do	Railway Terrace, Alltwen	do	178..13	22..17
Thomas J. Richards	Mills Superintendent	Danycoed, Dyffryn Road	do	333	45
George Webb	Tinhouse do	The Laurels, Swansea Rd.	do	269..2	30
William Evans	Annealing Foreman	Ynysderw Rd.	do	269..2	–
David C. Jones	Cold Rolls Superintendent	Arthur Terrace	do	228..16	–
H. J. Munro	Asst General Wks Manager	Lyndhurst, Uplands	do	700	200
C.A. Hardy	Mill Manager	St. Dunstans, Brecon Rd.	do	560	–
Wilfred Williams	Draughtsman	c/o Mrs Worthing, Oakfield Rd.	do	339..3	–
Stephen Davies	Mill Foreman	Bettws y Coed, Uplands	do	333..9	–

Joshua Davies	do	Old Road, Ynysmeudwy		273..4	–
David Rees	Mechanical Engineer	Bristol House, High St.	do	211..5	5
David Davies	Galvanizing Foreman	37, Swansea Rd.	do	224..18	–
Owen Davies	Steelworks Manager	Bryneithin, Uplands	do	436..16	1,377
Elias Morgan	Foreman Bricklayer	10, Grove Road	do	430	–
Wm Williams	Foreman Mason	4, Derw Road	do	370..10	20
Morgan Jones	Demurrage Clerk	Maesybedw, Uplands	do	169	10
Prosser Thomas	Tinplate Superintendent	Graig Road, Trebanos	do	257..8	10
Jno. Roberts	Foreman Mechanic	Vine Villa, Brecon Rd.	do	370..10	–
Ivor G. Harries	Metal Coating Manager	Brynbedw, Uplands	do	50	–

F. W. Gilbertson to Shareholders. **15 July 1918 [10 : 556-560]**

. . . the Twenty-third Ordinary General Meeting of the Proprietors of W. Gilbertson & Co. Limited . . . [when] . . . the Directors recommend:–

(1) That a final dividend at the rate of 7½% per annum on the present ordinary share capital of the Company be declared for the six months ending May 25th last and making together with the Interim dividend at the rate of 20% per annum on the old ordinary share capital paid for the six months ending December last a total distribution equivalent to 6¼% per annum on the present ordinary share capital.

* * *

N.B. The Directors desire to call the Shareholders' attention to the alteration in dividend following the increase of Capital. They are of opinion that it is important to conserve the Company's resources at the present time, and if the dividend they recommend is passed at the Shareholders' Meeting the position will be practically the same total dividend will be distributed for 1918 as for 1917.

The Shareholders should observe that the dividend is paid free of Income Tax, and so the actual Return to the Shareholders is somewhat larger . . .

So long as the profits of the Company and other conditions remain in the position they are now in, the Directors will recommend that the interim dividend be at the rate of 5% per annum, and of the final dividend at the rate of 7½% per annum free of Income Tax.

The Company is now erecting important new Works adding an entirely new branch of trade to its activities, but the resumption of normal conditions in the Tinplate and Galvanising Trades after the War is likely to be attended with serious difficulty and delay, and a large absorption of Capital in refinancing the working stocks of the Departments now idle. After the War, the Company's operations will be on a much larger scale than before, and some financial provision will have to be made for increased housing accommodation for the work-people.

Notice of Thirty-seventh O.G.M., 6 October 1922. 28 Sept. 1922 [10 : 580]

. . . at such Meeting the Directors recommend:

(1) That a Final Dividend of 3 per cent per annum on the present Ordinary Share Capital of the Company be declared for the six months ended 1st July last, making together with the Interim Dividend at 4 per cent per annum paid for six months ended December last, a total distribution of 3½ per cent per annum free of Income Tax.

I think I ought to let the Shareholders know that while the trading results of the past year showed a small profit, losses are being incurred today on a substantial scale, and the prospects of the Steel Trade are very bad.

As far as it is possible to forecast it would not seem likely that an interim dividend in the early months of 1923 can be declared.

The value of our property has been greatly increased during the past six years, if profitable trade to employ the plant should develop, but at present our new plant and our investments in colliery companies are idle or unproductive.

The Directors are doing their best to secure new outlets for the Company's products, and to assist in putting the staple trades on better footing, but it is extremely difficult and discouraging work at a time when the general demands for steel are not more than half the productive capacity of Great Britain.

F. W. Gilbertson

Cecil Gilbertson to T. Williams, Mill Superintendent. **16 April 1924 [10 : 589]**

You will remember a year ago we were owed some £10,000 by Messrs J. C. Hill & Co. They have gradually reduced this debt so that today the balance due to us is £1,824..3..6. We have been trying to get payment of this balance for some months, so far unsuccessfully. I wrote personally to Major Butler last week and received enclosed reply this morning. Do you think the suggestion is worth considering?

Frank Gilbertson to L. D. Williams. **22 Aug. 1924 [10 : 594-5]**

Thank you very much for your most efficient help last week & this.

I can hear no criticisms of our conclusions which is most satisfactory.

Would a letter like the draft below do for Mr. Leeder?

I hear they have bored into a seam at Cwmguinea 5'8" thick with a good roof & are going on boring. This section seems too thick for Rock Fawr, so we don't yet know where we are. The seam is only 60 yards below the one we are working.

To Leeders

"We expect to have our new Sheet Mills ready in a month & a few weeks later a Steel Furnace, [. . .] with up to date Producers. By the time these improvements are completed we should like to introduce a better method of calculating annual depreciation & to start a Plant inventory which would thereafter be kept up to date.

We should also like to know for our own information what is now the real value of our plant.

Will you please let us know what you would charge for a valuation with an inventory of plant. We presume the value would not be less than £450,000 or so, but would prefer the work done for a fixed fee. Probably we should be ready for the valuation to be made by November."

Cecil Gilbertson to W. J. Roberts, Engineer. **17 Nov. 1924 [10 : 596-7]**

Some time ago Mr. Frank went into the Salaries of all our officials and made reductions in almost every case. He told you that your Salary would have to come down . . .

Frank Gilbertson to Frank Rees, Llanelly Steel Co., Ltd. **9 Jan. 1925 [10 : 598-9]**

You once said very kindly that you would always be willing to discuss & compare costs with me.

Would you be willing to extend this to the extent of allowing Mr. Charles Giddings our Sec. to come down & really make a detailed comparison with your figures? I know of course that we have nothing to show you & you have plenty to show us, but I am a little uneasy sometimes at our failure to earn an adequate return on the very large sums we have spent on our Steel Works while we can hold our own very well in Tinplates.

We have a meeting of the Stabilization Special Committee on Tuesday next, at which Bond & J. C. D. will be present & I really hope we shall now make headway & start fresh. Firth is really a friend of mine, but in business we dont always pull together & to my mind he has during the last two months queered the pitch most frightfully!

"Mr. W. J. Firth's conception of a tinplate market in which conditions are regulated by a stabilization scheme is not quite so modern as might be thought . . ." The Metal Bulletin, 8 March 1927, quoted by E. H. Brooke, Appendix, 234.

Notice of Fortieth Ordinary General Meeting, 9 October 1925 in Great Western Hotel, Paddington. **1 Oct. 1925 [10 : 610]**

. . . The Directors recommend that a Dividend of 2½% on the Ordinary Share Capital of the Company be declared for the year ended 27th June last.

Dear Sir or Madam,

As the present conditions in the Steel and Tinplate trades are so serious, and the future prospects present no hope of any immediate recovery, the Directors would like to meet at our Annual Meeting as many of the shareholders as possible this year so as to enable the Directors to explain to them the position and prospects of the Company.

Realising that it is inconvenient, and often impossible, for many Shareholders to attend the Annual Meetings when held at our Registered Offices, Pontardawe, they have decided this year to hold the Meeting in London on Friday, 9th October, and the Directors hope that as many of the Shareholders as possible will endeavour to be present.

Yours faithfully,
Chas. Giddings
Secretary

Cecil Gilbertson to G. N. Tregoning, Bynea Steel Works. **26 Jan. 1926 [10 : 613]**

I wonder if you would tell me in confidence your cost of Bars at Bynea for the last 6 months. We have just got our results out and I am rather disappointed, we are just on the wrong side.

Our new materials cost	£3.. 8..6 including yield
Conversion to Ingots	1..13..8
Ingots cost	£5.. 2..2
Conversion to Bars	1.. 3..3
Bars cost	£6.. 5..5 f.o.r.

Our conversion to Bars is 3/- higher than our previous quarter as we had a very bad loss in yield but even if we get this yield right I cannot see a lower cost than £6..2..6 in front of us.

C. Giddings to N. F. E. Knapp, HM Inspector of Taxes, Swansea. **n.d. [May?] 1929 [10 : 629]**

Employee	*Description*	*Salaries/Wages Year ending 5 April 1929* £	*Bonus/ Commission* £
F. W. Gilbertson	Director	1,615	Bonus 1,615
C.F. "	" "	2,000	" 2,500
C.G. "	" "	2,000	" 2,000
G.N. "	" " }	500	None
" "	Selling Agent }		Comm. 237
L. D. Williams	Director	250	None
H. Vivian	Engineer from Oct 1/28	750	"
C. Giddings	Secretary	900	Bonus 1,100
D. J. Bowen	Accountant	750	" 750
I. G. Harris	"	900	" 100
T. George	"	500	" 200
S. Rutter	"	650	None
J. J. Emanuel	"	488	"
A. Palmer	"	322	"
D. Davies	"	280	"
Edgar Jenkins	"	274	"
Sidney Hopkins	"	260	"
Daniel Lewis	"	239	"
Harry Jenkins	"	243	"
Oswald Jenkins	"	232	"
Wilfred Morgan	"	218	"
Thomas Jenkins	"	294	"
Ed. Hudson	"	211	"
Sidney Davies	"	211	"
Daniel Suff	"	196	"

Employee	*Description*	*Salaries/Wages Year ending 5 April 1929*	*Bonus/ Commission*
		£	£
Muriel Jones	Typist	180	"
C. M. Jenkins	Accountant	411	"
David Morgan	Tinplate Mgr.	500	Bonus 250
W. R. Jones	Accountant	390	None
Gethin Jones	St. Wks. Manager	1,200	None
G. W. A. Doe	Welfare Supervisor	500	Bonus 50
D. H. James	Accountant	180	None
Capel Bubb	"	168	"
Thos. Richards	Mill Supt.	348	Bonus 40
W. J. Roberts	Engineer	462	None
W. Palmer	Bar Mill Supr.	356	"
Geo. Webb	Tinhouse "	252	Bonus 110
Wm. Evans	Annealing "	195	None
W. I. Williams	Mill "	311	"
Jno. Roderick	" "	345	"
J. H. Beckett	Chemist	371	"
Hopkin Williams	Mill Supr.	168	"
Joshua Davies	"	439	"
Daniel R. Jones	"	292	"
Edwin Suff	Timekeeper	234	"
D. C. Jones	Cold Roll Supr.	253	Bonus 58
Ed. Edwards	Tinhouse "	250	None
E. Thomas	Draughtsman	355	"
T. D. Thomas	Electrician	182	"
Stephen Davies	Mill Supr.	398	Bonus 18
Elias Morgan	Foreman Mason	361	None
Dd. Davies	Galv. Supr.	372	"
T. Ayres	Yard Foreman	269	"

TABLE 1: Returns to Special Commissioners of Taxes, 1892 - 1907

Tax Year to March Adjusted from Company's year to June	**1892** £	**1893** £	**1894** £	**1895** £	**1896** £	**1897** £	**1898** £	**1899** £	**1900** £	**1901** £	**1902** £	**1903** £	**1904*** £	**1905*** £	**1906**** £	**1907**** £
Profits	11,842	9,851	11,788	11,919	14,251	4,212	8,011	19,248	14,125	10,891	29,943	18,880	23,577	34,524	66,414	59,915
Depreciation Adj.wef 1906															4,235	4,077
Adjusted Profits															62,179	55,838
Interest on Loan							355	355	89							
Debenture Interest	512	512	512	362	362	362	362	362	615	700	700	700	700	700	700	700
Wayleave	56	56	56	56	56	56	56	56	56	56	56	56	56	56	56	56
Income Tax Sch. A.	40	78	80	81	85	85	79	90	107	138	144	111	126	135	144	144
Income Tax Sch. D.	546	584	492	341	334	378	291	267	487	770	883	824	990	1,193	1,278	2,038
Ground Rent	137	137	137	137	137	137	137	137	137	490	490	490	490	490	490	490
	13,133	11,218	13,065	12,896	15,225	5.230	9,291	20,515	15,616	13,045	32,216	21,061	25,939	37,098	64,847	59,266
Earnings before Interest & Tax	12,940	11,025	12,872	12,703	15,032	5,037	9,098	20,322	15,423	12,499	31,670	20,515	25,393	36,552	64,301	58,720
Interest on Loan	0	0	0	0	0	0	355	355	89	0	0	0	0	0	0	0
Debenture Interest	512	512	512	362	362	362	362	362	615	700	700	700	700	700	700	700
Earnings before Tax	12,428	10,513	12,360	12,341	14,670	4,675	8,381	19,605	14,719	11,799	30,970	19,815	24,693	35,852	63,601	58,020
Income Tax	586	662	572	422	419	463	370	357	594	908	1,027	935	1,116	1,328	1,422	2,182
Net Earnings	11,842	9,851	11,788	11,919	14,251	4,212	8,011	19,248	14,125	10,891	29,943	18,880	23,577	34,524	62,179	55,838
Earnings per share (E.P.S.)	£16·92	£14·07	£16·84	£17·03	£20·36	£6·02	£11·44	£27·50	£20·18	£15·56	£42·78	£26·97	£33·68	£49·32	£88·83	£79·77
E.P.S. as percentage of Nominal Value	33·83%	28·15%	33·68%	34·05%	40·72%	12·03%	22·89%	54·99%	40·36%	31·12%	85·55%	53·94%	67·36%	98·64%	177·65%	159·54%

* In 1905 the Surveyor of Taxes queried the charges for depreciation included in the Profits Returns [5 : 388]. It appears that he insisted on the substitution of a wear & tear allowance for the depreciation figures appearing in the Company a/c., and this was put into effect in 5 : 510.

** From 5 : 880-3 (which shows apportionment of profit figures for tax purposes) the figure of £66,414 on the Return for 1906 is in fact for the 12 months to March 1907, similarly the figure of £59,915 for 1907 is for 12 months to March 1908. There appears to be no reason for these anomalies, although the dates given on some of the letters appear to have been subsequently altered. It may be assumed that the data for each preceding year since 1892 have been declared in the same manner.

TABLE 2: Dividends payable on Ordinary Share Capital.

OGM	Year	Dividend Payable % per annum		
		Interim	Final	Total
6th	1890-91	-	20	-
7th	1891-92	-	10	-
8th	1892-93	-	10	-
9th	1893-94	-	10	-
10th	1894-95	-	22½	-
11th	1895-96	-	20	-
12th	1896-97	-	17½	-
13th	1897-98	15	10	12½
14th	1898-99	5	15	10
15th	1899-1900	20	40	30
16th	1900-01	20	20	20
17th	1901-02	20	20	20
18th	1902-03	-	-	-
19th	1903-04	-	-	-
20th	1904-05	30	60	45
21st	1905-06	80	100	90
22nd	1906-07	100	150	125
23rd	1907-08	100	50	75
24th	1908-09	50	50	50
25th	1909-10	-	50	-
26th	1910-11	50	50	50
27th	1911-12	50	50	50
28th	1912-13	50	50	50
29th	1913-14	40	40	40
30	1914-15	12½	17½	15
31	1915-16	17½	22½	20
32	1916-17	17½	32½	25
33	1917-18	20	7½	6¼ *
34	1918-19	7	8	7½
35	1919-20	7	9	8
36	1920-21	-	-	-
37	1921-22	4	3	3½
38	1922-23	-	3?	3
39	1923-24	4	6	5
40	1924-25	-	-	2½

* Apparent fall is due to capital reconstruction [q.v. 8 : 543-4, 10 : 405 & 10 : 537, 540-1].

Chapter 5

MAN MANAGEMENT

The Employers and Workmen Act 1875, which repealed the Master and Servant Act 1867, produced not only a radical change in the designations of the parties to the employment contract, but just as fundamentally altered their relationship to that of equal partners to a civil contract. Any breach of contract by either party was no longer a criminal offence, and any agreement, however informal, was valid and enforceable, provided it did not infringe a statutory provision. The master-servant model had implied the servant's subordination to the master's control, reinforced by sanctions which would be administered by the local magistrates, who were often masters themselves. After 1875 the same magistrates courts and the county courts could be used by employers and workmen to obtain civil remedies for breaches of contract and to impose damages.

Arthur Gilbertson continued to refer to himself as 'master' long after 1875, and his attitude and behaviour towards his 'servants' displayed his rejection of the egalitarian values and expectations inherent in that statute. His relationship with line management and his workforce generally was personal and direct, and his letters to them were uncompromisingly forceful. Whilst his authority was legitimised by customary tradition and reinforced by his sole control of the factors of production, his sons were constrained by the need to manage in a less deferential environment and to adjust to new social values and unprogrammed structural and technological changes which demanded greater professionalism and differentiated roles.

The letters in this chapter deal with the organisation, direction and control of labour from 1890 to 1924 and illustrate several of the constituent elements of what was later to emerge as a specialist personnel function. They include the employment, promotion and termination features of manpower planning and such resource control elements as standard setting, wage incentives, discipline and rule enforcement.

Arthur Gilbertson to William Veitch, Steel Works Manager. **13 Nov. 1890 [1 : 31-2]**

I don't want to add to your annoyance, which I feel must be great, at your complete failure to keep your word.

You ought to have confessed your ignorance of the practical mechanical work of a new Steel Works. You sent me a detail cost of £41 for last 24 hours – during that period I conclude you got out 50 tons of Cold Ingots?

I have merely to say that unless you roll Bars on Monday, the Steel Furnace must stop, and I must try another manager: you have misled me dreadfully.

Have the flooring plates come to replace those stupidly made wrong?

Arthur Gilbertson to Editor, *South Wales Daily News*, Cardiff. **26 Nov. 1890 [1 : 34]**

"Practical outside manager for Siemens Steel Forge required . . . Please insert the foregoing . . . & forward us the replies.

Arthur Gilbertson to William Veitch. **31 Dec. 1890 [1 : 57-8]**

As our definite arrangement comes to an end with this year, we write to say, that the same may continue, with this alteration, that it be subject to three months notice on either side, or payment of three months salary, in lieu of notice, at any time. This is our usual form.

We are disappointed at your want of outside practical knowledge, and have had consequently (& shall have) a large amount of personal trouble which ought to be done by yourself.

Third Steel Furnace. Remember you are bound down to complete & get to work, at end of February. You can employ more Masons if needful.

Third Rolling Furnace. We await your advice as to this.

Mixtures. We see no reason why ⅔rds. steel shearings, should not be used – it saves ore.

Gas Tubes. Should be kept clean.

Gas Producers. Should all be on the Tons. You pay these highly. Could not some improvement for facility of working be made?

Memos. Look through letter book receipts & reply to AG.

Arthur Gilbertson to William Veitch. **9 Feb. 1891 [1 : 74]**

We have come to the conclusion we shall do the outside management of our Works best without your assistance, and we therefore relieve you, from today, from further duty here.

Upon giving up your House, you will receive payment for unexpired term of your notice, it being understood that should we require to consult you, during that period, you will give us your assistance without further expense.

Arthur Gilbertson to George Lawrence, Cheltenham. **13 Feb. 1891 [1 : 76]**

. . . The Steel Works are going fairly well, but an awful worry – I have paid off Mr. Veitch, the Engineer, as he calls himself! We shall do better without him.

Arthur Gilbertson to W. H. Forester. 2 Jan. 1892 [1 : 165]

Who of our Workmen applied for £2..2..0? We don't allow it & return the check.

As regards the Cigars many thanks, but I really don't want them. My Sons wont smoke them – they very seldom smoke a cigar, but then it must be A1.

Best wishes of the Season to you.

Arthur Gilbertson to W. H. Forester. 5 Jan. 1892 [1 : 166]

I have your note of yesterday. You know presents to us, and our Workpeople are against our rules & have been for many years. I fully appreciate your kind intentions, but I should be more pleased if you struck our name off your list, and if you told your Clerks in future they will be responsible for not offering us, what is in a way, an annoyance. Our wishes to you & yours.

Arthur Gilbertson to David Morgan. 15 Jan. 1894 [1 : 281]

I am sorry I cannot allow you to remain in my Office.

All my Clerks have grown up with me from Boys, they respect and trust me. This is essential in my Clerks, because their duties are [confidential?]. You have taken the great liberty of writing to me, for your Parents, a most insulting letter, and you must go.

Mr. Jno. Davies will pay you a month's wages in advance, and you will leave today.

Arthur Gilbertson to Oliver Adams, Steel & Tinworks Accountant. 7 Aug. 1894 [1 : 300]

We received your notice this morning with considerable surprise. We could only accept it, as if there is not mutual confidence, you are useless to me.

Your agreement is a monthly one – not three monthly, and we enclose your check for one month's wages in lieu of notice. We shall probably be able to give you a bonus for past period, when "discounts" made out, but it is a matter at our discretion entirely.

Check enclosed for £10..3..4d.

Arthur Gilbertson to David Smith., Agent to H. Lloyd 8 Aug. 1894 [1 : 301]

To my intense surprise yesterday morning Adams gave us a written notice to leave. From what he said and from what I can find out he considered the worry of management outside too much for him, that men did not carry out his orders, and he, of course, incurred censure from me, as I employed him to relieve me.

In these days absolute economy is needful in manufacture, and must be resolutely carried out, and not only talked about.

I wished to let you know the facts.

Arthur Gilbertson to Oliver Adams. **26 Sept. 1894 [1 : 309]**

We enclose £15 bonus for last half year. The state of trade, in fact, would need a quarter reduction, but I do not care to make it.

As regards your period of notice, all our Employés are paid monthly, and the notice necessitated on each side, is therefore only a month.

We have had a great deal of loss & trouble from Harris & Pearson's Bricks turning out a very mixed lot, some much underburnt & consequently worked badly with fully burnt ovens.

Arthur Gilbertson to Henry John Williams & others **31 Oct. 1894 [1 : 312-3]**

Glynbeudy Workmen

I received your telegram, and letter, and am doing my best to get orders for Tin and Terneplates.

If I succeed the Works shall start on Monday.

You can understand the competition I named to you from Works, where they are able, from certain allowances, to save 6d. a box in cost, renders your position and mine very difficult and unless I can cover loss, I cant keep working.

I shall come & see you & talk these matters over again if I cant get orders without loss.

Arthur Gilbertson to A. Wolfe, Glynbeudy Tinplate Works Manager. **31 Oct. 1894 [2 : 23]**

I received the Books today. You did very wrong in taking them away from Glanbeudy Office without my consent. I am obliged to ask you, have you kept any copies or details of these Books, or any copies, or details, of costs &c of Glynbeudy. Please say simply yes or no, I trust the latter.

Arthur Gilbertson to A. Wolfe. **31 Oct. 1894 [2 : 24]**

At last Monday's meeting it was decided that you should have notice, that after three months from this date, your engagement would be subject to the notice of one month, on either side, which please note. We think work may be resumed on Monday next, so please hold yourself in readiness for a telegram at any time.

Arthur Gilbertson to Dd. Roberts, Rollerman, 6 Tower Street, Morriston. **28 Dec. 1894 [1 : 318]**

You were dismissed because you did unsatisfactory work, turned the Mill badly, and did not prove the good Rollerman you represented yourself to be. I thought possibly there was some friction between our Foreman & yourself, and therefore wrote to you as I did. I have however further investigated the matter and find you are considered a reckless roller, and that your Tongs going into the Rolls, nearly caused an accident to the Machinery – our Head Mechanic confirms this & that you treated the matter contemptuously.

Under these circumstances the Rules of our Works render you liable to dismissal, and you can take any steps you think fit.

Arthur Gilbertson to Oliver Adams. **4 Jan. 1895 [1 : 323-4]**

I have your letter, and am very glad Mr. Smith's call led to this matter being discussed – it has been much on my mind, and coupled with the sudden way in which you determined to leave, and with the distinct statement of one Foreman, and also the evidence of the Tin Yield Paper & the delivery book made things look very serious. You were of course <u>responsible</u>, whether you knew or not, what was going on, and you had no right to allow the "transfers" you admit – it was the very way to cause laxity, and should have opened your eyes as to the reason why some Pots got short of Tin. The fact which Mr. Howel discovered is this, that altho' the "Total Tin used" on Yield Sheet agreed with Total of "Tin delivery Book", no single item of Tin delivered to each Pot agreed with the same item on Tins delivery book, and it was evidently an organised plan.

I will go further into the matter, with the light thrown upon it by your letter, and you shall then hear from me again.

Please let Mr. Smith read this.

P.S. If your account of the transfer is correct, you should have had the Black Tin delivery Book set right – I understand you interviewed Llewellyn Jones, the night before last. This was not wise of you – I have only just heard this.

Arthur Gilbertson to Oliver Adams. **9 Jan. 1895 [1 : 326]**

I regret to find you have been privately to both Foremen, instead of meeting them before me. One says you knew about the Tin Yields being "cooked", the other says you did not. His statement however made since you saw him, does not accord with his previous confession. However <u>you</u> admit you knew about transfers of metal, and therefore the weekly yields could not agree with Tin delivery Book on your own admission.

You made a serious error and should have put the matter before me.

I shall not discuss the matter further.

Arthur Gilbertson to Thomas Turner, Shelton, Stoke-on-Trent. **19 Jan. 1895 [2 : 51-2]**

Thank you for your very frank letter, to my eldest Son, of 15th inst. You may rely upon our treating your information with strict confidence.

I have been poorly for a few days & unable to attend to business, hence the delay.

We shall be glad to pay you £31..10..0 for information, and would £2..2..0 a day pay you for coming down here to superintend & advise, on the Basic Siemens Fce, to include your travelling expenses, the days spent in travelling to be charged?

We note we shall hear from you as to Dolomite and suitable Pigs & Scrap, and you will also find out who will buy our Slag in Truck at Pontardawe, to begin with, and also keep your eye on two good first hand Furnacemen accustomed to Basic work.

Birmingham. Thank you for giving us names of your friends. We feel sure there is a business to be done there in our commodities, and if you decide to locate yourself in Birmingham you might take up our Agency on some footing. We are now trying the man we told you about, and shall probably give him a small Salary for a year & pay rent of small Office & Stores, to see what we can do. We have, in fact, promised him a trial on these lines. Perhaps a little further on, you may be able to tell us definitely what you decide upon doing as regards Birmingham. We know our Agency would not produce you enough by a long way, but you might combine business of another class, with it.

J. P. Davies to John Roberts, former Butler, Primrose Row. **26 Jan. 1895 [1 : 328]**

Mr. Gilbertson instructs me to tell you that your son will not be required as post boy after today but for sake of your wife & children they will be allowed to remain rent free in Primrose Row for a couple of weeks while you are looking out for a situation & I enclose balance of your wages to 6th Feb. when your month's notice expires. I also add at the rate of 10/- per week for your board from the day you left Glanrhyd to the expiration of your notice.

2 weeks from Jan. 19 to Feb. 2	1..19..0
From Feb. 2 to 6th	11..5
Board Jan. 25 to Feb. 6	1.. 0..0
	3..10..5

Arthur Gilbertson to John Roberts. **4 Feb. 1895 [1 : 329]**

Take notice that I shall require the Cottage you occupy in four weeks from this date. I have learnt what you said about me, and to my Workmen in the Public Houses.

Just for the sake of your Wife & children, you may have labouring work in the Works.

Frank Gilbertson to William Thomas. **12 Feb. 1895 [2 : 62]**

Referring to your application to Mr. Thomas Turner of Shelton, who acts for us. We will engage you as 1st hand to work a Basic Furnace at £3 a week.

Can you be down so as to begin making the bottom on Monday week?

Can you bring a good steady second hand at £2 a week?

Arthur Gilbertson to Rees Jones, Landore. **5 March 1895 [1 : 335]**

The Carpenter you name will suit me well, and I can give him a Cottage up here at 10/- a month, himself to pay rates. His wages 4/6 a day & to come at once.

Frank Gilbertson to John Rees. **15 April 1895 [2 : 85]**

We are starting a Siemens Basic Furnace, about 14 to 15 Tons. We have not a first class Furnaceman & want one who can work the Furnace to ° 120% Carbon, for Tinplate Bars, he must be able to work the Metal without tapping it "wild" or "piping" in the moulds.

A Solid Ingot is essential, weight about 10 cwts, he must therefore know the due proportion of Ferro Silicon required for each charge.

He must pass his own samples for Phosphorus.

Our idea of rate is about 14d. a Ton, to include passing Phosphorous, divided between the two first hands.

These Works work very regularly & there are a very decent lot of men.

Would you like to come, if you can satisfy us on above points?

Mr. Thos. Turner, to whom you wrote on Feb. 6th, was then acting for us.

Works Notice from Arthur Gilbertson. **3 May 1895 [1 : 342]**

25% reduction Landore
Morwoods Works giving up Board of Control

The above is very serious – it means a reduction of just sixpence a Box in cost, and I must now ask the assistance of our Workmen in meeting the matter, or our orders will be taken from us by the above people.

I therefore propose reducing Wages 10% from Monday last (29th April) on all persons getting more than 21/- per week – any one objecting could give notice on Monday.

Works Notice from Arthur Gilbertson. **3 May 1895 [1 : 343]**

Steel Works

I am told most of the Steel Works are now working at a reduction of 10%, and I am obliged to ask our Steelmen to help us to meet the competition, so that we may keep our Sale Bar Trade.

I should be glad if our men would tell Mr. Richards what they can do.

J. P. Davies to David Harris, Sunnybank, Glanamman. **27 May 1895 [1 : 357]**

I have your letter of 23rd inst, and am prepared to try your Son Ivor as Pay Clerk, he would get 20/- a week, and Bonus, twice a year possibly £10 each time. If you would like him to come, it must be at once.

Arthur Gilbertson to Thomas Turner, Tower Hills, Kilmarnock. **4 June 1895 [1 : 361]**

. . . Our trouble has been that in working the metal long enough to reduce Carbon & Phosphorus, the metal gets sticky and the tap hole closes up. The Men's excuse is, that in all works where Siemens Basic is made, that every now & then, metal with high carbon is tapped which clears the Furnace. I hope I am right in this? The Brymbo people say this is not so, that they always work low. I have interviewed the Furnacemen personally, and am not impressed favourably.

I believe they are careless. Why they should wish to spoil the process I don't know.

Arthur Gilbertson to Thomas Evans, Tinman. **18 Nov. 1895 [1 : 395]**

I understand you are the Father of a child expected to be born to a girl in Rock.

I wish to know whether you are going to marry her & when?

Arthur Gilbertson to William Thomas, Mill Foreman. **16 June 1896 [1 : 447]**

In order that you may give more attention to stop Wasters & make a good yield, I have decided that you shall be Foreman over No. 10, No. 9, No. 8, No. 7 & No. 5 Mills. You, and David Jenkins, will divide the orders between you, and separate accounts will be kept, as if distinct Works. Wasters must be reduced.

If you carry this out well, I shall further consider your wages.

Arthur Gilbertson to Messrs. R. P. Morgan & David, Neath. **10 Aug. 1896 [1 : 470]**

First item. The £2..7..6 is an amount claimed from the day Rock left, to the day he says a month's notice should count from. He received his Pay up to the day he left, as we explained to you.

There is abundant evidence that we were justified under rule 8 in dispensing with his Services, but if absolutely needful Mr. F.W. Gilbertson, assistant Manager, can prove that Rock said he couldnt do better and must go & that he then went, when Mr. Gilbertson said then you had better go.

Rock came back one day (July 10th) and paid our Book keeper some money which had been lent to him – he said he would like to see Mr. Gilbertson, but made no claim, or deduction from his debt. Perhaps Mr. David had better propose a day & drive over to see Witnesses – it is important.

Arthur Gilbertson to Morgan & David. 5 Sept. 1896 [1 : 476]

. . . I never suggested asking Rock in Court about the affidavit. I only wanted you to know it was false, to find out why such an effort was made to bring the case to Neath, and who backed him up.

I dont care a button about your professional etiquette, I want to get at the bottom of the matter, and conclude you cant do so.

Arthur Gilbertson to Mr. M. King. 15 Sept. 1896 [1 : 479]

Mr. J. P. Haynes has written to us about you. We are going to put up a Galvanizing Pot as an experiment, and it may be possibly followed by an extension.

We want to employ a practical man, and think you would suit but as we have to get the Pot & other things ready, we should not require you to come yet but would like to engage you to come, when we are ready, and meanwhile, to consult you on several things.

Do you advise the Galvanizing Pot made by John Thompson of Ettingshall, or Thompson Bros. of Bilston?

What wages do you ask as Galvanizer, and for advising us generally?

Do you prefer Mureatic Acid or Sulphuric Acid?

Do you know George Tompkinson's Annealing Furnaces for sheets?

Are you now in work?

Arthur Gilbertson to Mr. T. E. Davies. 20 Oct. 1896 [2 : 263-4]

Nelly Webb & myself opened dear Nurse's cupboard today, and found the enclosed papers together – Post Office Savings Bank Book, No. 15563, which shows £32..7..0 – Penny Bank cards, amounting to £33..3..9½ to end of December 1895 (and it now amounts to £36..3..9½) also Perpetual Investment Bldg. Society, memo's all dated July 1896 for £3..12..7, £10..19..9 & £50..11..8. I dont understand them, but no doubt the Secretary can explain. These are all the documents I can find, of value – a bag of only private letters I have burnt. There will be several Boxes of Clothes & various things, which I will get off as quickly as possible to you, a brooch & two earrings, I gave Nurse, after my dear Wife's death, I have kept, as Nurse had endorsed them "For Mr. Gilbertson if I die" – it seems the dear Woman, thought she would die, when she left my house, Nelly Webb tells me, and that she burnt many letters that day. There is an old oak dresser, of no value, but perhaps you would say if you would like it sent anywhere. Some common Jugs & cups on it (mostly from our Christmas Trees

& little presents), are not worth the trouble of packing & carriage, but might be given to Nurse's few old friends in the Village, if you would like it done. Mrs. Thomas's bill is correct, the Cloak (£1..4..5) is in one of the Boxes.

Arthur Gilbertson to William Thomas, Mill Foreman. **15 April, 1897 [1 : 497]**

I have been disappointed with your attention here lately. The Pickling & Annealing has all been put straight by my Sons & myself without any help from you, and you have allowed the Mill Yields to go back and did not know about it.

You must now consider whether you will wake up, or whether it is best for you to remain altogether at Glynbeudy. Let me know what you wish on Tuesday next.

Arthur Gilbertson to William Thomas. **5 July 1897 [1 : 523]**

I have sent out for you several days, and cant get you.

Dr. Jones says he does not think it would be well to move your Wife, and that it is best for her to remain at Brynamman, it is therefore no use for me to go on paying Rent for Rees's house, and I had better give him notice to stop it.

I am very sorry your Wife remains so poorly.

Arthur Gilbertson to Davy. **18 Oct. 1897 [2 : 311-2]**

. . . You are not justified in saying I wish to make other arrangements. Considering all you owe to me, I am surprised at your saying such a thing – but for the Works Manager, to give notice to resign twice in a couple of months because the Managing Director wishes certain retrenchments to be carried out (because the Works is making a loss), is manifestly absurd – after strong pressure from me, you carried out those reforms, and the last Quarter shows a small profit. You dont reply how many Tinpots were at work to produce the 1150 boxes? but I conclude you mean

2 Machines @ 8 hours &
2 " @ 12 hours & all idle on Saturday?

It is clear you are getting tired of the trade, or you would not have made the suggestion of resigning twice.

If I am right in this you should at once honestly say so, it is very unfair & unworthy of you to put it on the score you do & it is really absurd. I enclose key to stamp the certificate for Mr. Cecil.

Arthur Gilbertson to John Davies. **14 April 1898 [1 : 623]**

On the understanding you will keep regular office hours, be responsible for Clerks & general office work, and examine Pays & report on economies monthly, see letters properly copied & put up (I should advise copy letter books for the important letters, of thicker tissue paper). You shall have the assistance of Ivor Harries every morning (and he shall assist John Lewis every afternoon). I think Ivor Harries will have to take up some of Charles Giddings work, and Charles must assist you. I dont see how this can be done without Charles being let into our private matters? I think he must, and I will speak to him about absolute secrecy. He can then help you about posting the Books.

Copy this letter in our private book.

Arthur Gilbertson to D. B. James. 20 July 1898 [1 : 656]

We enclose you £10 in lieu of notice as you are incapable of carrying out the work you undertook to do, or at any rate you have not done it, and balance of Pay, up to date.

Arthur Gilbertson to David Jenkins, Grove Villas, Penrhiewtyn, Neath. 14 Nov. 1898 [1 : 744]

I have your letter – our Cold Roll work is much reduced. We want a man as foreman over the Cold Rolls & he is also to drive the Engine.

I am quite willing to take you if you like to come, but can only pay £2..0..0 per week & bonus half yearly according to results. I have no work for Justin, but something may turn up after a bit.

P.S. I think I could give Justin work in our Office.

Arthur Gilbertson to William Thomas, Mill Foreman. 13 Nov. 1899 [1 : 923]

Quarter (4 months) ending Octr. 7th.

Bars delivered Mills	5906 Tons
Blackplates as per Tom Harris a/c }	5025 "
	881 for Shearing
	1255 actual Shearing
	374 Tons difference

How do you account for this? We also find a loss of finished materials, nearly 200 Tons!!

How do you account for this?

Are the monthly Mill Yields wrong?

This a/c adds 1 cwt per Ton to Mill Yields, for the worse, per month.

Arthur Gilbertson to Mr. T. H. Harrison, 24 Cotterill Street, Hereford. 2 March 1900 [1 : 961-2]

We are prepared to give you 50/- a week as general Traffic Manager. We can hardly specify all your duties, but you will have to look after working the traffic, Platelayers, Loco Drivers, Shunters, and to see to the delivery of materials to the various departments – if this was well done, you would have no reason to complain of your situation, and it would no doubt be permanent. If by any chance it were not so, we would use our influence with the Midland Ry. to take you back.

Arthur Gilbertson to Andrew Little, 143, Firpark Street, Dennistown, Glasgow. **5 March 1900 [1 : 965]**

We have your letter of 2nd inst., and are prepared to engage you at a Salary of £250 a year, subject to one month's notice on either side.

We should be glad if you could come in three weeks. We conclude you know the mode of lining & levelling Sheet Mills & double Crank steel shafts – also that you give a hand yourself with your men.

Arthur Gilbertson to A. Little. **9 March 1900 [2 : 976-7]**

I am sorry not to be at home, when you start, but my Sons will attend to anything with you. I wish to tell you you will find, I am afraid, Babcock Boilers, Economisers &c, not very well kept, and a great deal of Waste in Tallow, Oil, Paraffin, Stores &c. for Engines. William Roberts, our late Foreman, who has left of his own account, for an easier berth we imagine, was many years ago one of our Engine Drivers, we put him on as Foreman, because his health became delicate, the Works were very small then & the Steel Works not built and Roberts was able to do what was then required. We want now a greater alteration in things & our Locos, Engines, Boilers, Mill Machinery, Fitting Shop, Smiths, Carpenters &c &c. kept in better & cleaner state. Our Dynamos and Electric Shed are in a neglected state and want more systematic management – the Babcock Boilers & Economisers especially want attention, and regular cleaning.

We also want more automatic appliances about the Works & Steel Works, when time admits. You will find leaks about the Boilers, Fittings & Steam pipes & culverts & passages drawing old air, from Fces to Boilers.

Wm. Thomas, the second man, was one of our Engineers & knows all the Works, pressures, arrangements, &c, and you will find him useful. The Locos want more care & more frequent washing out of Tubes (copper). We want some overhead Traveller & Hydraulic over Pit at Steel Fces to lift up "messes". Mr. Gilbertson Jnr. has a plan for new Shops, for Fitters, Smiths &c., which you should look over.

My Sons will give you every support & assistance.

Arthur Gilbertson to Captain Lindsay, Chief Constable, Glamorganshire. **23 July 1900 [3 : 82]**

Could you supply us with a good Constable to look after our extensive premises here? We understand he could live at the Police Station & be under the Supervision of the Inspector here.

Please say what we should have to pay for his salary & send him as soon as possible.

Arthur Gilbertson to Messrs the Glanrhyd Tinplate Co. Ltd. **24 July 1900 [3 : 83-4]**

I have gone over your a/cs. I believe from bad working in Mills, bad Yields & cutting up sheets in shear by grindstone, for all which Dd. Gwillym was dismissed, you made a loss on Blackplate sold, which should have covered cost, if properly worked. We find Bars were charged you at an average of £7..1..0 for the 4 months ending July 7th. – W. Gilbertson & Co. Ltd. debited their Tin Works for the same period @ £6..17..6 & sold Bars to outsiders up to £7..5..0.

As you have made such a serious mess & Dd. Gwillym has been dismissed, W.G. & Co. Ltd. will grant you a rebate of £375..0..0 on the 4 months – you may increase price of Tin in Pots by £300 on stock schedule. This will show a few pounds profit on the 6 months.

The loss of 2T. 2C. 0 . 0 Black Tin (in addition to the loss on weekly yields), distinctly points to dishonesty, and the Works will therefore be closed & all Employees dismissed.

P.S. The prices of Bars charged you, after the rebate, will be 1/6d. a Ton less than W. G. & Co. debited their Mills for the same period.

Arthur Gilbertson to Messrs the Glanrhyd Tinplate Co. Ltd. **24 July 1900 [3 : 85]**

Notice

In consequence of the extraordinary high cost of making Plates in these Works, bad yields, cutting up plates in Shears, bad "outputs", large quantity of Wasters made, losses of Tin in yields, and losses of Tin from Stock!! we are unable to get orders unless at a loss of capital. The Mills will therefore stop on Saturday, and the finishing departments after the Stocks are worked up, and then the Works will be shut down & closed, and all Employés dismissed.

Arthur Gilbertson
Director
The Glanrhyd Tinplate Co. Ltd.

Arthur Gilbertson to M. Morgan, Tinhouse Foreman, Glanrhyd Tinplate Co. Ltd. **13 Aug. 1900 [3 : 99]**

Not only have you allowed a large quantity (over 2 Tons) of Tin, to be lost from stock, but you have not had the Pots put to gauge, and another large loss has arisen.

You will be dismissed and paid off at once and you may consider you are lucky not to be prosecuted.

Arthur Gilbertson to Jos. James, Glantawe Works. 17 Aug. 1900 [3 : 105-6]

Perhaps the notice was not clear to you. You may have a month's wages in lieu of notice, from tomorrow & you may hand over keys &c. to my Senior Clerk, Mr. Philip Davies, who will call at Glantawe at 10 a.m. tomorrow – if you have not cash you may draw a cheque, and I will sign it. I may draw your attention to the fact, that the unexplained loss of Block Tin, while you were in charge, is so serious, that I should be justified in declining to pay you anything.

Arthur Gilbertson to the Glantawe Men. 21 Aug. 1900 [3 : 112]

I have your letter of the 18th inst. I can probably see you at my Pontardawe Office at 10.30 a.m. on Monday next.

I am sorry all you Glantawe men have treated with contempt all my warnings & suggestions for several years.

I never knew any one of you, ever do anything I asked of you, and now the blow has fallen – the losses of "Capital" were so severe the last three months, that I was unable to go on working.

As the Mills cannot make plates for Tinning at a profit, you had better consult together how the Big Sheet Mill could be started again.

I spent a great deal of money on it, and you only broke up the Rolls &c., to repay me, for my outlay.

It is a sad pity you did not come to your present state of mind several years ago.

I dont care "twopence" about the anonymous letters, such silly disgusting rubbish only hurts the man who writes them, and the man who suggests them. They dont influence my opinion in the least degree.

Unfortunately some of the letters have let out that they are written on behalf of Glantawe & D. Gwilym, and therefore some of your party should try to find out who pretends to be your friend.

Arthur Gilbertson to Dd. Rees, Pickler. 27 Nov. 1900 [3 : 148]

We understand you refuse our offer – we therefore withdraw it. We should be justified in dismissing you at once, under our Rule 8, and will enforce Rule 4.

We will however give you notice to leave in four weeks from December 3rd., but we warn you that if you neglect your duties or waste our materials during the period you will be stopped.

Arthur Gilbertson to Colonel Lindsay, Chief Constable. **15 Jan. 1901 [3 : 184]**

We have severed our connection with the Tinplate Works [Glanrhyd] which gave us trouble, when we decided to employ a private Constable & we find we require his services no longer, so after the 29th March we shall not want Constable Toye.

He is a smart man, and has been very satisfactory.

Arthur Gilbertson to Robert Watts, 12 Lower Mill Row, Pontypool, Mon. **18 Jan. 1901 [3 : 185]**

Your letter of 16th inst, is satisfactory and if you can with truth say, you are a sober man (not an abstainer) we are prepared to engage you on the terms you ask, from & including the Pickling to loading into Trucks, you need not do any Office work. Provided you will give us good References at once.

Arthur Gilbertson to Robert Watts. **11 Feb. 1901 [3 : 212]**

You will find the Galvanizing Shop in some disorder, and a dreadful quantity of Defective sheets.

Our late Foreman drank, and neglected his duties, I am afraid. Several of his Relatives are in the Galvanizing Shop.

Evan Griffiths, the stretcher, is the Secretary of the Union, he can give you assistance, if he likes.

There is too much labour in the Shop – after a few days you can report to me.

Arthur Gilbertson to Messrs Selby Bigge & Co. **11 May 1901 [3 : 277]**

Electrical Generator & Engine

We want to know how much Steam at 100 lbs pressure, per indicated Horse power per hour, our Engine should take? We also want to know officially, if Thornton thinks we have sufficiently skilled men, attending the Engine, and if it is in a good state. We wish to learn this from you and we shall keep it & Thompson's report quite private. A. Little knows nothing about this.

Arthur Gilbertson to Jenkin Jones, Solicitor, Swansea. **15 July 1901 [3 : 327]**

A youth in our employ has been putting fictitious names in our Time Book, cashing their cheques himself & spending the money. If this was proved before the Bench, could he be sent to a Reformatory?

Frank Gilbertson to Jenkin Jones. **17 July 1901 [3 : 330]**

. . . The youth in question is between 16 & 17 years old. The case is one of serious fraud. He has cheated us to the extent of £12 odd during June, which sum he appropriated.

If the Magistrates could not send him to a reformatory what would the penalty be?

We shall be obliged by your advice as we dont want to make him a hardened criminal.

Arthur Gilbertson to A. Little, Engineer. **13 Aug. 1901 [3 : 367]**

After our interview of yesterday, we very much regret to say we are unable to retain you in our employ. In lieu of a month's notice we will pay you a month's salary upon your giving up our House in a month's time, and you will not return to our Works after today. The same will apply to your Son. We cannot alter this determination.

Arthur Gilbertson to Messrs
The London & Scottish Boiler Insurance Co. Ltd. **13 Aug. 1901 [3 : 368]**

We have your report of the 12th inst. and will ask you to point out to us, what you suggest should be done to our Locos & Boilers? Do you consider the Locos & Boilers are well & carefully kept?

We may say an alteration is about to take place in our Head Engineer, responsible for this work.

Arthur Gilbertson to William Roberts. **19 Aug. 1901 [3 : 379]**

We have your note, but we do not intend again to employ a Mechanical Engineer like Mr. A. Little.

We intend to divide the work, and look after it more ourselves, with a good working Foreman, in each department.

Arthur Gilbertson to Wm. Morgan,
26 Castle Street, Merthyr Tydfil. **20 Aug. 1901 [3 : 381]**

We have your application. You seem to have had the experience needed.

Please say where you are a native of? and what positions you have held since you were a youth, and what you have done since you left Cory Bros. & whom you are now employed by? We shall treat this as private.

Frank Gilbertson to A. Little. **21 Aug. 1901 [3 : 383]**

In reply to your letter, we are very sorry that after what has transpired we could not give you a satisfactory reference.

We advise you to return to Scotland & refer to your previous Employers.
Should any firm, to whom you may apply, refer to us, we should answer any questions as favourably as we are able.

Arthur Gilbertson to W. Ricketts, 110 Victoria Road, Middlesboro. **23 Aug. 1901 [3 : 388]**

Please say your age, and where you were apprenticed, and what situations you have held. Where had you charge of Babcock Boilers?
Did you serve your time to an Electrical Engineer? or what experience and where, did you get Electrical knowledge?
Do you work yourself?

Frank Gilbertson to Messrs Summers & Sons, Stalybridge. **4 Dec. 1901 [3 : 504]**

Our Sheet Millmen are agitating for a readjustment of rates claiming that the rates settled by the South Wales Association do not include the lighter gauges, such as the Rangoon specification of 300 6ft. sheets to the Ton.
Might we ask you if you would let us know what you pay?

Arthur Gilbertson to William Evans, Tinhouse Foreman, Glantawe. **3 Jan. 1902 [3 : 517]**

I hope you are very careful to see that 2¼ lbs of Tin, at least, is put on the Parsons Coke plates, and that the finish is right up to our standard.
Some serious complaints have come, and it would be serious to us & your present Employers if the brand lost its name.

Arthur Gilbertson to W. Griffiths. **7 Feb. 1902 [3 : 544]**

Referring to our interview today, we are prepared to give you a Salary of Two Hundred a year, as Manager &c. of the Slag Works from 1st July and a half yearly Bonus according to profits. Three months notice on either side.
When our Port Talbot Works begin to grind Slag, we hope to make an arrangement to employ you as Manager &c. for both Works.

P. Davies to W. Griffiths. **10 Feb. 1902 [3 : 548]**

We cannot alter the terms we offered you on the 7th inst. – we hope to be able to employ you also when we start working at the Port Talbot Steel Co. Ltd., and think it would be rather unwise of you not to avail yourself of the opportunity, but you of course know your own business best – please let us have your decision.

Arthur Gilbertson to Mr. Elias, 17 Victoria Terrace, Cwmavon. **23 July 1902 [3 : 693]**

Yours of yesterday. We dont want any information about your Employer – it would be dishonest. We only asked your wages & your work, to decide if we could give you a bonus for the 10 weeks.

As your Wife has been confined again, we send you £5 – you need only simply acknowledge it.

Frank Gilbertson to Augustus Lewis, HM Inspector of Factories, Swansea. **30 July 1902 [3 : 704]**

We wish to work our whole Works next Monday as we had them idle for the whole of the first Coronation week, & they will be idle on August 9th. Can we do so, seeing that we have not given the notice under Par. 33 of the Act?

Arthur Gilbertson to W. Griffiths, Slag Department. **19 Sept. 1902 [3 : 726]**

We find the "labour" too costly per Ton, at the Slag Works – please look into this & <u>bring it down</u>. You know what you indicated, including your Salary & the Clerk.

Please send a list of cash which will come in by end of this month.

Arthur Gilbertson to W. Griffiths. **29 Sept. 1902 [3 : 732]**

We sent for a/c. this morning & find you had not arrived at ¼ to 11 am.

Is it not needful for you to be early on Monday to see starting the week off at 9.30?

Arthur Gilbertson to Robert Watts, Galvanizing Foreman. **8 Oct. 1902 [3 : 741]**

We now find out that the Canada Plates sent to Canada are absolutely bad and we have serious claims.

We have pardoned you so often that we cannot go on with you further. <u>You must be stopped at once</u>, and you will be paid a month's wages in lieu of notice, although we should be justified if we stopped you, as Foreman, without notice or payment.

You are not to enter into the Works again, and you will be paid off the balance when you leave the House.

We give you notice of four weeks from the first Monday in November to quit our House.

Frank Gilbertson to G. B. Hammond, Melyn Works, Neath. **9 Oct. 1902 [3 : 743]**

Mr. Hodge asked for certain of our rates paid to Basic men, as he had got an incorrect list from someone here.

We pay exorbitant rates, above the North Country ones, which date from the time when we had trouble at starting the process.

We think Mr. Hodge wishes to establish ours, as Standard Basic Rates for South Wales, & we would suggest that you might enter a protest if you pay them.

We are not disposed to fight them at present but it might be necessary for us some day to adopt the North Country rates.

P. Davies to C. Bevan Jenkins, Solicitor. **24 Dec. 1902 [3 : 766]**

Robert Watts, the late foreman in our Galvanizing Department, behaved himself abominably. We gave him a month's wages and allowed him to stay in our house for a month, instead of working his notice, as he was found drunk in the works and constantly left the works during the day.

We have now got to know from our Canadian Agent what this man Watts has caused us by his wilful neglect. We have to pay £500 to £600 to the buyers of our Galvanized Sheets in Canada – they were disgracefully made under Watts' supervision. An arbitration took place in Canada, and we are convinced that Watts sent very bad sheets. Can we sue him for damages? But possibly it would not be worth the trouble.

You might write him that unless he vacates our house by Tuesday, 1st January, we shall sue him for damages for his neglect which has caused us to lose over £500, when he was our responsible Foreman.

Frank Gilbertson to Stanley Davies, Apprentice. **29 Dec. 1902 [3 : 769]**

It is agreed that Stanley Davies be apprenticed to W. Gilbertson & Co. Ltd., as Steel Works Chemist – Stanley Davies agreeing to remain for three years, with W. G. & Co. Ltd., unless he desires to return to school after the expiration of two years.

He agrees not to leave the firm for any other purpose than completing his education, until three years from Nov. 1st 1902.

His remuneration is to be 6/- per week for the first year, 12/- for the second & 18/- or 20/- per week for the third.

Arthur Gilbertson to Messrs Sutton, Reading. **5 Oct. 1903 [4 : 123]**

Mr. Gilbertson wants a Head working Gardener who understands Orchids, Forcing Muscat Grapes, Peaches &c. under Glass, also forcing Rhubarb, Sea Kale &c. Mr. Gilbertson is an experienced Gardener himself, and expects the Head Gardener to work & be active. Three men are kept in the Garden. The Head must know thoroughly about forcing Grapes &c.

Can you recommend a man? Say wages & references. There is a nice Lodge, but the Gardener supplies his Coal. Say if married, and ages of children.

Arthur Gilbertson to James Exell **n.d. [Oct. 1903] [4 : 124-5]**

I like your letter, and send you a telegram this morning "I give 26/- and Lodge, would you like to try my situation". Half a dozen Gardeners are recommended to me from Florists and they ask 25/- a week. My Lodge is good, and Coal is cheap in this District but my Gardener supplies his Coal & light. I tried my second Gardener as Head, and has injured the Vines, Peaches &c. so he leaves me on Friday, 30th inst. My second Gardener is a respectable man and lives in the Bothy – the Bothy is very nice & Electric light – there are three good bedrooms & sitting room. I would not be illiberal if I found you satisfactory.

I prefer my Gardeners to go to Church once on Sunday. I have built a Church near my House. Would you like to try a month? You could live in the Bothy for that period.

Frank Gilbertson to W. Griffiths, Slag Works Manager. **2 March 1904 [3 : 977-8]**

Mr. Gilbertson has now considered the terms of your engagement & we propose the following, from the expiration of the notice running:

(1) Monthly salary calculated at rate of £150 per annum.
(2) Bonus of 6d a ton upon all sales delivered at prices not less than 30/- & 25/- f.o.t. for the respective qualities, up to 6,000 Tons per annum.
(3) Bonus of 1% of nett profits.
(4) Engagement terminable by 3 mos. notice.

Please say if you agree.

Frank Gilbertson to W. Griffiths. **5 March 1904 [3 : 980]**

We are in receipt of yours of 3rd inst. & note that you agree to the terms specified in ours of 2nd.

We understand there will be no necessity in future for such extensive travelling as last year, but we wish you to consult the writer or one of his brothers on each occasion before incurring travelling expenses.

The profits are now cut very fine, and as many sales next year as possible should be made by correspondence.

Cecil Gilbertson to the Secretary of the Board of Trade. **7 April 1904 [5 : 9]**

A certain section of our Workmen, numbering about 10, called Barcutters, demand an increase on the tonnage rate that we offer them for the work they have to do.

It has been decided to submit the matter to arbitration and to ask the Board of Trade to appoint an Arbitrator.

The points that we wish to have decided by the Arbitrator are as follows:

(1) The tonnage rate that should be paid for this work.
(2) Our claim for damages, consequent upon the men refusing to work in accordance with an arrangement made between Mr. T. Griffiths of the Steel Smelters Union on the men's behalf and ourselves.

Frank Gilbertson to Stephen Davies, Mill Superintendent. **11 May 1905 [5 : 126]**

We propose in order to give you a definite interest in results to substitute for your present bonus a scale as follows:

(1) 2/6 a week for each Mill that turns out its full make, without any breakage of Standard Roll, Spindle, or bedplate.
Full make to be calculated as over 610 boxes in big [?] Mills & 500 boxes in Nos. 8 & 9 & not to be counted as full make if any turn is idle for want of men.
(2) £5 a quarter if yield below 1.4.2.0 on quarter accounts, £10 if below 1.4.0.0.
(3) £5 for any month that establishes a new record in output.

What do you think of this proposal?

Frank Gilbertson to Messrs. Wenham Brothers & Co. **15 June 1906 [5 : 299]**

With reference to your circular in connection with the Iron, Steel & Allied Trades Federation. We are not quite sure whether you require our total wages, so we give them in such a form that you can take out what you require.

Last year	
Steel Works	£34,000 of which ⅓rd may eventually belong to galvanized sheets.
Mills	£39,000 of which ⅚ths belongs to galvanized sheets.
Galvanizing Department	£12,000.

Cecil Gilbertson to Stephen Davies, Mill Superintendent. **20 Nov. 1906 [5 : 388]**

You must send for Lewis the Rollerman and I will see him this afternoon at 2.30. In future you are to understand that the rules of the Consultative Committee must be kept, and no man may be stopped until he has been down to the Office to see one of us, unless it is a case of drunkenness or disobedience. I find that on Friday Lewis could not be called drunk and although he did disobey orders at first, he afterwards complied with them and was allowed to finish the rest of his shift. I cannot therefore see any reason why you should have stopped him contrary to the rules of the Committee.

Frank Gilbertson to W. J. Onions, Pontnewydd Sheet & Galvanizing Co., Ltd. **29 July 1907 [5 : 502]**

Could you very kindly allow 2 representatives of our Workmen & 1 of our own to see you working 72 x 36 sheets, 30 gauge, on eights?

Our men wont believe it possible without undue labour.

Frank Gilbertson to J. Trevor Owen, MA, Swansea Technical College. **14 Nov. 1907 [5 : 584]**

Would you very kindly send me a report upon the work & ability of Gwilym Lewis, of Pontardawe, who lately finished 1 year's course?

Also would you give me your advice as to whether a further course is desirable & whether he could specialise in Iron & Steel? We want him to be pretty well equipped & shall then employ him in our laboratory, as his father is an old & valued workman.

Frank Gilbertson to Mr. Owen, School Master, Rhydyfro. **1 June 1908 [5 : 736-7]**

We have considered the matter since Mr. Owen Davies & the writer interviewed your son.

We think he is anxious to get on & to work hard, & it is on this assumption that we make the following proposal – That you should send him to Sheffield to study iron & steel at the University, & we will pay him £50 for his first year. If he gets on well, & we are satisfied, we may give him £50 for each of the two succeeding years of the course.

During the holidays we should expect him to spend a lot of his time in these works so as to become thoroughly acquainted with the practical side of his work.

If he gets on well, we may be able to give him employment when he leaves Sheffield.

We wish you to understand that this scheme will fit him for more important work than mere analysis in a Laboratory & that if he is to make the most of his opportunities he must think more of the practical processes of steel making than of Laboratory work, & must visit all the Works he can in Sheffield & keep his eyes open, studying the theory of all he sees done in practice.

Cecil Gilbertson to Wm. J. Williams, Bethel Road, Llansamlet. **11 Feb. 1909 [5 : 570]**

We have decided to accept your application for the post of Mill Foreman in our new Tinplate Works, at a salary of £4 per week. We will advise you when we shall require your services but this will not be for some months yet. Probably we shall want you to start with us when the Mill machinery is being erected which we hope will be in about 3 months time.

We should like however to have a talk with you as soon as possible on various matters in connection with the New Mills, and if you will please suggest one or two days next week or the week after when you could manage to come up and see us here either in the morning or afternoon we will try and arrange an appointment.

Frank Gilbertson to Morgan Jones. **11 Dec. 1909 [7 : 168]**

We have decided to offer you the job at 35/- a week on the understanding that if you effect a considerable improvement, & give us satisfaction, we will add something in the form of a Bonus.

The work is to keep account of the trucks going under demurrage, & to follow up those that require to be discharged with the Foreman concerned.

At present our Demurrage is a disgrace & we are probably the worst works in the trade, & I feel sure it will be easy for you to make some improvement.

Frank Gilbertson to H. Summers, Stalybridge. **24 March 1910 [7 : 240]**

The helpers in the Welsh Mills, about here, are agitating to be placed on tonnage rates.

Would you very kindly tell me how many helpers you employ, if any, in your Welsh Mills & the rates.

Would Mr. Onions also be willing to let us know the tonnage rates & the number & conditions of the helpers at Braby's, when working an order like 72 x 36, 30 gauge, which is worked largely in South Wales also.

I think I gave you the rates we have been paying, sometime back, so I need not repeat them.

I may say Melyn work 72 x 36 with one helper only.

Frank Gilbertson to Trevor Owen. **11 April 1910 [7 : 256]**

We enclose £25 which represents the reduced amount we have promised to allow you for your Second Year's course. I am glad you have got a part job with Vickers & hope you will be successful at the next exam.

Frank Gilbertson to The Surveyor of Taxes, Neath. **5 Oct. 1910 [7 : 425]**

An employee of ours Mr. J. R. Roberts was late in sending in his Income Tax return, & fears that he has lost the chance of Abatement.

I hope you will be able to make an exception in his case, without sticking to the actual letter of the law, as he has no income except his wages & these are returned by this Company, so that there is no doubt whatever as to what his income actually is.

Please do the best you can for him.

Frank Gilbertson to Stephen Davies, Mill Superintendent. **15 Oct. 1910 [7 : 438]**

Confirming the promise we made you of a bonus on output.

From now on, at the end of each quarter, the output will be compared with the average output of the same quarter in the 3 previous years, & a bonus of 1/- a ton on any improvement will be paid you.

For the tax year ending April 1911 Stephen Davies earned £249 and bonuses of £75 [7 : 596]

Frank Gilbertson to David Morgan, Belmont, Coleshill Terrace, Llanelly. **12 Dec. 1910 [8 : 466-7]**

We now decide to offer you the situation as Superintendent of our Tinplate Mills at a salary of £17 a month, & a bonus upon results that will be fixed later on, when you have got things into order.

We have a house that will suit you well, & the rent will be 36/- per month inclusive of rates & taxes.

If you accept the position we should like you to give notice at once, & although it can only date from the first Monday in January, you might get your Employers to let you off as soon as they have found a successor.

We should like you to start as soon as you can get off.

Please keep your engagement private, as far as you can, as if our present Roll Turner hears of it he will be upset, & it will be no hardship for him as we shall let him go back to roll if he wishes to.

Frank Gilbertson to David Morgan. **15 Dec. 1910 [7 : 469]**

In reply to your letter of yesterday.

The rent of the house is high, but it is what we pay ourselves for it. It is an exceptionally good house, with many conveniences. Houses are so scarce that we thought we were fortunate to have it in hand for you to start in – you could move if you wished to, after you had settled down here.

We are prepared to increase the Salary we offer to £18 a month.

There will, later on, be a bonus on results as soon as you have got things right.

We hope these amended terms will enable you to accept the situation.

On 28 December D. Morgan rejected the appointment.

Frank Gilbertson to Stephen Davies, Mill Superintendent. **12 April 1911 [7 : 536-8]**

The work of our Sheet Mills is so very bad compared with other Works that we have got to make some drastic changes if this Works is to continue to live.

Sheets are coming in from the Melyn 7 lbs per box heavier than you are rolling from the same Iron.

The breakages are even worse than ever.

The Grease has been allowed to reach disgraceful figures.

The Yield generally is as bad as ever it was in spite of the fact that the defectives are now included in the weight.

If things are allowed to drift any longer, I can see no way except to stop a number of Mills, and choose out the best workmen to man the rest of the Mills and begin afresh.

This could be a very unfortunate step to have to take, and it has occurred to us that there is one alternative that might be tried first.

You are keen enough at times, but you do not show steady perseverance.

We are therefore prepared to try the effect of giving you a direct interest in the results of your work, and we will pay the following bonuses to you and give this system a full trial before we decide upon any other steps.

(1) Present bonus arrangements to be cancelled.

(2) Weekly bonus and Monthly bonus

- (a) Every week you will receive 5/- for each Mill that has worked without breakage of Rolls.
  10/- to be deducted for every breakage.
- (b) The average output of each Mill will be taken over the last 12 months to form a basis – taking into account an estimated week's work, for any weeks Mills are idle for strikes and annual holiday. The 12 months average will be divided into two sections:

(1) April to Sept.
(2) Oct. to March.

Every month the make of each Mill will be compared with the basis make for that particular Mill and you will have 1/- a ton upon any increase make in any Mill.

No. 8 & 9 will be calculated in boxes and the bonus ½d a box.

(c) Every quarter you will have a bonus on Yield

below 1 – 4 – 2 – 0	£5/-/-
" 1 – 4 – 1 – 0	£7/10/-
" 1 – 4 – 0 – 0	£12/10/-

(d) We will arrange a bonus on all sheets worked on sixes if we can settle with the men.

(e) 2½% of any saving in Grease during a quarter compared with last quarter's yield of grease.

Frank Gilbertson to Owen Davies, Steel Works Manager. **6 June 1911 [7 : 582]**

Private

Now the extensions in the Steel Works are beginning to come into work, we propose the following additions to your remuneration.

Standing Salary £6 per week instead of £5..10..0.

Weekly bonus of ½d. per ton upon any output in excess of 1200 tons of ingots.

Tube Steel. If this develops, a bonus of 2d a ton same as for special hard steels.

We take this opportunity of saying how much we appreciate the careful work you perform – you manage your department in an admirable way, & we greatly value your faithful services.

At the same time we must remember your responsibility is growing, & with the increased output we shall have, & the 2 Mills working together, your department will require more supervision than ever.

The Income Tax returns for the year ending April 1911, dated 16 June [7 : 595], show that Owen Davies received a salary of £414 and bonuses of £60.

Frank Gilbertson to C. Johnson, HM Inspector of Factories. **3 Nov. 1911 [7 : 705]**

I sent you a statement of the evidence I wish to give to the Committee on the night employment of young persons. It would be of great assistance to me if you would let me know as early as possible when my attendance in London is required. If there are any matters upon which you consider the Committee will require information, within my knowledge of the trade, & not covered by my evidence, I should be glad if you would make any suggestions that occur to you.

Charles Gilbertson to Tom Lewis, Galvanizing Superintendent. **10 Nov. 1911 [7 : 712]**

I have been speaking to Mr. Frank about your wages, & we propose that your standing wages should be £4 per week instead of £3 per week, in return for the saving which will be gained owing to your patent "carriers".

Should this "carrier" be patented, you will get a share of the Royalties paid by users in other Works.

Your spelter & tonnage rate remain the same as at present.

Charles Gilbertson to Harold Trubshaw. **22 Nov. 1911 [7 : 728]**

In reply to your enquiry over telephone this afternoon, about W. J. Williams, roll turner. He was engaged by us when we started our new tinplate works, & came to us with excellent recommendations.

He met with a great number of difficulties, which always occur in the starting of a new works. We felt that matters were not getting on as well as they ought, & we decided to make a change, as we were anxious to lose no time in getting things straight. We had nothing really against Williams, except that we felt we might get a man better able to tackle the difficulties of starting the new works.

He was undoubtedly an experienced roll turner, as is clear from the references which he had from other employers, & he was a very respectable man.

Frank Gilbertson to W. J. Williams. **15 Dec. 1911 [7 : 776]**

W. J. Williams has worked under us for a number of years, at different times. First as a tinplate Rollerman, then as a Sheet Rollerman after his return from America, & last as Tinplate Mill Roll Turner.

He is a very competent & good workman, but found the starting of six new Tin Mills, with new & inexperienced labour, too much for him.

He is a superior man with a good influence among his men.

Frank Gilbertson to Stephen Davies. **12 Jan. 1912 [7 : 813-4]**

Referring to our conversation yesterday, & the period of trial we have allowed you.

You must distinctly understand you have a free hand to effect improvements & reduce breakages.

You may suspend any men who dont come in to work without satisfactory reason.

You may suspend any men for bad work provided you do not transgress the Association rule, given below – you must be careful to conform strictly to it.

If there is anything you want & cant get from other departments, you must send in a written complaint on each occasion.

Apart from these limitations you have a free hand to manage the Mills & to reduce cost in your own way if you can.

Association Rule "In the event of any Millman being suspended for any "breakages of or stalling of Engine, he shall be given an opportunity of "defending himself before the Management, on the day of such breakages or "stalling, or not later than the day following the suspension; should the "Management not be able to investigate the matter upon the day "following the suspension, the Millman has the right to continue working "until the day appointed for the investigation – No Millman to be finally "dismissed for breakages or stalling until the representatives of the men "have had an opportunity of investigating the case."

Frank Gilbertson to C. A. Hardy, Springfield, Baglan. **9 April 1912 [7 : 876-7]**

I am much obliged to you for your information with regard to H. Jenkins. We have carefully considered the question, & have come to the conclusion that if you came here now, you would not have a fair chance with our Roll Turner, or with our men.

We think it would be better for us to give our Roll Turner fair warning that unless he can produce satisfactory results by the middle of June we shall bring in fresh blood.

We would then be disposed to appoint you & give you the opportunity of bringing a Roll Turner with you.

This procedure would prepare the men for a change, & prevent any suggestion of unfair treatment to our present Roll Turner, who has been with us for many years.

He undoubtedly has a following among the men, & might create an amount of sympathy among them that would render his successor's position very difficult.

The only difficulty about this proposal would be that if our Roll Turner got things straight you might be disappointed at the time your notice at Briton Ferry expired. This is not likely, & we could probably give you a good idea of what was likely to be the result before the end of May.

Frank Gilbertson to C. A. Hardy. **25 April 1912 [7 : 890]**

Private

The Welshmen here decided not to re-start the Staffordshire Mills after the coal strike, & they are going to work 6 hour shifts in the Welsh Mills.

This leaves a clear field for the re-start of the Staffordshire Mills, one by one, with Monmouthshire men.

Could you tell us when Whitford [Steel & Galvanizing Works, Briton Ferry] are changing the 2 Mills to Welsh style & what prospects there will be of getting a good gang of these men, thrown out at Whitford, to start one or two Mills here?

Frank Gilbertson to C. A. Hardy. 1 May 1912 [7 : 906-7]

We are now in a position to offer you definitely the situation of Outside Manager in our Sheet Mills & Shearhouse at a salary of £400 a year.

We should like you to start on June 2nd if you can manage it.

We have spoken to our Roll Turner & given him to understand that his future depends upon his working hand in glove with you in the Welsh Mills, & making an improvement under your management. We may say that if you carry on the work well, you may look upon the position as a permanent one, & it is very seldom that any of our officials desire to leave our service. We should like you to make arrangements, if you can, for the restart of 2 out of our 3 Staffordshire Mills with men you know on June 3rd, & with your own choice of a Roll Turner & we should wish to work them under Staffordshire Board, if you would tell us to whom to apply for Membership.

The Third Mill could be started at a later date, & if desirable we would arrange to increase the steam pressure from 110 lbs. to 140 or 150 lbs. to get extra power for the 3 Mills.

We suggest that your appointment should be on a 3 months notice on either side.

Frank Gilbertson to C. A. Hardy. 7 May 1912 [7 : 916-7]

. . . We have spoken to Stephen Davies, who will be careful in future to give the correct impression to any men that come over. We do not think it was from him that your men heard the rumour you refer to. You can assert with confidence that our intentions are never to work Welsh style again in those Mills.

We have applied to Mr. Dan Jones for particulars of the Midland Board, & he asks if our men have agreed to join in our application, & if they have had any communication with Mr. Cox. We are replying that you are coming to manage our Mills & will communicate with him.

The new boiler has been sent off & we shall probably be ready with 150 lbs pressure at the end of this month, but it might be advisable to work at 120 with 2 Mills & keep the higher pressure in reserve for when the 3rd Mill starts.

Frank Gilbertson to David Jenkins, Mill Foreman. 5 Sept. 1912 [8 : 21]

There is a small amount due to you on account of Royalties = £7.

I think justice will be done by giving you £25 for the past 2 years.

I have sent out to the Millmen to give them notice that unless they take an interest in the machines & reduce the consumption of grease we shall have to remove them, as they no longer pay for their maintenance.

Charles Gilbertson to William Baker. **3 Jan. 1913 [8 : 139]**

I was greatly surprised & disgusted to receive the report this morning that you were found taking small pieces of wood out of our Works yesterday, concealed under your coat.

You must have known, at the time, that you were acting dishonestly. You must also know well, the rule of the Works about men taking things away, without an order.

It is because I feel certain that you will never do anything of this kind again, that I shall do nothing more than warn you this time. But you must understand that it would be a most serious thing for you, if it ever happened again.

After what we have done for you, you are the last person in the Works who one would have suspected of such behaviour.

Frank Gilbertson to the Chief Constable of Glamorgan. **26 Aug. 1913 [8 : 323-4]**

Private

We have reason to suspect one or more of our Employees of habitual theft & sale of Brass & other valuable metals.

Could you let us have the services of a really capable Detective for a time? We should like a man whom we could pretend has entered our employment, & who would come in daily, in working clothes, to do a few light jobs to explain his presence.

We have also reason to believe that the Dillwyn Arms is now very badly conducted, & is the resort of betting men from Swansea.

Betting has such a bad effect upon our Workmen, that we should be glad to pay for the service of the Detective to watch what goes on in that House in addition to the matter of theft in our Works.

We think a Detective could carry on both observations at the same time, as the men we want to watch frequent the Dillwyn Arms.

We dont want the Inspector at Pontardawe to know we have a man, as we wish for the greatest secrecy.

Frank Gilbertson to the Chief Constable of Glamorgan. **2 Sept. 1913 [8 : 326]**

Could you let us know by wire tomorrow if you are sending a man? The men we suspect are working nights this week & this is the time they should be watched.

Frank Gilbertson to the Chief Constable of Glamorgan. **13 Sept. 1913 [8 : 342]**

. . . Unfortunately it leaked out that a Detective was to come into the Works, & we believe he therefore left.

We however received information from a resident that enabled us to make a report to the Police at Neath & has led to two arrests. It now appears that the thefts of brass &c. have been going on systematically for about a year.

We hope no stone will be left unturned to ascertain from the Railway Co. who were the Receivers of the brass, during the full period.

Frank Gilbertson to R. & C. B. Jenkins & Lloyd. **15 Sept. 1913 [8 : 344]**

We are very anxious to get at all the Receivers of the stolen property we can.

We hope you will be able to find out from the Railway Co. all the names to whom Heywood had been sending parcels during the past 12 months, even if no evidence can be found to enable a prosecution to take place.

Frank Gilbertson to R. & C. B. Jenkins & Lloyd. **29 Sept. 1913 [8 : 355]**

. . . We consider the punishment was much too lenient in the case of Heywood, who appears in the character of a newcomer to the place bringing temptation to weak men.

Is there any chance of bringing the Receivers to book?

We are much obliged to you for the care you have shown over the matter.

Frank Gilbertson to The Melyn Tinplate Co., Ltd. **6 Oct. 1913 [8 : 358]**

Private

We are obliged by your private lines of yesterday.

We work all 72 x 36 with 2 helpers as has always been the case here.

The 100 lb. substance are all worked here on twelves & not on eights. The twelves do not present any extra difficulty in opening but do give a shocking yield due entirely to bad workmanship. Sometimes a shift gives excellent results but only with the very best men.

Frank Gilbertson to W. D. Johnson, Bynea Steel Co. **26 Oct. 1914 [8 : 798-9]**

It was agreed between you & me that you should take no men from our Works without my sanction, in recognition of the fact that you had gained all your outside experience here & that we could therefore expect friendly consideration from you.

Dan Thomas was specifically mentioned in this connection.

Hearing that he was going to Bynea, after David Williams had been here, I wrote to Mr. Tregonning & have his reply today.

He says it is too late to cancel Dan Thomas's engagement, & that he was referred to me before he was promised his job. I must say this is not correct. No one has asked me if I am willing to allow Dan Thomas to go to you & the only time I have seen Dan Thomas was when he asked me on the first Tuesday in the month to allow him to give notice to date from the first Monday. I did not even ask him where he was going & did not think he was likely to be going to you.

I must now express myself quite plainly & say that if you do not cancel Dan Thomas's engagement I shall consider it an unfriendly act & a breach of your promise to me when you left us, & that from this time our friendly relations between our Companies must be at an end.

Frank Gilbertson to C. S. Tregoning. **5 Jan. 1915 [8 : 856]**

Thank you for your letter & for taking the matter up again & settling it.

All the men Johnson has taken are good steady men & most are abstainers & just the sort of men we want to keep, to preserve a decent spirit in the shop.

I dont think I have ever heard of a case of worse ingratitude on the part of any man?

I am sorry to have to change the opinion I always held of Johnson – I can only suppose that success has spoilt him.

However, I am grateful to you for what you have done.

Charles Gilbertson to The Central Liquor Control Board, Piccadilly, London. **25 June 1917 [10 : 359]**

Proposed Canteen

We beg to enclose plans, 6 Tenders, Specification, and priced Bill of Quantities in respect of the lowest Tender, namely the one from Messrs. Thos. Richards, of Swansea.

As the Firm is a good one, we recommend the acceptance of their Tender.

Referring to your letter of the 3rd May, Ref. 2013/17, we notice that you considered that our estimate of cost was too high, and you suggested certain modifications which would reduce the cost.

All these modifications have been included in the tenders submitted herewith, and yet the cost is going to be £3,031 for the Canteen alone.

May we ask if you will be good enough to reconsider the amount which in your letter you suggested you would recommend to the Ministry should be written off against the earnings of our Establishment during the Control Period, namely a sum of £2,000.

We should be glad if you would favourably consider this point . . .

Frank Gilbertson to Mrs. Stanley Davies, Widow of Analytical Chemist. **24 Oct. 1917 [10 : 436]**

I enclose cheque for £120 which represents approximately what Stanley would have earned had he been in our service for another month. I think it is due to his long & faithful service that we should send you this.

As you know we had the highest possible opinion of Stanley who worked so hard & successfully all the time he was with us, & whom we regarded more as a friend than a servant.

I do not think we can reproach ourselves with not having recognised his work in the remuneration we were paying him which was much more than Steel Works pay their Chemists & Metallurgists.

I am afraid it must be very difficult for you to make your plans, but hope in time you may be able to decide what is best for you & your child.

Charles Gilbertson to S. Crook, Works Laboratory. **27 Oct. 1917 [10 : 451]**

I had a talk with Mr. F.W.G. this morning, and as our present arrangements in the Lab. can only be looked upon as temporary, we have decided to recognise your extra hours of work by a half yearly bonus, and not by any definite increase in salary. At the same time we wish to let you know that we appreciate the way in which you are tackling the work, and helping to tide over the present difficulties.

Frank Gilbertson to Mr. Salt. **7 Dec. 1917 [10 : 441-2]**

I am sorry I have delayed replying to your letter of 12th ult., but I have been very busy. Now I dont want to hurt your feelings, but your letter, coupled with what I hear, makes it quite clear that you & Mrs. Davies hold an exaggerated estimate of poor Stanley's services to us.

We never had & shall never have a more capable hard working fellow, but he did not introduce or invent any new departure in our Works.

He carried on the work that was originated by Mr. Johnston & myself, & he & I worked out many matters together, but the idea that the Firm is benefiting & will always benefit from some discoveries of Stanley has no foundation of fact.

Progress is made in all Works that have efficient staff & progress has been made here since poor Stanley's death, but at no time has there been anything more than gradual evolution as our experience & experiments proceed.

If Stanley had left a widow & family badly off we should most certainly have given them all necessary assistance, but I understand that Mrs. Davies is in no want of assistance or likely to be.

If circumstances change, we shall deal with Mrs. Davies in the same way as we should deal with the widow of any member of our staff, but we should not consider this case one for any special treatment.

Frank Gilbertson to C. A. Hardy, Mill Manager. 29 Dec. 1917 [10 : 486]

Mr. Charlie spoke to you some time ago about your future position.

We have decided to make a change in regard to the Management of the Sheet Mills when they start again.

We do not wish to upset you at a time when it is impossible for you to obtain another position, but you should keep your eyes open on the chance of something offering. My object in writing to you is that we must appoint a Manager for the Slag Works at Panteg, & cannot delay doing so.

If you cared to apply for the position I would endeavour to get you appointed, as we have full confidence in you & believe you should carry on that work well. We are not however satisfied with your capabilities as an outside Mill Manager.

If you should decide to apply please let me know at once.

The salary would probably be £300 a year.

Frank Gilbertson to Mrs. Davies, 8 Nov. 1922 [10 : 581-2]
Widow of Philip Davies, Company Secretary.

I saw Mr. Morgan Davies one day with Mr. John Isaac Edwards.

I was glad to see Philip had left quite a substantial sum of money pretty well invested although some of the securities are not paying dividends.

I suggest seriously to the Executors that they should obtain the best professional advice because with the present prospects of trade it might be wise to sell some of them at a sacrifice & reinvest, before worse balance sheets come out & further depress values. I suggest to you the need of facing the situation & drastically cutting down expenses until perhaps the coal trade improves & your income increases.

It is better to face a cut at once than to delay it till absolute necessity compels a change.

For an indefinite period you may stay rent free at Danygraig if you wish to do so – at the present moment the Executors owe this Firm £148.

I propose to cancel this debt & to pay you £250 in quarterly payments starting at Christmas.

This time next year we will review the position & talk it over with your trustees & yourself.

This is of course only a business letter, but I do hope you are all getting on bravely.

J. P. Davies died in September 1922 and was replaced by Charles Giddings from 6 October 1922 at a salary of £1,600 p.a.

Frank Gilbertson to Pilliner, 25 April 1924 [10 : 590-1]
19 Fairfield Road, Crouch End, London.

Bowen has shown me your letter of 23rd.

I am just off abroad (including Roumania) & shall not be back till the middle of June.

Before going I should like once more to say how extremely highly we all value our old connection with you.

No Firm was ever represented better than we have been by an Agent who has given us wise guidance & helped as much as we could have done to keep the reputation of our Firm high.

We should ask you to allow us to arrange a pension of £250 a year with just two reservations. The first is that we should year by year be able to afford it, & the second is that we should perhaps supplement it in times of extra prosperity.

I shall hope to arrange a meeting with you on my return & perhaps we may be able to make the acquaintance of your wife.

Cecil Gilbertson to J. Roberts, Head Mechanic. 17 Nov. 1924 [10 : 596-7]

Some time ago Mr. Frank went into the Salaries of all our Officials and made reductions in almost every case. He told you that your Salary would have to come down, but you asked him to leave it for the time being. Mr. Frank has been away so much since then that the matter has been allowed to drag on, but it must really be brought to a head now. I do not propose making any very drastic reduction, but a fairly substantial one necessary from two standpoints:

1st. In fairness to our other foremen who have suffered a decrease.
2nd. As you are not able to do the full duties of a Head Engineer.

By the letter I mean that you are not able to personally inspect the overhead machinery in Gantries, Chargers, Magnets, etc., now a most important part of our Works plant.

I propose therefore to make a reduction of £1 a week, and to give 10/- a week of this saving to one of our best workmen and make him responsible for the overhead Machinery. The man I have in mind for this post is Ivor Davies if you think him sufficiently capable & painstaking.

Of course I am quite willing to hear anything you may wish to say on both these matters, but I must insist that a reduction is both necessary & fair.

Chapter 6

LABOUR RELATIONS

The letters reproduced in this chapter span the years from 1892 to 1916, a period which witnessed the emergence of new unionism and its challenge to traditional managerial prerogatives and unilateral job regulation. Whilst many of the letters refer to specific work disputes and are addressed to trade union leaders, solicitors or supposedly interfering newspaper editors, there is also commentary on events of significance to employers generally, such as the implications of the Taff Vale judgement (1901) and the pre-war emergence of syndicalism with its militant ideology for workers' control. Unlike his father, whose attitude to unionists was invariably confrontational, Frank Gilbertson developed a more pragmatic recognition of the need for strong union organisation to help curb dissident elements and maintain a disciplined workforce. Other characteristics of the period were the development of joint consultation and collective bargaining, and there is reference to the creation in September 1901 of a Consultative Committee in the steelworks which lasted until the company joined the South Wales Siemens Steel Association in 1906 and the Committee's function was subsumed in the more formalized conciliation machinery of the Association.

Arthur Gilbertson to John Hopkin John, Editor of *The Industrial World*, Swansea. **29 Feb. 1892 [1 : 178]**

I appreciate the courteous tone of your note of 27th inst.

I don't think there is any agitation among my men.

I pay very liberal wages, and afford absolutely regular work. I did not avail myself of the reduction in wages, when others did, but the terrible competition just now compels me to reduce my costs. I trust it wont last long.

Arthur Gilbertson to John Hodge, General Secretary of the Steel Smelters' Union, Glasgow. **16 March 1892 [1 : 180]**

I have your letter of 14th inst.

For 32 years I have conducted these Works and I do not fear criticism from any one – and your reckless remarks had better have been withheld.

Arthur Gilbertson to Thomas Phillips, General Secretary, Tinplate Workers' Union, Llanelly. **26 April 1893 [1 : 235-8]**

I am told you attended a meeting of men at Pontardawe on Saturday evening last, when the question was discussed as to the advisability of our Workmen giving notice to close these Works, in which some 900 persons are employed, which with wives & families mount up to over 2000 persons, dependent upon these Works. In fact the Village of Pontardawe with its Shops, Public Houses &c. is mainly supported by our Workpeople. I feel it therefore to be my duty to point out to you, the gravity of the position, if any such foolish step is taken. You know my character as a Master during a long series of years, and you know the unexampled prosperity of these Works & consequently the good fortune of the men in our employ.

You probably know now the facts connected with the assorters, who gave me notice & left my employ, many months ago, and who refused my urgent personal request to withdraw their notices. You are also aware these men took the step "without the authority of the Union".

From the fact that the bulk of my men supporting me, you have probably arrived at the conclusion, that there must be some distinct justification for my course of action!

I am perfectly prepared to put the details before the General Public, and am confident in the rectitude of my position.

In these difficult times I can only carry on these Works, providing my men with work from years end to years end without intermission, if the Workmen loyally support me, & I cannot work the Ship with a mutinous crew, as you well know. I am astonished that men who have abused me as some of these men have done for months past, in print, and otherwise, should even wish to be again in my employ. They can have but little self-respect. I have been in these Works 33 years, and a new generation has grown up around me, and I cannot keep on extending the Works any more, so as to give employment to all the youngsters – some of them must seek work elsewhere.

Everything that can be done for the moral welfare of our people, and their healthy recreation, is attended to. I have given more regular employ than any Works in South Wales. I have (altho' well known in the United States) stuck to Wales. The whole quarrel arose because I tried to keep our Plates up to the standard which was needful to maintain our position against McKinley.

I don't wish to threaten, but simply to say that if, after all this, a set of youths are to close our Works, they must do so, and accept the consequences.

Arthur Gilbertson to Edward Edwards. **6 June 1893 [1 : 243]**

I should like you to know that Thomas Phillips threatened to give in "notices" yesterday. I did not see him at all & only Mr. Adams saw him. He was told to give

April 26th 93
Mr. T. Phillips. Llanelly.

Sir: I am told you attended a meeting of men at Pontardawe on Saturday evening last, when the question was discussed as to the advisibility of our Workmen giving notice to close these Works, in which some 900. persons are employed, which with Wives & families mount up to over 2000. persons, dependant upon these Works. In fact the Village of Pontardawe with its Shops, Public Houses &c is mainly supported by our Workpeople. I feel it therefore to be my duty to point out to you, the gravity of the position, if any such foolish step is taken.
You know my character as a Master during a long series of years, and you know the unexampled prosperity of these Works & consequently the good fortune of the men in our

Letter from Arthur Gilbertson to Thomas Phillips, 1893
(West Glamorgan Archive Service)

in his "notices" & he went away for 10 minutes, and then decided not to give in the notices. I wish to say, that if in the future, Phillips does give in notices it will not stop the Works. I believe I shall have enough faithful men left to carry on the Works. Let the Unionists know this.

Arthur Gilbertson to Messrs Morgan & David, Solicitors, Neath. **6 June 1893 [1 : 244]**

Please say, if in the event of the Tinplate Unionist Secretary handing us in notices to terminate contracts on behalf (as he says) of our Workmen, such notices would be valid?

We should have no means of testing such notices & we are told men are induced to sign notices, or a "round Robin" for the lot, when under influence of drink.

We enclose a copy of our rules & Pay Tickets. Mr. Phillips (the Unionist) called yesterday & threatened to hand in notices. We said "very well", and then he altered his mind! and did not do so.

We conclude, if we accepted the notices or "round Robin" under protest, we could afterwards take steps to prove validity of Signatures?

Arthur Gilbertson to D. Randell, MP, Llanelly. 29 June 1893 [1 : 253-4]

As my Workpeople are your constituents, and I believe you are interested in the Tinplaters' Union, I think I ought to trouble you with the enclosed correspondence. The difficulty I have to counter in dealing with the Union is the entire disregard to truth displayed by the persons interested. I cannot bring myself to believe Phillips letter of the 7th inst. was ever posted to me. If it was, it is very singular he took no further steps on getting no reply from me. Most certainly his letter never reached me. The copy he sends is no reply to my letter of 26th April and might have been scribbled off in 5 minutes at any time. The men who left my employment . . . I begged them personally to withdraw their notices. They said "they did not dare", indicating that the "Union" was behind them. In due course they applied for their money and left. Sometime after it transpired in the Industrial World, that they had given notice without the instructions of the "Union" at all!! It seems they now wish to come back, and I have no room for them. Their only sensible course is to get work elsewhere. If the "Union" give notice to close my Works, they will enter into a long period of idleness. I am confident of my rectitude in the matter.

I am taking Mrs Gilbertson away following a long illness for change and will be unable to give any further attention to this Works matter.

Arthur Gilbertson to Captain A. L. Lindsay, Chief Constable, Cardiff. 31 Aug. 1893 [1 : 270]

You know our Works are on strike. We have 4 extra Constables here now, and we are paying for their Board & Lodging. Next week (Monday next) we are starting part of our Works with a few faithful men, and we want extra protection for next week, to give these men courage. I think six more Constables are wanted as day & night duty is needful.

I have summoned some dozen men for intimidation about three weeks past, as a lesson.

Arthur Gilbertson to D. Davies, Beaufort Tinplate Company. 26 Sept. 1893 [1 : 272]

Would you mind trying 50 Tons of our Siemens or Bessemer Bars @ £4..7..6 & £4..5..0 delivered less 2½%. You would find the quality excellent.

It would help us a little in dealing with our men. You have probably heard that we are successfully contending against the tyranny of "the Union", and our men are gradually giving way.

The same letter was sent to the Yniscedwyn Tinplate Company. [1 : 273]

Arthur Gilbertson to J. M. Price, Station Master, Brynamman. **19 July 1894 [2 : 9]**

I have treated the Glynbeudy men with great patience; they are a bad, ill-conditioned lot.

⅔rd of the Works belongs to me & my friends, and altho the concern has been, and is, a paying one, I should be glad to get out of it. I don't know whether you & your friends would like to consider buying us out? For my part I would accept "Par" say £300 each for my shares, and would sacrifice my proportion of the Reserve Fund. I however attach to my offer the stipulation that the same price should be paid my friends, did they wish to sell upon my retirement.

Mr. Price made no reply, or offer. AG. [Pencilled annotation]

J. P. Davies to J. M. Price, Brynamman. **24 July 1894 [1 : 298]**

Your letter to Mr. Gilbertson of 21st inst.

Mr. Gilbertson has gone from home for a change, but I may say that I know that Glynbeudy men are to learn a lesson before they start again.

Arthur Gilbertson to The Editor, *Western Mail*. **13 Aug. 1894 [2 : 13-14]**

I am compelled to say that the report about the stoppage of the Glynbeudy Works in your issue of today is incorrect, and in order that the Tinplate Workmen generally should not be deceived, I shall feel obliged if you will allow me to say, as Managing Director of these Works, that the Works are entirely closed because the Workmen gave us 24 hours to cease working, and we accepted it.

The reason they put forward was, that one Tinhouse was kept partially idle, we told them we could not help that, as we would not get <u>Tinplate</u> orders unless at prices yielding us a loss of 4½d. a box, while we could get Blackplate orders just to cover cost: thus giving the Workmen, half a loaf instead of none. We also said that as they would not turn out as much work as the Machinery (of a very costly & first rate description) was capable of, they did not assist us in reducing "cost".

So that on the one hand, they said, "we insist upon you keeping your Tinhouse at work, at a loss", on the other hand "altho' for <u>several months we did follow your machinery</u> to the utmost output of which it was capable, we will do so no longer", thereby causing us additional loss.

It is absurd that machinery capable of turning out 45 Boxes in 8 hours, should be crippled down to machinery only capable of turning out 36 Boxes in 8 hours.

This would give a blow to all enterprise and make it still more difficult to meet the American, and other competition, where the best machinery is being fully utilized.

If the Tinplate Union Executive (whatever that means) are going to order a strike for such a cause & to support the men from the central fund, the public will be able to form an opinion as to the desperate state of this Trade.

A Leading Metal Manufacturer

Arthur Gilbertson to D. Randell, MP, Llanelly. 26 Sept. 1894 [2 : 18-19]

I see from the papers, you are embarking in the Tinplate Trade with Sir T. J. Jenkins, and it occurred to me to write and ask if you are inclined to go in for the Glynbeudy Tinplate Works, Brynamman. There are 4 Mills, Galloway Boilers, Galloway Engine, excellent Railway arrangements, 5 acres freehold Land, good house, cheap Boiler Coal, and most modern arrangements – Players & Struve Patent Tin Pots. In fact I don't think a better arranged & equipped Works exists. They can as easily turn out 45 to 50 Boxes per Mill in 8 hours, as Yspitty for instance could do 32 Boxes in 8 hours.

My reason for wishing to get out of the Works is, I am too far off to get influence over the men, who are ruled by Thos. Phillips & J. H. John, and altho' I have afforded good work to these Works, all thro' the depression, I am now sick of them, and should be glad to get quit of the place. Myself and friends hold ⅔rd of the shares.

I should say the Works & freehold site ought to fetch some £18,000. They have cost us just £20,000.

If you are prepared to consider the matter, I would call a meeting of the Shareholders.

Arthur Gilbertson to J. M. Price, Brynamman. 16 Oct. 1894 [2 : 21-2]

I am sending you some cuttings from American & other papers. There may be some sensible Workmen at Glynbeudy, who may appreciate them. The Union Leaders, who are absolutely ignorant & untruthful, are doing their best to ruin the South Wales Tinplate trade. I am convinced some Workmen are giving concessions to their Masters of 4d or 6d. a box in wages by giving extra sheets to each Box – thus Tinplates are sold f.o.b. Swansea at 6d. a box under Glynbeudy cost & we cannot compete.

I believe I could now work Glynbeudy without loss upon Blackplate for Europe (not America) and occasional lots of Tinplates, if the men would heartily work with me, but the few men, who only last week, sent me an impertinent letter (you may know who they are) had much better go to the Collieries. You may make any use you like of this letter.

Arthur Gilbertson to Henry John Williams & Others. **31 Oct. 1894 [1 : 312-3]**

Glynbeudy Workmen

I received your telegram, and am doing my best to get orders for Tin and Terneplates. If I succeed the Works shall start on Monday.

You can understand the competition I named to you from Works, where they are able, from certain allowances, to save 6d. a box in cost, renders your position and mine very difficult and unless I can cover loss, I cant keep working.

I shall come & see you & talk these matters over again if I cant get orders without loss.

Arthur Gilbertson to J. M. Price, Brynamman. **5 Nov. 1894 [2 : 27]**

I want to interest the Workmen in Glynbeudy Works and contemplate turning all the shares into £50 each. That is calling in old shares, and issuing six shares of £50, for every one share of £300. Eight shares of £300, are not issued, I propose to change these into 48 shares of £50 each, and offer them to the Workmen! If they took them, they would be interested in making profits. What do you say?

Arthur Gilbertson to J. M. Price, Brynamman. **7 Nov. 1894 [2 : 28]**

Please read enclosed –

I cannot get a Tinplate order beyond 10/- IC 20/14 f.o.b. Swansea and our cost there is 10/9d!!

What are we to do? If we could save 3d. by working plates bare of "Tin" & saving in Mill Yield &c, there would then be 6d. against us.

There seems no hope unless men will give 15 to 20 sheets free, as other Works must be doing.

Perhaps then we could work Tinhouse full & no Blackplate.

Will you show all this to the men?

Arthur Gilbertson to D. Randell, MP, Llanelly. **16 Nov. 1894 [2 : 32]**

Referring to our recent conversation & correspondence, I have now come to the conclusion to sell Glynbeudy Works, freehold, & house – my idea is £16,000 and small amount of stocks at a valuation. I am obliged to make this offer subject to confirmation at the meetings to be held under our Articles, but I may say I control a good majority of votes. Possibly some of the local Shareholders would join a new company.

The Machinery, Buildings, Siding &c are first class. I find the place too distant for my personal care, and I am getting old!

I make you first offer, as you have had some trouble about it.

Arthur Gilbertson to Thos. Lewis, 107 Dinas Road, Plas Marl, Landore. **17 Feb. 1895 [2 : 66-7]**

You wrote to me asking some aid for the men out of work. I replied, but you did not answer. It is odd that while men are asking for aid, they should also be anxious to increase the number of unemployed and to play into the hands of our Foreign Competitors, by closing all the Works! It seems to me too silly, even for "The Industrial World" to suggest.

It is also stated that the Tinplate Union have given £5000 in relief not in strike pay – this is very surprising, because the men "on strike" only received a few shillings from the Union, in cases which came under my personal notice.

If you like to give me particulars of this £5000, and also a copy of the Union Balance Sheet, proving the payment, I shall be glad to send £25 to the unemployed "thro no fault of their own" at Morriston.

I reserve the right to publish this letter, if I think fit.

Arthur Gilbertson to Frank Nevill. **4 Sept. 1896 [1 : 475]**

I am so disgusted with the Tinmen at Glynbeudy, that I have called a meeting of the Shareholders for next Wednesday, when I intend telling them I wont trouble myself further at Glynbeudy, and that the Works must be sold. I, & my friends, hold 2/3rds. and the 5 acres are freehold.

We have never made a loss any year, & have built up a "reserve fund" of nearly £6,000. One Engine & 2 Boilers work the whole Works (4 Mills).

After next Wednesday I will write you as to Machinery on order.

Arthur Gilbertson to Glynbeudy. **26 Sept. 1896 [1 : 480-1]**

I have gone over your estimated profit & loss sheet, it is very carefully & accurately made, and we must admit shows an aggregate loss – also the allowance for Pickling loss must be counted @ 5/6d a Ton, and you may so deal with it. As you know Messrs. W. Gilbertson & Co. have let you have Bars, many shillings under market price, to help you but this cannot continue.

Therefore at the expiration of your notice, the entire Works must stop, unless the Millmen & Tinmen &c &c agree to 20% reduction or give in sheets (as other Works do) to help us, to meet the loss incurred by Railway rates to the Port so long distant and which now tells so heavily against us, when matters are cut so fine.

I am very sorry, but the men cannot expect us to go on at a loss.

You may read this to the men and tell them some orders lose us as much as 8% & 10% a Ton.

Arthur Gilbertson to H. Llewellyn Smith, Labour Department, 44 Parliament Street, London, SW. **5 Sept. 1898 [1 : 697-8]**

Your letter of the 31st. ulto. had caused us great surprise, as we had no dispute in our Works, which is not controlled by the miserable & discredited so called "Union" of Tinplaters in South Wales. This "Union" is virtually bankrupt and powerless.

But from some incidents which have occurred during the past few days & your query, we begin to think a man named Thomas Phillips has been attempting to make mischief in our Works by means of a few starving Tinplaters whom we took in from Morriston lately.

Our Machinery was nearly broken on Friday night, and we have dismissed all three men.

There is no dispute existing. We shall consider your silence as admitting the man Phillips sent you the libellous statement.

Arthur Gilbertson to H. Llewellyn Smith. **8 Sept. 1898 [1 : 702]**

Your favour of yesterday. We presume you refer to a paper called The Industrial World, and if you attach the least importance, or give any credence to its deliberately untruthful articles & statements, you are simply wasting your time & getting all false information.

Arthur Gilbertson to John Hodge, Steel Smelters' Association, Manchester. **24 April 1900 [3 : 12-13]**

Private

The enclosed letters have been sent to my Coachman, – and by a cowardly black-guard to Mrs. Frank Gilbertson. Similar letters were sent to me and our Clergyman, – we both threw them in the fire, but when I found letters were sent to Mrs. Frank, I thought I should take some action.

First of all – Letters were posted at Swansea Docks on Saturday afternoon last.

Secondly – They are written in copying ink, which indicates some place, where men transact some business in Swansea.

Thirdly – who can be such a vindictive liar, and who can be at enmity with us?

Fourthly – The writer knows Pontardawe, and even our Domestic relations.

These considerations fix upon a Pontardawe man, and the only man we know, who could owe us a grudge, is Thomas Hodge – the rollerman, whom you will remember, he wrote last week asking to come back to the works and we replied, distinctly declining to have anything to do with him, then came these Blackguard letters.

We are very sorry to name this man, but we cannot think of any other man, who is at issue with us – these letters are very much in the style of the old days of the Industrial World.

I fearlessly say, that no Master in South Wales has done more than myself for the welfare of his Workmen. I don't know what steps you will take in the matter, but possibly you will put it before your Local Branch here and they might send us a resolution repudiating the Writer and his letters and saying that he is a Liar.

Arthur Gilbertson to John Hodge. **4 May 1900 [3 : 16-17]**

We thank you for yours of the 3rd inst, with enclosures of Anonymous letters. We thought the action needful, beyond putting them in your hands and leaving the Union Branch of Pontardawe to deal with them.

We never allow such communications to affect us in any way whatever – the remarks in the daily papers arose from the foolish action of the police, whom it seems, had received letters also, the police acted without any instructions from us.

We are sorry to say, the Sheet and Tinplate trade seems to get duller daily, we are getting no enquiries at all, and although, we yesterday, authorized our Agents to reduce for special lines of sheets, to try to keep our mills going, they say today, they cannot find any buyers in consequence of the present American tactics – it looks like stopping of the mills in a very short time, simply from lack of orders, a thing that has hardly happened with us for a very great number of years. It must be aggravating to the English workman, as well as to the Employers, that the Americans shut out our plates by the enormous tariff, and dump their surplus output upon Great Britain and Canada.

We are losing all orders for Galvanized sheets from Canada, because the Americans sell their Galvanized sheets, delivered in Canada at a lower price than they charge to their own consumers in the United States. We cannot understand why British Labour and its representatives, do not take up this matter.

Arthur Gilbertson to John Hodge. **25 Jan. 1901 [3 : 191-2]**

Private

I have come to the conclusion that we must have a capable up-to-date Mill Foreman, for our Sheet Mills, who can superintend "turning" and by attention to his work will gain the respect of the Millmen, and who can help them to improve their mode of working, so as to avoid Waste of Steel & Wasters.

I would pay a good salary. Can you tell me of such a man?

You will see by ours of yesterday, that our Millmen are simply ruining us.

Arthur Gilbertson to John Hodge. **25 April 1901 [3 : 264]**

I enclose you copy of statement of Palmer.

I may tell you privately that if we added 5% to the loss, on our Capital, for interest – we lost £2000..0..0 in Mills & Galvanizing Department, in the 3 months.

If we had sold our Steel, instead of working the Mills, we might have saved all the loss.

Some of the £2000 was due to the "strike", and "bad output" before the 6 hour Turns – No wonder Ynismeudw & Foxhole failed.

Arthur Gilbertson to John Hodge. 22 July 1901 [3 : 341-2]

Private

You have seen the copy of my letter to the "Mills", sent you last Saturday.

I have made a great effort to get orders for our Mills, direct from Foreign places, instead of placing ourselves in the hands of middlemen, which means reduced prices and therefore less wages, but the constant stoppages in our Mills from the ignorant interference of James & Palmer, has placed us in a serious position. We are now losing 70 Tons a week in Mills from this cause. I have therefore decided to enclose you some letters received by this morning's post.

Our financial year ended 15th ulto, and the loss on the Mills & Galvanizing is very serious indeed. Had we closed the Mills, and been saved an infinity of trouble, we could have disposed of our Steel (instead of wasting it in our Mills) at a small profit.

Unless Palmer & James can be brought to a right mind, we shall cease entering orders for our Mills, and gradually let them go into disuse.

Frank Gilbertson to Messrs Strick Bellingham & Hanson, Solicitors, Swansea. 23 July 1901 [3 : 344]

The House of Lords judgement in the Taff Vale case in today's papers, causes us to think you may be able to advise us further on the matter the writer called on you about, last Saturday. The local branch of the Union decided that two of our men should break the rules, & consequently 2 Mills are idle. Is not the whole Association liable for the action of their local branch?

We enclose copy of a letter sent today to the Society's head Secretary at Manchester.

Frank Gilbertson to Messrs Barlow & Barlow. 30 July 1901 [3 : 343-4]

We are very glad to see the Lord Chancellor's statement that "Unions" may now be sued for damage caused by their illegal action, and are responsible for the action of their Branches.

The Union Branch No. 2 Pontardawe, prevented two of our Rollermen changing places, which we were at liberty to order, under our printed rules, consequently we stopped the Engine, and the Mills became idle, after a few days Mr. Thos. Griffiths, Organizing Sec for the District came up, and appealed to us not to insist upon the change of men, on our refusing, he said he considered the men had not been unreasonable in their action and he regretted being unable to settle the matter.

The next important communication came from the Head Office (John Hodge), saying "I have today wired the men, instructing Dd. Jones to change Mills under protest, so that the Mills can be kept running and the matter be left open for discussion between you and Mr. Hodge at some future date".

After the men received this telegram, the local branch refused to obey the instructions of the Head Office and our Mills remain idle. When we found this out, we gave notice on 23rd inst. to Head Office (John Hodge) that we held their Association responsible for loss and damages. We also telegraphed to Head Office on the 24th inst. "that the losses are £10 every 24 hours which you will have to pay".

We want you immediately to write formal notice of the damages to John Hodge, 88 Bignor St, Manchester. We enclose one of his letters for your guidance.

The damage is still going on and must be calculated as £10 per 24 hours (day and night) since 18th inst. (5½ turns of 24 hours per week) – £55 per week.

We should say the above damage does not include claims from Customers on non-performance of our contracts, or damage to our reputation, or loss of orders and prestige.

Frank Gilbertson to Messrs Barlow & Barlow. 31 July 1901 [3 : 357]

We understand the head Union & the No. 2 branch at Pontardawe are prepared to swear they did not authorize the action of our two Rollermen which resulted in stopping our Mills.

We don't believe this, as a matter of fact, but we should have difficulty in proving that the Union are responsible for the matter.

We think therefore it will be better for us to prosecute the two rollermen who personally infringed our rules, claiming damages.

When these men find that the Union have thrown them over, they may disclose something – we therefore wired you as at foot, & should appreciate your advice in the matter.

If we decide to summon the 2 rollermen, we presume we had better do so through Messrs Strick & Bellingham.

Could they act for you as Agents in South Wales in this matter, as we should like the matter to go through you?

Telegram

Don't write Hodge today further matter has turned up.

Frank Gilbertson to Messrs Barlow & Barlow. 7 Aug. 1901 [3 : 358-9]

Your favour of yesterday. The notices of which we enclose you a copy, were handed in on Monday by the whole of the Sheet Millmen including the 2 men "on strike".

You will see they give us reason for this action, & we therefore wrote the Local Sec, and received his reply, as per copies enclosed.

He gives us reason, but fixes the onus on Mr. Hodge, who at our interview last week suggested no settlement of any sort, his main idea apparently was to repudiate any liability for the strike of two men, on the part of the Union – yet he attended a meeting of the men afterwards & these notices, without any reason stated, are the result – Do you think we should prosecute these 2 men at once? The damages from their action to us, is about £50 a week & they have been on strike nearly 3 weeks – or should we at once suggest arbitration on the whole matter, with the £500 fine to the Swansea Hospital?

If so please give us a draft of what you propose.

We enclose a copy of our letter of 2nd inst. to Mr. Hodge, his reply received today, & our own further reply.

We hear Mr. Hodge is coming here on Saturday to coerce the Steelmen, as our action whatever it is to be should be undertaken at once.

Frank Gilbertson to John Hodge. **7 Aug. 1901 [3 : 360-3]**

Your letter of 6th inst. As regards the effect upon the men, of the written statements of Mr. Gilbertson Senior, we quite disagree with you – We trace the insubordination of the men to the period when he was ill, & in consequence gave way so much to them, that they thought they might get any concession they wanted, & behaved disgracefully – you remember Dd. Jones himself struck work because we wished him to work in another Turn in the Mill.

We are surprised you think the 2 Rollermen did not act illegally; our Rule No. 13 states "Every Workman in the various departments of the Works, will when required by the Manager or Agents, perform such duties as may be deemed necessary in case of emergency, other than the special work he may be engaged in" – and the custom of the trade leaves it entirely to the discretion of the Manager to say at what Mill a man shall work. As we have suffered great loss from their action, & you repudiate the liability of the Union we have nothing open to us, but to take legal measures for damages against these 2 men. We cannot understand what your notices to cease work, received last Monday, mean, unless they are to support the illegal action of these men.

You know the changing of the 2 Rollermen was not a punishment in any way – it was only to prevent Dd. Jones being dismissed.

We conclude a man would not intentionally break Rolls, but when you consider that the Rolls broken in the last twelve months amounted to over £2000 in value, you will admit we had to do something to check such gross carelessness. But you will be surprised to hear the fines inflicted during that period amounted to only £12..2..0, of which £6..2..0 was put to our "sick fund" & has all been spent in benefits to sick Workmen!

No. 10 & 11 Mills. You do not refer to the Second Helpers having repudiated the settlement made by us with your Mr. Griffiths. The continuance of the stoppage of these Mills causes us great damage, & the Union ought to pay these damages. How can you pretend that your Union enforces discipline while these Mills are still idle, and the 2 Rollermen continue to disobey your instruction, while you now support them by sending in notices from all the Sheet Mills to us?

We may remind you that Mr. Gilbertson Senr. has got on with his men for 40 years, before your Union appeared on the scene, and you know his reputation in Glamorganshire as a successful Works Manager.

We may also remind you that he, & we, have never had any difficulty at all with our Steel Men (who include many well experienced in the methods of the Steel Smelters Union) or the Dockers Union!

This will probably indicate to you that something must be wrong among the men of the Sheet Mills in <u>your</u> Union.

At this point John Hodge visited Pontardawe and his autobiography, published some 30 years later, presented a bland account of the episode. He stated that he instructed his assistant secretary, J. T. Macpherson, to "go down and tell these men that the old order has passed away, that we have rules for the government of the Association and no branch can be permitted to act without executive sanction . . .". Macpherson's inquiries led him to conclude that the men were in the wrong, and attempted to gain admission to the meeting between Arthur Gilbertson and his rollermen, but was ordered out. John Hodge, Workman's Cottage to Windsor Castle *(Sampson Low, 1931), 111-3.*

Telegram to Acquaint Manchester [J. Hodge]. **n.d. (c. 20 Aug. 1901) [3 : 382]**

Mr. Gilbertson senior away today. Your letter will be considered tomorrow. You no doubt understand he is very indignant at your attempt to coerce us by the forced notices from our Steel Works and the misleading and unfair statements given to the Press by MacPherson. Gilson.

Frank Gilbertson to John Hodge. **22 Aug. 1901 [3 : 386]**

Our Mr. Gilbertson Senior has considered your letter of 20th inst.

We are willing to allow all notices, on each side, to be withdrawn, and to start the Mills, as soon as the Engines can be ready next week, if you will enforce your letter of 22nd ulto, & make Dd. Jones & J. M. Davies change Mills, for a month's trial say, under protest if you like, to enable us, & you, to see if Dd. Jones can work in an easier Mill.

If this is agreed to, we wish a Consultative Committee appointed, say 6 officials to be nominated by us, & 6 by the Workmen to consider any disputes, or questions arising. This should put an end to difficulties in the future.

The first meeting of the Consultative Committee took place on 21 September 1901 and its minute book shows that Arthur Gilbertson did not attend. The company was represented by Frank, Cecil, Colin and Owen Davies, the steelworks manager, and there were six employee representatives. At its first meeting Frank explained that it was to be a forum for the discussion of points of difference between the firm and the workmen, but added that it "must not be considered in any way a Committee of Management". He hoped that "it might conduce to a better feeling between the Firm and the Men, and that the latter might realise that the principal aim of the Firm was to secure cheapness of production, which was equally in the interest of the workmen and the Company". The Committee considered roll breakages, fines, labour deployment, wage issues, production problems and welfare cases. The Council was a symbolic recognition of the relevance of employee opinion and maturity, but its abandonment in 1906 when the company joined the South Wales Siemens Steel Association suggests that there was no place for formalized consultative machinery in the managerial strategy of the Gilbertson family at that time. John Hodge was later to deplore the cessation of the Consultative Committee (British Steel Smelters' Reports, 1909, 91), *but Frank's view was that although it had served a useful purpose "the machinery existing between the Tin Plate (sic) Association and the union now supplies the want that the Consultative Committee was formed for* "(Evidence, 1913, Questions 6003 & 6004).

Colin Gilbertson to His Honour Judge Austin. 10 Sept. 1901 [3 : 410]

We have received an intimation from the Board of Trade that your Honour will kindly act as Arbitrator between us and the Steel Union of which Union our Workmen are members and are represented by Mr. Hodge . . .

Arthur Gilbertson to Barlow & Barlow. 2 Nov. 1901 [3 : 476]

You will be interested to read the enclosed, which please return. We took infinite trouble in arranging our "brief"! Messrs. Frank, Cecil & Colin Gilbertson represented our Company. Mr. Hodge produced a number of witnesses for the Union, but fortunately they were shown to be untruthful.

The Judge said Mr. F. W. Gilbertson ought to be a Barrister!

The decision is very fortunate for the Manufacturers in South Wales.

Arthur Gilbertson to His Honour Judge Austin. 3 Dec. 1901 [3 : 499-500]

I trust it is not improper to let you know, that your award on the dispute between our Firm and the Steel Union has had a most satisfactory result, as regards our Works & Workmen.

During the month when the Arbitration was pending, our Men were told by Mr. Hodge & his men, that they would win, and consequently the men broke our Rolls "for fun", causing us loss of £400 in that month.

As soon as the award was made in our favour, the men got frightened and ceased breaking the Rolls in a most remarkable way.

We believe the award is saving us over £2500 per annum, and indirectly it is an advantage for the foolish men.

Mr. Hodge in his monthly report, is reported to have said, as per cutting enclosed.

The Writer gave every fair play to Mr. Hodge, when Hodge first appeared in South Wales. The Writer is disappointed & disgusted with him. Apologizing for troubling you.

Frank Gilbertson to John Hodge. 30 Dec. 1902 [3 : 770]

We should like to know what success you have had in negotiating with our neighbours using the Basic process, about whom we spoke to you at our last meeting.

We hear they have 4 or 5 furnaces now working & it is quite unfair that they should be paying much lower wages than ourselves, for example, & competing in the same market.

Frank Gilbertson to Messrs C. B. & R. C. Jenkins, Solicitors. 30 Jan. 1903 [3 : 784]

Will you kindly peruse enclosed & advise us as to the responsibility of the Union in view of the fact that the picklers' helpers mentioned have given 28 days notice terminating tomorrow to cease work?

Cecil Gilbertson to Messrs R. & C. B. Jenkins, Solicitors. 24 Feb. 1903 [3 : 796-800]

We have a dispute with some of our Millmen, who have in consequence stopped work and unless they resume their work before the end of this week, we intend issuing summons against them, before doing so however, we shall be glad if you will kindly give us your advice upon the matter.

The duty these men have to perform is to roll sheets of such size and gauge as we may specify in our No. 11 Mill. We have lately adopted a new method of rolling certain specifications called the "American method", by which an increased output may be produced. In order to gain the full advantage of this method extra helpers are required because the work is heavier, but the method may be worked without any extra help, in which case it is doubtful whether any advantage would be gained. For the last fortnight we have been trying this method and as it was an experiment and the men were not accustomed to it, we have paid the extra helpers for them, but during this time we only paid the Millmen their tonnage weights based on an average of their previous months' work, the custom in America being that the Millmen pay the extra helpers themselves and are compensated for so doing by the increased make.

Towards the end of last week, we saw that the process was capable of being worked successfully and we therefore put out the following notice:–

> "It is now clear to us that the American principle is capable of being successfully worked, increasing the output of the Mill without overheating the rolls. We shall therefore, as stated at the Consultative Committee, pay the extra helpers ourselves up to the end of this week, after which the workmen must pay them themselves."

On Monday last, this notice came into force, and in consequence, the men refused to start work in No. 11 Mill and same is still idle.

Our point is that the men are obliged to work such specifications as we may choose to give them, and as there is no agreement to the contrary they must work that specification in any particular manner we may desire, they therefore had no right to stop work on Monday and if they objected to paying any extra helpers they should have started working the process with the old number of hands, we therefore propose to issue summons against them for having stopped work, and to formulate a claim for damages.

Frank Gilbertson to John Hodge. **25 April 1903 [3 : 818-9]**

We saw James & Palmer yesterday, & as they were unable to agree to any name, as Umpire, without your approval, we agreed to send you two names acceptable to us, for your selection.

Mr. Riley. We have no objection to him, but the work will not be much as his experience would help him to judge of.

Mr. Wm. Evans. The latter is unknown to you, but his name occurred to us as one who would be acceptable to the men, & his knowledge of Mill Works would enable him to gauge the statements of each side accurately.

He was our Mill Foreman, before we made sheets, for a number of years, & is personally known to most of our Millmen, among whom he was always popular.

He is now managing a Tinplate Works at Resolven, & since he left us, some 12 years ago we have had no connection at all with him.

The qualifications we consider he has, that will enable him to give a decision superior to Mr. Riley's, for permanence are

(1) His complete knowledge of Mill Work
(2) He has no connection with sheet rolling
(3) He is a Welshman, & well known to our men.

We press you very strongly to agree to Mr. Evans, on the score that his award must be a better informed one than Mr. Riley's, & therefore more likely to be lasting.

Arthur Gilbertson to Geo. Palmer & Dd. Jones. 19 May 1903 [3 : 828]

We enclose copy of our letter of 18th inst. to Mr. Wm. Evans [Arbitrator] roughly stating our case about American Process, of which we enclose a copy. Now you can write to him stating your ideas & please send us a copy of your letter. This will clear the air, and bring the matter to a very small contention. We ought (you & ourselves) to come to an arrangement – it would be a pity to drop the American Process without further trial, especially as Trade in Sheets and Galvanized, <u>is slacking off greatly</u>. No orders come to hand, and every one is trying to cut under another Manufacturer.

Frank Gilbertson to Messrs R. & C. B. Jenkins. 13 Jan. 1905 [5 : 85]

Your letter of yesterday re Glynbeudy & J. H. John.

We are extremely pleased at the results & congratulate you upon it.

We hope John will be made to pay up quickly – we dont know the resources of the Union, but John's must be small.

Colin Gilbertson to J. Charles, Dockers Union. 8 March 1906 [5 : 238]

We have your letter of yesterday, with which we quite agree.

We enclose a letter to the Board of Trade, & would be glad if you would sign it & send it on if you agree.

You will remember we also arranged that the men must peg. Please make this clear to them.

Colin Gilbertson to The Secretary, The Board of Trade. 8 March 1906 [5 : 239]

Being unable to agree as to the wages to be paid men engaged in a certain process at the above Works, we would be glad if you would appoint an Arbitrator to fix a price for doing the Work in question on contract, which price we have both agreed upon to accept.

Frank Gilbertson to The Editor of *The South Wales Daily Post,* Swansea. 2 May 1910 [7 : 269]

Your action, in making public a communication that we addressed to our Workpeople, has caused us the greatest annoyance.

Such action is calculated to have a very bad effect upon the relations existing between our men and ourselves, and has resulted in making public a comparison between two Works that amounts to a breach of privilege on the part of the Writer.

We beg you will not refer to the matter again in your columns and we hope you will see the propriety of consulting us in the future before you interfere in our relations with our employees.

A letter from Frank Gilbertson to John Hodge had been reproduced in the local weekly newspaper Llais Llafur and on 30 April 1910 the South Wales Daily Post had given it national coverage. Frank Gilbertson had written that the output of the Raven Works in Glanamman had exceeded that of Pontardawe because of the "enormous number of rolls broken by our millmen", allegedly 109 rolls broken in 12 sheet mills during the past year, in comparison with 6 rolls in 6 mills in the Raven Works. Output at Pontardawe was consequently "400 tons less than it might have been", losing the company £6,400 and the men £1,000 in wages.

Frank Gilbertson to H. Folland, Grovesend Steel Works. **2 May 1910 [7 : 270]**

We beg you will accept our apologies for the scandalous way in which the South Wales Daily Post has given publicity to a communication we addressed to our Workpeople. What we said was quite proper as affecting our relations with our Workmen, but most improper when made public property, & we regret the occurrence very much.

We have expressed our annoyance & asked the paper to print nothing more on the matter.

Frank Gilbertson to The Editor of *The South Wales Daily Post.* **6 May 1910 [7 : 286-7]**

You do not in the least appear to appreciate how serious your interference has been. If there had been a dispute at the Works there would be no reason why the press should not publish any proper information in regard to it. There was and is no dispute in this case, but your action in making our letter public will be the cause of any trouble that may arise.

The letter that we wrote to Mr. John Hodge, and circulated among our Workpeople, was of a private nature and concerned them only, and it is intolerable that such a communication should have been put into the hands of the public. The publication in "Llais Llafur" was of no importance, as the paper is read by a small number of people in the immediate locality. The whole aspect of the issue was changed when you saw fit to give prominence to it and it was from your paper that it has been copied all through the country.

The Raven Tinplate Co. are naturally indignant at the publicity that has been given to their working, and we are not able to express our annoyance at your behaviour.

Your letter of yesterday shows that you do not in the least appreciate the importance of the matter from a commercial standpoint, and we are not going to let the matter rest where your letter leaves it.

Frank Gilbertson to Messrs. R. & C. B. Jenkins. **6 May 1910 [7 : 289]**

Would you kindly ascertain & let us know the names of the Directors of the South Wales Post Newspaper Co., Ltd?

Frank Gilbertson to Tom Griffiths. **7 Sept. 1910 [7 : 404]**

Mr. Summers tells us he gets 50 tons per Mill per week from his Welsh Mills on 30 gauge.

We also hear of 70 cwts and 74 cwts in 2 shifts at Grovesend 72 x 26 x 30 gauge. We wish you would convey these figures to our men.

In several of our Mills there is a good Engine for 2 Mills only, & we do not see why every one should be doing better than we are here.

We are afraid our men are allowing themselves to be beaten around, & you know what the end always is for a Company that starts to be beaten by its competitors.

Frank Gilbertson to Henry Clement, Secretary, Welsh Plate & Sheet Manufacturers' Association. **26 Sept. 1910 [7 : 411-2]**

We have told you before, we believe, that we attribute all our troubles with our Millmen to one Roller J. M. Davies.

This man turns No. 7 Mill.

On Saturday he & some other Turners came to our Foreman & asked that they should be allowed to turn on Sunday mornings instead of Sunday nights.

We told our Foreman to say we would give their request our consideration upon the return of our Engineer from his holiday. J. M. Davies then said he wouldn't come in again on Sunday night.

He actually did not put in an appearance & 2 other Turners also absented themselves but the latter had the excuse of illness. Will you please advise us? We should very much like to get rid of Davies, but we feel that such action now would only make him a Martyr in the eyes of the men.

Do you consider that being employed as a Turner at 30/- a month, we can prosecute him for leaving his work without notice. We should like you to give your views to Mr. Philip Davies tomorrow.

At present our Millmen are in a very troublesome mood, & although Davies is the cause of all the trouble, we must not give him the chance of recovering the sympathy of the men, which he has rather lost over the late mistake he led them into.

We enclose a letter which shows how we have dealt with the summonses.

Frank Gilbertson to Messrs R. & C. B. Jenkins. **28 Sept. 1910 [7 : 416]**

Will you please apply for 14 days adjournment of the summonses against our Rollermen, next Friday. They have still under consideration a proposal we have made them, which if accepted will mean that we proceed no further.

Frank Gilbertson to H. Clement. **28 Sept. 1910 [7 : 417-8]**

We are much obliged by your letters of yesterday.

Millmen. We have reason to believe that J. M. Davies refused to be one of the deputation that Tom Griffiths suggested. Please keep this quite private, but we are writing Tom Griffiths for the names.

The proposal was for a "round table talk", not for the purpose of considering fresh grievances but for the purpose of improving the spirit of the men.

If J. M. Davies is not present, he will only criticise the action of the others, & will destroy any good effect that such a conference might have.

We think we are entitled to demand that the ordinary Works Representatives should be present.

We should be very glad if you could make it convenient to come when the date is fixed.

Boxers. We quite agree with your suggestion.

Frank Gilbertson to Messrs R. & C. B. Jenkins. **10 Oct. 1910 [7 : 433]**

The Rollermen have agreed to our terms & we therefore will not proceed with the summonses against them.

Frank Gilbertson to Tom Griffiths. **3 Dec. 1910 [7 : 462]**

We want a first class Tinworks Smith for our new Tinplate Works.

The new Blacksmith's Shop is now ready, & none of the youngsters in our old shop is good enough to go on.

We also want a member of your Society as we prefer dealing with your Union. Can you find us a good man at once?

Cecil Gilbertson to Messrs R. & C. B. Jenkins. **29 May 1911 [7 : 574]**

Please issue summonses against the 25 men named below for damages occasioned by their stopping work without notice.

Ten shillings each will do, but you may understand privately that the cases are not likely to come into court.

We should like service to be made as soon as possible.

Cecil Gilbertson to Messrs R. & C. B. Jenkins, Solicitors. **30 May 1911 [7 : 577-8]**

Your favour of yesterday.

Summonses. We thank you for your prompt attention. We are glad to say the men have given in, & have returned to work "unconditionally". Under these circumstances we do not wish to proceed with the summonses. Will it be sufficient if we let the men know that they need not attend the Court, as we shall not proceed with the claims?

Eli Skidmore. We have now given you the exact address & occupation.

He promised to pay quarterly "a sum equal to the rent of the house". Could you estimate from this what would be a safe sum to claim.

We did not propose to charge interest, as we do not usually do in such cases.

We wish to proceed with our claim in this case, to show that if men are prepared to act vindictively against us they cannot expect favours from us.

He is a bad man.

E. Skidmore was employed as a Packer and was the local Branch Secretary for the Dockers Union.

Frank Gilbertson to Messrs R. & C. B. Jenkins, Solicitors. **13 Nov. 1911 [7 : 713]**

Annealers. When the adjournment summonses come on, would you please tell the Court that we are parties to an annual agreement made by the masters and the men in the Tinplate Trade, under which conditions of labour are settled every summer for the ensuing 12 months and that the Unions agree never to stop work, and never to hand notices even till the matter has been before the Conciliation Board.

Also, that we have had a great deal of trouble [. . .] owing to the men throwing down tools without legal notice, and in defiance of the undertakings given by the Union leaders at the Annual Conciliation Board Meeting; and that we are tired of this behaviour which is causing much concern to the Chairman of the Board, and in future intend to go before the Court for damages when contracts are broken.

Frank Gilbertson to T. W. James, Solicitor, Swansea. **31 Jan. 1912 [7 : 826]**

I am troubling you personally to ask if you could see your way to prevent incorrect paragraphs appearing in the Daily Post about our Works.

Two years ago I wrote as strongly as I could to Mr. Davies protesting against the publication & discussion in the Paper of a private letter I had given our Workmen, which resulted in a very awkward situation for myself & the reproaches of my fellow manufacturers. Last Saturday a ridiculously incorrect paragraph appeared in the "Post" of a meeting I had with Mr. Hodge & some Workmen, & which I only attended upon the understanding that nothing I said should appear in the Press. I am constantly being annoyed in this way, & it adds very much to my difficulties in managing our Workmen, besides giving information of any changes we make to our competitors.

I feel very strongly about it indeed, & should be very grateful to you if you could help me.

Frank Gilbertson to Messrs Barlow, Barlow & Lyde, London. **29 Nov. 1912 [8 : 106]**

We are much troubled by a local newspaper which publishes paragraphs about any labour difficulties in these works.

It usually happens that the reports are incorrect, and in the last two instances this was the case.

If the reports are incorrect, and if they are such as would lead Merchant firms to think we are unreasonable employers constantly having unnecessary friction with our men, would this damage to our reputation be sufficient to enable us to proceed against the newspaper?

The newspaper is the local Conservative organ, and I have tried to get protection from the Directors, but they are tools in the hands of the Editor who is an impertinent bumptious little fellow.

Frank Gilbertson to The Editor of *Llais Llafur*, Ystalyfera. **11 March 1913 [8 : 190]**

I must again ask you kindly to allow me to refer to "Birks" note in your issue of 8th inst.

In no year in the history of this Works have the profits approached the figure mentioned of £97,000.

The Financial News has no means of ascertaining what the profits of this Company may be, & if my notice had been called to the statement I should have corrected it.

"Birks" is evidently sincere in believing he had authority for his information, and I would point out that a great deal of harm & much misapprehension follows the common failing of believing all one sees in print.

Frank Gilbertson to Messrs R. & C. B. Jenkins. **5 April 1913 [8 : 211-2]**

According to our best estimate of damages due to our Furnacemen's failure to work the furnaces on Easter Monday, we should claim the following:

Actual loss of output of Steel Ingots = 500 Tons.

A Furnace	90 tons
C "	90
E "	60
F "	150
H "	110
	500

Consumption of coal per ton of ingots increased 4 cwts = 250 tons at 14/- = £175
Extra cost due to General Charges at 5/- per ton upon 500 tons lost = £125

As the furnaces got cold during the stoppage they were unable to tap the best quality of steel during the remainder of the week, which occasioned the complete stoppage of our Billet Mill for a whole week.

We estimate our loss from this cause at £100.

The total claim therefore, excluding loss of profit, amounts to £400.

Frank Gilbertson to Messrs R. & C. B. Jenkins. 23 April 1913 [8 : 220]

Mr. Hodge has called & has practically promised us in future the same conditions as our competitors enjoy.

Under these circumstances we will abandon our contemplated action.

His promise is of more value to us than a successful action would be, as in the latter case the men would continue to take the holidays after putting themselves in order by giving us legal notice of their intentions!

Frank Gilbertson to T. Mansel Franklen, Clerk to Glamorgan County Council. 27 Sept. 1913 [8 : 350-1]

I write to you with some hesitation, but I think you will understand my difficulty & perhaps be able to advise me whether I should write officially making my complaint to the Education Committee. There is a Teacher at the Trebanos School whose influence in the place is exceedingly odd – he is an atheist, & calls himself a syndicalist, & is very active in propagating his views among the young people of the district.

His name is Abraham Jones.

He has now commenced to interfere actively with our Workmen – he interests himself in any little difficulty that arises, & his influence is most hostile. He has even got himself elected Chairman of our Galvanizing branch of the Dockers Union. On public grounds he is a menace to the life of the place, but our own position seems to be very hard, as we are the chief ratepayers of the parish, & we are practically contributing largely to maintain an unscrupulous enemy in our neighbourhood.

Business is difficult enough under the best conditions, but I am afraid the future of industry in Pontardawe is going to be influenced by the teaching of such men. The socialist element is immediately destructive of good workmanship, apart altogether from its encouragement of petty strikes & disputes.

Frank Gilbertson to Messrs R. & C. B. Jenkins & Lloyd. 20 Jan. 1914 [8 : 488-9]

Referring to 'phonic conversation, and our interview with your Mr. Davies, we enclose list of names of the packers who stopped work irregularly last night, and we shall be glad if you will issue summonses against these persons, in addition to the list handed to Mr. Davies, but the amount of damage in the case of the packers does not exceed £2/-/- each, please claim accordingly.

Names and addresses of Packers who stopped work irregularly last night, January 19th 1914.

Alec Williams, James Street, Pontardawe
John Jones, Edward Street, Alltwen, Pontardawe
Elias Thomas, Balaclava, Glais
John Rees, Lycod Terrace, Rhydyfro, Pontardawe
Evan Davies Commercial Road, Rhydyfro, Pontardawe
Edward James, Glen View, Rhydyfro, Pontardawe
Edwin Rapsey, Church Street, Pontardawe
Arthur Suff, c/o Mrs Gordon, Ynisderw, Pontardawe

Frank Gilbertson to John Hodge. 30 Jan. 1914 [8 : 465-72]

I am writing you a private and unofficial letter to tell you my point of view in the present dispute in Pontardawe because I think some far reaching influences are on their trial, and I believe you and I would agree that it is to the mutual interest of Employers and Employed that these influences should now be checked finally.

The dispute originated in the Galvanizing Department and the Dockers Union.

We were starting up an additional Galvanizing Pot, as often happens in the Spring of each year. We had to select 2 Dippers for the Pot from the ranks of the Tankers, as is customary.

We put on as one of the Dippers a young man named Phil Humphreys. This man is a full member of the Dockers Union, a son of the Treasurer of the Sheet Mill branch of your Society and both a good Unionist and a capital workman.

Our reasons for choosing him as one of the 2 new Dippers were that he was a competent workman, and had had the same promotion to dip last year, at the end of February, when we put on a fresh pot for the Spring trade.

The local Works secretary of the Dockers Union objected to Humphreys going on, upon the score that a young man named Harding was senior to him.

. . . You may judge from the foregoing that there is something more at stake than the simple case of Humphreys versus Harding, it is the position assumed by the little clique led by Jeremiah the Checkweigher, and Abraham Jones the Schoolmaster.

Abraham Jones has actually been Chairman of the Dockers Branch for a year, and he and Jeremiah are so blinded by hate for us that they have taken a step I believe you will strongly disapprove of. It would seem that the Steel Smelters Society with its Rules and its Head Secretary does not permit of sufficient Authority being wielded by Thomas Jeremiah, so a new organisation has been formed called "The Industrial Council" with Jeremiah as Chairman and Abraham Jones as secretary.

It is composed of delegates from all the Smelters and Dockers branches in our Works, and it seems to me can only exist to promote discord or to usurp the proper functions of the different Societies' officials.

You know that I have always been a strong believer in a strong Union, and in collective bargaining.

I am a strong supporter and loyal member of the Tinplate Conciliation Board.

Now I utterly fail to see how that board is going to last if we have more of these unauthorized "down tools" strikes in Pontardawe, and if we have an "Industrial Council" to reckon with, which is not a party to the annual agreement, and does not admit the authority of the Central Executive Committee of the Unions, unless their orders happen to coincide with the wishes of the "Industrial Council".

I do not see how your Society is going to maintain its great position and reputation if it allows a man like Jeremiah to wield an unauthorized authority in its midst, or a bitter, disappointed Schoolmaster to interfere in industrial matters that are beyond his knowledge, in the name of an ally and almost an officer in your Society.

Once the Galvanizers stopped work the dispute passed into the hands of Jeremiah and his "Industrial Council" and I should like [to know?] what he said at the large protest meeting . . .

The Dockers were no doubt spoiling for a fight, and they had notices running which would have terminated tomorrow and which they refused to withdraw so as to render the appointment of a Committee possible, but you will see how serious a matter we are faced with, how prolonged a stoppage is probable, when you realise that I regard the fight as one not with a Union, but with all the anarchical forces of discord that threaten the great Unions as much as the employers.

The "Industrial Council" is now busy in trying to get the Steel Works to "down tools".

Abraham Jones wrote to me on the 24th asking me to receive a deputation of the Council and I replied that I could only recognise the authorised leaders of the Unions that were parties to the Conciliation Board Agreements, and I spoke in the same strain to a Committee of 4 from the "Industrial Council" that waited on me on Tuesday last. I may say that as an employer who tries to find employment for his old men and maintains a regular pension list, I have been very much hurt at Jeremiah's speeches that "we have no use for any one over 40 years old, who we then throw on the industrial scrap heap". A great deal of untruth and misapprehension is rife here, and I wish you would find time to give the men a little education.

As things are drifting now a long & bitter strike is coming in these Works, if indeed this is not it.

In calling this a private letter I do not mean that I wish you to keep any part private that you would like to use.

Frank Gilbertson to Messrs R. & C. B. Jenkins. 10 Feb. 1914 [8 : 483-4]

Your favour of yesterday re. John Joseph & Ed. Thomas. We shall be glad to arrange with Mr. Jenkins about the witnesses tomorrow.

Both these men started work today.

Joseph is a blackguard & one of the chief agents in all the trouble here.

Ed Thomas is a very decent fellow & has simply been terrorized.

We should like, if you can see your way clear, for us to retain the wages due to these two men, & then for you to destrain upon Joseph for half the balance. The other half owing by Thomas we should not press for & eventually should let him off.

With reference to the other fines already inflicted. How can we obtain payment? It is possible to make further application to the Court for leave to deduct from wages earned after work has been resumed?

Frank Gilbertson to Sir Walter Lawrence, Bt. 11 Feb. 1914 [8 : 488]
22, Sloane Gardens, SW.

. . . We are in the middle of a very big strike here – it has been brewing for 2 or 3 years as the result of a few "Syndicalists" getting influence.

It is certainly a blessing in disguise & has come at a time that suits us. Our attitude is quite correct, & the men have not the support of their Unions.

They have nearly had enough of it now, & I think peace will come next week & that one or two of the leaders will lose their influence, & will never enter the Works again.

Frank Gilbertson to John Hodge. 24 Feb. 1914 [8 : 504-6]

I am much obliged by your private lines of yesterday & note the strong & correct attitude you have adopted.

Mr. Ben Tillet wrote the Galvanizers a strong letter yesterday practically ordering the men to resume work immediately, & it was carried to the men by Mr. Hughes, who says he used his best efforts, but the men refused to start work "until Mr. Hodge had been down".

Evidently there is a connecting link somewhere between your No. 2 Branch & the Galvanizers.

After lighting up the Galvanizing Pots at considerable cost, we have therefore to cool them down again.

On the whole I think it better not to approach the No. 2 Branch for an interview. If I asked for a deputation, I know it would consist of men that I could not trust to carry back the strict truth to the Branch, & I would prefer our official letter of 20th inst. to stand as our intimation to your Society of our action in the matter.

With regard to the carrying back of truthful statements, I may say Tom Jeremiah's account of his meeting with your Executive is

> "He had a magnificent reception & addressed the Committee for 1 hour (this has now grown to 2 hours) & that the Executive quite agreed that a case lay against us in law, but it might be impolitic to fight it.
>
> He also took the opportunity to rub some home truths in to Mr. Hodge, with regard to the expenses he incurred in foreign travel & other ways."

Now of course I give this account for what it is worth, but it is based on strong rumours. I hope very much that in any final decision you may be able to insist on ballot voting. The whole case is a very sad one, & much suffering will result from the wild ambitions of one man, for that is really what it comes to.

Frank Gilbertson to F. Edwards, Capital & Counties Bank. **24 Feb. 1914 [8 : 507]**

Private

Owing to the strike hanging up our finishing departments, our stocks are temporarily increasing very rapidly, & it is probable that we shall require some accommodation unless we realize investments which we do not wish to do.

We are aware that you will give us the accommodation, but we mention the matter as it is possible our account may be overdrawn £2/3000 at the beginning of March.

Frank Gilbertson to Henry Holford, Capital & Counties Bank. **27 Feb. 1914 [8 : 511-2]**

Thank you for your letter of yesterday. I wrote to Mr. Edwards as I had had some conversation with him before, over our investment in the Galvanizing Co. of Roumania Ld. We shall probably require some further accommodation when we pay our calls on these shares, as the prolonged strike is locking up a great deal of Capital, & we have no desire to realize our "Gilt Edged" investments. I am in hopes that this strike, in which our attitude is entirely just & correct, will give us some years of peace in future.

We have been much troubled by a small group of Syndicalists here, & the lesson our men are learning may lessen their influence in future.

Frank Gilbertson to John Hodge. **4 March 1914 [8 : 516-20]**

. . . I can quite believe that by the end of that wretched strike of bundlers Jeremiah, seeing the game was up, used his influence towards a restart.

The strike lasted a fortnight, and my charge was that he prevented the boys accepting Mr. Whitehead's advice on one occasion during the stoppage.

I had better tell you what my information is and I should like to hear whether Mr. Whitehead says it is right or wrong.

You must not make too much of what men say about tale bearing because there are plenty of men in the Works who look upon my brothers and myself as better friends than any they have outside.

. . . I must take the opportunity you have given me to express the great surprise I felt at the defence you put up for Jeremiah. I have too high an opinion of your integrity to doubt that you genuinely believed Jeremiah was a better man than you thought, and that you honestly believed his influence had been used for peace in these Works.

Now I must claim a far more intimate knowledge of his character than you have, and if I am wrong how can Mr. Tom Griffiths have been misled, forming his opinion from a directly opposite point of view and knowing what Jeremiah has said at Meetings I know nothing of?

Mr. Griffiths has said in the most emphatic manner that there can be no peace at Pontardawe with Jeremiah!

The men say freely "Jeremiah is a lamb in the Office, but a roaring lion outside".

Now I must conclude that he acted the part of a lamb before you and that other steps were very deliberately taken to persuade you that he was unjustly treated.

I say most seriously that if you have not succeeded in transforming Jeremiah's character you will live to learn that he has deceived you as he has in the past deceived me.

I would also say that whatever their individual characters may be, a group of men like Abraham Jones, T. Jeremiah, Dd. Evans and half a dozen more, who go about ridiculing religion and turn the Sabbath into a day for nothing but the propagation of Syndicalist and Atheistic views of life, is a group that is sowing the seeds of great unhappiness for the next generation, and is not a man that should receive encouragement from a man of your large and experienced views.

Frank Gilbertson to John Hodge. 17 March 1914 [8 : 530-1]

Private

I have to acknowledge your personal letter of the 12th & 13th inst, and I am obliged to you for the trouble you have taken.

With regard to yours of the 13th inst, there was no occasion for the Millmen referred to to be accompanied by any representative as we had no intention of inflicting any penalty at all upon the men.

With regard to your paragraph referring to Mr. Hardy, Mr. Hardy informs us that your information is quite incorrect. I may say we have no objection to Jeremiah forming one of any deputation that we may receive in the Office as formerly, and we are quite prepared to agree to receive a deputation on behalf of any man whom we intend to punish in the absence of sufficient explanation for any fault. I am, however, determined to limit Jeremiah to the opportunities given him by the document he has signed, and I think it well that the matter should be cleared up quite definitely without delay and before incidents have arisen that may render its interpretation difficult.

I agree that Clause 4 can properly be read to mean that Jeremiah can form one of a deputation. I must insist, however, most strongly that he is only to form one of a deputation of two or more, and I am not prepared to receive him in the Office by himself as a deputation of one. He would then find it necessary to adhere strictly to the truth in reporting proceedings to the Branch which might very easily be a help to him in reforming his old habits and character.

If Jeremiah is ever to gain our confidence it can only be by his actions in the future, and it is quite certain that in the past he has not carried out strictly true reports of proceedings that have taken place in the Office, and his behaviour inside and out has hitherto been most inconsistent.

If you wish my firm to write you an official letter embodying part of what I say to you now, please let me know.

Frank Gilbertson to John Hodge. **20 March 1914 [8 : 534-5]**

With reference to the matter of Tom Jeremiah accompanying men to the Office.

We may say that in the case referred to there was no necessity for the men to be accompanied by any Official, as we did not intend inflicting any penalty upon them.

With regard to the future, we have no objection to Jeremiah being one of any deputation of two or more that we receive in the Office, and we are prepared to receive deputations as in the past.

We are not prepared, however, to receive Jeremiah alone, and this was not provided for in the Document that governs his scope of action for the future.

Of course, so long as he is Secretary of the Branch we shall recognise and reply to letters written by him on their behalf.

We take this opportunity of asking you to instruct the Branch to prepare a list of Doublers, Furnacemen and Behinders, say twelve of each grade, in the order of seniority. Perhaps, also, six Rollermen, in the order of their claim for promotion to Shearing.

We will then check the list, and make any comments we desire, and it can then be taken as our basis when promotions occur, and will save considerable discussion at times.

If we and the Branch agree the seniority of the men, the only matter remaining for discussion will be the individual's efficiency.

Charles Gilbertson to Tom Griffiths. **16 June 1914 [8 : 673-4]**

Private

We are given to understand that the Millmen have appointed an assistant check-weigher.

They have, of course, no right to do this without our consent.

If my information is correct, the man they have chosen is a good class of man, & one to whom we should not object.

But in order to secure our rights in the matter, it is necessary that the Branch should obtain our permission to appoint an assistant checkweigher, & that his name should be given to us for our approval.

Until this is done, we cannot recognise him officially.

If you find that our information is correct, would you please arrange that the right steps are taken by the Branch to obtain our consent.

I thought it wise to write to you privately on the matter, seeing that we do not object to the man appointed, but we do object to the method of his appointment.

Frank Gilbertson to Messrs R. & C. B. Jenkins & Lloyd. **7 April 1915 [8 : 899-900]**

. . . The facts (2) (3) (4) are correct.

(1) is not correct as it stands, the Strike originated in another department, but was prolonged by the Steel Smelters Branch of which D. Morgan Griffiths was a member. The fact that work could not be resumed until Mr. John Hodge had addressed this branch, proves that this branch was the cause of work not being resumed as soon as it might have been.

The Dockers were responsible for the strike, which might have ended in 4 weeks had not this Branch of the Steel Smelters interested themselves in the dispute & refused to resume work after a deputation of the Dockers had reached an agreement with us, thereby prolonging the strike by two weeks.

Frank Gilbertson to Tom Griffiths, 7, Queen Street, Neath. **5 Jan. 1916 [10 : 101-4]**

Private

I am writing this personal letter to you, in reply to yrs. which I received this morning. I appreciate that your object in writing privately to me, was to try & preserve peace in our mills, & I thank you for the effort which you are making in this direction.

I shall reply quite candidly, but in a manner which will prejudice you in no way, should you wish to show this letter to the men.

Mr. Hardy has made a genuine effort to keep on friendly terms with the men, & on the whole I believe that his efforts have been appreciated by the men.

But I fear that his efforts in this direction have been misinterpreted by a certain section, as a sign of weakness, with the result that the Branch have taken too much upon themselves.

There is a section of the men, I believe a small section, headed by Jeremiah & David Evans as Branch officials, who seem to resent any action taken by the Management. I take it that the officials of the Branch are not called upon to interfere with the Management, unless they consider that we are doing something contrary to the rules of the Conciliation Board agreements, or unfair to the men.

As it is now, they seem to look upon any action taken by Mr. Hardy, necessary to the maintenance of proper discipline in the Mills, as a hostile action – and one which they must meet with another hostile action on their side.

I am anxious to treat the men in the Mills with as much consideration as possible – but it is absolutely necessary for us to retain proper control without unnecessary interference from the Branch officials.

No doubt the officials of the Branch think that they are serving the men's interests best by combating the Management on every possible occasion.

But I am sure that they are wrong. If they will reserve their opposition for occasions upon which we are guilty of unfairness or breach of Conciliation Board rules, they will be acting entirely within their rights, & the feeling of unrest & hostility at present existing, will die down.

As far as we are concerned, I shall endeavour to see that the men are treated with fairness & without harshness, but if we find it necessary to penalize men for breakages etc., for which they are responsible, our action must be taken as the natural outcome of management, & not as demonstrating any hostile feelings towards the men or any particular man.

It is very seldom that Mr. Hardy ever takes a step of any importance without first discussing the matter with me first, but I have not so much time, as formerly, to devote to the mills personally.

I do not think, however, that this effects the position much.

I must say that I find the officials of the sheet mill Branch very difficult to get on with, & I don't believe the fault lies with me!

Today David Evans sent in a man to work in his place, without leave from Mr. Hardy – not even a message supported by a Doctor's Certificate.

We cannot allow this – but I only mention it as an illustration of the way in which some of the men appear to disregard the Management entirely. I shall do my best to keep the peace, within responsible limits, & feel sure that I shall receive yr. support.

Frank Gilbertson to A. P. Townsend. **13 June 1916 [10:181]**

Private

Your favour of yesterday re. E. Griffiths.

This man was employed by us for many years, but having attained an official position in his Union it was impossible to dismiss him, although he was unsatisfactory in every way.

We at last closed a department in which he worked as much to get him out of the Works as anything else!

Unless adversity has changed his nature you would regret taking him on.

Chapter 7

HEALTH AND SAFETY

Factory legislation in the nineteenth century evolved in a piecemeal and empirical manner until 1878 when, as a result of a Royal Commission review, the law was consolidated and a comprehensive Factory and Workshop Act was passed. This was followed in 1880 by the Employers' Liability Act which placed an employee injured at work in the same position as a member of the public injured by the employer's negligence. This Act was passed for seven years and renewed annually to 1897 when a new Workmen's Compensation Act replaced the common law doctrine of negligence and substituted the principle that the employer must, subject to certain limitations, insure his workmen against the risks of their employment. It remained the basis of workmen's compensation until 1925.

One of the sections of the 1878 Act was cited by Arthur Gilbertson in 1891 when he remonstrated with Augustus Lewis, the factory inspector, urging him to replace Dr. Griffith Griffiths, a local general practitioner who also held the public offices of Certifying Factory Surgeon and Medical Officer of Health, with a more amenable works doctor. When works injuries or accidents could lead to compensation claims, employers may have wished for a compliant works doctor but at the very least would have expected impartiality. It appears that Dr. Griffiths displayed an independence of spirit, and his alleged "animus" against Gilbertson was forcefully expressed in several of the letters which follow. Other letters refer to workmen's insurance, the appointment and remuneration of works doctors and nurses, the control of a typhoid outbreak in 1895, ambulance and hospital provision, and the use of the Gilbertson family home at Glanrhyd as an auxiliary hospital during the war.

Arthur Gilbertson to Howel Cuthbertson, Coroner, Neath. **5 Nov. 1890 [1 : 29]**

Would you be so good as to inform us in the event of any Inquest which may unfortunately arise in connection with our Works, by whose instructions the panel is selected, and we wish, in such cases, to have our Works Doctor, Dr. Grice-Jones, as a matter of course, summoned to attend, under any circumstances.

It is known to all in the district that the other local Doctor (Dr. G. Griffiths) does not work in accord with us, or with Dr. Grice-Jones.

To Augustus Lewis, HMI Factories, Swansea. **5 Nov. 1890 [1 : 30]**

In reply to yours of yesterday. Certainly Marshall was in our employ, and the scene of the accident was on our Railway Siding, which is without the precincts of our Factory. Should you be coming up here to view our Steel Works, you can be shown the spot . . . We are instituting inquiries into why our Works Doctor had no notice of the Inquiry.

Arthur Gilbertson to Augustus Lewis. **17 Feb. 1891 [1 : 79-80]**

I before told you I objected to Dr. G. Griffiths being our Factory Doctor in consequence of his animus against myself. You will understand how unpleasant it is to have such a person coming into my Works & Office. When I told you that he has the impertinence not to reply to my greeting when I meet him on my own property I conclude the Factory Doctor is for the Works & not the Works for him, and the Owner of the Works should be able to consult the Factory Doctor. I again ask, in the interests of the better working under the acts, and in courtesy to myself that our Works Doctor, Dr. Grice-Jones, be appointed our Factory Doctor.

Arthur Gilbertson to Augustus Lewis. **24 Feb. 1891 [1 : 83]**

. . . I am unwilling to take the step you suggest, but having put the matter before you, I thought under Sec. 72 of 41 Vict. Chap. 16 you have power to appoint further officers, or to revoke any such appointments.

Perhaps the difficulty might be met by your further appointing Dr. Grice-Jones.

The matter is now fully before you.

The legislation referred to was the Factory and Workshop Act, 1878.

Arthur Gilbertson to Augustus Lewis. **4 March 1891 [1 : 89]**

. . . I am desirous of avoiding anything which would lead to further animosity on the part of Dr. G. Griffiths, and have more than once given him the opportunity to resume more friendly relations, but I cannot submit to be insulted in my own Works.

I think the best way would be to further appoint Dr. Grice-Jones to our Works, without removing Dr. G. Griffiths & we could then avail ourselves of Dr. Grice-Jones assistance & advice.

Arthur Gilbertson to W. Robinson Smith, Solicitor, Swansea. **2 July 1891 [1 : 121]**

Your favour of yesterday. The Rev. Williams (brother-in-law), the Father-in-Law of Jonah, and Jonah's Father called on me this morning. They all distinctly state that

Mr. Leyson was engaged to watch the medical evidence, and distinctly not to attempt to set up any claim under Employers Liability Act. The question therefore is, who did instruct Leyson to act as he did?

I want this traced. The three men mentioned on other side would stake on oath, they did not so instruct him – my short hand Clerk took down their statement.

I enclose for your private perusal & guidance, Dr. Thomas' letter to use. I wish to send out enclosed circular at once to my Workmen. I conclude no objection?

Arthur Gilbertson to Augustus Lewis. **8 July 1891 [1 : 124]**

The Inquest on Jonah Williams about whom we wrote on 30th ult. is adjourned to the 14th inst.

The matter is of such importance that we hope you will kindly attend if possible.

You will hear such evidence as will enable you to form an opinion as to whether Dr. G. Griffiths ought to be forced upon us, as Factory Doctor, any longer. In any case, after this Inquest, we shall have to take such steps in the matter, as we may be advised.

Arthur Gilbertson to W. Robinson Smith. **28 July 1891 [1 : 143]**

. . . I enclose copy of my letter to Mr. A. Lewis at the time he refers to. Of course, we dont know what he said to the London Chief. I take it Dr. G. Griffiths has taken good care to ingratiate himself with Aug[ustus] Lewis. It seems absurd that the Testifying Surgeon should not speak to the Owner of the Factory!

Aug. Lewis now has before him, the evidence he heard at the Inquest and I call upon him to appoint a further Doctor. You know the "Act" & I believe he has power. Should you find he is not prepared to advise a further appointment please drop the matter & I will proceed thro' London.

Arthur Gilbertson to Dr. F. Grice-Jones. **14 Sept. 1891 [1 : 152]**

We have now received Messrs Robinson Smith & Son's bill of costs in case of Jonah Williams dec[eased]. The bulk of the charges (which are very moderate) are for protecting yourself, but under all the circumstances we intend paying them ourselves, without asking you to contribute.

Arthur Gilbertson to Messrs W. Robinson Smith & Son, Swansea. **15 Sept. 1891 [1 : 153]**

Costs	re Dr Griffiths	8..16.. 5
	re Jonah Williams decd.	14.. 4.. 1
	re Steel F'ces	1..17..11
		£22..18.. 5

Arthur Gilbertson to Augustus Lewis, HMI of Factories. **13 Aug. 1892 [1 : 203-4]**

You will remember an Inquest on Jonah Williams, one of our Workmen, in July last year. The man's leg was broken & internally bruised, by a weight of plates falling on it. You were at the Inquest. The relations very foolishly yielded to the insinuations of some persons, and employed a Mr. Leyson & afterwards Mr. D. Randall M.P. to attempt to fasten the responsibility for the death, upon our Works Doctor, Dr. Grice-Jones.

Under the circumstances we let the Relations take their course, and did not volunteer the assistance in money, we usually give voluntarily. We were unable to ascertain definitely who first started the rumour that Dr. Grice-Jones was to blame, altho' we were certain, from our knowledge of his practice & skill during several years of Ambulance lectures (when a large body of Police &c &c availed themselves of his lectures & demonstrations of bandaging &c and took certificates in the annual examinations before one of the first Surgeons in South Wales) that Dr. Grice-Jones was not to blame.

Having recently learnt that the Relatives regretted their action, and that they had abandoned all charges, I saw the Father-in-Law and the Widow, and afterwards wrote the letter, of which enclosed is the copy & received the replies also annexed.

Under the circumstances, I again ask you that Dr. Grice-Jones be added as additional Factory Doctor to our Works, and failing your being able to accede to our request, we will put the matter before our London Solicitor.

Arthur Gilbertson to Dr. F. Grice-Jones. **22 April 1893 [1 : 233]**

Please let me have your Bill for attendance & medicines for my family, and servants in Glanrhyd House. I prefer paying please as I told you before. I know it is the custom where Doctors have their money collected in Works, to attend the Manager gratuitously, but I dont wish to avail myself of it. Thank you all the same.

I find we collect money for you from about 700 persons, entailing 700 entries in Pay Book and also on Pay Tickets per month, and also a "Ledger a/c" – we, in fact, collect your Bills from 700 Patients & you make no bad debts!

There are many small matters you can & do oblige me in, especially reporting serious cases & when you need a Consulting Doctor. These I like to hear about.

Arthur Gilbertson to R. P. Morgan & David, Solicitors, Neath. **16 Aug. 1893 [1 : 262]**

Please read enclosed rough notes. I want summonses against all the men named for "following & hooting".

I attach great importance to subpoenas being served on Dr. G. Griffiths and his party.

Perhaps Mr. David could come over here tomorrow & see me about midday at this office.

Arthur Gilbertson to R. P. Morgan & David. **17 Aug. 1893 [1 : 263]**

At considerable inconvenience I attended at this office until 20 to 1 this morning and cut one Director's meeting, but no telegram arrived, or Mr. David.

I have now to go off for another meeting. The instructions, I conclude, are so plain that you can act on them. I dont want the summonses returnable any sooner than needful, but I want them served.

I think it will be sufficient to subpoena Dr. G. Griffiths & Mrs. Griffiths, and Dr. Williams.

Arthur Gilbertson to R. P. Morgan & David **25 Aug. 1893 [1 : 265]**

Yours of yesterday. We dont think, upon consideration, that we need employ a Barrister. The case seems plain, does it not?

We find Inspector Giddings was with the Constable near our entrance gate, to protect our Foremen, and he was pushed aside & hustled by the gang. This is surely "disorderly"? It almost amounts to assaulting the Police?

Arthur Gilbertson to R. P. Morgan & David. **31 Aug. 1893 [1 : 268-9]**

Yours of 28th inst. We think the men will employ Mr. D. Randall M.P. or Howells of Llanelly, the latter is a blustering Bully. If Mr. David thinks well, we believe Mr. Nicholas of Llandilo is the best Police Court advocate we know. Could you employ him with you?

We conclude you will notify Witnesses, as to meeting? You have no doubt noted the point, about Rees Edwards, being your employer?

Dr. G. Griffiths will be an unwilling & unreliable witness. We think you should write to Mrs. Griffiths, Bryncelyn, Pontardawe, about Wednesday next saying "Madam,

As we believe Dr. G. Griffiths will be able to give sufficient evidence as to mob of intimidators, we shall not trouble you to come into Court, but if Dr. G. Griffiths evidence is not sufficient, we may have to call you, and must therefore ask you to hold yourself in readiness during the sitting of the Court."

We think this will help to keep Dr. Griffiths up to the mark.

Arthur Gilbertson to R. P. Morgan & David. **1 Jan. 1894 [1 : 279]**

Miss Jane Asman (aunt to William Baker) died some months ago at Pontardawe, leaving her property between W. Baker, Sarah Baker, another sister of W. Baker, and a cousin. Something near £200 I believe. W. Baker lives in my House. Dr. G. Griffiths is unfortunately the only Surviving Trustee. W. Baker is an Executor. Dr. G. Griffiths got Baker to sign some paper before C. & B. Jenkins (Clerk to Guardians here). Dr. G. Griffiths has the Will, he says to Baker he sent it to Cuthbertson &

Powell, Neath. Baker does not know if it is proved. It is too bad of Dr. G. Griffiths to put poor people to such costs.

Baker wishes this money to be handed to me.

Kindly look into matter & save all costs you can as a matter of charity.

Happy New Year to you.

William Baker to Dr. G. Griffiths **1 Jan. 1894 [1 : 280]**
[in Arthur Gilbertson's handwriting]

Sir,

Be good enough to hand to Mr. A. Gilbertson of Glanrhyd the amount coming to me under the Will of my late Aunt, Miss Asman.

(Signed in my presence: Godfrey Wolfe, Clerk in Holy Orders, Danygraig, Pontardawe).

Arthur Gilbertson to Dr. Grice-Jones. **9 Aug. 1895 [1 : 385]**

I have seen Mrs. Davies, the Widow today. I should feel much obliged if you would kindly let me know, in writing, of any serious cases of illness among our men. When you come to consider the immense saving of time to yourself in our system of collecting for you some £320..0..0 per annum, and no bad debts! I am sure you wont mind the time taken up writing me information as to sick people.

Arthur Gilbertson to Dr. W. Williams, **23 Nov. 1895 [1 : 398-9]**
County Medical Officer, Neath.

I am obliged by your letter of yesterday. I have now a record of 39 cases from the beginning – Several cases of 4 in a House, and one of 5 including the Wife dead. I shall be glad to know what list Dr. G. Griffiths sends you. I just hear of a fresh case at Craig Llanguicke, child of man named Battenbow, whose Wife was confined yesterday.

It seems a great pity the empty Sanatorium at our huge empty Workhouse was not utilized temporarily. From what I can find out the first case was a tramp at the Workhouse in September last – Possibly excreta from the Earth Closet was thrown out, before the case was pronounced Typhoid, and the popular idea is, rain washed this Soil into the drinking water supplying the Northern division of Pontardawe, to which District the Fever is confined. This water supply was cut off, no doubt you have the date, I should guess 6 or 7 weeks ago. What then kept the Fever going, if the excreta <u>from the first</u> was absolutely disinfected? The inference is, it was not properly done. Some trace the continuance to the drains at Police Station being cut into, by some Navvies, but altho' those living at the Station have suffered, their near neighbours have not, and the Fever has appeared some little distance off, <u>on same water circuit</u> – but I have ascertained this morning that some stinking earth, excavated by the Navvies by Police Station, was carted to Steadman's garden, and there are bad cases of Fever around it!! This stuff (if this report is true) was dug up under Dr. G. Griffith's nose, and was it disinfected? doubtless not: I offered Copperas by the Cartload on 4th Novbr, none was sent for until a few days ago.

I have cut short Typhoid with only one case (imported) among my own Tenants, in a crowded cottage, by seeing myself that a load of Copperas was put in the garden and all excreta covered with it.

The fact of 40 cases alone proves neglect on part of officers on the spot.

Arthur Gilbertson to Dr. W. Williams. **24 Nov. 1895 [1 : 400]**

I have just heard of the death of one of our Workmen, 3 of his children are still ill & one dead.

They are close to Steadman's garden.

Today Mr. Morgan has sent for 3 loads of Copperas, which I give. If I can be of any use to you, I should be glad to see you, but I have no official status on any "Councils" &c, as altho' I am a man of 35 years business experience, & the chief support of this prosperous Village, the Dissenting Preachers & their flocks think that as I am a "Churchman", I know nothing about drains, water, rates &c.

Frank Gilbertson to S. B. Barlow. **23 Nov. 1898 [1 : 751]**

We should be glad if you will let us have the digest, as promised, of the Workman's Compensation Act, as soon as you can.

A poor fellow has lost his life in these Works – a shunter by occupation – carelessly trying to uncouple some trucks, while in motion, himself standing in one of the trucks & leaning over to uncouple, instead of waiting till the train was at rest.

Apparently he has no relatives whatever & no one dependent upon him, with the exception of an illegitimate child, whose mother the man was shortly to marry.

Will you kindly give us your opinion on this case?

Arthur Gilbertson to Dr. Grice-Jones. **18 Jan. 1899 [1 : 795]**

I am very sorry to bother you when you are so ill, but I feel sure you will say yourself you will not be able to resume your duties as Works Doctor, until you have had some weeks change. Therefore I feel I must ask what you propose doing to serve the men (who pay a large sum) and your private Patients?

Do you propose to keep Dr. Barber? In that case he would be single handed here, for sometime, and I should like to know about his training, certificates &c, and I should like Dr. T. Griffiths to have an interview with him, as soon as possible, and to report to me.

I sympathize with you greatly, and will do anything I can to help you.

Arthur Gilbertson to Dr. Grice-Jones. 23 Jan. 1899 [1 : 798]

I have your letter of yesterday, and altho' I deeply regret it, I feel you are right in your decision.

Please note that the new Doctor will have to take on your house, and pay the full rent of £30..0..0, and taxes, also we shall require him to pay his own Consultant Doctor when needful & to attend the Manager's family free of charge.

The Works appointment to be subject to three months notice on either side.

Testimonials, & personal interview with myself, to take place before the Works appointment is decided upon – it is now a valuable one.

Dr. Llewelyn Rees was appointed Works Doctor.

Arthur Gilbertson to Messrs Andrew & Thompson, Solicitors, Swansea. 30 Sept. 1899 [1 : 905-6]

Your favour of the 27th inst. to hand. You refer to some letter from A. Palmer to us? We have not received any letter from him & when the Writer sent for Palmer about ten days ago, with reference to further medical treatment & a spring cork leg, which would enable him to resume his proper occupation here, as Steel Works outside Clerk, he made no reference to any letter from him, nor did he refer to the fact that he was taking legal advice.

The work he was at, when the accident occurred, was not authorized by us, but it seems he had undertaken it, by paying half of the proceeds to a man to teach him, with a view to his ultimate advancement.

He received weekly wages from us as Clerk, and had no permission from us to take other jobs.

The accident occurred in May last, and the weekly wages of Palmer have been sent ever since to his mother & several donations.

Arthur Gilbertson to Strick, Bellingham & Hanson. 3 Oct. 1899 [1 : 908]

Your favour of yesterday re. A. Palmer & we write as you suggest to his Solicitors today.

We are not insured, we place an amount annually to an "Insurance Fund" in our own accounts.

Arthur Gilbertson to Dr. Ll. Rees. 29 June 1901 [3 : 314-5]

Geo. Palmer is malingering as regards his hand – he wants to remain idle for 4 weeks, when he hopes then to claim under Act.

I dont think his general health is good & he has been really taking a Holiday. What do you say as to his health?

I expect you keep a Diary – if not, please do so for all Works cases, as you might have to give evidence on oath, in Law Court.

When did Palmer come to you first? and how many times & when? & what is the real injury, if any? I conclude he could have done "overlooking" work, all the time, without using his hands?

I saw him this morning, and thought he looked "ill" – nothing to do with the hand.

Frank Gilbertson to Illtid E. Thomas, 14 Castle Square, Swansea. **1 July 1901[3 : 316]**

Please quote us again the Provident Clerk's terms for insuring our Workmen. We have now decided to insure. We think you have particulars of our number of workmen & wages.

Frank Gilbertson to W. A. Ford, Provident Clerks Insurance Co., Swansea. **31 July 1901 [3 : 356]**

We should be very obliged if you would kindly give us your advice upon the enclosed statement of claim. The accident however occurred before we insured with you and for which of course we shall pay. Wm. Rapsey's earnings for the last three months he worked, averaged £2..14..9 per week, he has been idle 10 weeks and we are prepared to pay him £8 for wages and any expenses he has been put to, we are also willing to give him employment of a non-dangerous character @ 5/- per day or to pay him a lump sum of £100 to assist him to start a business which we think he would prefer to work. Would you kindly say if you consider our proposal is a fair one as we wish to be liberal to the man but have no experience to guide us in arriving at the amount.

P.S. Please return enclosures after perusal.

Frank Gilbertson to W. A. Ford. **14 Aug. 1901 [3 : 373]**

Referring again to your letter of 1st inst. We wrote Wm. Rapsey as per enclosed copy & have the enclosed letter from Mr. Hodge, the Union Secretary.

We wish to know if you would be good enough to correspond with Mr. Hodge to settle the matter for us, & we would pay your Company whatever you think right for the service.

If you would do so we will give you a free hand, but dont want legal proceedings.

Colin Gilbertson to W. A. Ford. **2 Sept. 1901 [3 : 396]**

W. Rapsey

Thank you for your letter of 31st ulto, & we note you have settled with Mr. Hodge for £182.

We regret we cannot send your cheque today, as our Secretary is absent, but will post it tomorrow.

Arthur Gilbertson to Dr. Ll. Rees. **31 Oct. 1901 [3 : 471]**

We dont know whether you understand that if you require a Consultation Doctor, that it has been our practice to allow £1..1..0 for this, and that we are always advised by you at the time.

We understand Dr. Brooks has charged Thomas Davies £4..4..0!!

Arthur Gilbertson to Dr. Ll. Rees. **2 Nov. 1901 [3 : 477]**

Please read the enclosed from Dr. Dahne, he saw some one at this Office yesterday, and said he would like to rent "Gwynfa", which is advertised to be let & he would pay the rent asked – today he has written to fix the matter.

No doubt a Doctor to take up some Patients of Dr. Griffiths is needed, and I would advise you to be on friendly terms with Dr. Dahne. You could probably work with him.

Philip Davies to Dr. C. F. Logan Dahne, Clasemont, Morriston. **2 Nov. 1901 [3 : 475]**

Mr. Gilbertson has received your letter and instructs us to say that you can have "Gwynfa" @ £25 per year from 1st January next, rent to be payable quarterly and three months' notice on either side . . . Taxes excepting water rates, to be paid by Landlord, and tenant to keep the place in good repair.

Arthur Gilbertson to Dr. Ll. Rees. **16 July 1902 [3 : 690]**

We knew nothing about your Locum Tenens, his certificates & antecedents &c, & therefore the Writer did not employ him at Glanrhyd. It has always been the custom of our Works Doctor, to put before us the above, before we consent to stop money for him in our Books & Office.

Arthur Gilbertson to Dr. Ll. Rees. **21 July 1902 [3 : 692]**

I have not time to go over all the Nurses applications – will you select half a dozen & submit them to me. I dont want a woman over 30 years of age, and I dont want a Midwife. I want a nice, well-educated woman, like Nurse Jackett. We pay entirely her salary, it is not deducted from fund paid by the men, for medical attendance.

Arthur Gilbertson to Nurse Sampson-Sage, Wallingford. **23 July 1902 [3 : 694]**

Our Works Doctor, Dr. Rees, has sent us your application from advertisement in "Hospital".

We employ & pay the Nurse, and she works under the Writer & Dr. Rees. We pay £75 per annum, Nurse getting her own Lodgings. It is a nice village, a pretty place, with Midland Rly. from Pontardawe to Swansea (9 miles).

Would you kindly state your age, if a Churchwoman? The work is not hard, very often there is little to do.

The Daughters of the Writer, are always ready to see the Nurse, if she wishes.

Arthur Gilbertson to Miss Sampson-Sage. **28 July 1902 [3 : 700]**

Your letter of 24th inst. and we are prepared to engage you at the rate of salary we named to you, on notice, on either side, of four weeks. Our Nurse has been with us for some years, and leaves on 3rd. August, to be married.

You could come here on 1st. Septbr. and get Lodgings at Mrs. Ryall, Swansea Road, Pontardawe, please write to her for terms, &c.

Arthur Gilbertson to Nurse Sage. **20 Nov. 1903 [3 : 924]**

We are very sorry to get your letter of 18th inst. You have done such good work in our Village, and we shall miss you greatly, but you are quite right about your duty to your Parents and we quite appreciate your views.

Arthur Gilbertson to Messrs R. & C. B. Jenkins, Swansea. **23 Nov. 1903 [3 : 928-9]**

We are surprised by your letter of 20th inst. The trial took place at Pontardawe Sessions over 8 weeks ago, & we have not been advised that an appeal would be lodged . . .

We cannot understand why we were not told weeks ago that they were going to appeal, & we think this is not fair.

We enclose copies of correspondence with Mr. A. Lewis, & you will note in his letter of Oct. 13th he did not say anything about "Appeal".

We will fight this strenuously, & we want you to do the very best you can.

We believe the root of this matter is Spite. Probably the Sub Inspector is a friend of Dr. G. Griffiths, & as a Factory Doctor he ought not to have been on the Bench.

Could you tell us who is the Counsel retained by Treasury? Will the Trial be in Assizes or Quarter Sessions, & when? . . .

CONTRACTORS TO INDIA OFFICE, ADMIRALTY, WAR OFFICE, &c.

SIEMENS STEEL TIN BARS.
BLOOMS FOR WELDLESS TUBES.
TIN TERNE & BLACK PLATES.
ROOFING SHEETS.
STEEL STAMPING SHEETS.
BEST GALVANIZED STEEL SHEETS.

SHIPPING PORT.
SWANSEA.

COPY.

Nr. Swansea.

Telegrams -
GILSON, PONTARDAWE.
CODES USED
ABC 4TH EDITION & AI
Nat. Telephone 607

Postal Address
PONTARDAWE, R.S.O.
GLAMORGANSHIRE.

October 1st 1903.

Mr D. James.

Langland Bay House,
Mumbles,
Glamorgan.

Dear James,

I am so grieved to hear of the death of George Palmer, I employed his Father many years, and George was one of my small boys in my choir over twenty years ago. Under Providence I saved the life of his wife, many years ago, by sending her to Ilfracombe for several weeks.

I understand old Dr G. Griffiths attended to George - I cannot understand why this was done? You know I introduced a new Doctor in Pontardawe because I was not satisfied by the attention given by Dr. G. Griffiths, on our old Platelayer and several other cases which died- and I insisted, in serious cases, a good second Doctor from Swansea should be called in, Griffiths would not agree - so I dismissed him - I beleive I have saved many lives.

Yours respectfully.

(signed) Arthur Gilbertson.

Letter from Arthur Gilbertson to D. James, 1903
(West Glamorgan Archive Service)

Arthur Gilbertson to S. B. Barlow. **6 Jan. 1904 [3 : 945-6]**

Mr. A. Lewis, the Factory Inspector in this District, took proceedings against us some months ago, in Petty Sessions at Pontardawe. The Magistrates dismissed the case – our point was, that we were building up a new Works, outside of our Works, and the new Works was not "a Factory".

A youth was killed, in a small portable Engine – the letter we wrote to the paper "Ironmonger" will explain all. We sent the letter to Mr. A. Lewis, which he did not like!! and some time after he appealed.

Mr. Hodge, in a letter dated Nov. 13, has refused our offer of £50 for the widow.

PONTARDAWE STEEL, and TINPLATE GALVANIZING WORKS.

Dear Fellow Workmen,—

You know, we, Gilbertsons, work our brains, as you do in manual labour, to keep Pontardawe Works "going," from the beginning of a year to its end, so I address you as "fellow-workmen" with me and my sons. I want you to think about "thrift" when you are in good work. I was told a few days ago that the poor widow of George Palmer (with four small girls), had applied for assistance from the Parish poor rates. I am distressed, and surprised, about this, that the widow and girls should become paupers. THIS OUGHT NOT TO BE.

I have taken out of our pay-book, what Palmer earned during the last twelve months, the sum being about £147. He could have earned more—(another rollerman in Palmer's mill got considerably more)—but I understand Palmer lost work attending to the Union. I believe Palmer, as Secretary for the Union, got £25 a year, thus making £172 per annum. He ought to have put money by for "rainy days.

Now, can we not make some arrangement by "insurance" of our lives, when the toilers earn good wages? I want you to consider this carefully; and we, Gilbertsons, would help you.

I suggest that men should insure their lives for £100, to be paid at the age of 60 years, or on death at an earlier age.

I have applied to the Alliance Insurance Company, London (in which I am myself insured), and they say the premiums per year would be as per list on next page. If a man were 25 years of age, his annual premium would be £2 9s. 5d. We could deduct from his wages 3s.10d. per month, and pay it to the Alliance Co.

As regards the widow of George Palmer, we are corresponding with Mr. John Hodge, and have suggested that the widow should start a small shop, to prevent her becoming a pauper; that we would give her fifty pounds, if the Central Union at Manchester, would also give an additional fifty pounds, to match our fifty pounds. Oddly enough, Mr. Hodge did not thank us for our generosity, but made some suggestions which did not satisfy us.

We said our workmen had paid such a large amount of money from our works—(and our works never stop)—that the fifty pounds must be provided from the Manchester Central Fund. I understand Mr. Hodge has placed our offer before the Council, and we shall hear soon.

Mr. Hodge said that 70 widows and 250 children had been provided with money from his Union, to prevent them going on the poor rates! I asked him, why did he not keep the widow and children of Palmer in the same way? He has not replied. Palmer did good work for the Central Union, and sent a lot of money from our workmen.

Yours truly,

ARTHUR GILBERTSON,

Notice from Arthur Gilbertson distributed in the Works, November 1903

Mr. Bevan Jenkins was our Solicitor and engaged Mr. Villiers Meager (a sharp & decent Barrister in Swansea) for the case at Pontardawe Petty Sessions. As the Americans say, it is impossible to make "Fool-fenced". This poor youth was a Fool.

We enclose the copies between ourselves, Mr. A. Lewis & Messrs. Jenkins, and we would like your opinion.

When we opened our New Works on November 23/03 we put up the printed notice that it was a Factory.

Arthur Gilbertson to Dr. Ll. Rees. — 11 Jan. 1904 [3 : 950]

We have your letter of 9th inst. The Writer was misinformed about the amount you get. You are quite correct, so we will pay you £115 per quarter from 1st inst.

The <u>certain</u> Income from a Works is a very nice nucleus, no bad debts! and no difficulty collecting money.

Arthur Gilbertson to Dr. Ll. Rees. — 15 Jan. 1904 [3 : 953]

We have your letter of 12th inst. accepting our terms.

We think we shall engage a Nurse again, we understand the people miss the Nurse.

Could you find the address of Nurse Cruickshank, or the Brecon Nurse, thro your paper? both of them had very good certificates. We must pay £75 a year.

Arthur Gilbertson to Nurse Cruickshank, Grasmere, Westmorland. — 30 Jan. 1904 [3 : 965-6]

Dr. Rees is our Doctor for our Steel Works, we employ about 1000 people. We engage the Nurse, and pay her every month, at the rate of £75 a year – notice, on either side, three months. You can get decent lodgings in this village. We like a churchwoman who attends to our church.

The Daughters of the Writer, would like you to call at Glanrhyd, their Residence, when you come to Pontardawe.

You could come here, as soon as you like acknowledging this letter, and writing to Dr. Rees, about lodgings.

Frank Gilbertson to S. B. Barlow. — 4 May 1904 [5 : 19]

We are very much obliged by your letter of congratulation. We are very pleased at the result of the appeal, because we felt we had done all that was reasonable to protect the temporary machinery, which would be removed in 3 months. It would be absurd to have to fence the donkey engine & mortar mill as permanently as a Mill Engine!

The obstacles the poor fellow surmounted to reach the dangerous position he did, were almost incredible, & as a matter of common sense the machinery was as safe as if it had been permanently fenced under the supervision of the Inspectorate.

Frank Gilbertson to Iltyd Thomas & Jenkins. 29 July 1904 [5 : 51]

Workmen's Compensation

We are very sorry we have come to the conclusion not to insure at all this year.

The rates of 12/6 would mean £500 to £600 in premiums & we are sure it is wiser to take our own risks under these circumstances, & not to insure at all.

It is a pity the Insurance Cos. have put up their prices so greatly, it will mean Works running their own risks, because unlike Collieries, they are not liable to wholesale accidents.

Frank Gilbertson to Dr. Rees. 27 Dec. 1905 [5 : 215-6]

Before the receipt of your letter we had a request handed to us by the representatives of the men to be allowed to choose the medical man they individually wished to employ.

We were given to understand that a certain number of the men whose subscriptions are deducted by us for you, were in the habit of paying separately for Dr. Dahne's services.

There is no doubt the size of the Works now justifies the men having a call on 2 medical men, & of course we cannot interfere with the workmen's wishes in this matter if they are definitely expressed to us.

I have talked it over with my Father & we have come to the conclusion that those men who have been paying Dr. Dahne privately hitherto, should not be compelled to pay twice over, & if they express a wish to have their subscriptions deducted for Dr. Dahne we must do so.

Frank Gilbertson to R. & C. B. Jenkins, Swansea. 22 June 1906 [5 : 302]

Re. John Jones

We have your favour of yesterday with copy of Dr. Stephens' report on this case, which we are glad is so conclusive. We did not obtain a Doctor's certificate in May last that this man was suffering from dropsy, but such information reached us from another source.

We shall now stop paying compensation, the man has no order from the Court upon us.

P. Davies to R. & C. B. Jenkins. 30 June 1906 [5 : 304]

Referring to enclosed, we are paying a compensation of 9/9 weekly to the person named since September 1904, and recently obtained a Doctor's certificate that the man was unable to follow his occupation, upon which we asked him to produce a certificate as to whether he could do light employment, which we are prepared to offer him. This he promised to do, but he has now evidently decided to take another course of action.

The man came up from Clydach from time to time for his compensation, and we do not understand the statement that one of his eyes has been affected through the accident, because it was only through the blindness of one eye that the accident occurred, a shunt of trucks having approached him on the blind side, knocking him down. We shall be glad if you will take up the matter for us, and perhaps it will be advisable to have an independent examination of the man.

Frank Gilbertson to The Secretary of the Swansea General & Eye Hospital. **Nov. 1906 [5 : 368-9]**

One of our workmen took his Father David Davies to the Hospital yesterday afternoon, with an "out-patient" letter signed by us.

David Davies is an old man, 72 years old, & has been a mason all his life. Amputation of the forearm was recommended but it was stated that the operation would not be performed without payment unless he could truthfully declare that he was unable to pay for the operation privately.

David Davies was then told to go to Mr. Brook as the operation must be performed privately & Mr. Brook named a price for it.

We do not know whom David Davies saw in the Hospital, but we wish to point out that our Workmen contribute a very large sum on the understanding that they have a right to free treatment in the Hospital.

Probably it would be possible for any working man to raise £10..10..0 for an operation, & although he could not sign the declaration in the strict sense of the letter, it is obvious that such a sum is beyond his reach in the ordinary sense of the word.

We may say that if working men are not going to be treated free, our men will probably cease subscribing, & we shall not try to influence them.

Frank Gilbertson to G. Reginald Rowe. **19 Dec. 1906 [3 : 410]**

. . . We have now gone fully into the matter & regret that our opinion is unchanged. We find that the experience of the last 3 years is, that our liabilities under the Act barely exceed half of the premium based on 8/-.

We have had sufficient experience now to lead us to believe that no advantage can be gained in such a works as ours by insurance at today's premiums.

The difference in cost to us during the last 3 years provides a considerable fund towards large & unusual accidents. We are sorry we are not able to put the business your way.

Frank Gilbertson to G. R. Rowe. **4 Jan. 1907 [5 : 422]**

. . . At present, judging from 3 years experience our cost of compensation equals a premium of scarcely more than 4/-.

We therefore do not see the use of insuring, unless we could get a rate of 5/- to 5/6, & this is manifestly impossible.

Therefore we decide to bear the risk ourselves.

Frank Gilbertson to Percy Player, Clydach. **5 Feb. 1907 [5 : 400]**

I am sorry influenza prevented my replying before.

Our Firm will also give £10 if it is understood the Motor Ambulance will be available in this district.

Frank Gilbertson to Dr. W. Owen Evans. **3 Aug. 1907 [5 : 523-4]**

Your favour of yesterday addressed to the Writer, who will reply to items (1) & (2) privately. With regard to (3).

We hold strong objections to the right of any workman, or sections of workmen in our works, to employ any medical services they desire, because it is only by the adoption of the majority's wishes, by all, that the post of "Works Doctor" is rendered attractive to the best men. We consider in our case that the number of men employed is a just reason for the connection of two Medical Men with the Works, but not more than two.

Who these two are to be is a matter that concerns the Workmen, excepting that Dr. Rees has certainly a prior right to being the principal Doctor in the Works.

Should a majority of the Workmen make known to us, through their representatives, a desire that your name should be the second Works Doctor, we should respect it.

Dr. Evans was Dr. Griffiths's son-in-law.

Frank Gilbertson to Dr. Ll. Rees. **19 Aug. 1907 [5 : 517]**

Several people have spoken to me about Nurse Davies since the trouble on Saturday night.

I am inclined to think that it is time for a change.

A Nurse is no good unless she is trusted by all & made use of generally.

Will you please give me your advice if possible today?

Frank Gilbertson to Nurse Davies, Brecon Road. **21 Aug. 1907 [5 : 519]**

We have come to the conclusion that it will be better for you to resign from your position, & start fresh somewhere else.

If you will be good enough to send down to the Office, your salary to date, & also 4 weeks salary in addition, will be ready for you.

Frank Gilbertson to Dr. J. Ll. Rees. 8 Sept. 1909 [7 : 144-5]

When our new Tinplate Works gets into full swing there will be 300 to 400 extra men in our employ & we have also started some extensions to the Steel Works.

Your income from these Works is now larger than it ever has been since the Works started & we think you will have to be prepared for a new condition of affairs.

Dr. Evans has again made application to be allowed an official standing, & if any body of men approach us on his behalf we hardly see how we can refuse, seeing the way the number of men here is likely to increase.

Our own idea is that Dr. Evans should be allowed the same privilege as Dr. Dahne. In that case all newcomers would be put into your list, & only those who make formal application to have their money deducted for Dr. Dahne & Dr. Evans would be outside your list.

This would ensure you a good preference among all newcomers, & it would relieve us of having to ask you to keep an assistant, as we otherwise might have to do when the Tinplate Works is in full swing.

Frank Gilbertson to Dr. W. Owen Evans. 17 Feb. 1910 [7 : 205]

We have decided that in our new Tinplate Works, which is entirely separate from our old Works, any men who desire their contributions to be kept for you may have this done, on signifying their wishes to the Manager, Mr. David Morgan.

With regard to the old Works, we are not prepared to make any alterations without having the wishes of the men expressed through the ordinary channels, their Trades Union Lodges.

We hope that our decision with regard to the new Works will be satisfactory to you.

Frank Gilbertson to Dr. J. Ll. Rees. 17 Feb. 1910 [7 : 206]

A number of men in the old Works have asked to have their contributions collected for Dr. Evans.

We have decided not to accede to their request as the application has not come from the mens' Trades Unions.

With regard to the new Works, which are quite separate, we have decided to give Dr. Evans the same liberty that Dr. Dahne now enjoys in the old Works.

All men in the new Works will be considered your men, unless they individually express a wish to be attended by Dr. Dahne or Dr. Evans.

Cecil Gilbertson to Dr. Ll. Rees. 6 June 1910 [7 : 332]

The following men who are Dippers in our Galvanizing shop have been burnt by explosions in the Galvanizing baths lately. They tell me that the burns are of a deeper & more lasting nature owing to a new sort of flux that we are using.

We cannot see how this can be as the chemical composition of the flux is the same as before.

Would you please let me know whether you consider that their burns are more serious than such as have occurred in the past? Do they take longer to heal? Do they leave a worse permanent mark? The men are Phillip Humphreys, Fred Davies, Amos Davies & Arthur Chilcott.

P. Davies to R. & C. B. Jenkins, Swansea. **27 June 1910 [7 : 343]**

Workmen's Compensation Act – Griffith Lewis

We enclose copies of recent correspondence regarding the above case.

Griffith Lewis met with an accident in our Smelting Shop on February 19th/1906, and has been receiving compensation at the rate of £1/-/- per week until recently when he was given light work for which we paid him 24/- per week.

You will see that we are now asked to pay in addition to his earnings at his present employment a further 50% of the difference between such earnings and his average weekly earnings previous to his accident, and these were over £3/-/- per week for a period of 3 years. Under the circumstances we should prefer to commute this case if possible.

Frank Gilbertson to Morgan Davies, Solicitor, Pontardawe. **10 Aug. 1910 [7 : 374]**

Would you kindly represent us at the Inquest on the poor boy E. Williams who met with a fatal accident last night.

We do not know that more can be done than to express our deep regret at what appears to be an entire accident.

Our Mr. Giddings can tell you how it occurred.

Frank Gilbertson to Dr. Ll. Rees. **6 June 1911 [7 : 581]**

It is so important for Johnnie Roberts not to have any stiffness left in his leg, & his services are so valuable to us that we should like Mr. Brooks to see him, however little it may appear necessary.

It is a case in which I should like to feel that everything possible had been done, & also it is important for us that he should not be away longer than necessary. Would you kindly arrange it?

Frank Gilbertson to J. Aeron Thomas. **12 July 1911 [7 : 620]**

. . . I had meant to write to you before & to tell you that in the course of the year we intend to send you a donation towards the Hospital extensions.

At present I consider we have given as much as I should like our Company to bear, in various charitable objects.

P. Davies to R. & C. B. Jenkins & Lloyd, Swansea. 1 Dec. 1911 [7 : 745]

We have your favour of yesterday, and regret to note that you are unable to come to an arrangement with the British Steel Smelters & Tinplaters Association in the matter of reduced compensation for Thomas, but as he is a strong, healthy individual we are fairly sure we shall be able to offer him some suitable light employment in course of time. At the same time, if you can arrive at a reasonable lump sum payment to pay him off altogether we would not object to this, and intimated our willingness to the British Steel Smelters and Tinplaters Association some time ago to pay such a lump sum, but were confronted with a demand for £300 which we considered quite out of the question, and with a possibility of our being able to find suitable light employment for him, we do not feel inclined to go beyond an amount of about £125.

Frank Gilbertson to C. B. Jenkins. 1 May 1912 [7 : 904-5]

It appears that a Dipper, Watkin Jones, is going over to Neath to give evidence for Ball. He will probably say that he considers it is the boy's duty to do any work he is told to do about the Pot.

Mr. Meager should know his character.

He is a lazy man who undoubtedly orders his boys to do work that is not in their province & is a regular bully to them. He even expects them to fetch him a piece of red hot coke to light his pipe!

It is however absolutely certain that the Boy Ball was not supposed to do any work whatever round the Pot, except to hold the slack of the chain when the Dipper was raising the machine, which he had not even started preparations for when Ball was injured.

The boys in Ball's position are paid day wages, & have no interest in the tonnage or work of the Pots.

All the other men & youths round the Pot, who have work to do at the Pot, are paid piece work.

If Watkin Jones says it was the Boy's duty to touch the machine or to attach the bridle to it, he will be telling a lie, although it is very probable that he has bullied his boy into helping him, at times when the Foreman was not present.

T. J. Ball, aged 17, sustained the accident by going on top of the galvanizing pot to hitch hooks, allegedly on the instructions of dipper W. J. Brown. Following the hearing, P. Davies sent T. J. Ball a cheque for £8..9..5, another for £17..1..2 for his Solicitor, and compensation of 8/11d weekly [7 : 923].

Frank Gilbertson to Messrs R. & C. B. Jenkins. 30 Oct. 1912 [8 : 78-9]

. . . We enclose a letter. T. Thomas died of heart failure 15 or 20 minutes after stopping work.

He was quite active & jolly up to the moment he fell down.

When you are next in Pontardawe perhaps you would telephone for our Mr. Hardy to come across & explain the circumstances. We do not think we are under any liability, but we had already arranged to help the widow by allowing her 6/- a week for 1 year, 5/- for the second & so on for 6 years, as she has sons who will be earning more wages each year.

P. Davies to Edward Harris, Swansea. 27 Dec. 1912 [8 : 135]

We have your favour of the 24th inst regarding accident sustained by Geo Hill. We have given him an opportunity to qualify himself for the position of weigher in our Galvanizing Department, and the light work already performed has been of no advantage to us, he has been learning to perform the duties of weigher along with another man.

As soon as he is able to do the work himself, we will pay the 3/- per day, and also 50% of the difference between that amount and his former wages.

We will pay arrears of compensation provided a receipt is given in full settlement of claim, subject to the memorandum which you propose to place to protect his rights.

Arrears of 14/1d per week were agreed and the daily rate was increased to 3/9. [8 : 144]. Additionally, compensation of 2/10d per week was paid. The injury was "the loss of half of the right thumb, which cannot be a very serious matter . . . we consider he is still capable of doing manual work" [8 : 252]. On 28th June R. & C. B. Jenkins were instructed to offer £20 in full settlement [8 : 253].

Frank Gilbertson to Messrs R. & C. B. Jenkins & Lloyd. 29 March 1913 [8 : 206-9]

We enclose a letter received from Mr. Hodge & copy of our reply.

A test case, with the Union's assurance that the liability of the other men should follow the test case, would be so much the most convenient course to take, that we think you had better wait for Mr. Hodge's next letter.

We are obliged by the information you give & your opinion.

Compensation cases

We often have instances of men, who receive some trifling accident, staying away for the 14 days, & then coming with a Doctor's certificate, signed on the 14th day, certifying that these men were still unable to follow their employment.

In many cases we are wholly convinced that the Doctor has been misled, or that he has given a certificate that he should not have done from sympathy with the Workmen.

Sometimes a Workman will bring one or more certificates given during his absence from work, which we should have liked to have checked if we had known of them before, because we have ample reason to know that some Doctors regard a certificate as a very light document. Can we, by giving any notice, insist that all Doctors' Certificates on which Workmen are going to rely, for compensation claims, must be produced to us within 24 hours, so that we can have the opportunity of sending the Workmen to Dr. Stephens if we think fit?

The fact is that these Certificates have become such a scandal that we want to force a couple of cases into the Courts, to give publicity to the Doctor's actions . . .

P. Davies to R. & C. B. Jenkins & Lloyd. 11 July 1913 [8 : 291]

Replying further to your favour of the 5th inst, we have ascertained that George Hill was insured under the National Insurance Act, in The Loyal Order of Ancient Shepherds, Ashton Unity, meeting at the Public Hall, Pontardawe, Secretary Mr. Lewis Evans.

Frank Gilbertson to Col. Ll. Morgan, Swansea. 29 May 1914 [8 : 635]

I want to bring a matter to your notice that requires careful handling but does call for some change I think in the Hospital Committee's Rules.

Our Workmen contribute handsomely to the Hospital and it would be a mistake to do anything that would given them an excuse for reducing the rate of their subscription, but it does seem very wasteful that Representatives of the men should constantly attend meetings, charging the cost of such attendance against their subscription fund. One of our workmen is now attending practically every week and receives out of the subscription 14/- a day and 1/5d train fare. There is some temptation for such work to be delegated to one who is not in strong health and who prefers to receive 14/- a day for attending a meeting in which he can take little part, for doing a day's work for this wage.

Charles Gilbertson to Herbert Lewis, St. John Ambulance Association, Cardiff. 29 May 1917 [10 : 338]

<u>Private</u>

In reply to your letter, with regard to Clydach.

Mr. Philips, Transport Officer, has told Mr. Player that until the Clydach people make their own arrangements for Transport, we will undertake the work.

But we cannot agree to do this indefinitely, as if Clydach wish to remain out of the joint Union Scheme (which is all to their advantage, and throws a heavier burden on us at Pontardawe, seeing that they only maintain 35 beds at a maximum, leaving 140 beds for us) they must expect to shoulder the burden of transporting their own wounded.

At the moment, as your promised ambulance has not arrived (so far as I know) we have only one ambulance, provided by ourselves. I really do not see how Clydach expect to make use of our Ambulance and Transport facilities, when they refuse to take an equal share in the support of the Union Hospitals.

As a matter of fact, the whole trouble has arisen from the fact that your Association did not make it clear to the local people that they, the local people, would be expected to defray the expenses of the Hospitals. Had this been done, at the start, I believe that there would have been no difficulties.

The only thing that is now necessary is for Clydach to appoint their Transport Officer, and for them to inform you as to what his name and address is, so that he can be communicated with direct, when a draft arrives for the Quarr.

Charles Gilbertson to Colonel Hepburn, 3rd Western General Hospital, Cardiff. **30 Aug. 1917 [10 : 406]**

I am writing to you in my capacity as Chairman of the Committee responsible for supporting and financing the Glanrhyd St. John Hospital in this place.

Our Committee has done everything possible to arouse local enthusiasm in the Hospital, and the people of the place are very anxious to make it a success.

We have been disappointed at the small number of patients which we have received, and it is difficult to make people realize, when there are only a very few of the beds occupied, that it is necessary to raise considerable Funds, in order to run the Hospital finances satisfactorily.

I have never taken it upon myself to approach you in the matter, considering that it was outside my province to do so.

But I am writing to you now, because I hear from the Matron in charge of the Hospital, that you have been informed by someone, that we did not want to have any more patients at present, and that the Hospital was under-going cleaning operations, and for this reason the Hospital was being kept bare of patients.

I think that you will agree that I am entitled to ask from whom you received this information, as it is a matter which touches our committee very closely, and myself personally, seeing that Glanrhyd is our own House, and in conjunction with the Matron and the local Committee, I and my family are anxious to make the best and fullest use of Glanrhyd as a Hospital.

We have spent a good deal of money on the house, to make it suitable for a Hospital, and it is a great disappointment to us to see it made such little use of.

As you possibly know, the local Workhouse Infirmary is also partially prepared as Hospital, and is intended to take from 30 to 40 beds I understand, and although the children have been moved out for the last 3 or 4 months to make room for the Wounded, nothing further has transpired. Our committee is also responsible for these patients, when they arrive.

Glanrhyd House, Pontardawe, adapted for use as an auxiliary hospital, 1917
(West Glamorgan Archive Service)

Frank Gilbertson to Lord Chilston, 83, Pall Mall, London. **13 Feb. 1918 [10 : 514]**

Thank you for seeing me today.

I shall be giving notice to Mr. Herbert Lewis, County Director of the St. John's Association for Glamorgan tomorrow, of my family's withdrawal of Glanrhyd as an Auxiliary Hospital.

You will understand that if any arrangements can be made for transferring Glanrhyd to the Red Cross Authorities, my family will bear all expense of any sort, including, if necessary, purchase of existing equipment or the re-equipment.

If such an arrangement can be made, my family will not withdraw Ynisderw House, which has been placed at the service of the Poor Law Authorities, in order to free the Union Infirmary as a St. John Auxiliary Hospital.

Should a transfer be impossible, Glanrhyd will be offered to the Red Cross Society when vacant.

If the arrangement I suggest can be carried out, the village of Pontardawe will then have one hospital under St. John and one under Red Cross, which will ensure local peace.

V.A.D. Detachments of both organisations exist in Pontardawe, and my daughter, Mrs. Vivian is Commandant of the Red Cross Detachment.

The local Committee, which incurs expenses of £60 and upwards per month, will, no doubt, willingly agree to a proper apportionment of its funds to each hospital, on the basis of the beds in use.

I anticipate no local difficulty, but rather the removal of existing ones.

Glanrhyd has proved an exceptionally popular hospital to the men.

There are in use about 75 beds, and many opportunities for recreation.

The Matron who has recently been driven to resign, Mrs. Royle, has had charge from the commencement, and proved herself to be a most efficient lady, and has given every possible satisfaction to the patients, and to the district, while maintaining excellent discipline.

Voluntary Aid Detachments offered patriotic ladies the opportunity to serve as unpaid nursing orderlies, performing menial but often essential complementary nursing care in hospitals and at the front line.

Frank Gilbertson to the Viscount Chilston. 20 Feb. 1918 [10 : 518]

I am sorry to trouble you again, but a matter has come to my knowledge in connection with the business upon which you gave me an interview last Wednesday that I wish to bring to your notice, and to strongly urge that proper enquiries be made.

You will remember I spoke very highly of the late Matron of the Glanrhyd Auxiliary Hospital, and I felt bound to speak in disparaging terms of the Secretary of the St. David's Centre of the St. John's Association.

Mrs. Moore-Gwyn of Dyffryn, Neath, who is arranging for a new Red Cross Auxiliary Hospital to be opened at Neath, saw Miss Swift in regard to the appointment of Mrs. Royle, the late Matron at Glanrhyd.

Miss Swift informed her that the Secretary of the St. David's Centre had so reported upon the late Matron and staff at Glanrhyd, that their names had been struck off her lists.

If this is so, a most abominable injustice has been done, and I am astonished that such an action should be possible upon the report of a gentleman like Mr. Lewis, without confirmatory evidence.

I will, in the course of a day or two, submit you evidence of an entirely different nature, but I can assure you, personally, that everybody connected with the work in this district, held the very highest opinion of Mrs. Royle and of the staff.

It would be impossible to imagine a hospital in which the patients were more comfortable, and better discipline maintained, and everyone connected with the hospital in this district has expressed the greatest regret that Mrs. Royle and her staff should have been driven to resign.

If the report I hear from Mrs. Moore-Gwyn is correct, I must ask that a proper enquiry be made, and I am sure you will agree with me that the matter cannot remain where it is.

Frank Gilbertson to Hugh M. Ingledew & Sons, Solicitors, 4 Mount Stuart Square, Cardiff. **25 Feb. 1918 [10 : 528]**

Private

. . . I am very sorry, so far as you and I are concerned, that the matter has gone too far for us to reconsider our decision.

I have never had any connection with Mr. Herbert Lewis before, and know nothing about him, but he has made a mistake in the way he has dealt with the affairs of Pontardawe.

My brother and his wife, and also my wife, have taken a good bit of interest in Glanrhyd, and since I have looked into the matter myself, I have become convinced that the opinions they formed were correct.

With quite negligible exceptions, the people in Pontardawe, who have taken an interest in the work, have formed the same conclusions, and, at a fully attended meeting of the local Committee last Friday, a resolution was passed nem.con. cordially approving of the action we had taken.

I think the matter probably started by your people backing the wrong horse in the person of Dr. Evans who does not make for peace in any direction at any time, and Mr. Lewis backed him against the very excellent Matron who was first appointed to Glanrhyd.

You will notice that we have taken no action in regard to Ynysderw House, so that as soon as Glanrhyd can be started under the Red Cross Society, it will be possible for the adherents of St. John and of the Red Cross to work their own hospital independently, and I will use my influence as far as I can, to ensure equitable distribution of local funds.

After the Hospital has been closed, but not before, I should be perfectly willing, if the Committee wished me to do so, to attend before them, and discuss the matter, but as we are quite determined, with the cordial support of the Local Committee, to transfer the Hospital to the Red Cross, if the latter will accept our offer. I am not prepared to discuss the matter before.

I shall be in London on Thursday morning, staying at the Great Western Hotel, and shall be disengaged until 10:45, but I little doubt whether, from your point of view, it would be wise for me to see Sir Owen Phillips. I will, however, do so if you would like me to, either with you or with you and Mr. Herbert Lewis, but you must understand that since I have become involved in this matter, I have formed unfavourable impressions of Mr. Herbert Lewis' methods and our relations will not be cordial.

I am inclined to think that you have not formed quite the correct impression when you say that Cardiff relied too much on the Local Committee, and did not exercise sufficient supervision over the internal management of the hospital.

You may, of course, have been misled by reports from Mr. Evans, but my view is that St. John did not attach sufficient importance to the views of the Local Committee, and, as I said before, backed the wrong horse.

I may say that I did not take the strong action I did until I had satisfied myself that it would meet with the fullest approval of the great majority of the Committee, of both the Doctors, other than Dr. Evans, of the more responsible of the Clergy and Ministers, and the Labour Leaders in the place, and public opinion here is quite solidly behind us.

You will of course understand that this storm in a teacup has to be dealt with, but the sooner I can relieve myself of any added work, the better I shall be pleased, and that nothing that has transpired, or may transpire, must be allowed to interrupt the friendly relations that exist between yourself and myself.

Chapter 8

A COMPANY VILLAGE

With the industrialisation of Britain the mill, the pit or the manufactory became the dominant influence in the dependent settlement which coalesced about it. Basic survival needs could be satisfied only by a commitment to the work demands of the owner-manager or his agent who came to exercise considerable power and authority in such closed and often remote communities. Owners, managers, workers and their families were obliged to live in close proximity, and class segregation became difficult if not impossible to maintain. Daily contact between management and workers, and their respective families, extended into every area of community life to a degree which would have been considered socially unacceptable in the more contractual and functionally specific relationships which typified urban factories. In these solidaristic environments a belief in social duty was more easily accepted, whilst shared experiences both inside and outside work would have served to heighten the awareness of some owners and managers of their social responsibilities.

In many ways, their works replaced the parish as the basis of social organisation. In 1847 a government enquiry into Welsh education stated that "when parishes were first instituted, it was every man's interest to think what parish he belonged to, because his rights of relief, employment, and redress, were all parochial or manorial, so now does the same interest make him think of these or those works, and not at all, or very remotely, of the parish. In the works is his sick fund, sometimes his benefit society; in the works is his hope of employment; in the works (by a tolerated system of fining) is his ordinary court of justice".[1] In such a context the employee saw the works master in much the same way as his ancestors would have regarded their manorial lord, and their communities became "the industrial analogues of the rural estates."[2] Thirty years later, James Shaw, one of William Gilbertson's successors at the Cwmavon Works, wrote to *The Times* about what he called 'Patriarchal Administration in Wales' and admitted that "The fiat of my predecessors, as of myself, is final, whether it be in great matters or in small . . . I am not ambitious of playing the part of a petty German Potentate of past years. I would infinitely rather that the inhabitants managed their own paving, lighting, gas, water and sanitary arrangements; but I have asked them to do so in vain. I am completely puzzled as to the future – shrinking from all this responsibility, yet powerless to escape it . . . Nevertheless, it is despotism".[3] Not only did the owner-manager inherit the prevailing ideology of authority, but community expectations could be met only if he assumed the obligations inherent in his status.

On the occasion of Frank Gilbertson's marriage in 1896, a local columnist, with a touch of hyperbole, referred grandly to Pontardawe as "The model little town", adding that it was "the creation of the Gilbertson family".[4] The letters selected for this chapter reflect the heterogeneous range of community issues which attracted the interest and involvement of Arthur Gilbertson and his sons, and include commentary on the local gas company, the post office, electricity and water supplies, pollution, housing and leases, the inadequacy of roads and the extension of the railway system. This chapter, together with the following two chapters, show how they interpreted their community roles and attempted to fulfil their responsibilities.

Arthur Gilbertson to D. B. Turberville, Solicitor. 3 Dec. 1890 [1 : 39]

I think the time has come when Pontardawe Town ought to be lighted with gas.

When I resigned the Chairmanship of the Gas Works, I think the "reserve fund" to pay off the Mortgage amounted to £200. I believe the present management have eaten up this reserve & more!

I can only imagine that after next Balance Sheet (end of this year) "Liquidation" must ensue.

What is to be done? or the shops, churches, etc. will be in darkness. Supposing the Company could be increased and put in working order, until "Gas Rate" for lighting streets &c be made?

The Pontardawe Gas Company had been registered as a limited company in 1869 with Arthur Gilbertson as its Chairman. He had later resigned from this position although he retained his shareholding.

J. P. Davies for Arthur Gilbertson to Messrs The Pontardawe Gas Co. Ltd. 15 Jan. 1891 [1 : 62]

I wish to transfer the following shares held by me in your company.

No. 79 to John Philip Davies

No. 80 to Oliver Adams

& I enclose transfers & the Share certificates. Kindly issue fresh certificates.

Arthur Gilbertson to D. B. Turberville. 31 Jan. 1891 [1 : 68]

I enclose your Balance Sheet of the Pontardawe Gas Co., in which I am a shareholder. Messrs. Davies & Adams my Clerk are also shareholders & will attend Meeting on Monday night. Can you attend on my behalf? I wish to know how the late Secretary became possessed of the £125..15..11?

I enclose copy of letter to Auditor.

Is the Company solvent?

Arthur Gilbertson to Samuel Taylor. 31 Jan. 1891 [1 : 69]
Auditor, 5 Castle Street, Swansea.

Pontardawe Gas Co.

Referring to the Articles of Association, are the Directors justified in making personal loans to the Co? and are they justified in allowing the late Secretary to hold at any time such a sum as £125..15..11? How could it arise in such a small affair?

J. P. Davies to D. Smith, Agent to H. Lloyd, Alltwen. 2 Feb. 1891 [1 : 70]

Mr. Gilbertson has instructed Mr. Turberville to attend at the Gas Meeting this evening on his behalf & Mr. Turberville has suggested that you should be asked to attend. Will you kindly do so? Mr. Gilbertson wants to know how L. Evans got such a sum in Cash in his hands as is shown on the balance sheet & if the Company is solvent.

Arthur Gilbertson to D. B. Turberville. 11 Feb. 1891 [1 : 75]

I dont care to bother myself further about the Gas Works, but think it best to let them go on to "collapse" naturally. It would not be wise to turn out the present Directors. Let them solve their own muddles.

Thanking you for attending for me.

Arthur Gilbertson to D. Jones & Co., Bank, Llanelly. 26 Feb. 1891 [1 : 87]

One of our Workmen named David Morris has separated from his Wife apparently.

The Mother-in-Law (Mary Davies) we understand became "Surety" to yourselves for a loan of £140 to the said David Morris. He has now sold the House to another man, it is said for £200.

We have tried to heal the breach, but without success, but thought it best to let you know what we have gathered, so as to protect the surety.

Arthur Gilbertson to J. James, Secretary, 3 Feb. 1892 [1 : 170]
Pontardawe Gas Works.

Beyond being interested generally in the well-being of Pontardawe, I am not interested in the Gas Works as a Consumer.

Dr. G. Griffiths seems mixed up in the Company as a lender of money, while being a Director – I cannot have any communications with him.

It seems to me you should go to your County Councillor for assistance, who is interested as a Gas Consumer, and I conclude a representative of the Executors of the late Mr. G. Lewis.

Arthur Gilbertson to J. James. 8 Feb. 1892 [1 : 172]

. . . Dr. Griffiths having ceased to be a Director, does not absolve him from transactions carried out by him. Probably the Mortgagee will require ultimately an explanation as regards Mr. Hedley, it clearly is more his part than mine, to take up the matter and he can act for his Wife or qualify by taking shares from the Executors.

If I were a Director I should acquaint the Bankers & the Mortgagees of the position of things and invite the County Councillor to call a Meeting of the Inhabitants and point out to them that unless they did something, the Town would be in darkness.

Arthur Gilbertson to J. James. 12 Feb. 1892 [1 : 176]

Yours of yesterday. If you cannot get Mr. Hedley to help, I see nothing for it but to wind up the Company.

You ought to forewarn the Principal users of Gas, if you decide upon that step.

Arthur Gilbertson to Herbert Lloyd. 6 May 1893 [1 : 239]

Siding for Cinders is progressing well now & Surveyor is making a "Plan" of this additional piece of ground, and piece for Reading Room & Gymnasium, which I will take up to London next week, and consult our Solicitor whether we shld. have a Lease, or an agreement, & as soon as this is settled, we can pay the entire sum for Bridge, which will be equivalent to purchasing the extra land, as a 99 years Lease, I think.

Water supply for drinking. Our Workpeople keep applying for this & Sanitary Board "put it off", so I am thinking of putting a pipe from our supply opposite Baptist Chapel to the Works, but this would leave no water for outsiders.

I am going to bring water from Glanrhyd to Primrose Row, temporarily, at my own expense at once.

Arthur Gilbertson to Herbert Lloyd. 8 May 1893 [1 : 240]

Thank you for your letter & that of 17th ulto. from Mr. Hedley, apparently written on behalf of Primrose Coal Co. You would observe he does not name the old Road nor would his reply bind the Primrose Co. He is very crafty!

However, I will close the old Road, as soon as new is completed, and if I were you, I would not settle a Lease for Primrose Wharf, until the above has been done.

Water Supply. You need not trouble, I have got a splendid supply to Primrose Row today from Glanrhyd thro' my old Gas Pipes, but it wont be fit to drink for a few days & I am arranging drinking water for this district, with Artesian Pumps & "lift" to cross Canal, to water supply from Level under Dan-y-Graig & shall expect a vote of thanks from Sanitary Authority!!

Hope you will have a pleasant trip.

Arthur Gilbertson to Barlow & James, Solicitors. 2 June 1893 [1 : 242]

. . . You are right, the Reading Room is already on our Leasehold so we only have to deal with the additional piece marked Brown which Mr. Lloyd gives us on Lease, without rent, on our paying him £80 extra, for additional cost of New Bridge.

Must a Lease or agreement be drawn up?

Arthur Gilbertson to David Bowen, Gellyonen Uchaf. 27 Sept. 1894 [2 : 20]

I want to take up land to build a block of 2 Cottages, facing Swansea road on Trebanws Farm, and to plant a ring of Trees round the field next . . . I wont inconvenience you in any way, and of course allow for land taken up.

My son, Mr. Frank, would show you what I want.

The Cottages will be adjoining those now built.

Arthur Gilbertson to S. B. Barlow. 5 Dec. 1894 [2 : 37-8]

I enclose further letter from Sir Douglas Fox & copy my reply, also a humbugging letter from Mr. Randall to which I dont reply.

Douglas Fox was fellow Pupil with my brother in law Russell Lloyd, and Douglas Fox's son was down here surveying: he only made Lloyd's acquaintance at the end of his visit, and Lloyd afterwards told me (I conclude from conversation with young Fox) that some one connected with the scheme, thought it fun to spite me! Anyway, the proposed railway simply ruins my Cwm, and my two Villas of Cwmdu & Gwynfa are within the "line of deviation" and the surrounding banks are to be cut down, and carried away, to form filling for an enormous embankment all up the Cwm to my waterfall. I got this information from Mr. Morgan, our Highway Board Surveyor who is preparing tracings of the plans for me. He says the two Villas and the whole Cwm will simply be destroyed.

Sir Douglas Fox evidently knows nothing about it, as I cannot imagine he would make a false statement. Randall I dont trust in the least.

I think now I shall ask you to call on Sir Douglas Fox, or write to him.

I must oppose it, in toto, or get very heavy damages.

I propose going on with additions to Cwmdu Lodge in the Spring, for my Son's residence – there is absolutely no other spot.

I dont know who the Promoters are? I think myself, the extension of the Railway, over Ynisderw upon an enormous viaduct, and the viaduct tunnels &c in my Cwm, render the project absurd. At an interview you might learn what reality there is about it.

Arthur Gilbertson to S. B. Barlow. 13 Dec. 1894 [2 : 39-40]

. . . Sir Douglas Fox has given you quite a wrong impression – the railway is to go up the right Bank of the river (not the left, as he told you) i.e. looking up the Cwm, against the flow of the river if you look at my plan (tracing). You will see both Gwynfa & Cwmdu Lodge will be destroyed. They are built on the edge of a precipice, along which surface cutting is to go.

The Cwm will simply be destroyed and it is my only freehold building ground.

I think you should at once let Fox know this.

Please kindly understand the matter is of great importance to me.

The Works siding is not my private affair and is of doubtful expediency for W. Gilbertson & Co. Ltd., for several reasons too lengthy to go into now.

I enclose notices received today: kindly advise me as to replies. I object "in toto", and must oppose.

Fox seems to have omitted to tell you why I was not consulted on the spot, as the chief Landowner and as to Lean's explanation, it is simply a lie, it was well known to him, that the right side of Cwm (looking up river) and both sides further up, are mine.

Kindly look over the correspondence & papers I sent you.

There are no "ancient" footpaths (see Lean's excuse). I made the Paths & Bridges rustic for my own use.

The Neath, Pontardawe and Brynamman Railway Bill proposed a twelve-mile connecting line, including a viaduct 500 yards long and 90 feet high over the Swansea Valley, a tunnel 500 yards long and a viaduct 89 feet high over the Upper Clydach at Cwmdu.

Arthur Gilbertson to S. B. Barlow. **3 Jan. 1895 [2 : 44-5]**

Your wire to hand. I have had now some weeks to think over this proposed Railway, and to consult with capable men knowing the District well. We are of opinion the line might be made from Neath to Pontardawe, but we dont see enough traffic to make it pay. The extension from Pontardawe to Brynamman, seeing cost of viaducts, tunnels & compensation, and the small amount of traffic to be gained is simply absurd: what coal there is, is problematical & quality also.

I dont believe this latter portion will find people foolish enough to support it.

The idea of a Hydraulic lift for our Works traffic (120 Trucks daily of 12 Tons each) is absurd, and we decline any connection with our Works.

As regards my Cwm, your blue line would save "Cwmdu Lodge" (which is about to be enlarged) but you would cross the Highway at the back & get into Mr. Jeffreys property, which I imagine is not applied for in line of deviation?

I returned cards "dissenting".

I believe the Promoters are men of straw & simply Speculators.

Please dont go to any expense which can be avoided, as I dont believe the line can be made in my Cwm, and I should not get expenses paid, for interviews with Douglas Fox &c.

The Midland Ry. will of course oppose – a man named Daniel [?] Thomas, I believe with a little Colliery on way to Neath, is absolutely without means, and a most plausible Humbug, and utterly unreliable. I think he is a prime mover.

Arthur Gilbertson to Sir Douglas Fox, Bart, London. 8 Jan. 1895 [2 : 48]

I understand from Mr. Barlow, you will be visiting Wales and I should be very glad if you would spend a couple of nights here. I can show you & tell you more about the locality than most people, as I have lived here 34 years.

I must tell you I am entirely against the Railway project, but you might perhaps like to hear my views on the spot.

Arthur Gilbertson to S. B. Barlow. 9 April 1895 [2 : 270, 276-7]

Thanks for your letter. Sir Douglas Fox & my brother-in-law, Russell Lloyd, were articled Pupils to Sir Charles Fox together. When Douglas heard how I had been treated he wrote to express regret and offered a visit of explanation, at same time promising he would give me time to oppose, if I desired to do this; he put off his visit several times, and forgot his promise about time to oppose in the Commons (this shows he is somewhat a "broken reed"!) but he stayed here last night & was very friendly. I walked him over my Cwm and pointed out the House I specially wish to save – he now sees another route might have been taken under Mr. Jeffreys land, merely cutting thro' my Cwm, at North pine end of "Gwynfa" (red brick house). I think you also suggested this, but as I told you it went beyond the line of deviation, and Mr. Jeffreys is a man who would rather see my property carved up, than his, altho it would damage me, and not him. Sir Douglas now sees the incivility of Lawyer Randall & the Surveyors, in not consulting me, has lead them into adopting a doubtful route thro' dangerous ground, and ruining the picturesqueness of part of my Cwm. Sir Douglas will now report to his Employers, and seems inclined to try to arrange with Howel Jeffreys – meanwhile no offer is made me, and Sir Douglas says he is only Engineer. He says I can yet oppose in the Lords, and he would explain the non-opposition in Commons was his fault.

You know I want to save this cost & anxiety – having very much to attend to, and it occurs to me whether you should not now approach the Promoters for an offer? I think £3,000, as the houses have cost £1,000 – the building site will be destroyed, and part of the "Cwm" shaken to pieces & spoilt. As regards the section Neath to Pontardawe, I dont care to oppose that. They can come to our Works, if they chose, but I doubt the possibility of working the traffic, and we dont want them.

Fox says the opposition in Lords, would be just as good as in Commons.

Any way, no further delay must take place now.

When I say £3,000, I dont see my way to share it, and perhaps with view to a split, we should say £4,000, in first instance. Jeffreys charges £150 an acre for his land adjoining & my Cwm is 15 acres.

Arthur Gilbertson to S. B. Barlow. **11 April 1895 [2 : 80-1]**

. . . I should be very sorry to think Sir Douglas Fox came here for hospitality, meaning to hoodwink me. I am glad you are writing him what I have reported to you. I conclude the Bill has not gone before Committee yet? First of all, I want them to go out of my Cwm (merely crossing it at end of Gwynfa – red house) & then to tunnel under Gellygron Farm, on northern side of Highway. (I send you "Bill" Promoters on page 3). If this route were adopted, £1,000 for Gwynfa House & £750 for spoiling & taking up land & interfering with the "amenities" (to use Fox's word) would do – but if they adhere to present line of deviation, they ruin also Cwmdu Lodge upon which I am now spending £1,000 in addition to its original cost of £500, and with the additional severance & destruction of property & building sites & absolute damage to the Picturesqueness of my residential property, another £750 must be added, making £4,000 in all – I told Fox, I could not delay developing my building property, while they were delaying & that the £1,000 would be spent this Summer – he said the sooner you go on the better – they must pay you for any damage to buildings.

Arthur Gilbertson to S. B. Barlow. **17 May 1895 [2 : 88-9]**

Glanrhyd purchase of freehold, and cost of House, Lodge, Stables, gardens, &c is about £7,000. The Cwm as you know forms part of the "amenities" (as Fox called it) and affects the "letting" or selling value of my property – the Cwm is laid out with paths, rustic Bridges & specimen trees & is 15 acres on the side of the river to be affected by the Railway. Mr. Jeffreys, the adjoining Landlord now asks £150 per acre for his land.

I enclose particulars of my outlay. You see a large sum is involved, or indirectly affected.

No doubt you remember my letters to you of 9th & 11th. April, but additions to Cwmdu Lodge are now in progress.

Glanrhyd property, House, Lodge, Stables, Glass Houses, gardens, ornamental water &c.	£ 7,000..0..0
"Cwm" the 15 acres affected by Railway @ £150 per acre	£ 2,250..0..0
"Gwynfa House" in Cwm – cost	£ 750..0..0
Cwmdu Lodge in Cwm, cost, and	£ 500..0..0
foundations are now made, and contract signed for outlay	£ 1,250..0..0
Orchard, cost, with clearing, fencing	

& walling £ 150..0..0

£11,900..0..0

Arthur Gilbertson to S. B. Barlow **2 July 1896 [2 : 246-8]**

1st You know all the facts, what do you advise me to do? It is no good wasting money & trouble if we have taken up an untenable position.

2nd You have sent me two copies of the same thing, viz Defence of Jno. Harris, why?

3rdly You have not sent a copy of Statement of Claim!

4thly What does Harris mean by saying I am not owner of Cwmdu? & not entitled to Riparian rights?

5thly The Duke of Beaufort as Lord of the Manor claims rights to make Weirs on the river, but surely I have right to flow of water, altho the Tucking Mill may have right to "pond"?

6thly Supposing Jno Harris's statement in clause 3 is correct as to 40 years, does that give him power to continue "pollution"? Does not his letter saying he is taking steps to stop Pollution give him the lie?

7thly Does not his letter also give the lie to his statement under clause 4?

8thly Did my letter saying I would be satisfied if the Dye were turned into the River at night, give me away?

9thly If I fail, can the District Council, or County Council, tackle Harris, under Pollution of Rivers Act?

10thly Counsel's opinion refers to John Jones Defence – I have no copy of J. Jones Defence!

11thly "Easement to Pollute" (Counsel's opinion) altho no doubt this pollution has increased greatly, since new machinery put up, I have no means of proving what it was before, and plenty of Welsh Liars will be found, to swear it is not increased.

12thly I conclude my Conveyance of the Estate & plan would be sufficient (see Counsel's opinion).

13thly But how can Defendant throw over his letter (you have it) admitting all, by "asking time" to remedy the nuisance?

Kindly answer these seriatim. It seems to me if I go on, I must employ a local Solicitor (Bevan Jenkins) to get up evidence for you?

If we lost the case, what might it cost us?

Arthur Gilbertson to Post Master, Swansea. **12 Jan. 1897 [1 : 498]**

We feel the time has come, when this place should have a Post Office & a Post Master, whose business it shall be to attend to the Post Office alone. Only a few days ago a telegram was wrongly sent in, to extent of £150. Letters are daily [delayed?]. There is no room, in the present little place for the men Messengers, and when Mails come in, the place is blocked simply.

It so happens the Writer has never once seen the Sub-postmaster in the Post Office!

What steps should be taken to get a proper Post Office and Post Master whose duty shall be to attend to it?

A post office, run by shopkeeper John Owen, had originally been established in Pontardawe in 1848. Kelly's Directory for 1895 (p.755) refers to "an Express Delivery & Annuity & Insurance Office" in Pontardawe with Esiah Jordan as postmaster.

Arthur Gilbertson to Post Master, Swansea. **15 Jan. 1897 [1 : 490]**

. . . It is no use our giving particulars & receiving the stereotyped apology.

Arthur Gilbertson to Post Master, Swansea. **18 Jan. 1897 [1 : 491]**

. . . when a matter of £150 is at stake & other serious matters, it is no help to us, to hear "the party in fault has been reprimanded". The "copy" (impress) of the message handed you at Swansea was quite clear & correct.

We cannot see how the girl here, can give proper attention in a small Box of a Room, with several young men (Postmen) lounging about.

Would it be any use if we got Sir J. T. D. Llewellyn, to back up our desire for a proper & separate Office?

J. P. Davies to Messrs R. P. Morgan & David, Neath. **24 Feb. 1897 [1 : 494]**

Please prepare a Lease for 15 perches of land let to Essex Davies of Graig Trebanos, Blockman, for 99 years from Sept 29th <u>1895</u> at a yearly rent of £1..2..6, also a Lease to Llewelyn Salmon, Graig Trebanos, Blockman, the same in every respect, for one cottage each. The cottages have been built.

Arthur Gilbertson to James Evans, Ystalyfera. **11 Aug. 1898 [2 : 355-6]**

A letter dated the 10th inst, written on paper with a printed heading "James Evans", but without any signature has been sent to me.

I can say at once none of my Sons make use of disgusting language, or would say an untruth for any consideration.

My Son said he had been dining at Mr. Moores & you evidently did not hear correctly. My son was under the impression that the very reasonable rule, that traps should have lights at night applied to Breconshire, as well as Glamorganshire, but there now seems a doubt if this is the case. I will see that the matter of lights is brought before the Court at Brecon.

Should there not be a law as regards lights. My Son, who nearly had an accident from your trap, in the dark, was not absolutely justified in stopping your Horse, and regrets that he did so.

Frank Gilbertson to J. G. Harris, High Street. **8 July 1901 [3 : 322]**

In reply to your enquiry we would, subject to our Landlord's consent, sell the 2 little cottages in Herbert Street for 26 years purchase, which equals £331..10..0. And we would brush off the £31..10..0, so as to leave £300, with which we should have to build 2 new cottages elsewhere.

Frank Gilbertson to Richard Davies, The Emporium, Llanelly. **29 July 1901 [3 : 352]**

We understand you are willing to pay £300 for the two small cottages in Herbert Street.

We accept this sum, subject to your arranging with our Landlord, Herbert Lloyd Esq., Plas Cilybebyll, who informs us he is prepared to grant you a new lease at the usual ground rent subject to your satisfying him as to the plans of the building you intend erecting.

Arthur Gilbertson to Richard Davies. **24 Aug. 1901 [3 : 390]**

Our Landlord has consented to our selling you the Cottages, for you to pull them down, and erect a good Shop, on the site.

Our Lawyer must make the surrender on our Lease, and Mr. Lloyd's Solicitor must make your Lease.

On hearing from you, this shall be carried out.

Arthur Gilbertson to D. Smith, Alltwen. **27 Sept. 1901 [3 : 435]**

Please see enclosed from R. Davies & Co. & return it to us.

We are rather sorry an arrangement cannot be made, as the Cottages proposed to be pulled down, are not very creditable to the Village.

Frank Gilbertson to John Morgan, Engineer & Surveyor. **8 Jan. 1902 [3 : 520]**

We enclose the Neath & Brynamman Railway Bill sent us this morning. Will you please act for us in the matter? We shall have to see our Works sidings &c, and water-ways, are not interfered with, & that proper sidings be arranged for our Works.

Also we wish to know how far Mr. Gilbertson's property will be interfered with in the valley of the Upper Clydach, through his Cwm.

Will you please see the plans which we suppose are now deposited at the District Council office & report to us thereon?

Arthur Gilbertson to Messrs Barlow & Barlow, London. **30 Jan. 1902 [3 : 531]**

We enclose report from Mr. J. Morgan, our Surveyor, and plans, & copy of our letter to him.

What he states about the Railway as affecting our Works property is quite correct.

We conclude you will hear from the Solicitors of the Railway – if not, please take any step you think advisable for our interest, or Mr. A. Gilbertson's, asking payment of expenses.

Arthur Gilbertson to John Morgan. **30 Jan. 1902 [3 : 532]**

Thank you for your report of yesterday, re proposed Railway, which you brought to us. We told you the matter is entirely in the hands of our Solicitor, Mr. S.B. Barlow, 165 Fenchurch Street, and that nothing could be discussed by us, with Mr. Jockney, but that you might point out to him, that if they entered into Mr. A. Gilbertson's property at Gwynfa, – not damaging Glynteg or Stables, and tunnelling under Gellygron, something might be arranged.

Arthur Gilbertson to Henry Miers, Ynyspenllwch, Clydach. **9 June 1902 [4 : 37]**

Excuse my delay, I have been very busy & away.

I dont like a road over Gwrachllynau to a Quarry – please make your road in Coedgwillym Wood, which is not my property.

Quarry proposed on Trebanws Farm, by Rees Williams – I find my "conveyance" say damages by "arbitration" – if this Quarry is worked, the stone must be taken away by the Pheasant Bush Lane, and I think £5..0..0 a year should be paid me for spoiling my surface – this should hold good for a certain period, and if this is accepted by you, my Lawyer shall draw up an agreement.

Arthur Gilbertson to Rees Williams. **n.d. [c. 20 July 1902] [4 : 50]**

Mr. Miers says that as I only bought the surface of Trebanws & Gwrachllynau, the Stone quarry belongs to Mr. Gueret with the coal. I am not certain he is right about the stone, but I dont want my surface damaged, if the stone is not mine, and I am not anxious that building should go on now. I believe when the Electric trams come up, my property will become more valuable. To help Mr. Miers, when he sold his property, I gave a ridiculous amount for the Farms, they dont pay me 2 per cent.

Llangavelach Parish **- Schedule A Assessments**

No.	Description of Property		Rateable Value		
817	1 Cottage	E. Suff	7	10	-
818	"	J.H. Elias	8	6	-
819	"	S. Ryall	3	6	-
820	"	Evan Davies	6	14	-
821	"	Rees R. Williams	7	10	-
1013-1014	Tin Works		1,125	-	-
1041	Steel Works		666	14	-
1187	Sheet Mills		135	8	-
778/787	10 Cottages	Primrose Row	57	10	-
806 + 1048	Ynysderw House + Garden		28	-	-
810	Ynysderw Farm		59	-	-
811	1 Cottage	A. Richards	6	14	-
812	"	J. Evans	8	16	-
813	"	R. Grummery	4	4	-
815	Danygraig		27	10	-
816	1 Cottage	T. Lloyd	6	14	-
			2,158	16	-
	Llanguicke Parish				
133/4	Cottages	Herbert Street	22	10	-
304/31	"	Thomas " }	56	10	-
"	"	Arthur " }			
548	Ynysderw	Meadow	8	13	-
692	Gwynfa House		11	13	-
			99	6	-
		Total £	2,258	2	-

P. Davies to J. W. Symons, Surveyor of Taxes, Swansea. **7 July 1902 [3 : 678]**

Frank Gilbertson to John Morgan, Surveyor & District Council Engineer. **13 Feb. 1903 [3 : 791]**

Following our interview, we confirm our request that you will carry out the necessary drain connections for our houses in Thomas St, Arthur St & Herbert St at the Schedule prices given us.

Kindly also arrange for the building of the necessary closets at £6..10..0 each.

Please consider this to apply to Mr. Gilbertson's houses in High St. also.

Frank Gilbertson to John Morgan. **14 Feb. 1903 [3 : 792]**

The Writer visited Thomas St. yesterday & was surprised to find that the present closets were as substantial as they are. Please therefore alter the arrangement we made, & cancel our order for the building of new closets in Arthur St & Thomas St with the exception of any cases where the existing closets are wooden – kindly have all connections carried out as arranged.

Arthur Gilbertson to T. Mansel Franklen, Glamorgan County Council Offices, Cardiff. **11 March 1903 [3 : 802-3]**

Your favour of yesterday. We, and the Writer, are anxious to do anything to facilitate the Light Railway.

On the plan sent us, we notice House (112) must come down, and old Turnpike House (111D) – we conclude these would be valued?

Trees on 113. This is really a nice avenue, and the inhabitants of Pontardawe make use of it. Mr. Herbert Lloyd, our Landlord, saw the Writer about it, as he & us are anxious the Trees should not be cut down, and Mr. Lloyd was going to suggest to your Council that a retaining wall should be made by the Trees, and we said the Council could have our Steel Works Slag, to build up the wall, free.

We should not ask anything for our interest in the land given up, if we were paid for the two Cottages and the Trees were spared.

Arthur Gilbertson to Gwillym Lewis, Grocer, Herbert Street, Pontardawe. **10 Dec. 1903 [4 : 135-6]**

I was surprised to get your Book this morning saying I owe you £6..2..6. I knew I paid you a cheque since the date 1901. I had the trouble to look over my cheque ends, I find I paid you £1..11..8 up to date on Jany. 22, 1902 & you did not credit this amount. Under these circumstances, I cannot allow you to supply anything unless cash is paid for the articles.

From this date, I give you notice I will not pay for book debts – I cant be bothered with this. If any of our Servants ask for articles, you must say, they must pay cash.

Frank Gilbertson to Messrs R. & C. B. Jenkins. **4 Dec. 1906 [5 : 402-3]**

The Canal Engineer of the GWR wishes us to sign an agreement with respect to a new doorway we are making in our wall, on to the towing path.

This is merely in substitution for an old doorway which has been in use for 60 years so far as we know.

He also wished us to sign an agreement for openings in the wall bordering the Cricket ground. This we have done, as after consulting Mr. Herbert Lloyd, we came to the conclusion that the wall, though built by us, was on the GWR property. But in the case of an opening in our Works wall we are disinclined to enter into an agreement.

The Wall is ours, & the towing path has been in use as a right of way by our Workmen since the works was built.

If we sign the agreement, we admit the power of the GWR to close the entrance by giving notice, & our idea is that some customary right to an entrance from the towing path must now exist.

Will you please advise us, & correspond with Mr. H. Saunders on our behalf.

Cecil Gilbertson to Inspector J. Gibbon. 11 June 1907 [5 : 482]

I have been told that Dealers in old clothes etc. are in the habit of remaining in Ynisderw Road near Syd Richards' House, & that they are often there after dark.

Syd Richards is a Blacksmith in our Works, & my Informant although possessing no definite proof is rather suspicious of him. Possibly one of your men might make some enquiries as to the object of the frequent visits made by these Dealers.

Frank Gilbertson to Jack Lloyd. 26 Oct. 1908 [5 : 864-5]

Would you have any objection to getting Charles Thomas to insert the advertisement below in 1 or 2 Building Papers & 1 or 2 Daily Local Papers?

If you would agree we would pay the cost, as the object would be to assist us.

If you agree I suggest that the advertisement be inserted immediately.

> "To Builders. A new Tinplate Works is in course of erection at Pontardawe in the Swansea Valley. A large influx of Workmen is expected & new houses will be required. An opportunity is offered to Builders who are in want of work. Application for suitable sites should be made to the Cilybebyll Estate Office, Pontardawe RSO, Glamorgan."

We would much prefer not being compelled to build ourselves, but unless at least 50 new houses are built within the next 12 months, we shall be in a difficulty.

P. Davies to Messrs J. M. Leeder & Son, Swansea. 23 Jan. 1908 [5 : 949-50]

We beg to enclose Schedule of Rents receivable from our tenants & which, with the exception of one, are to be included in our new lease.

Schedule of Rents receivable from:

Name of Occupier			
Philip Davies	Danygraig House	Rent Free	
Samuel Williams	Primrose Row	11 14 –	Tenant pays Poor Rate
Emma Sinfield	"	7 16 –	do

William Jones	"	6	10	–	do
Thos. Thomas	"	6	10	–	do
Thos. Lloyd	"	7	16	–	do
John Jones	"	Free			
William Richards	"	6	10	–	do
John Lewis	"	Free			
Sarah Francis	"	6	10	–	do
John Jones	Herbert Street	16	5	–	
Mary Ann Jarman	"	5	4	–	
John Grubb	"	7	16	–	
Geo H. Jones	Ynisderw Farm	9	2	–	
Thos. Jones	"	7	16	–	
Rev. J. Rowland Thomas	Ynisderw House	20	–	–	
Sarah George	Old Tollgate House	3	–	–	
Thos. Lloyd	Ynisderw Lodge	5	4	–	
Jno. Harris	"	6	10	–	
Edwin Suff	Nr. Tollgate House	9	2	–	
Jas. Barrow	"	11	14	–	
*Evan Davies	Swansea Road	7	16	–	

*Not to be included in new lease

P. Davies to R. & C. B. Jenkins, Solicitors, Swansea. **23 March 1909 [5 : 1003]**

Mrs. Alice Lewis, High Street, Pontardawe has fallen in arrears in payment of ground rent to our Mr. Arthur Gilbertson and we shall be glad if you will write to her pressing for payment. We give you particulars of amounts due at foot, and in need you may proceed against her for recovery of these amounts.

To 1 year's ground rent of Cottage due Dec 31st/06	£1..14..0
Paid on account Dec 9th/07	6..0
	£1.. 8..0
To 1 year's ground rent due Dec 31st/07	£1..14..0
" 1 " " " " Dec 31st/08	£1..14..0
	£4..16..0

Frank Gilbertson to J. H. P. Lloyd. **2 April 1909 [7 : 4-5]**

Replying to yours of yesterday, we give below the rents we have been receiving in respect of the properties you name, which we are not including in our new lease. We understand the rent payable under the new lease will be £700 per annum, & the lease will include some of the property now in the occupation of the Primrose Coal Co.

Will you please let us know if we are correct in thinking we are to have the whole of the Primrose premises this side of the river, & that the Primrose Co. will become our tenants for their offices?

We wish to express our thanks to Mr. Herbert Lloyd for granting us a larger and longer lease, & we are quite satisfied that the method adopted, of employing the most capable surveyor in Swansea to value all our interests, was the fairest possible way of arriving at our new rental.

With regard to the meadow at Rhydyfro we should like to take this at a yearly rental of £12, but not to be included in the lease. Is this agreeable to you?

		pr. annum			**Collected to**
Evan Davies	Cottage Swansea Rd	£7 16/-	& rates payable	monthly	Mch 13
Edwin Suff	Land	£4	"	quarterly	" 25
David Lewis	do	£5	"	"	" "
Jno Jones	Cottage Herbert St	£16 5/-	"	monthly	" 13
Jno Grubb	" " "	£7 16/-	"	"	" "
M. A. Jarman	" " "	£5 4/-	"	"	" "
Concert Hall		£3 10/-	"	half yearly	" 25

Frank Gilbertson to Messrs The South Wales Primrose Coal Co. Ltd. **14 April 1909 [7 : 6]**

We understand that you agree to your premises on this side of the river being included in our new lease from Mr. Herbert Lloyd & we wish to thank you.

We presume you will become our annual tenants for your office & will pay us £10 a year as hitherto.

We shall not disturb you & shall consult your wishes as far as possible. As long as we can cope with the traffic, we shall also give Messrs Lloyd Co. Ltd. facilities for getting their coal out as we now do.

Frank Gilbertson to C. B. Jenkins. **11 June 1909 [7 : 75-6]**

Referring to John Harris & Sons difficulties & the sale of Nant Rickett farm, minerals, & Shop in High Street.

For various reasons we are anxious to help them not to lose their business or their interest in the minerals underlying the farm.

I am informed that the total amount of the Mortgage to be paid off is £3,500 to £3,700, & that the surface of the farm is likely to fetch £1,700 or £1,800.

If both these suppositions are correct, & if there is no doubt as to the title of the minerals & there are no charges on the minerals or the Shop in High Street, my Father will lend £2,500 on Mortgage on the following terms:

(1) That interest be paid at the rate of 4½% per annum
(2) That the £50 per annum dead rent now paid by Dr Howell Rees be assigned towards the interest on the loan.
(3) That the Shop in High St (Leasehold I presume) & the Freehold minerals under Nant Rickett be security for the loan & a proper mortgage drawn up.
(4) That when the minerals are developed the royalties are used to reduce & eventually wipe off the loan, before Mr Harris or his representatives handle the royalties.

If you can properly secure the £2,500 on these properties my Father will advance the money forthwith, but we do not wish to have anything to do with the surface of the farm. If it realises £1,700 or £1,800, Mr. Harris will in this way be able to pay off Mr Glasbrook & will have a little capital left over which is wanted for the business.

Frank Gilbertson to The General Manager, Midland Railway, Derby. **19 Aug. 1909 [7 : 133-4]**

Private

We have to complain of the way the business at Pontardawe Station is now carried on.

There is constant friction with our people and your Station Master misrepresents facts in his correspondence.

In our large business we cannot be bothered by the careless or wilfully incorrect statements in your officer's letters, and we expect him to enquire sufficiently into the matters at issue to ensure his letters containing the truth. As it is now we have to examine every statement he makes because he is so frequently mis-informed.

Apart from our experience in business there are general complaints of the way the public is now treated at the Pontardawe Station. Many people have failed to catch trains owing to the booking office not being opened in time and on certainly one occasion the booking office was closed when a second relief train came in and a large number of people were unable to travel to Swansea.

Yesterday the Writer accompanied a child to the Station to send her off to Moorhampton and when he arrived at the Station the train was just coming in, but the booking office was closed and if the Writer had sent a servant with the child instead of going himself she would have been put into a most awkward position. The Station Master said his instructions were to close the booking office so that the clerk would attend to the train. If this is so, please cancel these instructions as they are quite inapplicable to a Station that serves so large a population as Pontardawe does. Generally speaking complaints of the present state of affairs are heard everywhere and we are getting tired of the treatment we are receiving.

We should not make a complaint lightly and we beg you will understand we are serious in stating that business with your Coy is now rather difficult and irritating.

Frank Gilbertson to David Jeremiah. 11 Nov. 1910 [7 : 450]

With reference to the shop you are building. The road is a private road, & in order that we should retain our rights, you must pay us a penny a year for the use of the road passing the shop.

Frank Gilbertson to Messrs R. & C. B. Jenkins. 5 Dec. 1910 [7 : 463]

At 4.0 p.m. on Saturday one of our Watchmen turned out of the Works Daniel Davies & David Williams, of no abode. On Saturday or Sunday night, we are not at present sure which night, another Watchman turned out David Lloyd, Daniel Davies & David Williams at 8.0 p.m. & again at 1.0 a.m.

These three are great blackguards.

Can we prosecute them?

If so we wish to do so.

Frank Gilbertson to The Clerk of the County Council, Cardiff. 10 July 1911 [7 : 618]

We are asked to supply electric current for a few shops & also power for some small industries in Pontardawe.

Would you kindly tell us whether the formalities connected with the crossing of the main road with overhead wires, are considerable, & how long it would be before we could obtain permission.

Frank Gilbertson to Messrs Barlow Barlow & Lyde. 5 Sept. 1911 [7 : 664]

Do you consider that we ought to make any addition to our Articles of Association before selling electric current to small consumers in the village?

Frank Gilbertson to L. G. Jeffreys & Co. 11 Jan. 1912 [7 : 812]

<u>Electric Light Extension from Gellygron</u>

We understand you have already been approached upon the above matter.

Could you conveniently let us have an early reply, and state terms upon which you will allow us to run the wire over the Quarry road and place one post in the field.

The letter referred to was written by one of our Clerks, Mr. T. George, whose house we are prepared to light by electricity if you give permission to fix a post & cross the lane.

Frank Gilbertson to Messrs J. M. Leeder & Son. 25 May 1912 [7 : 931]

We enclose notice to treat.

Will you please act for us in negotiating with the GWR?

We think they will damage the value of Ynisderw house.

We had understood that they were going to take Ynisderw house & use it.

It would suit us if they took the House as we should then throw open the remaining ground for building Workmen's houses.

Frank Gilbertson to Messrs Williams Bros. 31 Oct. 1912 [8 : 81]

. . . We do not object to granting you a 21 years lease of your premises & the extra ground you require, if you undertake that no impurities or drainage enters our water supply, & if you make a culvert to our satisfaction with the necessary manholes.

We think however that you ought to pay a reasonable price for such an excellent site & we suggest £10 a year.

Cecil Gilbertson to Messrs Williams Bros. 28 Jan. 1913 [8 : 168]

Re. New Offices

We thank you for your offer of a reduction of £100 off your original quotation, bringing your price down to £3,528.

Even with this reduction you are still considerably above other quotations we have received, but as we would prefer giving the contract to a local firm we will give you the chance of accepting it at the price of £3,500 (Three thousand five hundred pounds).

We leave this offer open for reply by return.

P. Davies to Messrs R. & C. B. Jenkins & Lloyd, Swansea. 7 July 1913 [8 : 285]

We are attempting to put a stop to a growing practice on the part of the Village boys to carry away pieces of Scrap from our Yard, and after a number of warnings, we are determined to make an example of one of the offenders . . . who was caught by our Watchman carrying away a piece of Scrap of the value of fourpence from one of our trucks on our Yard.

Will you kindly proceed against this boy, as we should like to have him dealt with as a first offender . . .

Frank Gilbertson to Morgan Davies. 14 July 1913 [8 : 292]

Fred Bendle has spoken to us about his difficulty.

We do not know the conditions of the Government Loans, but we have always understood that ¾ths of the value of a Workman's house would be lent by the government after the house had been built.

If this is so, we are quite willing to lend the value of the house until such time as the loan from public funds is secured, provided we have the security of the house during the period of building.

We are not prepared to advance money on mortgage for more than a limited time.

Frank Gilbertson to R. & C. B. Jenkins & Lloyd. 19 July 1913 [8 : 300]

. . . We are sorry to hear . . . turned out to be such a small boy.

We were influenced by the constant & regular pilfering that goes on.

Hardly a rag & bone cart goes down to Swansea without an old bicycle on it, & most of them come from the scrap in these Works.

Frank Gilbertson to Messrs R. & C. B. Jenkins. 25 July 1913 [8 : 304]

The Water Works on the mountain above the Star Inn at Cwmgorse & the prospect of further works jeopardises the water supply of these works.

Have we any protection against the diversion of water that has hitherto come down the Clydach river? Many years ago we purchased the factory at Maesiago to insure our getting all the water that the River carried.

Frank Gilbertson to Messrs R. & C. B. Jenkins. 21 Aug. 1913 [8 : 320]

Referring to our letter about the deviation of water at Cwmnanthopkin farm. We are afraid we shall have to go closely into this matter.

Could Mr. Jenkins name a day when it would be convenient for him to talk the matter over & drive up to the spot?

Frank Gilbertson to Messrs J. M. Leeder & Son, Swansea. 2 Dec. 1914 [8 : 832]

In your recent letters re GWR Railway you have not referred to my request that work should be stopped till the fences are complete.

I may say my sheep are straying over adjoining property all the time, & there is nothing to prevent them getting on the public roads.

I am caused considerable trouble by this. Mr. Blundell made an appointment to call on me at 10 o'clock this morning but did not do so.

He telephoned about 11.0 instead & I thought his manner was very unconciliatory.

Frank Gilbertson to Mr. Phillips, Road Surveyor. 8 Jan. 1915 [8 : 857-8]

The roads from Pontardawe to Neath & to Swansea are in the most appalling condition.

Ever since the Motor Buses began to run these roads have been steadily getting worse, & no attempt is made to meet the new conditions. I cannot get anywhere on my business without annoyance, & unnecessary cost of tyres, & what is my experience must be the experience of all the thousands that use these roads.

I think it is too bad that these conditions are permitted by the Road Committee to continue.

A few loose stones scattered over the road without any attempt to fill definite holes causes extra cost to every user with Rubber tyres, & does practically no good to the road.

I cannot understand how the Committee sanctions the expenditure on any material except tarmac, & such material, which is proved now on these very roads to be the only material that will stand the wet & the heavy wear.

I am a very large Ratepayer through Steel Works, & I feel that I have a most serious grievance when I can hardly use the roads in any direction from Pontardawe.

I travel a good bit by road & I know of no district in England that can compare with the west side of Glamorgan for hopelessly bad roads, & an apparent absence of any policy for dealing with the situation.

Frank Gilbertson to Mr. Phillips. 11 Jan. 1915 [8 : 860]

Thank you for your letter of 9th. I am afraid it is very disappointing, as it indicates that although water bound macadam is unsuitable for these roads, no clear programme of renewing the surfaces with Tarmac has yet been adopted by the Road Committee.

Can you not make representations to the Committee that a drastic alteration in their policy is immediately required?

I do not see why we who live in this part of the world should have to suffer as we do, & the injury is quite as great to those who use the roads purely for commercial purposes as to those who use them for business & pleasure.

Frank Gilbertson to Messrs Barlow, Barlow & Lyde. 7 June 1915 [8 : 945]

A Chemical Works producing Sulphuric Acid immediately adjoining our Works appears to have introduced a new process last Saturday.

A new Chimney was put to work that day & ever since a volume of irritating white vapour has been emitted. The smoke is either volatilized H_2SO_4 or SO_2 & is heavy, & it is impossible to breathe freely in that part of the village when the wind blows the smoke.

We cannot, today, sit in our office unless the windows are closed.

We have reported it to the Home Office Inspector of Chemical Works, & wish to know from you what steps we can take ourselves if the nuisance continues.

Once these things start it seems difficult to stop them & we want to make no mistakes in any initial steps we may take.

P. Davies to W. Pennant Jones, Branch Manager, Atlas Assurance Co. Ltd., Cardiff. **15 Dec. 1916 [10 : 276]**

Private Dwelling Insurances

Referring to your favour of the 13th inst. we are now sending the Schedule giving the amended amounts for the private dwelling Insurances which we shall be glad to have covered in the new Policy to be issued in substitution of the above.

We are sending herewith Policies: 5102396; 5426416; 5221554.

You have already 452830 in your hands.

Also letter re Policy 452831 herewith.

Messrs W. Gilbertson & Co. Ltd.
1/5426416

All private dwellings

Rhyn-dwy-Clydach			
	9 in Primrose Row		1,900
	Anr. ditto occd. by D. Price		275
	"Ynisderw Lodge"		140
	another ditto		200
	1 in Francis St. occd.	– I. James	275
	1 ditto	– Thomas Russell	425
	2 in Uplands		850
	1 Glanrhyd Lodge		200
	1 Brynbedw		700
	1 Bron-y-gan		425
	1 Ty-Gwyn		140
	1 Gatehouse		75
	1 All Saints Cottage		350
Rhyn-dwy-Clydach			
2/5221554	Graig-y-rhedyn		900
	Stable near		75
3/452830	Dan-y-Graig & 2 Cottages		2,500
3/452831	do Ynisderw		3,200
4/5102396	do "Graig Ynisderw" (Owen Davies)		550
	Ynisderw Cottages		350
Llangiwg			
1/5426416	6 in Thomas St.		1,700
	2 ditto occpd. by P. Hopkins and J. Emmanuel		850
	2 in High St.		550

1 St. Dunstan 700

P. Davies to J. M. Leeder & Son, Swansea. 18 June 1917 [10 : 351]

With reference to your letter of April 10th. addressed to Mr. J. H. P. Lloyd.

We are prepared to purchase the two plots mentioned for the sum of £720.

We notice on your plan that you apparently leave room for a roadway alongside the plots coloured green and blue. Is this necessary, as we should like to have our own free access from these two plots to the rest of the farm we have bought behind?

If, for any reason, it is absolutely necessary to leave a road joining up with Tawe Terrace, it would suit us better to have it on the opposite side, in order that our new purchase should be practically joined up to our ground behind.

We want you, if you please, to negotiate with the Lessees of the Pontardawe Inn, for permission for us to run a railway through the back of their premises, crossing the main road at the foot of the Tawe Bridge. The railway would have to be at the level of the main road, which would practically mean purchasing the corner of their back field, and making suitable arrangements for giving them access from the level of our railway to their backyard. The matter is rather urgent.

With regard to the right-of-way along the Tawe River, behind Ynisderw Road, does anything stand in our way of constructing a railway on this road, as we do not suppose it is a public right-of-way, but merely a road giving access to the property, of which we are now the owners?

If your representative could arrange to come up one day when our Engineer is in the Works, it might be well for him to be shown exactly what our proposals are.

It seems probable that, to meet special requirements of the Ministry of Munitions, we may, before long, have to construct a Works on the upper side of Herbert Street on the ground we have purchased, and we want to put in the railway connection at once so as to prepare the site.

We have written to the Clerk of the Glamorgan County Council in regard to crossing the main road by a level crossing.

Frank Gilbertson to Messrs Deloitte, Plender & Griffiths, Bute Docks, Cardiff. 25 June 1917 [10 : 361]

The Chairman of the Tawe Gas Company informs me that about £1,100 of shares in that Company are in pawn at a Bank in Swansea, and suggests that it might be to our interest to acquire them, as we are the competing lighting authority of the district, and for another reason.

I think a Colonel James, of Windsor Place, Cardiff, is the person principally interested in the Gas Company, and it was at his office that I met Mr. Morgan, the Chairman, in regard to the price of gas and electric light.

Could you make some enquiries quite at your convenience and ask Colonel James for any information necessary, in order to give us a little advice?

We do not want to throw away £1,100, or whatever the shares might be bought for, but there are certain reasons why it might be to our interest to have a little direct connection with the Gas Company.

Charles Gilbertson to George Webb, Tinhouse Foreman. **5 Dec. 1917 [10 : 467]**

I have put before Mr. Frank your application for an advance of £360 towards the purchase of a house.

He agrees to advance the money, but as it is such a large amount, we shall have to charge you interest upon it, at the rate of 4½% per annum, and we shall have to ask you to lodge with us the Title Deeds, until the advance is cleared.

Will you also please sign the enclosed.

We are glad to be able to show our appreciation of your faithful services by assisting you in this matter, but you will understand that it is necessary for us to charge the interest in this case, as the amount is such a large one.

You can get the amount from Mr. Philip Davies at any time in return for the enclosed agreement signed.

Charles Gilbertson to Messrs R. & C. B. Jenkins & Lloyd, Swansea. **23 Feb. 1918 [10 : 523]**

We desire to purchase the 2 houses and freehold ground of Nos. 10 and 12 Ynisderw Road – owner, William Davies, Engine driver, Grove Road, Pontardawe, and shall be glad if you will kindly negotiate for the purchase of property as early as possible.

We leave the question of price entirely in your hands, to make the best bargain you can.

Both houses were bought for £750 [10 : 531]

NOTES

1. *Reports of the Commission of Enquiry into the State of Education in Wales 1847,* Part 1, R. R. W. Lingen, 12-13.
2. I. G. Jones, *Health, Wealth and Politics in Victorian Wales* (Swansea University College, 1979), 28-29.
3. *Times*, 1 December 1877.
4. *Cambria Daily Leader*, 24 April 1896.

Chapter 9

ORGANISED RELIGION

The contribution of industrialists to the religious life of their local communities found its most tangible expression in the churches which they built and endowed. In Pontardawe the tinplate manufacturer William Parsons built St. Peter's Church in the Parish of Llangiwg between 1858 and 1862 at a personal cost of £10,000. Soon after his arrival in Pontardawe, William Gilbertson built a Reading Room for the English congregation which was licensed for divine service and he paid the officiating clergyman. Both William and Arthur Gilbertson were devout Anglicans and gave liberally of their time, money and energies to promoting the spiritual well-being of Pontardawe's population.

Like his father, Arthur Gilbertson was an accomplished church organist and in 1866 donated the organ to St. Peter's. He followed his father as honorary organist there and in 1873 he edited a book of responses and hymns for the Festivals of the Church Choral Union. His personal legacy to Pontardawe was the building of All Saints Church in the Parish of Clydach in 1886 as a memorial to his father. It was intended to be used by the English speaking inhabitants and is an imposing stone building which cost approximately £3,000 to build. Its nave is large enough to hold 370 worshippers and the belfry contained a peal of tubular bells given by the local inhabitants as a testimonial to William Gilbertson. The living was a curacy whose value, in the gift of Arthur Gilbertson, was £150 p.a. The church was transferred by Order in Council to the Parish of Llangiwg on 24 June 1903.[1]

The following letters show how successive curates and their pastoral duties were rigorously monitored by him, as were the maintenance and improvement costs of All Saints. Also included are references to the untidy state of the graves, donations to other churches and chapels, the provision of a new marble chancel floor and choir stalls for St. Peter's and a dismissive note to a nonconformist minister expressing his objection to the local provision of secondary education. Frank Gilbertson continued to maintain All Saints Church and to support churches and chapels attended by his employees, and with his wife contributed largely to the building of St Mary's Church, Ynysmeudwy, in 1912-13. On the broader stage, he helped to frame the Constitution of the Church in Wales (1917), was appointed to its Representative Body, Finance Committee and Governing Body. He also chaired the St. David's Diocesan Board of Finance and most of its main committees, and was prominent in the deliberations which led to the creation of the diocese of Swansea and Brecon in 1923.[2] Unfortunately, the only reference in the Letter-Books to his influence in Church affairs is a brief reference to his position as Secretary of the Church Congress in 1909.

Arthur Gilbertson to Rev. Godfrey Wolfe, Curate of All Saints Church. **2 Dec. 1890 [1 : 37]**

Would you please see Arthur Saunders at Pheasants Bush & David Price (near old Methodist Chapel) and arrange a share of relief for him?

I think Wm. Williams (Aaron's half brother) also wants help. You may give 20/- in each case, as a start please. Cash enclosed.

Arthur Gilbertson to Rev. J. T. Davies, Minister of Tabernacle Independent Chapel. **30 Dec. 1890 [1 : 56]**

Thank you for your letter.

I can't say I am much interested in intermediate education. In fact I don't quite know what it means! The high standard now attained to in the schools (National & Board) with evening science classes, seem to supply all that is required, but there is a fad for these Intermediate Schools and persons who wish to make themselves prominent, take the matter up, regardless of expense.

I am of opinion, that to assist the evening science classes in the Village, would be quite sufficient at present.

Thanking you for your good wishes.

An Intermediate School was established in neighbouring Ystalyfera in 1896, but not in Pontardawe until the opening of the Higher Elementary School by Frank Gilbertson in 1913.

Arthur Gilbertson to Rev. G. Wolfe. **13 April 1893 [1 : 230]**

Referring to your Tenancy of Dan-y-Graig, seeing that you are giving up a portion of the garden at end of this year, and that you now make the big room "a Parish Room", we shall reduce the rent you pay from £15 a year to £5 a year, to date from 25th March past.

Arthur Gilbertson to Rev. G. Wolfe. **4 Jan. 1894 [1 : 280a]**

I return Rev. D. Jones [Vicar of Llangiwg, 1860-92] letter of April 1889. He had better have consulted me, but I suppose it would accord with his views of Priestly dignity! – the Layman should only provide the money!!

However it is not of much consequence, as it happens, but in <u>future</u> as Easter is coming on tell Mr. Jones I prefer Clerk & All Saints being omitted from the minutes – he can appoint Baker as Sexton to All Saints Burial ground, if he likes, with certain fees & no salary.

Arthur Gilbertson to Rev. G. Wolfe. **15 Jan. 1894 [1 : 282]**

Trade is worse than I can remember since I married, and I have determined not to go to the expense of rearing Pheasants this year, and in several ways to economise. My dear Wife's illness causes me great expense.

I do not therefore feel that I can promise to pay you a stipend of £150 & House, after June next. I will do so until then to give you ample notice.

After June, the stipend will be £120, and House = £150. I feel this is much better than many Livings, considering the outgoings a Vicar or Rector have to provide as a rule from their stipends for Parish & church expenses.

Arthur's wife Ellen died on 15 March 1894.

Arthur Gilbertson to Rev. J. Griffiths, Vicar of Llangiwg. **12 June 1894 [2 : 6]**

I think I wrote to you about the chancel, but seem to have omitted to copy my letter, and I dont find any reply from you.

I want things to be perfectly understood before I instruct the Architect, so write to say, you undertake to proceed at once, with repairs of fabric, for which Mr. Hedley has a considerable sum in hand, and I am to be allowed to place a "Brass" in chancel, stating I make the improvements in memory of my Father & Mother, and I agree to spend £250 on the complete job.

Kindly confirm this by letter.

I expect you this afternoon.

Canon James Griffiths was Vicar of Llangiwg from 1892 to 1913. The memorial to William and Eliza Gilbertson was placed on the north wall of St. Peter's Church.[3]

Arthur Gilbertson to Messrs Buckley, Wilson & Moxham, Architects, Swansea. **n.d. c. 12 June 1894 [2 : 7]**

Referring to our interview yesterday. You will take very careful measurement please, and give attention to the Organist's seat.

The choir stalls being in Pitch Pine, will reduce estimate, and please remember the £250 is to cover everything, architect's commission & charges included. I hope you will send me "section" in a day or two.

Arthur Gilbertson to Messrs Buckley, Wilson & Moxham. **4 Aug. 1894 [2 : 20]**

I was glad to find the work already done at St. Peter's chancel, did not have Mr. Wilson's approval. It is very rough & uneven. Your reputation is at stake in this matter, and if well executed is likely to be of advantage to you.

All Saints Church, Pontardawe *(W. H. Booth)*

I must call your attention to the fact, that I look to you to see the work is executed well, and I think you ought to run up for an hour by train now & then, to see if it is being properly done.

Arthur Gilbertson to Rev. J. Griffiths. 4 Aug. 1894 [2 : 11]

I had a cheque in my pocket for £50 yesterday for the Architects, but I thought it best to withhold it, until they have had the work properly done by the Contractor.

If you would allow me to suggest, if I were you, I would not step between them & the sub-contractors in any way, or the job will be damaged.

Let Wilson & Moxham do & arrange everything themselves.

Arthur Gilbertson to Rev. G. Wolfe. 3 Jan. 1895 [1 : 321]

I enclose All Saints Church a/c. which as I expected has a deficit. Kindly return it tomorrow morning. I intend presenting it, as I think a great many persons forget the cost.

Arthur Gilbertson to Rev. G. Wolfe. 4 Jan. 1895 [1 : 322]

I write Revd. Smyth Rees suggesting 3rd Feby, as his first Sunday here. I will write you directly I hear.

Offertory. Of course I know fell off for want of my gold. I meant others to know it too!

Account. The cash items are strictly accurate from our Books, but "2[?] Years" is wrong – it should be accurate with items being left out in broken periods & carried forward.

Churchyard needed attention.

Arthur Gilbertson to Rev. Evan Davies, Vicar of Clydach. **5 Jan. 1895 [2 : 46-7]**

The Revd. W. Smyth Rees, Curate of Blaina, has officiated at All Saints most satisfactorily, and has excellent references.

Following the precedent of Mr. Wolfe's appointment, I have offered Mr. W. Smyth Rees, the appointment to my Church, and I have notified my selection to the Bishop, and shall be obliged if you will write and confirm the appointment to the Bishop's Secretary. Mr. Rees cannot enter upon his duties before April 4th and as Mr. Wolfe wants to leave at end of this month, he must, if he goes, find a locum tenens.

Arthur Gilbertson to Mrs. Ann Thomas, Gwynfa. **11 Jan. 1895 [2 : 49]**

In consequence of family arrangements I may want Gwynfa next Summer, and shall have to ask you to give up the Tenancy in three months from 25th March next.

Revd. G. Wolfe is leaving Dan-y-graig, and in future I mean to have an unmarried Curate, who will lodge somewhere, so that I can make you the offer of Dan-y-graig instead of Gwynfa – the rent of Dan-y-graig should be £30, but you may have it for £25, yourself paying Taxes, on quarterly notice. Mr. Wolfe, I believe, made several pounds a year out of the Fruit & garden.

If you go there, would you care to take the Curate as a Lodger?

Arthur Gilbertson to W. Smyth Rees, The Vicarage, Blaina. **11 Feb. 1895 [2 : 61]**

I have your letter. You have not acted rightly in this matter. You have broken your written word, and none of the considerations you name can justify such conduct.

That your Vicar does not counsel you to perform your promise, is to me very sad, but as your training for the Priesthood has been under him, I think there is room for doubt whether you would have turned out all I had looked for & I therefore absolve you from your engagement.

Arthur Gilbertson to Mrs. Thomas, Dyffryn. **14 Aug. 1895 [2 : 100-1]**

Thank you for your letter. I would not object to put a thousand pounds or so, into the South Wales Primrose Coal Co. Ltd., if upon investigation I found it a satisfactory concern.

All the interests of my Sons & myself are centred in Pontardawe. I should ask to see the last audited Balance Sheet, the Articles of Association, the amount of last annual dividend, to read the Colliery Engineer's report on the whole taking, to see the plans, to be put into communication with Company's Lawyer, and to have any questions answered to my London Lawyer and a Colliery Surveyor – Mr. Arthur Lawrence of Cardiff. Also are the shares fully paid, and what do you ask for them? I conclude "par" value.

I have often been surprised at the constant absences of Mr. Hedley – I could not carry on my business that way. I conclude he commands the majority of votes.

E. H. Hedley, JP, Alltycham, was Managing Director of the South Wales Primrose Coal Co. Ltd.

Arthur Gilbertson to Rev. J. C. Thomas. 17 Aug. 1895 [2 : 105]

Thank you for your letter: any information you give me shall be kept strictly private.

I should like to know who hold the Debentures and what per cent you pay, and if you ever have to overdraw on your Bankers? also how long your mineral agent says your coal will last? at rate of 600 to 700 Tons a day – some Colliers say from 7 to 10 years only.

Unfortunately I am fully engaged for a few weeks & house full, but if you would kindly reply, we can get on.

Arthur Gilbertson to Rev. J. C. Thomas. 20 Aug. 1895 [2 : 106]

To save you further trouble I think I ought to say at once, I have decided not to invest in the Primrose Coal Co., because I understand the Coal may not last much over seven years, and this would not be worth while sinking capital for.

Arthur Gilbertson to Rev. S. E. Cornish, Curate of All Saints Church. 20 Aug. 1895 [1 : 388]

I think it is all settled now with Hopkin Williams, and it only rests with him to say when you can enter. Please give the date (to W.Gilbertson & Co., Ltd.) when you enter into possession. It is understood you pay us £5 per quarter, tenancy subject to three months notice, at any time, on either side.

I have told Hopkin Williams to make the path & gateway, and he is to pay Taxes.

You will hold the premises from us (W. Gilbertson & Co. Ltd.)

Arthur Gilbertson to Rev. J. C. Thomas. 24 Aug. 1895 [2 : 112-3]

I thought I might have seen you yesterday & did not therefore write. I did not understand one sentence in your last letter, about "hoping no harm had been done".

You will remember I told your Wife & yourself, all the details, if you thought fit to answer my questions, would be kept absolutely private and so they will be. I have not even shown them to my eldest Son who is my confidant in most things.

The time of duration of present workings is common talk among your Colliers and others.

I may be entirely wrong, in my ideas, as I don't profess much colliery knowledge, but my impression is no man of business experience would now invest in the Collieries, at "par" value of shares. I keep this opinion to myself, and trust you may carry out the arrangements you wish.

Arthur Gilbertson to Richard Davies, Builder, High Street, Pontardawe. **20 Sept. 1895 [2 : 126]**

The tiles are very badly layed in the Cottage [of All Saints Church], and I wont pass them.

Several loose stones in walls, and crests badly finished off. It is very foolish of you not to have the work done thoroughly, as it will not lead to more jobs.

Arthur Gilbertson to G. Halliday, Architect, Llandaff, Cardiff. **27 Sept. 1895 [2 : 130-1]**

Your letter of yesterday & tracing, has been read and explained to my Builder, John Griffiths, who quite agrees to all your suggestions, and so do I. Please do as you suggest as to Bridgend stone for Windows (East and two side ones) & ashlar work – and get Tender for it, ready for fixing, delivered at Pontardawe Station, on Midland Ry.

Jno. Griffiths will begin building on Wednesday and would soon want the ashlar for binding as work goes on.

Choir Seats. J. Griffiths will tender for, and also Principal & roof from your drawings to be supplied – Mr. Clarke to do the carving.

I like your ideas very much.

Arthur Gilbertson to G. Halliday. **11 Oct. 1895 [2 : 133]**

Yours of 4th & 5th inst. and plan & specifications of roof. I have come to the conclusion this is too elaborate for my carpenter, so I am posting you back the plan & specification today and will you kindly get a Tender from your carpenters for them.

Goody Cripps & Co. I like your idea & return sketch. I conclude when they say "Tiles" they mean marble ones. I also enclose a letter from people I deal with (A. & N. Stores). Their price per superficial foot might enable you to make Cripps & Co. reduce. You remember a certain portion of floor will be required between new choir stalls – I shall be glad to see ashlar stones coming on – no doubt you know Bridgend quality varies.

Arthur Gilbertson to Richard Davies. **n.d. (c. 15 Oct. 1895) [2 : 135]**

I have your a/c. showing £160..15.7 (and old materials &c) for All Saints Cottage without Porch.

Payments to deduct	
Cash on a/c	£100.. 0..0
Mortar	4.. 0..4
Paving Porch like Glanrhyd Lodge	2.. 0..0
	106.. 0..4
balance	54.. 15..3
	£160..15..7
and I enclose check for	£ 54..15..3

I cannot say the work was carefully done, and had I not troubled over it a good deal, it would have been worse.

Arthur Gilbertson to W. Dodds, Mason. **22 Oct. 1895 [2 : 138]**

You must not write me impertinent letters. You have sold some of my Stone, and you must pay me, or the Bath Stone Firms for what you have taken, and I will pay them for what I have taken, and I will pay you a fair amount for expenses &c, which John Griffiths shall advise me upon.

Arthur Gilbertson to G. Halliday. **30 Oct. 1895 [2 : 143-5]**

Thanks for yours of 28th inst & drawings. I like the East end & Rheredos much.

I have jotted down the Totals, enclosed – are they about correct? If so, I am prepared to go to that amount. But please let me know.

1st. Is background of Rheredos panels to be in your gold work, like Nicholaston?

2nd. Is the stone for Rheredos to be Bridgend, or Pink Marble, or Caen? I had hoped some Pink Marble, it looks so warm.

3rd. What are "figures" to be made of?

4th. I should like Clarke to carve all figures – I suppose McGaul would employ him?

5th. If there is a wood freize on each side of Sacrarium, could you have one side "Let Saints on earth in Concert join", and on the other side "with those whose work is done" – I especially want it – my dear Wife's favourite Hymn – might the words be printed on?

John Griffiths will try his hand at roof estimate. Should he not give me a new estimate for structural work with ashlar? Will it make much difference? Is the ashlar lining cleaned down after roof on? or how is it kept nice? Can we not have a canopied figure each side of East window? – above side wings.

Sorry to trouble you so much. Hope your answer to this will settle all.

Shepton – Roof	–	£98.10..0
McGaul		
East Window	–	91.. 9..0
Shafts for roof	–	31.. 7..0
Ashlar & Side Windows	–	50.. 3..6
Rheredos	–	243.12..0
Side wings	–	100.. 0..0
New glass Windows Side & East	–	100.. 0..0
Structural Work Jno. Griffiths	–	150.. 0..0
New Stalls & floor & removing old floor	–	100.. 0..0
Goody Cripps – Marble		121.. 8..6
		£1,086.10..0

Arthur Gilbertson to G. Halliday. **6 Nov. 1895 [2 : 164-5]**

. . . My estimate of £1,086..10..0 of October 30, is really as much as I want to go to, but I do want the Pink alabaster, so I must allow Clarke to add the £99..8..6, and instead of marble from Goody Cripps, I will ask you kindly to send me at once, plan & specification of Steps & Sacrarium floor to me at Langham Hotel London (where I am going to tomorrow) and I will see several people about a nice plain mosaic. I think we ought to save a good bit off Goody Cripps, and it will help pay for the Pink Alabaster. I must have the Side Canopies & figures, but as I now authorize you to accept Clarke's tender of 5th inst., I hope he will add the two figures & canopies for £18 each. I think we said St. Peter & St. Paul. Can the names be cut under all the figures? I understand the Freize will have the 2 lines of the Hymn on it.

Ashlar. What extra should be paid for setting?

2 New window lights. East end, I conclude you leave to me & Ward & Hughes?

Roof. I notice Clarke erects but does not do slating.

Arthur Gilbertson to Jno. Griffiths. **18 April 1896 [2 : 226]**

. . . I have sent on your time a/c to Mr. Halliday, the Architect, he can judge how far it is fair. I say it is simply absurd – no one has been overlooking your men, and they have just idled as much as they like. You only began selecting the stones for East Window &c beginning of last week. Today your men are much more active, since my letter to you. You had better let them understand they wont be paid all this day time & that you are on contract. I enclose £40 on general a/c.

Arthur Gilbertson to G. Halliday **5 May 1896 [1 : 440]**

Please read enclosed.

I find Jno Griffiths is now putting up tracery of Window & does not want Clarke's man! How stupid they are – please let Clarke know his man is not wanted but he must pay Griffiths, what you consider right. Window will be up in a couple of days.

I am glad to find Clarke says two months (not four as you imagined) for Rheredos – it would be dreadful to have Chancel in present state for 4 months. So kindly let me know soon as possible about Marble floor.

Arthur Gilbertson to Rev. D. Williams, Vicar of Clydach. **6 May 1896 [2 : 233-4]**

The untidy state of some graves in the Cemetery adjoining my Church annoys me. I keep the grounds in order at my own expense. I now want some half dozen people to put "headstones" to their graves, but I find the Fees, somewhat deter them – as I undertake all expenses up here, do you think half fees might be charged? or if otherwise, perhaps I might be paid for keeping the Cemetery in order, and I could divide the money between the most needy.

Arthur Gilbertson to Rev. S. E. Cornish. **2 Sept. 1896 [1 : 472]**

I find you have not handed in the offertories for the last two Sundays and that your rent is due to end of June, viz £5..0..0. Will you please send these amounts at once – I dont like things to get irregular.

Arthur Gilbertson to Mr. Rees. **9 Nov. 1896 [2 : 268-9]**

Since you spoke to me here sometime ago, I have had a talk with several Parishioners of Cilybebyll, and find they are of opinion that the Churchpeople at the Rhos, already go to the Parish Church and it is not therefore advisable to add to the burdens of churchpeople by erecting & maintaining another building, with additional liability for stipend &c, and robbing the old Church of part of its small congregation.

I must say I quite concur with their view and advise you, for the present, to remain content with St. John's, Alltwen.

I dont quite understand Mr. Arthur Lewis' note, but I feel sure the Rector must consent before Cilybebyll is saddled with another church building. I dont gather that Mrs. Gwyn means to become responsible for the maintenance of the building & stipend?

I certainly advise you to wait.

St. John's Chapel of Ease at Alltwen, was erected in 1886-8 at a cost of £1,500 by

Howel Gwyn of Dyffryn, Neath. Mrs. Gwyn was a major landowner in the district in 1896.

Arthur Gilbertson to Rev. S. E. Cornish. **7 Jan. 1897 [2 : 277-8]**

I have yr. letter of 4th inst: it is not that you have "grieved me", but dont you see how dreadfully you have injured yourself, as a man bound by most solemn vows? You know you are absolutely culpable for entering into all these liabilities. I find they add up to £150 besides the £50 you owe me. Before I can form any opinion as to what to do, considering my duty to the church, I must have details of Brader's a/c. £12..10..0, Standen £5..7..0, Leary [?] £5..3..9, Mackmillan £7..3..6, Mowbray £3..2..8, Mr. Eddington £13..0..0, J.L. Williams £8..18..1.

I cant imagine why you ran these up?

I must also know about the G.F.S. "Balance Sheet" & the "Columbus a/c".

I hardly like to apply the word which seems applicable to your dealing with these funds.

I am willing to help honest misfortune, but I wont help anything which has to be called by another name, and you must judge whether to answer my questions or not. If answered at all I shall require every detail.

Arthur Gilbertson to Rev. S. E. Cornish. **11 Jan. 1897 [2 : 279-80]**

I have thought over the whole matter, with the deepest concern.

You know how I have the work at "All Saints" at heart, & that I expend personal time & money on it, you will not be surprised to hear, that I cannot in justice to the Flock & my young family retain your services. I must ask you to take notice, that your services will not be required at "All Saints" after 25th March, when your stipend will cease, and the tenancy of your House will also expire on that date.

I require a letter from you, saying you will conform to all this and will quit the House on 25th March & that during the intervening period, you will do your best in every way. If you send me this undertaking I will allow you to send in your resignation to the Vicar of Clydach which will be much better for you, than if any enquiry was held into my reasons, for wishing you to leave.

Arthur Gilbertson to Rev. S. E. Cornish. **14 Jan. 1897 [2 : 281]**

. . . The Licence is contingent on my paying the stipend – therefore if you send in your resignation notice at once, the three months may date from today, terminating on Thursday April 8th.

Considering you owed me £50, you had no right to buy pictures, books and an Instrument, and I cannot alter what I said in my last letter.

Arthur Gilbertson to John Griffiths. **21 Jan. 1897 [2 : 282]**

Mr. J. P. Davies has gone over your complicated accounts with me.

You have broken two contracts, charged extras at All Saints Church & Glynteg on an absurd scale, compared with the details you gave me, and I should be within my rights, in declining to pay you anything further, but under consideration for the position you have been placed in, by your failing health, I have determined to send you £50 in full discharge of all accounts to this date.

Arthur Gilbertson to Rev. D. Williams, Vicar of Clydach. **24 Jan. 1897 [2 : 283-4]**

Thank you for your letter. I enclose two from Mr. Cornish, which kindly read & return. His engagement here is to terminate on April 8th. If he has not advised you, kindly write him and say I have told you and that you conclude he has informed Mr. Barker, the Bishop's Registrar. We must keep him up to this point: he is a sad shuffler, and utterly without conscience as to defrauding others, I can use no other word for his conduct, from what is turning up daily.

Mr. Hampton seems quite worth following up, and I should like to see his references &c. when they come.

Thank you very much for your kindly action in this matter.

I cant help hoping a man of light & learning, may be appointed, as our Bishop, with Bishop John, of Swansea, for the Welsh work. It is more practical than dividing St. David's.

Arthur Gilbertson to Mr. Gronow. **8 Sept. 1897 [2 : 305-6]**

I have your letter of 6th inst. & now reply in detail.

I understand the Singers you name are educated & can read music & time – if so, I am willing to pay them £13..13..0 inclusive (Singers to pay their own travelling and accommodation in the Village). I enclose a list of the Music, they are to sing all of it, the church choir only doing the choruses, two of which have Solo part for your Soprano.

Perhaps Mr. Chubb could suggest a Bass Song to me? The Soloists would have to attend Rehearsal on evening of 3rd. Novbr. @ 7.30 at Church & sing at the two performances on the 4th. I prefer the men to wear Surplices, which I provide. I accompany on the organ, which is a fine instrument, the Church holds 450 to 500 persons, and is very nice. It was built by myself, and I provide every expense connected with it, and the Offertory collected is given to a Charity.

Thanks for the names of Harpists.

Arthur Gilbertson to W. G. Vowles, Bristol. 31 Oct. 1899 [2 : 396-7]

Referring to your visit yesterday.

Hydraulic. I fixed the head of water about 90 feet. Would this give 39 lbs. per square inch of pressure?

Swell Organ. I think I must have a "Clarion" added to Swell. I think a 4 ft. Reed?

This Swell Box must be absolutely muffled when shut, so it must be very thick – this is essential.

No. 3 in Swell, to be an 8 ft. wood flute.

Position. I want a door out of Bellows Room into new dark room (shown on following plan) and as the brick partition behind present Organ will be removed to allow back of Swell Box to come where present feeder is, I want the Organ constructed so that we can prevent draught blowing in, around Organ, from Lavatory &c. behind – we must close up to the sides tightly in wood partition I conclude.

I suppose your quotation of 12th inst. includes Delivery & erection? and you will now be able to quote for the complete Instrument, blowers & Hydraulic, as proposed, and submit to me "ground plan" & "elevation". I forgot to say there is to be a "Tremullant" (not "tremolo") to the Swell.

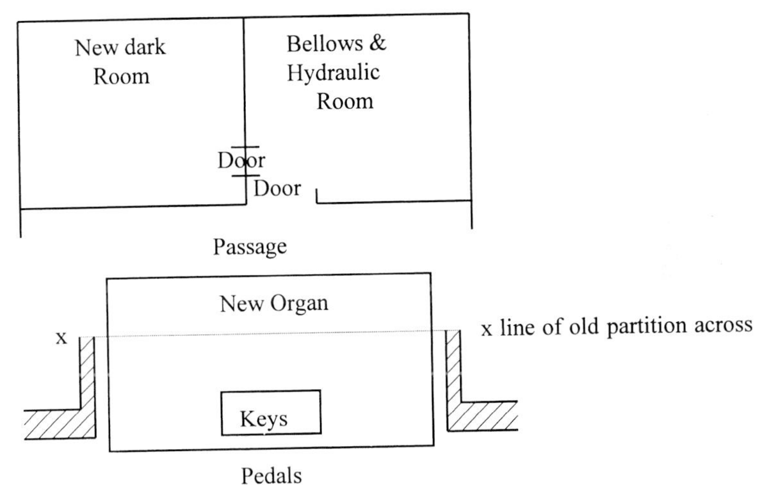

Red chalk shows new woodwork to be put by me instead of present partition & this woodwork must be kept close up to sides & back of Swell Box.

Arthur Gilbertson to Herbert Lloyd, Plas Cilybebyll. **8 Aug. 1905 [5 : 163]**

Our Workmen live in Alltwen & Cilybebyll parish, so we ought to help the Churches & Chapels.

W. Gilbertson & Co. will pay to the Rectory of Cilybebyll £10 a year, every year.

This was the last longhand letter written by Arthur Gilbertson to be copied in the Letter-Books.

Frank Gilbertson to Rev. James Griffiths, Vicar of Llangiwg. **22 Feb. 1907 [5 : 445]**

I have spoken to my Father & we agree to give £100 to the living of Cilybebyll in lieu of our annual subscription of £10. We understand this will enable you to receive £300 from other sources for the augmentation of the living.

Frank Gilbertson to Rev. D. Williams, Vicar of Llangyfelach. **10 July 1908 [5 : 784]**

We enclose a donation to the fund you are collecting for the Phillips family.

Frank Gilbertson to Rev. J. Harrison. **10 July 1908 [5 : 785]**

We enclose £50 to be applied as you may think fit in the work of your new parish.

Frank Gilbertson to the Rev. Prebendary Griffiths. **22 July 1908 [5 : 804]**

We desire to subscribe £10..10..0 annually to the general fund of Llanguicke Parish & enclose this amount for year ending Dec. next.

If you would kindly send us a reminder next January we will send the amount in that month in future.

Frank Gilbertson to Alfred Darby. **17 May 1909 [7 : 30]**

. . . I am Secretary of the Church Congress at Swansea this year, & have so little time left after my ordinary work, that I grudge going away at present.

Frank Gilbertson to J. G. Harris. **18 Nov. 1909 [7 : 163]**

We understand you are selling the Rechabite Hall.

As your ground landlords, at present, we should wish to be satisfied with the purchasers, so please submit the offers you receive to us, before committing yourselves to a sale.

Lambeth Palace. S.E.

19th October 1909

Dear Mr.Gilbertson,

I had been for days past meaning to write to you to say how intensely I realise, as I think over what happened at Swansea, the obligation which we all owe to yourself. Without under-valuing the service and devotion of others I know that to you more than to any other man were due the admirable arrangements which resulted in making everybody happy as well as, up to their powers, useful. That a gentleman so busy as you are should be willing to undertake this responsible and anxious work, and be able to carry it through with such extraordinary efficiency, fills one with thankfulness and hope. Let me add my own cordial thanks to those which you must have been receiving on all hands.

I enclose a note for Mr.Harris, which is better perhaps than a mere autograph, but he may like to have the latter as well.

I am

Yours very truly,

Randall Cantuar

Letter to Frank Gilbertson from the Archbishop of Canterbury, 1909
(Mrs Nanette Pearce)

P. Davies to W. B. Laws, Auditor, Cardiff. **2 May 1910 [7 : 278]**

Income Tax 1909/1910

. . . We enclose detailed statement of Subscriptions and Donations for year ending 13 March 1909 . . .

Abstracted from list:		£.. s ..d
Don to	Alltwen Chapel for Concert Tickets	1 1 –
Subn "	presentation to Rev. J. Harrison	7 10 –
Don "	Tabernacle Chapel for Concert Tkts.	2 2 –
Subn "	Pan Anglican Congress	10 – –
Don "	Rev. J. Harrison towards work in new parish	50 – –
" "	Rev. D. Williams " fund in aid of Phillips family	10 – –
Subn "	Llanguicke Ch. General Fd.	10 10 –
" "	Diocesan Inspector's Salary	2 2 –
Don "	Alltwen Chapel for Concert Tkts	2 2 –
" "	Diocesan Fund	200 – –
Subn "	Llanguicke Church	10 10 –
Don "	Methodist Chapel for Concert Tkts	3 3 –
Subn "	St. David's Diocesan Fund	5 – –
Don "	New Church @ Bonymaen	50 – –
Subn "	Gosen Chapel Organ Fund	10 – –

Frank Gilbertson to W. B. Laws, Cardiff. **7 May 1910 [7 : 290-2]**

. . . With regard to the subscriptions I enclose a few notes . . .

Churches & Chapels

Llanguicke Church Tabernacle Gosen Methodists & others included in sundry subs.	These are subscriptions to the Places of Worship actually attended by our Workpeople

NOTES

1. In February 1999 All Saints Church was advertised for sale at an asking price of £60,000, with the suggestion that it would be "Suitable for conversion to 2 or more units". *South Wales Evening Post*, 18 February 1999.
2. *Links with the Past: Swansea & Brecon Historical Essays*, ed. O. W. Jones and D. Walker (Llandybie, Christopher Davies, 1974), 245.
3. E. Iris Williams, *St Peter's Church* (Swansea, Origin, 1996), 12-13, 18, 20, 29.

Chapter 10

LEISURE PURSUITS

On the occasion of Frank Gilbertson's marriage *The Cambria Daily Leader* (24 April 1896) commented on his father's moral influence on the village:

> "Mr. Arthur Gilbertson's system of moral suasion has been of a very practical kind. He has recognised that to make workmen good, rational, sober men, they should have some other form of relaxation than that simply offered by the public-house. Many employers do not care a hard suet dumpling what becomes of the men as soon as they are outside the gates of the firm, and that is a policy which does more to breed bad workmen and bad citizens than anything else. Recognizing this, Mr. Arthur Gilbertson has taken an active interest in the method and form of relaxation open to his employees. He has built for them a comfortable reading-room, where they can foregather and read their papers, and smoke their pipes, and chat about politics and the topics of the day."

The following letters refer to a number of leisure activities which in some instances met with Arthur Gilbertson's approval, whilst others stimulated his angry response. The reading-room mentioned above had been provided by his father in 1869; attached to it were a well-appointed billiard room with three tables and "a rattling gymnasium" which was furnished with exercise equipment. Arthur had placed a large field at the disposal of village sportsmen with separate areas for cricket, soccer and rugby football. In 1892 he provided Pontardawe R.F.C. with a new ground adjoining the steelworks and later developed the site by providing a cinder track for cycling and athletics. As the rugby club's "live-wire President", he spared "no effort to promote the cause of Pontardawe rugby" and ensured that "no financial difficulties should hinder the club . . .".[1] All his sons played in village teams and Pontardawe Golf Club was patronised by the family. Music and choral singing were other forms of relaxation which he promoted enthusiastically and this interest culminated in the provision of the Public Hall and Institute in 1909 which remains a focal centre for social activity today. In contrast, several letters express his irritation over the sporting expenses of his sons, but his anger was more trenchantly reserved for less healthy diversions, amongst which were public houses, local fairs and poaching.

Arthur Gilbertson to Jno. Evans, Publican, Dynevor Arms, Pontardawe. **26 June 1891 [1 : 118]**

I am surprised you did not reply to my letter.

You know the money expended in Pontardawe comes mainly out of my Works, and I am surprised you should set me up defiance. I do not think you are wise or right to do so.

What Rent do you pay?

Arthur Gilbertson to David Smith, Alltwen. **31 Aug. 1891 [1 : 150-1]**

The Fair Committee at Pontardawe, in deference to my urgent request, have decided only to hold March Fair annually – it is admitted that one Fair meets all that is required, with Alltwen Fair. The Fair causes much drunkenness & brings bad characters into the Village for a good week.

I am told a few Publicans are trying to defeat our views, as they make such a profit in drink in the Fair week.

Would you aid the Fair Committee in stopping or at any rate reducing Sept Fair?

I think "no Fair" should be advertised & no special trains run. I will pay any printing & expenses. These Publicans pay their rent on Fair Day, it is said, & if so their assessment ought to be increased.

I told the Fair Committee if they would stop a second Fair, per annum, I would give £150 towards altering the Bridge over Canal for improving Pontardawe Village.

The Chairman of Board of Guardians & most respectable people in Pontardawe wish to reduce the Fair to one per annum.

Arthur Gilbertson to Inspector J. F. Giddings. **25 Nov. 1892 [1 : 207]**

This morning Jno. Jones, Glynmeirch, shot at & wounded a Pheasant on land belonging to his Mother adjoining Penlan. I saw him myself and am bound as a J.P., if for no other reason, to report him to the Excise, if, as I am told, he has not a Game Licence.

You must please find out if he has.

I need not give evidence myself (as being Sheriff I should prefer not doing) but three men with me can give evidence.

Arthur Gilbertson to J. Taylor, Supervisor, Inland Revenue, Neath. **n.d. (c. 26 Nov. 1892) [1 : 208]**

The Exciseman from Pontardawe called on me this morning. His manner was decidedly rude. I can only account for it by the fact that he is a tenant of Mr. Jordans, the Uncle of the man John Jones, who has been shooting game without a licence. This man Jones, and two other men, named Stanhope, are constantly out shooting Game and I believe only one Stanhope has a licence.

I cannot understand the Exciseman having taken no trouble to follow them up.

I think you had better come over and see my men, who know about this affair on Friday last.

Arthur Gilbertson to J. Taylor, Neath. **30 Nov. 1892 [1 : 210]**

. . . I concluded the Excise would feel obliged to me if I could indicate to them, how to carry out their duty in a certain case. The number of persons shooting game without licences is very considerable in this district.

I indicated to Inspector Giddings, a shooting party in Llanguicke & Llangavelach who are constantly out shooting together – only one of the three takes out a Licence. I am told one or more of this party were seen in pursuit of Pheasants a fortnight ago & two were shot. I believe Giddings has informed Sanderson to make enquiries. I know these men are only to be caught by careful watching. I dont know exactly what the duty of the local Exciseman is, in such cases?

Mr. O'Hara can see my old Labourer John Jones tomorrow, on application to my Butler at Glanrhyd, and he can see Morgan Jenkins at the Cottage Hospital which I am building.

Arthur Gilbertson to John Morgan, Tyn y Pant. **15 Jan. 1894 [1 : 283]**

I have your short note of this morning and will pardon your foolishness this once, but I cannot keep your Son in my Office. You can read the paper he brings with him.

I have decided not to rear Pheasants this year. We can only account for 80 or so, out of 200. I dont care to rear Pheasants for Jones & various Poachers to shoot.

You & Tom will therefore be able to do the work, and your Wife, as before. The servant, Esther, will not therefore be required by us after this Quarter ending March & her pay will then cease.

Arthur Gilbertson to J. Davies, Ironmonger, Pontardawe. **31 Oct. 1894 [2 : 25-6]**

Mr. J. P. Davies has told me the result of his conversation with you. Last evening J. L. Jones was very impertinent to Mr. Howel – I know Mrs. Jones would not desire that, but J. L. Jones is often affected by drink. To prevent squabbling with him it seems to me the only way would be to get a lease of Glynmeirch on the north side of the Highway, around Glanrhyd, including the Cottages which I should rebuild and I would give the high sum of thirty pounds a year, and let you have the shooting over Graig Ynisderw.

If no arrangement can be made, I must give up the footpaths over Glynmeirch (and you must cease going over my property as he does constantly), but this would cause me inconvenience, and would lead to a complete rupture with the Glynmeirch family, and the consequences would be probably disagreeable to them, in the end.

It is useless for me to preserve Game as things are, and I could only go in for Rabbits. One other course is open, if the shooting were let to me, over the portion I name, it would include the paths & might end the bother. In that case I would let Jones shoot over Graig Ynisderw.

Could you call on me, here or at the Office on Friday?

If you could bring the worry to an end I should feel personally indebted to you.

Arthur Gilbertson to J. Davies, Ironmonger. 24 Jan. 1895 [2 : 53]

I received the enclosed this morning. I declined Mrs. Jones offer of £10, as you know it is absurd.

I am prepared to pay the old wayleaves, or to give them up, as regards the paths it would be rather inconvenient, but I can manage to do so – I should look upon it as a very unneighbourly act of the Glynmeirch family, and I think the members of the family would suffer from it.

I am prepared to rent the shooting this side of the Highway, and to allow Mrs. Jones to have Graig Ynisderw shooting. If you would call at Glanrhyd or the Office, I could see you.

Arthur Gilbertson to J. Davies, Ironmonger. n.d. (c. 25 Jan. 1895) [2 : 55]

. . . I should be glad to see Mrs. Jones at Glanrhyd at 2.30 . . . will you please come with her.

I can only say that Mr. Jones, and his friends have more than compensated themselves for any damage my Rabbits have done, by shooting my Game & Rabbits. I do think Pontardawe Tradesmen, and adjoining Farmers owe something to me, for the prosperous Village and market for their produce.

Arthur Gilbertson to J. Davies. 25 March 1895 [2 : 72]

Referring to our talk today with Mrs. Jones, I agree to pay her £6..0..0 a year & £1..0..0 (for present water pipe) and £3..0..0 a year to Mr. J. R. Jones: also to make a good fence from the Chapel to Glanrhyd, also to give Mrs. Jones the grazing on the Graig field by Dr. Jones', and to let her have Penlan water over her big meadow, and the shooting over Graig Ynisderw. This being agreed to, I will pay her Ten pounds, for past year 1894.

On her part she gives me the shooting & fishing & rights of way, over the Glynmeirch property on this side of the highway & right to make a narrow road between Glanrhyd & Penlan. I am also prepared to take the Cottage at £9..0..0 a year, with the right of altering it, as I may see fit. The whole of the above to be put into a 21 years agreement.

If above is correct, I will have the agreement prepared by my Lawyer.

Arthur Gilbertson to J. Davies. **11 April 1895 [2 : 79]**

I enclose Lease for Cottage & for sporting, perhaps you will kindly get Mrs. Jones to sign Counterparts, and Mr. J. L. Jones as Witness. I quite hope now nothing may disturb our good relations, as neighbours, and I will do all I can to make things pleasant. To save a lot of writing in the sporting Lease, I have only recited the £9 – the remaining £1 is under an old agreement with Mrs. Jones; and will be paid of course – all other matters about water, roadway &c, will be, as per our correspondence.

I shall have to cut a few Trees in making roadway across field, close to the Hedge. I am now preparing a contract with some men, to do the fence along Highway.

As soon as Jno Jones can get a House, I shall set about rebuilding.

Arthur Gilbertson to Mrs. Jones, Glynmeirch. **12 April 1895 [2 : 83-4]**

I have sent the Leases to Mr. Davies for you. I have put the Game Lease for 5 years certain & then subject to a year's notice. I am sure you will agree to this because you would not expect me to lay out the money I am going to do on the 250 yards of your Hedge, without some understanding for five years. As regards Rabbits, I shall keep them down at Glanrhyd end, and only keep them at Penlan, and as I shall now be able to keep some Pheasants again, I shall reduce the Rabbits. If you had not made this shooting agreement with me, I should have been obliged to increase the Rabbits for my Sons to shoot. I may mention several Sheep & lambs are in your part of Cwmddu, and feeding on your Fields & doing much more damage than Rabbits. You know I am giving you the grazing of the Graig by "All Saints" Church & £10 a year.

Arthur Gilbertson to Lewis Francis,
Sporting Goods Dealer, Herbert Street. **13 May 1896 [2 : 237]**

I remitted you on Octr. 25/95 £ 4.. 4..1
" 28/95 £18..11..4

Surely £24..7..1½ is not due again? If so, you are indeed greatly indebted to my Sons' fondness for athletics, and their support of them must be the making of your shop?

Arthur Gilbertson to O. Lewis. **2 Nov. 1896 [2 : 266]**

If you bring any more men on my neighbour's land to shoot my straying Pheasants, I will dismiss every man in my employ connected with you (and there are a good many) and I will dismiss every man living on my neighbour's leaseholds &c, because he does not behave to me as a neighbour should. You must stop Jonah Jones &c.

Arthur Gilbertson's Cricket XI, 1903 *(Jeff Childs)*
Back row, left to right: Harry Thomas, T. Lewis, D. Evans, T. Jones, B. Thomas, W. Jeremiah, J. Jenkins, D. Lewis (Sec.). *Front row:* A. Bodycombe, A. Davies (Vice Capt.), C. Gilbertson, Arthur Gilbertson, Esq. (Pres.), J. H. P. Lloyd (Capt.)

Arthur Gilbertson to O. Lewis. 4 Nov. 1896 [2 : 267]

I have your letter. I dont believe any agreement was entered into between Mr. Jeffreys & Jonah Jones, until Dan caught Jones with the Poacher from Trebanos.

I understand you & Jonah paid Dan Morgan 7/6d.

I wish he had gone on with his case.

I cant imagine a Gentleman taking a paltry £2 or £3 a year, to enable another man, to poach in fact, his neighbour's reared Pheasants. I paid Jeffreys £12 for one Hare.

I have now instructed my Solicitors to offer to buy the Farms – I think it would be best for you, if this is carried out.

I find three of your Daughters are dependant on my Works for their Husbands' living, and altho' you always go against me (as you did in the river pollution matter) I certainly think you will be very foolish to provoke me further.

Arthur Gilbertson to E. H. Hedley. **18 June 1897 [2 : 297-8]**

Dr. Grice-Jones tells me the Drill Hall, he understands from you, is not to be used for Concert purposes, and I conclude has a Government Grant.

My reason for wishing to know is, that for sometime past, we have been thinking a larger Concert Hall is now needed for Pontardawe. The old building provided at the expense of my Father & myself has served, until now: it is capable of extension and I offered it on certain terms to Mr. John Morgan (Surveyor) to see if a public Co. could be formed to take it, and enlarge it. Something of this sort might be done if the Drill Hall will not meet the requirements . . .

Arthur Gilbertson to Lewis Francis. **21 Jan. 1899 [2 : 378]**

I have your accounts for 1898 & 1898 to 99.

I consider you should have had a good Balance from the Sports to help & I consider the Sports financially were grossly mismanaged as to prizes &c. The "gate" should have yielded a large profit.

If Mr. Cecil pays for <u>all expenses</u> except train fares, I consider it very liberal, and the men must pay their own travelling expenses, beyond what "gates" produce.

I enclose you therefore £25..11..0, deducting the travelling expenses, deducting £4..7..0 fares.

Now you will please understand Mr. Cecil's & my guarantee for expenses, ceases with this Football Season & before Cricket commences I must see you.

Arthur Gilbertson to H. Lloyd, Plas Cilybebyll. **24 July 1901[3 : 347-8]**

We are much obliged by your letter about the 2 Cottages.

The Wesleyans want now to buy our Concert Hall, to convert into a Chapel.

The sites on Herbert Street are becoming valuable, evidently.

The Concert Hall is seldom used and an expense to us – with improved education & facilities to "Empire" &c. at Swansea, the people dont care for tame performances locally!

If you allowed us to sell the Concert Hall, and would grant a Lease, to the Wesleyans, we would engage to spend the money on your property, under Lease to us.

Arthur Gilbertson to John E. Roberts, The Ferns, Alltwen. **14 Aug. 1901 [3 : 371]**

Referring to your letter of 20th ulto, we have consulted our Landlord about selling the Concert Hall, and he has given his consent for us to sell it, for the erection of a Wesleyan Chapel, and he would grant a Lease for the same.

We would accept £600 for the Building.

Arthur Gilbertson to Rev. J. E. Roberts. **24 Aug. 1901 [3 : 389]**

Please reply to my letter, or the opportunity may pass you for the site.

Arthur Gilbertson to J. Wignall, **27 Sept. 1901 [3 : 442]**
Secretary of the Dockers' Union, Dockers Hall,
Swansea.

The following men absented themselves from our Galvanizing Works last night, causing us considerable loss, probably £10.

They went to a Fair with certain leave and did not return altho warned at the Fair.

They should pay damages.

J. Carney, O. Taylor, A. Hodge, Fred Davis, D. Davies, D. Howells, J. J. Taylor, J. T. Lewis.

Arthur Gilbertson to John Davies. **9 Dec. 1901 [3 : 505-6]**

Thank you for your letter of 7th inst & trouble you have taken. Of course Mr. Jones knows, that when we cease to kill Vermin (as recently) & cease to preserve, there is nothing for him & his friends to shoot in the Coppice – it is supplied entirely by Rabbits &c. from Glanrhyd & Tynpant. However I dont like to press you too much, for the Glynmeirch family have always been willing to give me footpaths &c., which are convenient, and therefore I will accept your proposal for one year from 1st Jany next, with the option of a further period of five years on same conditions, if we find the arrangement suits me.

It is understood that the men who shoot with Mr. Jones, are not to <u>shoot Pheasants</u>.

We will, of course, not shoot any Rabbits on Glynmeirch, except on our portion on North of Highway.

Arthur Gilbertson to D. Smith, Alltwen. **7 Feb. 1902 [3 : 543]**

We have broken into the Cricket field for some railways & Turntable for our Steel Works – no permanent Building will be put up. We have arranged to pay £15 per acre additional, to our Landlord, for the portion taken up – please note this.

<u>Concert Hall</u>. I am inclined to pull down & sell materials, putting up elsewhere a Concert Hall of galvanized sheets & wood lining, to hold 800 people, what do you think?

Arthur Gilbertson to D. Smith. **6 June 1902 [3 : 639]**

We are anxious to support a New Concert Hall at Pontardawe, and therefore we offered our old Concert Hall to Mr. J. G. Harris, of the Rechabite Club at the low price of £300..0..0, and this is accepted by them, subject to the ground Landlord giving satisfactory terms to them. If this is carried out, we will put the £300 into shares for the New Hall.

Colin Gilbertson to D. Smith. **8 Sept. 1902 [3 : 718]**

Thank you for your letter of 6th inst. re. Concert Hall. We propose now leasing it to the "Rechabites" for 33 years at a rent of £4 a year. Is there any clause which you or Mr. Lloyd would wish us to insert in the lease, as to the uses to which the Hall should be put?

Colin Gilbertson to J. G. Harris, Albion House, Pontardawe. **8 Sept. 1902 [3 : 718]**

With reference to your letter of 3rd inst., we have now heard from Mr. Smith, & we can grant you a lease of the Concert Hall for 33 years, at a ground rent of £4 per annum. You can have the lease prepared as soon as you like now. There may possibly have to be some clause in the lease restricting the Hall to certain purposes, & have written Mr. Smith about this, but I should think there would be no difficulty about this.

Colin Gilbertson to J. G. Harris. **7 Oct. 1902 [3 : 739]**

In reply to your letter of yesterday, we will say £3/10/- for ground rent instead of £4.

For Electric Light, we will charge 2/- for each night used, you to supply lamps when worn out.

Arthur Gilbertson to D. Smith, Alltwen. **9 Oct. 1902 [3 : 742]**

Can you tell me if the Reading Rooms & Gymnasium (behind Baptist Chapel) are on the Tin Works lease? I think they are. The Rooms are so full, we are considering a further Room.

Colin Gilbertson to J. G. Harris. **13 Oct. 1902 [3 : 745]**

Your favour of 11th inst. re Concert Hall. We can give you permission to proceed with the repairs at the Hall on the understanding that payment will be made for the Hall as soon as the lease is completed.

We will accept your price of 1/- per night for the use of the Electric light, lamps to be supplied by you when required.

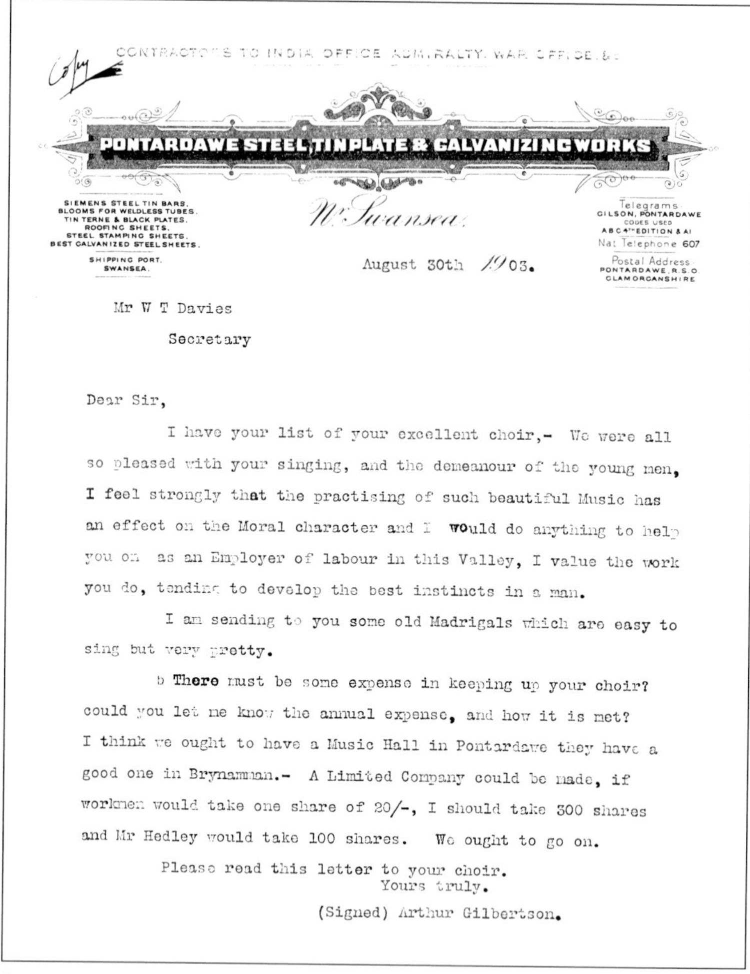

Copy

CONTRACTORS TO INDIA OFFICE ADMIRALTY, WAR OFFICE &c

PONTARDAWE STEEL, TINPLATE & GALVANIZING WORKS

SIEMENS STEEL TIN BARS.
BLOOMS FOR WELDLESS TUBES.
TIN TERNE & BLACK PLATES.
ROOFING SHEETS.
STEEL STAMPING SHEETS.
BEST GALVANIZED STEEL SHEETS.

SHIPPING PORT. SWANSEA.

Nr Swansea.

Telegrams GILSON, PONTARDAWE
CODES USED A B C 4th EDITION & AI
Nat Telephone 607
Postal Address PONTARDAWE, R.S.O GLAMORGANSHIRE

August 30th 1903.

Mr W T Davies

Secretary

Dear Sir,

I have your list of your excellent choir,- We were all so pleased with your singing, and the demeanour of the young men, I feel strongly that the practising of such beautiful Music has an effect on the Moral character and I would do anything to help you on as an Employer of labour in this Valley, I value the work you do, tending to develop the best instincts in a man.

I am sending to you some old Madrigals which are easy to sing but very pretty.

b There must be some expense in keeping up your choir? could you let me know the annual expense, and how it is met? I think we ought to have a Music Hall in Pontardawe they have a good one in Brynamman.- A Limited Company could be made, if workmen would take one share of 20/-, I should take 300 shares and Mr Hedley would take 100 shares. We ought to go on.

Please read this letter to your choir.

Yours truly.

(Signed) Arthur Gilbertson.

Letter from Arthur Gilbertson to W. T. Davies, 1903. A list attached to the letter named 10 First Tenors, 15 Second Tenors, 13 First Bass, 12 Second Bass and Conductor T. Jenkins, Treasurer John Daniels *(West Glamorgan Archive Service)*

Arthur Gilbertson to Tom Evans, Dynevor Arms, Pontardawe. — 11 April 1904 [3 : 995]

You have been trespassing on our land and our Leasehold for some months, and you have made a regular path on the North side of the River, on my property. You did not ask me for leave and I ought to have prosecuted you, for this.

We know now, that you went to Mr. David Smith, instead of us.

You must pay wayleave, if you are going on, and you must pay the "costs" for a legal contract. Let us know?

Frank Gilbertson to the Capital & Counties Bank, Swansea. **29 Oct. 1907 [6 : 1]**

Will you please open an account for "The Pontardawe Hall Committee" with Mr. Daniel Daniels, Railway Terrace, Pontardawe, as Treasurer.

Mr. Daniel will enclose cheques paid in, & cheques drawn on the a/c will be signed by the Chairman or Vice-Chairman, and by the Secretary & Treasurer.

P.S. Please place enclosed £15 on deposit, & also all other sums paid in until further notice.

Philip Davies, Hon Secretary, to C. T. Ruthen, Bank Chambers, Swansea. **15 Nov. 1907 [6 : 2]**

Pontardawe Public Hall & Institute

The Committee formed to deal with the matter of plans for above have decided to ask if you would care to submit the Plans & Specifications for their consideration, on the understanding that payment for same should be made only in case of acceptance, and the terms for the supervision of the work to be afterwards mutually arranged between us. It is proposed to build the Hall to accommodate 1,500 people, and the Institute would contain Club Rooms, Reading Rooms, Refreshment Rooms, Billiard Room, as well as a Residential part.

I may say that we are only approaching a limited number of Architects in this way.

I could give fuller particulars on application.

The same letter was sent to C. S. Thomas, Swansea; Messrs Jones & Peregrine, Port Talbot; W. Beddoe Rees, Cardiff; J. Cook Rees, Neath; Glendening Moxham, Swansea [6 : 3-7].

Philip Davies to C. T. Ruthen. **25 Nov. 1907 [6 : 16]**

I thank you for your favour of the 22 inst, and understand you accept my Committee's proposals with regard to plans for above.

The Hall is required to seat 1,500 people, and is to have a Gallery at the 2 sides and one end, and the other end is to be fitted with a platform to accommodate 150 persons. It is proposed that the Institute should include 2 Refreshment Rooms and Bar for non-alcoholic drinks, one Billiard Room for 2 tables and with a provision at one end for 12 newspaper stands, one Reading Room & Library to accommodate 50 readers, one Club Room suitable for friendly societies, to accommodate 150 persons, and to be supplied with movable partitions dividing into 3 equal rooms, Lavatory accommodation, also Residential part including 4 rooms and scullery. The Building will be in a corner fronting Herbert Street and with Holly Street running along one side.

If you can arrange to run up here I should be glad to meet you upon the proposed site, a plan of which will be sent you in a few days.

With regard to cost, this will have to be limited to about £3,500, which will fully tax our resources.

The drawings are required to be sent in the first week in January.

Philip Davies to Members of the Sub-Committee. 28 Jan. 1908 [6 : 50]

A meeting of the Sub-Committee will be held at Williams' Coffee Tavern, High Street, on Wednesday evening at 8 o'clock to further consider plans.

The plans will be submitted for inspection from 7 p.m. onwards.

Philip Davies to W. Beddoe Rees. 24 April 1908 [6 : 106]

. . . We have now men busily engaged clearing the trees on the site of the buildings, and Messrs Radford & Greaves have also commenced pulling down the old house.

17 June 1908 [6 : 131]

Copy of resolution adopted by the General Committee:

> "It was decided that four foundation stones be laid, and that a representative of Messrs W. Gilbertson & Co. Ltd., another representative of Mr. Herbert Lloyd, Lord Glantawe, and the oldest workman in the district be invited to perform the ceremony of stone laying. It was also resolved to lay a Memorial Stone, and that the Sub-Committee be delegated to carry out preliminary arrangements."

Copy of resolution adopted by the Sub Committee:

> "It was decided to ask the Trade & Labour Council to nominate three persons as the oldest workman in the district, from which list the Committee will decide upon the one to perform the ceremony of laying one of the foundation stones."

Philip Davies to W. Beddoe Rees. 17 June 1908 [6 : 134-5]

Your letters of the 15th and 16th instant, with drawings, have reached Mr. Gilbertson, but he had to leave for London today, and has asked me to send you the addresses of Mr. Evan Morgan and Mr. Walter Jones, which are as follows:

Evan Morgan, Derwen Road, Alltwen, Pontardawe

Walter Jones, Brecon Road, Pontardawe.

Mr. Gilbertson has noted your suggestion with regard to the working of Foundation and Title Stones in Blue Forest Stone, with sunk letters, and he personally agrees to this.

He also agrees to the wording being cut down as you suggest upon the Title stone, and you may proceed with the matter accordingly.

I shall be glad, however, if you will approach some Welsh Scholar in Cardiff, as to the proper wording of the Welsh proverb. I observe that upon your drawing it has been given as "A Fyddo Doeth Darllene<u>d</u>", but the form given to us was "A Fyddo Doeth Darllene<u>r</u>".

The date of the ceremony of the stone laying has now been definitely fixed for July 11th, at 3 o'clock p.m. Please prepare accordingly, and the gentlemen who have to perform the ceremony are Lord Glantawe, Mr. Herbert Lloyd, Mr. Francis William Gilbertson, and the oldest workman in this district – we shall let you have his name in a few days.

Philip Davies to W. Beddoe Rees, Architect. **1 July 1908 [6 : 146]**

A question has arisen this week regarding the ceremony of Stone Laying, which has necessitated a little change in our arrangements, and it has been decided to add to the memorial stone "This Stone was laid by Arthur Gilbertson Esq".

Mr. Radford called here today, and we put the matter before him and he undertook to attend to it. Will you kindly also follow it up. The wording previously given will have to be altered a little to meet this.

Philip Davies to Cecil Gilbertson, Abercrave. **11 July 1908 [6 : 166]**

I have your favour of yesterday, and thank you very much for cheque £10/-/- from Mrs. Gilbertson, and £50/-/- from yourself towards the fund of above.

The Committee, I am sure, will be greatly encouraged by these substantial donations, and your promise of further assistance, if required.

Philip Davies to Daniel Daniels, Alltwen. **30 July 1908 [6 : 170]**

I enclose cheque £250/-/- being the second donation from Messrs W. Gilbertson & Co. Ltd., towards the funds of above.

Frank Gilbertson to Frederick Edwards, Manager, Capital & Counties Bank Ltd., Swansea. **13 Oct. 1908 [6 : 186-7]**

Referring to my interview with you when you stated your willingness to advance up to £2,500 for the Pontardawe Public Hall, on the guarantee of the Trustees, myself being one, the time has now come when we require assistance. We have drawn some £1,700 from our account & have to find another £300 by the end of this week.

May we draw this cheque? You can take this letter as my personal guarantee for the £300, pending the formal arrangements that I presume the Trustees will enter into with the Bank.

I think I told you that we were spending £5,000 of which £2,500 was paid or promised.

May I ask, in consideration of the close connection of my firm with the New Hall, & of the use that our workpeople will make of it, that you should charge us the lowest rate of interest that you can?

The Trustees are now appointed & number 16 substantial names, so we are ready to execute the necessary documents.

Philip Davies to W. Howel Thomas, Treasurer, Gellinedd. **20 Oct. 1908 [6 : 196]**

We enclose accounts with cheques against same, kindly sign the cheques and enclosures as soon as possible.

You will be pleased to hear that Madam Patti will give a Concert to open the new Hall. I understand that she has given her word to Mr. C. F. Gilbertson that she will do this, and she is also arranging with Mr. Ben Davies to assist.

On 6 May 1909 the Public Hall and Institute was opened by Baroness Cederström, the eminent diva Adelina Patti, "amidst enthusiastic scenes" (Cambria Daily Leader, 7 May 1909).

Philip Davies to W. Howel Thomas. **21 May 1909 [6 : 381]**

I enclose cheque for £500/-/- being a further subscription from Messrs W. Gilbertson & Co.

Frank Gilbertson to Messrs R. & C. B. Jenkins, Solicitors, Swansea. **26 June 1909[7 : 86]**

Could you proceed with the Lease & the Trust Deed for the New Hall as soon as convenient?

Our Fire Insurance Policy is made out in the name of the "Public Hall Committee". Should it strictly be in the name of the Trustees?

Frank Gilbertson to Messrs The Pontardawe Skating Rink Co. **20 Dec. 1909 [7 : 172-3]**

Your favour of the 6th inst.

We confirm the arrangement recited in your letter.

We have asked Messrs R. & C. B. Jenkins to prepare a draft lease.

Can the lease be drawn in the name of Messrs Lewis Brothers, or members of your Company?

We do not care to grant a sub lease to a Limited Company.

We have discussed the question of Electric light with you, & we should be glad if you were able to arrange suitable terms for lighting by Acetylene or some other method, but if you cannot we will again consider electric supply.

In any case there would be no difficulty in supplying 1 horse power for an electric motor.

Frank Gilbertson to Messrs R. & C. B. Jenkins. **17 Feb. 1910 [7 : 207]**

Skating Rink

We think £5 per annum would be a fair sum to put in as Rent.

With regard to the clause relating to a possible use of the ground for Railways. We certainly think they should in that event have liberty to remove the whole building, & we should not like anything in the Lease to prevent them receiving proper compensation if a Railway Co desired to buy the ground, because not much of the building would pay to move. Perhaps we could arrange that without complicating the terms of the Lease?

P. Davies to W. B. Laws, Auditor, Cardiff. **2 May 1910 [7 : 278]**

Income Tax 1909/1910

. . . With regard to the Subscriptions to the Public Hall, this is really a Workman's Institute and there are certain tangible advantages to us as Employers that result from its use.

Abstracted from list:		£	s	d
Subn to	Public Hall & Institute	250	–	–
Don "	Male Voice Party for Concert Tkts	2	2	–
" "	Workmen's Annual Trip	1	1	2
" "	" " "	1	1	2
" "	Police Band Concert for Tkts	2	2	3
Subn "	Pontardawe Football Club	1	1	2

Public Hall & Institute – £250. As our object in promoting this Institute was to improve the habits & characters of our Workpeople, & to provide a place where Trades Unions could meet as an alternative to Public Houses, where the better class of men wont go, we consider the Company derives direct benefit from the expenditure.

Pontardawe Public Hall and Institute *(Jeff Childs)*

Frank Gilbertson to The Postmaster, Swansea. 3 Sept. 1910 [6 : 402]

Pontardawe Public Hall & Institute

As Chairman of the Committee I have been requested to write to you & ask that a Letter Box should be placed on the Boundary Wall of the Institute.

Will you kindly give our request careful consideration?

The Institute is very largely used & the Box would be a great convenience to the members & also to the public living in Herbert St, Holly St, & the adjoining district, which is increasing at a rapid rate.

Frank Gilbertson to Messrs R. & C. B. Jenkins. 24 Oct. 1910 [7 : 442]

Skating Rink

We have special reasons for extending favours to the Lewis family, & we do not think the clause will hurt us. We shall have no reason for disturbing them unless the GWR line came up the Canal, & we put this clause into the lease so that we might include the Skating Rink claim in any arrangement we should come to with the Railway Co.

First committee of the Pontardawe Public Hall and Institute, July 1909.
Front the left (back row): David Henry Jones, Charles Williams, Evan Thomas, Eli Skidmore, David Jenkins, Rees Gwilym, Ben Lloyd, David Williams, Tom George, Thomas Davies, Henry Thomas; *(middle row):* George James, William Davies, John Daniel, David Rees, John Jenkin Jones, Tom Price, Walter Jones, D. T. Williams, John Davies, David James, Tom Harris, David Thomas, Arthur Williams, John Owen Williams, William Davies; *(seated):* D. J. Williams, John Walters, Daniel Morgan, Gwilym Lewis, L. W. Francis, William Thomas, Morgan Jones, James Hinkin, F. W. Gilbertson, Philip Davies, T. W. Owen, John Thomas, David Lewis, Evan Morgan, Jonah Williams; *(on ground):* W. Richard Lewis, Jonah Jones, John Bodycombe, John Bowen. (From the *West Wales Observer*, 16 October, 1959)

Frank Gilbertson to Messrs Lewis Brothers. 13 Dec. 1910 [7 : 468]

Rink

Now you are using electric current for lighting we think our charges must be revised.

We make out that the organ for 2½ hours per day takes – 550 kW.

18 – 50 cp lamps for 4 hours a day = 5·40 kW.

This means 6 BT Units or 2/- per day.

Please give us your views & correct us if the times given above are wrong.

Frank Gilbertson to John Morgan, Surveyor. 24 April 1911 [7 : 551]

I do not like asking further favours after the kind reception the Council gave us last Thursday, but if it was possible without inconvenience to the Council to erect the new Offices on the upper side of the plot of ground, so as to give the Public Hall Committee the use of the plot adjoining the Hall for a Bowling Green, it would increase our facilities very much.

Would you kindly bring the matter before your Council again?

Frank Gilbertson to Frederick Edwards, 28 July 1911 [7 : 641]
Messrs Capital & Counties Bank Ld, Swansea.

I wish to make one further appeal to you about the Public Hall & Institute overdraft.

The concern is more than self supporting as the result of 2 years work. It is of great use to this growing village, & has been a success in every way.

You have the overdraft perfectly well secured, & we want to know whether you cannot be satisfied with 4% interest inclusive of all charges?

You were good enough to tell me when I first made the application that you would charge us as low a rate as you were able to do, which I understood to mean the lowest rate you charged any customer.

Frank Gilbertson to Messrs Lewis Bros. 4 Dec. 1911 [7 : 747]

I am sorry to hear that you let your Rink for a meeting of protest against the sentences passed upon the rioters at Tarenni, on Sunday.

Such a proceeding is opposed to our ideas altogether, & although we cannot control the use you put the Rink to, we have shown a desire to help you in regard to your liabilities under the lease, & in other ways, & we hope you will not allow the Rink to be used for purposes of which we obviously would not approve.

Tarenni Colliery in Godrergraig was about 5 miles from Pontardawe

Frank Gilbertson to Messrs Lewis Bros. **8 Dec. 1911 [7 : 757]**

We are much obliged by yours of 5th which quite explains the matter, & we are glad to know the facts.

Frank Gilbertson to Messrs Lewis Bros. **23 Feb. 1914 [8 : 503]**

Would you be willing to cancel the Lease we granted you of the Skating Rink & to take a new lease of a reduced area, excluding the Barn & the wooden shop, upon our making an abatement in rent equal to the revenue you now derive from that part of the property?

We would pay all legal expenses.

Charles Gilbertson to Charles L. Lawrence, **8 Nov. 1920 [10 : 573]**
3 Paper Buildings, Temple, EC

A special meeting of the Shareholders is hereby called for 10.30 a.m. on TUESDAY, 16th NOVEMBER, for the purpose of ordering the attachment of the Seal of the Company to a deed of gift of land to the Glamorgan County Council.

N.B. The land is to be used as playing fields for the County Schools, in furtherance of the objects of Mr. Fisher's Education Act [of 1918].

NOTE

1. J. R. Jones, *The History of Pontardawe R.F.C.* (Llandybie, Salesbury Press, 1985), 21-23.

BIOGRAPHICAL NOTES

Some of the Main Addressees in theText

BARLOW Stephen Babington: practised as a sole practitioner from 1869 to 1873 when he joined T. Westall and J. P. S. Roberts as a partner. By 1876 Roberts & Barlow were practising from 49 Lime Street, EC3 (to 1906), being joined by nephew George Barlow in 1898, and shortly afterwards by Henry Lyde. The practice specialised in insurance work. S. B. Barlow retired in 1907. Since 1930 the practice has continued under its present style of Barlow Lyde & Gilbert.

BOND Henry Coulson (1864-1937), educ. Rugby. Family company was Vivian Younger & Bond, a leading London firm of tinplate merchants. Partner in E. Morewood & Co. and acquired Morewood's South Wales and Cwmbwrla Works to establish the South Wales Tinplate Co. in 1896. Deputy Chairman of Richard Thomas & Co., Llanelly, and Chairman *ex officio* on death of L. R. Beaumont Thomas in February 1917 (to 1918) and again in the 1920s, retiring in 1931 to be succeeded by William Firth. President of National Federation of Iron & Steel Manufacturers, 1926-27 and Chairman of the Welsh Plate & Sheet Manufacturers' Association, 1928-32. High Sheriff of Carmarthenshire 1920-21.

DANIEL Edward Rice (1829-1905): b. Margam, educ. locally, Mining engineer, estate & mineral agent. Acquired, with his brother-in-law, Sir John Jones Jenkins, the Cwmfelin Tin Plate Works in 1883 and sold it in 1896; Director of Aber Tin Plate Works, Villiers Spelter Works, and the Swansea & Mumbles Railway. Swansea Borough Councillor for St. John's Ward to 1897, Mayor of Swansea 1882-3, Justice of the Peace, represented the Swansea Division on County Licensing Committee (Compensation).

ECCLES Herbert (1857-1928): Founder & Joint Managing Director of Briton Ferry Steel Co. in 1889 and Chairman from 1910 to 1928. Director (1898), Managing Director (1907) and later Chairman of Llanelly Steel Co; Secretary and prime mover of an Association of Steel Makers 1899, and founder and first Chairman of the South Wales Siemens Steel Association (1899-1918). First Chairman of the Tinplate & Sheet Conciliation Board from 1899 to 1928. Joined Board of Directors of Western Tinplate Works on death of E. Trubshaw in 1910. Justice of the Peace and High Sheriff of Glamorganshire 1905-06.

EDEN Charles Hamilton (1855-1921): b. Co. Durham, fourth son of Canon Eden, Rector of Sedgefield; educ. Haileybury and College of Physical Science, Newcastle. Mining engineer. Assistant to general manager of Vivian & Sons, 1890, and succeeded (with brother Gerald) to general management of works and collieries of Vivian & Sons, Swansea. Chairman of English Group of Spelter Manufacturers, Chairman of Swansea District Board of the Monmouthshire & South Wales Collieries Association and member of its Sliding Scale Joint Committee. Director of North Bitchburn Coal Co. Ltd., Darlington.

EDWARDS Frederick: b. Walton Court, Radnorshire; entered Gloucestershire Banking Co. in 1862, becoming Manager of the Berkley branch in the late 1870s. Joined the Glamorganshire Banking Co. as Manager in Neath in 1880 and appointed General Manager in 1884 when, "with moderation, discretion and calm courage", he guided the Bank through a financial crisis. He remained in post when the Bank was taken over by the Capital & Counties Banking Co. in April 1898.

FRANKLEN Sir Thomas Mansel (1840-1928): b. Swansea, son of Richard Franklen, JP, DL, and Isabel Talbot; educ. Harrow, Exeter & Merton, Oxford, graduating 1861. Called to Bar from Lincoln's Inn, 1865, practised on South Wales circuit. In 1878 became Clerk of the Peace for Glamorgan, and in 1889 the first Clerk of Glamorgan County Council, holding the office for 50 years to his death. Knighted in 1921, receiving honorary LL.D. from University of Wales in same year.

GIBBINS Frederick William (1861-1937): b. Neath, eldest son of Frederick Joseph Gibbins, scion of a Quaker family owning Melincryddan Chemical Works from 1813. Manager of Ynyspenllwch Tinplate Works, Glais, 1884-90, leaving to build the Eagle Tinplate Works, Neath, becoming its Managing Director in 1905 and Chairman in 1909. Chairman of Melyn Tinplate Co., Neath (1903) and Director of Melincryddan Chemical Works. A founder and Chairman of Welsh Plate & Sheet Manufacturers' Association (1910-24). High Sheriff of Glamorganshire 1908-09. Member of Parliament (Liberal) for Mid Glamorgan 1910. Member of Board of Management of the National Shell Factory, Landore, and of Glamorgan Appeal Tribunal & Excess Profits Commission. Chairman of Employers' Committee of Tinplate JIC (1920). Alderman of Neath Town Council 1922-28 and Glamorgan County Councillor for 18 years.

GIBBINS Theodore (1876-1952): b. Neath, brother of Frederick William. From 1903 to his retirement in 1933 was a Director, then Managing Director of Melyn Tinplate & Blackplate Works, Neath. Member of Executive Committee of Welsh Plate & Sheet Manufacturers' Association from 1910 to 1933. Acquired Glynbeudy Tinplate Works from Arthur Gilbertson in 1910 (to 1917). High Sheriff of Glamorganshire, 1928-29.

GILBERTSON Francis Bramah (1838-1921), second son of William Gilbertson, "known by all as F.B.G . . . & a bit of a headache for my Grandfather Arthur. He was given a job as Sales manager for WG & Co. Steel Products in Liverpool" (Family correspondence). Gore's Directories for Liverpool from 1870 to 1895 list him variously as a metal broker, iron & tinplate merchant and agent for WG & Co. During this time Liverpool was the main shipping port for tinplates until Swansea Harbour Trust developed its docks & facilities from 1889 to become the largest shipping port for tin, terne & blackplate in the world. He was a Trustee of the Company, a shareholder and debenture holder. From 1914 he lived at the Royal Hotel, Hoylake, where he died in July 1921.

GRIFFITHS Griffith (1840-1908): b. Tynycae, Alltwen, son of Rev. Phillip Griffiths of Alltwen; educ. Swansea Normal College, University College & University College Hospital, London; Gold Medal, Materia Medica, 1861, Silver Medal in Midwifery, 1862, Certificate of Honour, 1864 at UCH; MRCS Eng. 1864, LRCP & LM Edinburgh 1864. Temporary house physician at Brompton Hospital for Consumption. General Practitioner, also holding Pontardawe Union appointments as Medical Officer & Public Vaccinator and Workhouse Medical Officer, and the public offices of Certifying Factory Surgeon and Medical Officer of Health to the Rural District Council. Justice of the Peace; Member of British Medical Association.

HODGE John (1855-1937): b. Muirkirk, entered iron trade at Rochsollach Iron Works and later at Colville's Motherwell Works where a conflict in 1885 led to the formation of the British Steel Smelters' Association in January 1886 with Hodge as Secretary. Membership increased rapidly under his leadership, characterized by his moderation and belief in "common sense and reason". From 1890 he worked to end sectionalism among rival TUs. President of Trades Congress 1892 and twice President of the Labour Representation Committee. President of British Section, International Congress, Zurich, 1893. Member of Glasgow City Council in 1891 & 1898-1901. Parliamentary candidate for Gower 1900, Preston 1903 and Gorton (Lancs.) where he was elected in 1906, serving as a solid if unspectacular MP until 1923, Minister of Labour 1916-17 & Minister of Pensions 1917-19. Alienated Labour Party in 1918 over its war policy and advocated an alternative trade union party. Re-elected in 1918 & 1922 but his political commitment to the Labour Party remained strained, and he resigned in 1931.

JOHN John Hopkin (1853-1923): Started work at Morfa Copper Works at 13, and from 1877 was a tinworker at the Forest Tinplate Works, Morriston. With Tom Phillips and David Randell MP, he formed the South Wales, Monmouthshire & Gloucestershire Tinplate Workers' Union in 1887 which later became the Welsh Artizans United Association. From 1888 to 1898 he edited *The Welsh Industrial Times* and subsequently *The Industrial World*, the weekly newspapers of the Tinplate Workers' Union.

LAWRENCE Sir Alfred Tristram (1843-1936): b. Pontypool, eldest son of David Lawrence, surgeon; educ. Mill Hill and Trinity Hall, Cambs. Called to the Bar from Middle Temple, 1869, practised on Oxford circuit; Junior Counsel to Admiralty 1882; Recorder of Royal Borough of Windsor 1885; took silk 1897; Justice of the High Court 1904; Knight Bachelor 1904; President of Railway & Canal Commission from 1908; President of the War Compensation Court, 1920-22, and of the Admiralty Transport Arbitration Board from 1922. In 1921 he was appointed Lord Chief Justice, a Privy Councillor and created first Baron Trevethin of Blaengawney, Monmouthshire. He resigned in 1922 owing to increasing deafness. In 1875 he married his first cousin Jessie Elizabeth, daughter of George Lawrence and sister of Walter and Charles Lawrence.

LAWRENCE George (1806-1896): b. Monmouth. Original partner of William Gilbertson in 1861 and subsequently a major shareholder in W. Gilbertson & Co. Ltd. Lived at Moreton Court, Hereford, and from 1880 to 1896 in Cheltenham. Justice of the Peace for Monmouthshire.

LAWRENCE Sir Walter Roper (1857-1940): b. Moreton Court, Hereford, fifth son of George Lawrence. Educ. Cheltenham College and Balliol, Oxford. Passed first in open competition Indian Civil Service, 1877, entered BCS 1879 and appointed Settlement Commissioner in Kashmir. Resigned BCS in 1896 to become Chief Agent to Duke of Bedford. Recalled to India in 1898 by Viceroy Lord Curzon to become his Private Secretary in 1903. Awarded Knight Commander of Indian Empire, 1903. Returned to England for business & public life in 1903, but in 1905 was recalled as Chief of Staff to Prince of Wales on his visit to India. Created GCIE and first Baronet in 1906. Member of Council of India 1907-09. Appointed CB in 1917 and GCVO in 1918.

LLOYD Herbert (1838-1914): b. Corston, Pembs; educ. Marlborough & Trinity, Cambs. (1850). Studied Land Agency at Castle Troy, Limerick. Inherited Cilybebyll Estate from his father, Francis Edwardes Lloyd. Justice of the Peace for Glamorgan & Breconshire, High Sheriff of Glamorgan, 1877-8, Vice-Chairman of Quarter Sessions, member of Glamorgan Standing Joint Committee, Chairman of Pontardawe Board of Guardians (1878-1909), Chairman of Pontardawe RDC (1900-04), Chairman of the Executive Committee of the South Wales & Monmouthshire Poor Law Conference.

PLAYER John (1841-1931): b. Loughor, son of Alderman William John Player, mayor of Neath in 1867. Educ. Birmingham, Member of Institute of Mechanical Engineers. Took over Clydach Iron Foundry in 1871, erected blackplate mill 1874, commenced tinning in 1881, patented the Player automatic tinning pot 1886. By 1893 plant comprised 2 mills, and in 1905 four mills were laid down and a cold rolling plant erected. Title of firm changed to John Player & Sons in 1908 and registered as a private limited company in 1917 with £75,000 capital. Director also of Gyrnos Tinplate Co., Ystalyfera. Justice of the Peace.

RANDELL David (1854-1912): b. Llanelli, solicitor, MP (Lib-Lab.) for Gower constituency 1888-1900. Helped to re-establish Tinplate Workers' Union with J. H. John.

RITSON JHR: manager of Aberdulais Tinplate Works in 1893, previously Secretary of the Vale of Neath Railway (1851) and its General Manager (1865).

TRUBSHAW Ernest (1846-1910): DL, JP, iron founder and Managing Director of the Western Tinplate Works Co., Llanelly, 1879-1910 and in 1896 a promoter and first Chairman of the Llanelly Steel Co. (registered 1898) to 1910. Advocate and first Chairman of the Welsh Plate & Sheet Manufacturers' Association (popularly known as the Tinplate Association) from 1899 to 1910, a bilateral conciliation board to discuss and regulate prices, wage rates and conditions. Chairman of Llanelly UDC and the Harbour Board; Chairman of Llanelly Bench of Magistrates and vice-chairman of Carmarthen Quarter Sessions. High Sheriff of Carmarthenshire, 1901.

WIGNALL James (1856-1925): educ. Swansea National School, worked at Morfa Copper Works, Swansea. Borough councillor and JP, first Labour member on School Board, 1899, and its vice-chairman by 1903. District Secretary of Dockers' Union and President of Swansea Trades Council, first National Organiser of the Dock, Wharf, Riverside & General Workers' Union in South Wales & the West of England. MP (Labour) for Forest of Dean, 1918-1925, Member of Overseas Settlement Delegation, 1923.

WRIGHT Col. Sir John Roper (1843-1926): b. Croston (Lancs.), apprenticed at Soho Engineering Works, Preston, worked for William Siemens in Midlands, managed steel furnaces at Landore-Siemens Steel Co. from 1867. Built Panteg Steel Works & Engineering Co, 1873. In 1878 formed Wright Butler & Co. to produce open-hearth steel at the Elba Steelworks, Gowerton, 1878; bought Panteg Steelworks 1882 and the old Landore-Siemens plant. Became associated with Alfred Baldwin at Panteg c. 1886, leading to formal merger of Wright, Butler & Baldwins under the title of Baldwins Ltd. in 1902. The Port Talbot Steel Co. Ltd., was formed with Baldwins Ltd. & the Gloucester Railway Carriage & Wagon Co. Ltd. as main shareholders with Wright himself holding the lease of the works from W. Gilbertson & Co. Ltd. With death of Alfred Baldwin in 1908 and his son Stanley's interest in politics, Wright and his son Charles exercised control over Baldwins, becoming Managing Director from 1905-8 and Chairman in 1908 & one of the joint managing directors during the Great War. In 1909 erected Kings Dock Tinplate Works, Swansea, and in 1915 acquired all shares in the Port Talbot Steel Co. Ltd., and oversaw subsequent steel developments at Margam, the acquisition of Brymbo Steel Co. (1917), Briton Ferry Iron Works (1918), Eagle Tinplate Works (1921), Wern Tinplate Co. (1923). Resigned Chairmanship (1925) in favour of his son. Created baronet in 1920.

WRIGHT Col. Sir William Charles (1876-1950): only son of Col. Sir John Roper Wright. Appointed manager of the Port Talbot Iron & Steel Works when it restarted in 1907. Chairman of Baldwins Ltd, Deputy Chairman & Managing Director of the British (Guest Keen & Baldwin) Iron & Steel Co, succeeded Sir John Hunter as Controller of Iron & Steel Production in 1917. For his contribution to the war effort he was made a CB in 1918 and a KBE in 1920. With his father he helped to build up the Margam-Port Talbot steel complex, with blast furnaces also at Briton Ferry and Landore. Succeeded his father as Chairman in 1925. By the end of the 1920s rationalisation was economically imperative and resulted in the merger of Baldwins and Guest Keen & Nettlefolds in 1930, with Charles as Deputy Chairman and Managing Director, and Chairman in 1936. Succeeded his father as baronet in 1926, made a GBE in 1943 for his services to the steel industry. He was possibly the major influence in the discussions which led to the formation of the Steel Company of Wales in 1947.

GLOSSARY

Technical and Trade Terms used in the text

ACID PROCESS: A steelmaking process carried out in Bessemer, Open-Hearth or Electric Arc furnaces, and characterized by the furnace lining consisting of an 'acid' refractory, e.g. silica, and with additions of silica introduced during the refining process. The slag formed during the process (known as 'acid' slag) does not absorb phosphorus from the iron charges to the furnace. The process is therefore suitable for processing only low phosphorus iron.

ANNEALING: Heating steel and holding it at a suitable temperature, followed by controlled cooling to remove stresses introduced during the rolling process and so improving its softness, machinability and coldworking properties.

ASSORTERS: Experienced tinworkers responsible for quality control who carefully examined each tinplate sheet on both sides for flaws, classifying and segregating the sheets into quality categories, e.g. primes, seconds, waste.

BASIC PROCESS: A method of steel-making carried out in a furnace, either Open-Hearth, Bessemer Converter or Electric Arc, lined with a basic refractory such as magnesite or dolomite, and with additions of magnesite or dolomite during the refining process. In the basic process phosphorus in the steel can be reduced to negligible proportions by transfer.

BASIC SLAG: A slag produced during the conversion of high phosphorus pig iron into steel by the basic process. It has a commercial value as a fertilizer owing to its high calcium phosphate content. Acid slag consists principally of silica, whilst basic slag consists mainly of lime or oxide of iron.

BASIC STEEL: Steel produced by the basic process which is characterized by a slag rich in lime with the sulphur and phosphorus passing into the slag during the working of the charge.

BASIS BOX: The standard box of tinplates, equivalent to 20" x 14", 112 sheets, which is equal to 31,360 square inches of area, weighing nett 108 lbs. These are called I.C. The basis box was the standard (before 1964) for measuring tinplates and calculating prices.

BERTRAND-THIEL PROCESS: A now obsolete method of steelmaking, for processing pig iron with abnormally high phosphorus contents, and requiring a two-stage (primary and secondary) refining process.

BIRMINGHAM GAUGE (B.G.): A standard of thickness (substance) of metal. There were several different gauges giving rise to frequent misunderstanding.

BLACKPLATES: Iron or steel sheet, rolled, pickled and annealed but not coated with tin (for tinplate), or lead (for terneplate), or zinc (for galvanized sheet).

BOSH: A bath for pickling or quenching (i.e. cooling with water) operations.

BRAND: Products of a particular make or trade mark, showing ownership and/or quality. Tinplates, blackplates and terneplates were packed in wooden boxes which were branded with names and/or letters, e.g. IC, IX, etc., which showed the substance of the plates, and *coal* or *charcoal* to show the quality of the iron, or (later) steel, used. In 1893 Gilbertson's brands were: *Charcoal* – PONTARDAWE CROWN, AZ, LINCOLN, COMET, REGINA, GWYNEDD; *Coke* – GILBERTSONS, PARSONS. Arthur Gilbertson's GOM (for *Gilbertson's Old Method*) had a high reputation and 135 boxes of ic 14/20 tinned roofing plates, Gilbertson's old method @ $6·70 per box were supplied to roof the White House in Washington DC in 1886.

C.I.F.: Cost, Insurance & Freight. The value of imports is sometimes measured c.i.f., and includes all the costs involved in their movement from the country of origin.

COKES: Originally tinplate made from iron smelted in a coke-fired furnace. It later represented ordinary coated tinplates, the grade of tin coating adequate for common purposes; BEST COKES would signify a grade between coke and charcoal in coating and slightly more expensive.

COMMON CHARCOAL: Originally tinplate made from iron smelted in a coal-fired furnace. It later represented a grade carrying a heavier layer of tin coating than BEST COKES, and therefore of better quality and more expensive than coke tinplate.

COPPERAS: Iron vitriol, ferrous sulphate. The spent liquor from the black pickling department was crystallised and sold commercially as 'green copperas'.

CROSSES: Plates thicker than IC were called crosses. Each additional X after the first X (which indicates 28 lbs.) indicates an increased thickness corresponding to 20 lbs. for 31,360 square inches of area.

CUPOLA: The furnace most commonly used for the production of iron castings in the foundry or, as in some cases, for re-melting pig iron before charging in a molten state into a Bessemer Converter. It is a straight shaft furnace consisting of a circular stack of steel plates lined with firebrick.

F.O.B.: Free On Board. The value of exports is measured f.o.b., excluding transport and insurance costs, so that f.o.b. prices are lower than c.i.f. prices. The choice of measure affects the size of the deficit or surplus.

F.O.R.: Free On Rail.

GALVANIZING: The coating of iron, or, as later, steel, with zinc, generally by immersion in a bath of zinc, covered with a flux, at a temperature of 425° to 500°. The flux was a solution usually of zinc ammonium chloride to promote the addition of the zinc coating.

I.C.: Definition of thickness (expressed as weight) of a basis box of tinplates, i.e. 31,360 square inches, weighing 108 lbs, 0·0123 of an inch (0·315 mm).

I.X.: Definition of thickness (expressed as weight) of a basis box of tinplates, i.e. 31,360 square inches, weighing 136 lbs, 0·0155 of an inch (0·394 mm).

LACQUERING: Tinplates covered on one or both sides with lacquer which was usually brightly coloured, with gold lacquer being most extensively used. Lacquering was an additional protective coating involving an extra process which was charged for. Food and drink cans were often coated on the inside with lacquer to protect the tin coating being attacked and broken down by compounds in the contents.

LIGHTS: Often referred to as C.L. or C.L.L. were tinplates thinner than I.C. weight, the usual variations being 100 lbs. weight and variations downwards in steps of 5 lbs., but intermediate weights of light plates were often made to comply with foreign specifications.

MURIATIC ACID: A former name for Hydrochloric acid.

PICKLING: The process of chemically removing scale or oxide from metal to obtain a clean surface, usually effected by immersion in a bath of a hot acid solution.

PIG IRON: Crude iron produced by the reduction of iron ore in a blast furnace and cast into pigs which are subsequently re-melted and refined into steel, cast iron or wrought iron.

PRIMES: The standard of first quality tinplates in each grade after seconds and wasters had been separated and withdrawn.

SIEMENS OPEN HEARTH FURNACE: A furnace of reverberatory type used in steel making.

SILICA BRICKS: Bricks containing at least 92% silica, which is extremely refractory, with a melting point of 1,750°. The bricks were used to line acid open-hearth and other furnaces where resistance to high temperatures and the attack of acid slags was required.

SMALL LOTS: Usually a lot under 2 tons of special size.

SPELTER: A term formerly applied to all grades of commercial zinc. HARD SPELTER is an alloy of zinc and iron formed in the galvanizing bath by the reduction of the iron salts on the surface of the steel being galvanized.

STEEL: A malleable alloy of iron and carbon, the latter being usually less than 1·7%.

TAGGERS: Very thin sheets of tinplates, usually 30 B.G., 38·0 B.G. or 40·0 B.G.

TERNEPLATES: Rolled iron or steel sheets or blackplates coated with lead or an alloy of lead with up to approx. 25% tin.

TIN BAR: Flat rolled steel bar, 15 to 20 feet long by 9" wide and a thickness from ⅜" to ⅞", intended for the production of tinplate.

TINPLATE: Mild steel (originally iron) flat sheet with a protective coating of tin or a tin-lead alloy on each surface. It combines the strength of steel with the corrosion resistance of tin.

TIN POT: Container for molten tin into which iron or steel sheets were dipped for tinning (now obsolete).

TRADE MARK: A registered device or name marked upon or displayed in connection with an article, peculiar to and the sole property of the producer or manufacturer.

WASTERS: Imperfect tinplates with some defect or blemish, but which were suitable for some purposes and were sold at a reduced price. Deficient tinplates which were not up to a standard to be classified as wasters, but still useful for certain purposes, could be classed as WASTE WASTE.

APPENDIX 1

Index of Letter-Books

The ten Letter-Books are deposited with the West Glamorgan Archive Service at County Hall, Swansea.

D/D Gil 1/1	:	13 August 1890 – 6 April 1900
D/D Gil 1/2	:	5 May 1894 – 2 June 1900
D/D Gil 1/3	:	9 April 1900 – 19April 1904
D/D Gil 1/4	:	5 February 1902 – 11 October 1904
D/D Gil 1/5	:	20 April 1904 – 25 March 1909
D/D Gil 1/6	:	29 October 1907 – 9 June 1909
D/D Gil 1/7	:	26 March 1909 – 7 August 1912
D/D Gil 1/8	:	8 August 1912 – 5 July 1915
D/D Gil 1/9	:	19 January 1914 – 10 May 1916
D/D Gil 1/10	:	8 July 1915 – 7 October 1929

Additional W. Gilbertson & Company papers on deposit include:

D/D Gil 2 :	Correspondence concerning colliery workings south of Pontardawe, 13 June1883 – 20 December 1889.
D/D Gil 3 :	Correspondence with Sir George Barstow including discussion of tinplate for canning trade, list of British canners and details of plant at tinplate works at Pontardawe, Glanrhyd and Glynbeudy, 3 September 1930 – 23 March 1932.
D/D Gil 4/1, 2 :	Memorandum of Agreement between The Graigola Merthyr Co. Ltd., and W. Gilbertson & Co. Ltd., 14 January 1888, and Plan.
D/D Gil 5 :	Plan of area to east of Glais Pit, 30 July 1870.
D/D Gil 6 :	Plan of Old Bryncoch Pit Workings, n.d.
D/D Gil 7/1, 2 :	Plan of Bituminous Coal by Wernddu, n.d.

APPENDIX 2

The List of 1874

* Rolling	(List Sizes)	3s. 5d. per doz.
* Doubling	" "	2s. 9d. "
* Furnacing	" "	2s. 7d. "
* Behinding	" "	1s. 3d. "
* Shearing	" "	1s. 1d. "
+ Annealing	" "	12s. 0d. } per 100
"		14s. 0d. }
++ Black pickling	" "	6s. 0d. }
" "	" "	6s. 6d. } per 100
++White pickling	" "	5s. 6d. }
Tinning	" "	0s. 3d. per box
Washing	" "	0s. 3d. per box
Greasing	" "	0s. 1d. per box
Sorting (per day 3 sets)		6s. 3d. per box per day 3 sets.

Resolved 18th January that **xx** plates and upwards be paid at the rate of 140 lbs. per box in Mills and Tinhouses.

* Bar iron to be cut and delivered to the Mills.
  Furnacemen to open stickers.

+ According to class of work.
++Or by day as may be agreed upon.
All allowances for Houses and Coals will be discontinued when these are paid.

ARTHUR GILBERTSON
GEO. B. STRICK Chairman
W. R. QUICK Secretary

APPENDIX 3

The Pontardawe Girls' Friendly Society

In the Winter of 1893 Ellen Gilbertson wrote down the substance of her appeal to the works' girls to join her Girls' Friendly Society. Its content is redolent of the values which typified middle-class attempts to promote the moral improvement of the labouring poor during the Victorian period, and extols the Puritan values of hard work and a sense of duty, and the virtues of thrift, moral responsibility and self-discipline:

> "I want to speak to you for 10 minutes about a Society which I have been asked to try and interest some of the young girls in. It is called the Girls Friendly Society. Now you know what a Benefit Club is, like the Forresters etc., and the use of these Clubs is to help their members when they are ill. Well, this Society is a sort of Club and this is what it tries to do.
>
> The heads of this Society are called Associates and you girls are called Members.
>
> First understand what a Member is. It is a part of a body such as your arm is a Member of your body. You are all Members or parts of Christ's Church on Earth.
>
> Well, these Associates and Members are joined together into the Body to help one another and their Motto is:
>
> Bear ye one Another's Burden.
>
> I daresay you will ask How can we be helped by these Associates?
>
> I tell you by feeling their Sympathy for you and knowing that they will pray for you and help you if you come to them for Advice.
>
> What these Associates try and teach is dutifulness to parents, obedience to them, love to them and to try and remind their Members of what the parents did for them when they were young, poor, helpless Babies.
>
> Old age has its cares and worries and lucky is the parent who feels her girls try and lighten the burden.
>
> Then we have to teach you about Purity.
>
> Think what that means: Purity of Life.
>
> Something so White it looks like the driven snow you saw on the Mountains around you this week. Something so pure and beautiful it is like a lovely white

Lily, and above all think of Purity like the Angels with their Raiment, white as nothing on Earth can make them.

But we cannot hope to be like this beautiful thing when we do things we should be ashamed to be seen and when we feel in our own hearts we are staining those garments of purity and dragging the Lily into the Mud.

Should my girls be ill they are sometimes helped by this Society to go for a change and when they marry respectably they are entitled at the end of 12 months to a present.

It is to help in every way we can to remind you of the design of Immorality. Freedom with Men and boys and the Temptations which beset you poor girls in a way you often cannot help, that the Society has been formed these 11 years.

You must fight against your old enemy the devil, but remember the promise: If you resist the devil he will flee from you if you ask Christ's help.

Another way we can help you is by reminding you to do your Work as unto God and not to Men. Not with lip service but in singleness of heart.

Don't be ashamed of doing your work well whether you are praised or not. Your conscience will tell you when you have done your duty.

Try and remember to put by for a rainy day for as I have often told you the sun does not always shine, and try and never buy what you cannot pay for. Nothing is more miserable than to feel the chain of debt binding you closer and closer.

Well, I have not much to say about worldly advantages connected with it. In the first place you pay 1/- a year to belong to the Society and you cannot become a Member till you are proved to be really in earnest, for it is chiefly a Society to help those who wish to climb the ladder to that City that Jacob saw in his dream.

It is for all whether Chapel or Church. Each has a right to climb it and by God's help I trust some of you will try.

Mrs. Griffiths has kindly consented to take the Head in Pontardawe and Mrs. Wolfe and myself will be glad to receive any names of those anxious to join."

The manuscript of Ellen's address is annotated in Arthur Gilbertson's hand: "Written by my dear Wife, for the Works Girls, year before her death".

APPENDIX 4

27th December, 1933.

TO THE EMPLOYEES OF W. GILBERTSON & CO. LTD.

Our Employees will have seen in the local Press that we have concluded an amalgamation with Messrs. Richard Thomas & Co. Ltd. The effect of this will be that early in the New Year Sir WILLIAM FIRTH will become Chairman of this Company and direct its policy, my brother and myself continuing to act as local Directors.

We have taken this serious step after very careful thought and with a full sense of the responsibility we as Directors bear both to our Shareholders and our Employees.

We have passed through a period of world wide depression extending over several years, during which we, like many other similar Companies, have been unable to pay our Shareholders any dividends or to provide work for quite a substantial number of our regular Employees.

Although we have experienced an improvement in trade during the past twelve months we feel that a continuance of this improvement is by no means assured. The production of Tinplates in countries that were our customers is rapidly increasing, and America, whose competition in the export market during the past two years has been practically non-existent, having abandoned the Gold Standard is now making a determined effort to get a large share of this export trade again.

World production of Steel, Galvanized Sheets and Tinplates is far in excess of present consumption and of what one can reasonably assume consumption may be for some years to come.

New methods of manufacture are being tried, and heavy capital expenditure will, in our opinion, be essential for all Works that are going to keep their plant in line with the most modern ideas.

In amalgamating with Messrs. Richard Thomas & Co., Ltd., we are joining an old established Firm with a great reputation, one that is well managed, and ably directed by the outstanding personality in the Tinplate Trade in South Wales to-day, Sir William Firth. This Firm is by far the largest producer of Tinplates in the country and possesses a wonderful selling organisation. We feel that as part of this large Firm we shall have a better opportunity of keeping our Steel Plant and Mills at work, than we could possibly have if we continued to operate on our own, in view of the difficulties that lie in front of us.

We would, however, impress upon our Employees the absolute necessity, which will be even greater in the future than in the past, of co-operating in every possible way with the management to produce Steel, Sheets, and Tinplates of the best possible quality at the lowest possible cost. Remember we shall be one unit in an amalgamation embracing nearly 170 Tinplate Mills. While demand enables only 60% of these Mills to operate, many of them must be idle. Obviously only those Mills which produce the best article at the cheapest price will be operated in such circumstances.

Don't forget that geographically we are not well situated, and the heavy transport charges we have to bear on our raw and finished material between Swansea and Pontardawe must be compensated for by better efficiency and cheaper costs of production, to put us on equal terms with plants more favourably placed.

In our Sheet and Tinplate Mills we can produce as good a product as anyone else in the country, and we can to-day compete in costs. We appeal to our Employees for their own sake and for the honour of the Firm to prove this is the case, and so improve the prospect of a continuance of work in our Pontardawe plant, which is so vitally important for the future of the whole Village.

As this is the last occasion on which I shall address our Employees as Chairman of W. Gilbertson & Co. Ltd., I desire to express to you the great pleasure it has always afforded my brother and myself to work with you, and to thank you for the loyal service you have rendered the old Firm for so many years, which service and loyalty you will, I am sure, extend to your new Chairman and Directors.

In conclusion I should like to take this opportunity of expressing the hope that, for both Employers and Employees, the coming New Year and the future generally will be as prosperous as is possible, in the face of the adverse world conditions I have already outlined.

(Signed) CECIL F. GILBERTSON,
Chairman,
W. GILBERTSON & CO., LTD.

INDEX

Frank G. abandons autocracy for coop.ⁿ w/ steel unions (27-8.)

Letter-books sparse after 1918. (31)

FWG as educationalist in the region, promoting Swansea Uni. (32)

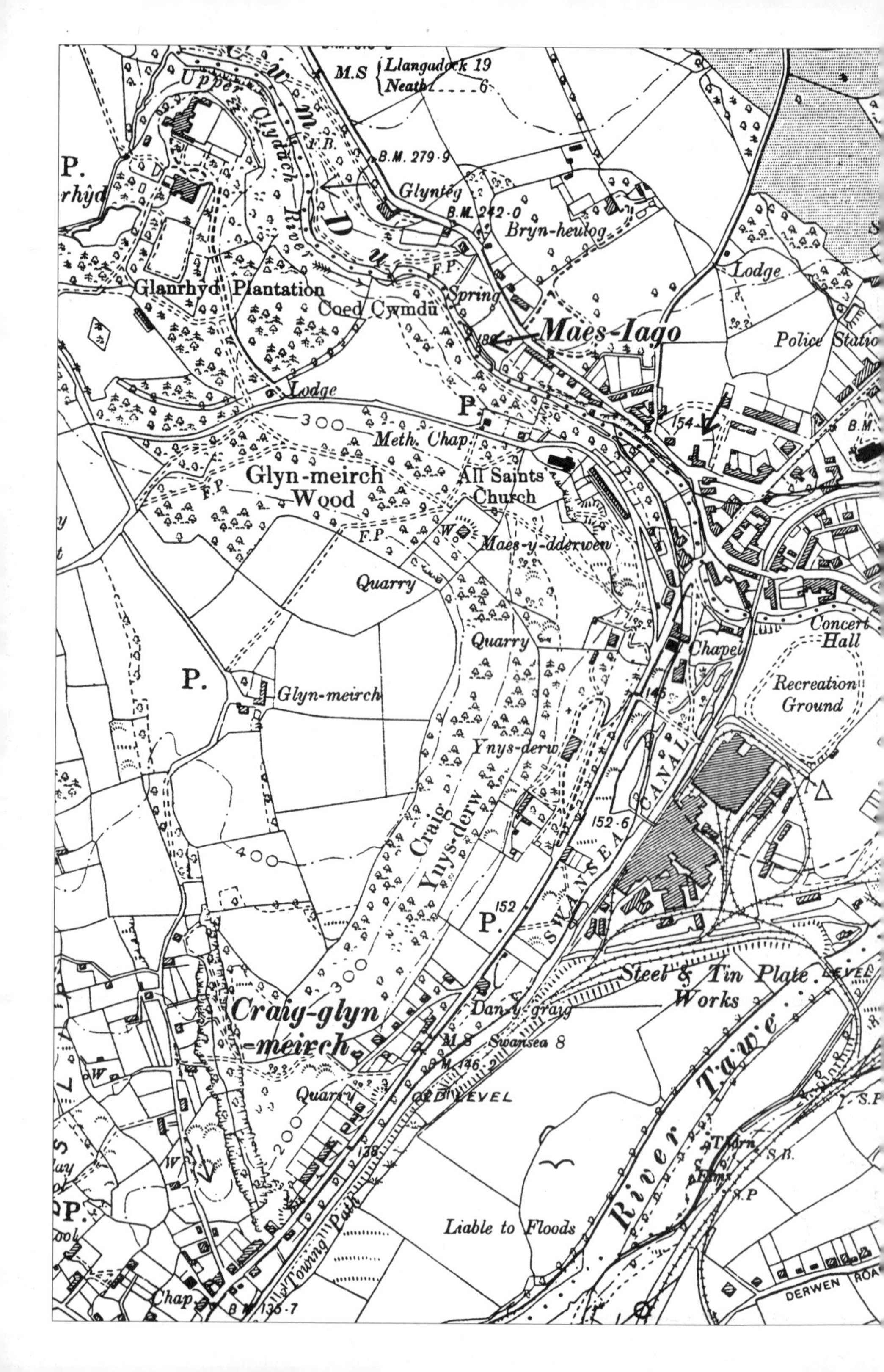

M.S Llangadock 19
Neath 6
Upper Clydach River
Cwm Du
F.B.
B.M. 279·9
Glyntêg
B.M. 242·0
Bryn-heulog
Lodge
Glanrhyd Plantation
Coed Cwmdu
Spring
Maes-Iago
Police Station
Lodge
300
P.
154
Meth. Chap
Glyn-meirch Wood
All Saints Church
F.P.
Maes-y-dderwen
Quarry
Quarry
Concert Hall
Chapel
P.
Glyn-meirch
Recreation Ground
145
Ynys-derw
Craig Ynys-derw
Swansea Canal
152·6
400
152
P.
300
Steel & Tin Plate Works
Level
Craig-glyn-meirch
Dan-y-graig
M.S Swansea 8
B.M. 146·2
Quarry
Old Level
200
River Tawe
138
S.B.
Liable to Floods
Towing Path
Chap
Derwen Road
135·7